Learning to Use the World Wide Web

Academic Edition

Ernest Ackermann

Mary Washington College

Franklin, Beedle & Associates, Incorporated
8536 SW St. Helens Drive, Suite D
Wilsonville, Oregon 97070
(503) 682-7668
http://www.fbeedle.com

Dedication

This book is dedicated to the members of my family—Lynn, Karl, and Oliver—who gave me their encouragement and support.

President and Publisher   Jim Leisy (jimleisy@fbeedle.com)
Manuscript Editor   Sheryl Rose
Production   Tom Sumner
   Karen Foley
Illustrations   Steve Klinetobe
Marketing Group   Victor Kaiser
   Sue Page
   Eric Machado
   Laura Rowe
Order Processing   Chris Alarid
   Ann Leisy

Manufactured in the U.S.A.

Rights and Permissions
Franklin, Beedle & Associates Incorporated
8536 SW St. Helens Drive, Suite D
Wilsonville, Oregon 97070
http://www.fbeedle.com

Library of Congress Cataloging-in-Publication Data

Ackermann, Ernest C.
    Learning to Use the World Wide Web : academic edition / Ernest Ackermann.
      p.   cm.
    Includes index.
    ISBN 1-887902-20-1
    1. World Wide Web (Information retrieval system)   I. Title.
TK5105.888.A26 1997
004.67'8--dc21   97-6198
                                          CIP

Preface

This book is written for people who want to learn how to use Netscape Navigator to access the World Wide Web and how to get the most from the resources available on the Internet. No prior experience with the World Wide Web or the Internet is assumed. We pay some attention to why things work the way they do, but the emphasis is on *how* to learn to effectively use the World Wide Web and associated services in a step-by-step, organized manner. The book can be used for self study, or it can be used as the primary or supplemental textbook in courses dealing with the Internet and the World Wide Web.

Work on this book began almost as soon as I finished writing *Learning to Use the Internet*, published by Franklin, Beedle & Associates, in April 1995. That book focuses on character-based (Unix) Internet services and software. It became clear to me and my publisher, Jim Leisy, that graphical World Wide Web browsers, like Mosaic and Netscape, would soon become the preferred and dominant mode of accessing information and services. The presentation and exercises in both books is derived from my years of teaching others in classes and workshops, and from my own experiences on the Web and Internet.

We use the Web browser Netscape Navigator to access the services and information available on the Internet. Netscape Navigator is the browser of choice because it's the most commonly used Web browser, and it is the focus of a lot of WWW development. It works well, it has integrated e-mail and Usenet news software, it can be modified to meet your needs and changes in Web technology, and it can deal with interactive elements such as Java Applets, JavaScript, and inline plug-ins. Not all Web browsers have these features, but most have enough in common with Netscape so that this book will help you learn to use any Web browser. The text, examples, and exercises were all developed on a personal computer using Windows 95. Instructions are included, where necessary, for working with previous versions of Microsoft Windows. You'll notice some differences if you're working on a Macintosh or Unix computer system, but things are not that different. Using Netscape Navigator on any of these types of computer systems is very similar.

Organization

The book is organized as follows:

Introduction to the World Wide Web and the Internet, Using a Web Browser	Chapters 1 and 2
Electronic Mail, Internet E-Mail Discussion Groups, and Usenet	Chapters 3, 4, and 5
Finding Information on the Web	Chapter 6
Writing Your Own Web Pages	Chapter 7
Telnet, FTP, Gopher	Chapter 8
Legal Issues, Ethical Issues, Privacy, and Security	Chapter 9

The book also has several appendices:

* Glossary of Internet and World Wide Web terms.
* Setting options and preferences for Netscape Navigator. Instructions and suggestions for setting Navigator's options and preferences.
* E-mail in a Unix environment using Mailx or Pine.
* E-mail using Eudora. Using Eudora and setting options for Internet e-mail on a personal computer.
* Java, Java Applets, and JavaScript. A discussion of the Java programming language and how to use Java Applets and JavaScript programs in Web pages. Includes examples, with source code, of Java Applets and JavaScript programs.

The first two chapters in the book are designed to quickly get you started using a Web browser to access the World Wide Web. The details of using the browser are in Chapter 2. Chapters 3, 4, and 5 deal with using the Internet for personal or group communication—electronic mail, Internet discussion groups, and Usenet news. We cover concepts and give the details of how to use the e-mail and newsreader software integrated with Netscape Navigator, version 2 and later. Other e-mail programs—Mailx, Pine, and Eudora—are covered in the appendices. Finding information on the WWW, either through directories or search engines, is covered in Chapter 6. Chapter 7 deals with the concepts, methods, and details of writing a Web page and getting it listed on the World Wide Web. Several Internet services—Telnet, FTP, and Gopher—are covered in Chapter 8. Some of the important ethical, legal, security, and social issues surrounding the use of the Internet and the World Wide Web are covered in Chapter 9.

All the chapters (except for Chapter 9), and appendices C, D, and E, contain step-by-step examples to demonstrate using the tools, services, and resources discussed in the text. By following the examples and trying them out the reader can gain firsthand guided experience. Including these examples is a bit of a risk because of the dynamic nature of the Internet and the World Wide Web. Nothing is frozen in place, and it may be that when you work with these, you'll see differences in the way information is displayed. Don't let that deter you. Using the World Wide Web and the Internet means you have to adapt to changes. Be persistent and use your skills to make accommodations to a changing, but important environment. One of the things that makes the Web exciting and vigorous is the way things are changing to make it more useful.

Each chapter contains several exercises to be used to explore the use of the tools and topics discussed. Doing the exercises is an important part of learning, and using the World Wide Web is a hands-on activity. The exercises deal with topics drawn from a variety of areas so that someone doing the exercises can be exposed to many of the resources that make up the World Wide Web.

Several of the chapters contain a section dealing with proper etiquette and responsible uses of the Internet and World Wide Web. Chapter 9 contains the most information on the subject, but rather than put all of that information in one chapter, it's dealt with in context in other chapters as well.

Supplemental Materials

For those teaching courses using this book, an instructor's guide is available from the publisher. A Web page is maintained to accompany this book at **http://www.mwc.edu/ernie/Lrn-web.html**. That page leads to individual Web pages for each chapter and appendix. These contain up-to-date links to all the Web resources mentioned in the text. They are periodically updated to keep the exercises current. Furthermore, since the material at a Web site can change, this gives access to the most recent versions of information on the Web.

Acknowledgments

This book wouldn't be possible without the support and encouragement from the members of my family—Lynn, Karl, and Oliver. Lynn has been encouraging, understanding, and given more help than anyone to this project. She deserves much more gratitude and acknowledgment that I can express here. Karl and Oliver, my sons, have helped me to see the Internet and World Wide Web through the eyes of another generation, and they give me the primary purpose for writing.

I want to thank my friends and students (and they're not necessarily separate categories) for the help they've given me and tell them how much I appreciate it. They've worked with me in preparing workshops, classes, and Web projects; they've given me good advice about my writing and working on the Web; they've listened patiently to my opinions and ideas, and in the case of my students, shown me new ways to teach and learn. There are too many to mention them all, but I want to give recognition here to a few. They are: Pastor Daphne Burt Carbaugh, who read and freely commented on early drafts of this book, Pete Clark, who wrote and documented the source code for the Java and JavaScript programs in Appendix E, Joseph Dreiss, who I can always count on for frank opinions about my teaching and writing and who has worked with me on many Web projects, Orland Gaithe, who answered my call for help for some materials related to this book, Steve Griffin, who in addition to being a great friend and supporter, let me use images of his painting "Fleeing from Flamingos" in Figure 7.25 and Figure 7.26, and Ryan MacMichael, who has developed several substantial Web projects—check out **http://www.mwc.edu/rmacmich**—and is always willing to help me or talk with me about my projects. I also want to thank CiCi Mills, Paul Everitt, Ryan Shriver, and Rob Page at Digital Creations in Fredericksburg, Virginia for their willingness to discuss issues and share information with me related to providing services on the World Wide Web, and to Larry Burgess of InternetSerF, Fredericksburg, Virginia who is always generous with his time and advice, and who is an example of an outstanding Internet service provider.

Franklin, Beedle & Associates is a very supportive publisher and has helped me greatly throughout this project. The people I've worked with directly are Steve Klinetobe, Jim Leisy, Sheryl Rose, and Tom Sumner. I recommend the company to anyone thinking about writing a book.

I also want to thank the following manuscript reviewers, whose contributions helped to make this a better book:

John McLain   *University of Indianapolis*
Tim Sylvester   *Glendale Community College*
Jane Turk   *LaSalle University*
Tom Wiggen   *University of North Dakota*

I hope you enjoy this book and find it useful. The World Wide Web and the Internet are great places to spend some time. Please feel free to send me e-mail to let me know your opinions, suggestions, or comments about this book. If you've got some time, visit my home page **http://www.mwc.edu/ernie** and drop me a line. I'm looking forward to hearing from you and seeing your home page on the Web.

Ernest Ackermann
Department of Computer Science
Mary Washington College
ernie@mwc.edu
http://www.mwc.edu/ernie

Contents

Preface iii

CHAPTER 1

Introduction to the World Wide Web and the Internet   1

The World Wide Web 2
   How the WWW Works 3
   What Is Available on the WWW 3
Key Terms and Concepts 9
   Hypertext and Hypermedia 10
   Uniform Resource Locator—URL 11
The Internet 19
   A Description of the Internet 19
Explanation of Internet Domain Names and Addresses 24
Your Internet Connection 26
Proper Network Etiquette 27
   How the Internet Developed 28
Summary 30
Exercises 32

CHAPTER 2

Using a Web Browser   34

What to Expect from a Web Browser 34
   Quick Review and Some Tips 35
Starting and Stopping the Web Browser 37
   Starting a Session on the WWW 37
   Ending a Session on the WWW 37
The Web Browser's Window 38
   Menu Bar 39
   Toolbar 41
   Location Bar 43
   Directory Buttons 43
   Content Area or Document View 44
   Scroll Bars 44
   Status Bar, Progress Bar, and Security Information 44
   Mail Icon 44
Getting Around a Page and the World Wide Web 44
   Moving Through a Page 45
   Moving Between Pages 45
Getting Help 58
   Online Help 59
   The Handbook 59
   Frequently Asked Questions (FAQ) 59
Saving, Printing, and Mailing Items from the WWW 60
   Saving Web Pages in a File 61
   Saving Items on a Page from the WWW into a File 63
   Printing Documents 64
   Mailing a Web Page 64
Using the Web Browser with Local Files 65

Bookmarks—Keeping Track of Favorite Places 65
Setting Preferences and Options 70
Where to Obtain a Web Browser on the Internet 74
Summary 74
Exercises 75

CHAPTER 3

The Basics of Electronic Mail and Using Netscape E-Mail   78

How E-Mail Works 79
Advantages and Limitations of E-Mail 82
    Advantages 82
    Limitations 82
Understanding Internet E-Mail Addresses 83
Dissecting E-Mail—Headers, Message Body, Signature 84
Finding Someone's Internet E-Mail Address 86
Sending E-Mail from the Internet to Other Networks 87
E-Mail Etiquette 88
Working with Nontext Files 88
Working with Netscape Mail 90
    Setting Crucial Mail Options in Netscape 92
    Getting Help 95
    Knowing When New Mail Has Arrived 95
    Opening and Closing the Mail Window 95
    The Netscape Mail Window 96
    Reading E-Mail 99
    Saving Messages 101
    Printing Messages 102
    Deleting Messages 102
    Setting Other Mail Options 105
    Composing and Sending E-Mail 107
    Replying to a Message 109
    Forwarding E-Mail 110
    Working with an Address Book 111
Summary 113
Exercises 114

CHAPTER 4

Internet E-Mail Discussion Groups   116

How to Join a List 119
    What Happens Next? 120
How to Communicate with and Contribute to a List 121
How to Leave a List 123
Requesting Services from Software that Manages a List 124
    Getting Help and a List of All Commands 124
    Getting a List of Subscribers 124
    Hiding Your Name from the List of Subscribers 124
    Temporarily Suspending Messages 125
    Switching to Digest Mode 125

Getting a List of Archived Files 126
Retrieving a File from the Archives of a List 126
A Summary of How to Work with Discussion Groups 127
How to Find the Names and Addresses of Lists **127**
Search the Names of All Listserv Lists by E-mail 127
Use Tools available on the World Wide Web to search for lists 128
Proper Etiquette or Behavior in a Discussion Group **128**
Internet Sources of Information about Discussion Lists **129**
Summary **130**
Exercises **131**

CHAPTER 5
Usenet—Reading and Writing the News   133

Introduction to Usenet **134**
A Quick View of How Usenet Works 135
Usenet Control Is at the Local Level 135
How the News Is Passed Around and Stored 135
How Usenet Articles are Organized **136**
Threads 136
Newsgroup Categories 136
Working with Usenet News **138**
What Is a Newsreader? 138
Netscape News 139
Starting a Usenet News Session 141
Ending a Netscape News Session 143
The Netscape News Window 146
Reading Articles **150**
Choosing an Article 150
Reading an Article 150
Marking an Article as Unread 151
Saving, Mailing, and Printing Articles **151**
Saving an Article to a File 151
Mailing an Article 152
Printing an Article 152
Writing to the Author of an Article **153**
Posting a Follow-Up to an Article **153**
Posting an Article **154**
Proper Usenet Etiquette **158**
Signatures, FAQS, and Finding Newsgroups **159**
Signatures 159
FAQs 160
Finding Newsgroups 160
Recommended Newsgroups and Articles **161**
Summary **162**
Exercises **163**

CHAPTER 6

Finding Information on the Web—Directories and Searching   165

Directories 166
    Directories of New and Interesting Web Pages 166
    Subject-Oriented Directories 167
Searching the World Wide Web 181
    Using a Search Tool 182
    Selected Search Tools 183
Summary 206
Exercises 208

CHAPTER 7

Writing Your Own Web Pages   211

Description of a Web Page 212
Viewing the Source Version of a Web Page 215
Introduction to HTML 216
    General Form of HTML Tags 217
    Structure of a Web Page—Head and Body 217
    Title 218
    Author's Comments 218
    Headings 219
    Paragraphs, Line Breaks, Shadow Lines 219
    Character Formatting—Italic, Bold, Emphasized 221
    Preformatted Text 221
    Quoted Text 222
    Special Characters 223
    Lists 224
    Links 230
    Images 234
    Table of HTML Tags 237
    URL Formats 238
Tools to Help Create Web Pages 248
Style Guides—How to Do It Right, How to Do It
    for Impact, and How to Make It Portable 249
Putting Your Information on the WWW 252
Resources for More Information on Creating Web Pages 253
Summary 255
Exercises 256

CHAPTER 8

Telnet, FTP, and Gopher   259

Telnet 260
    When and Why to Use Telnet 260
    The Form of a URL for Telnet 261
    Configuring Your Browser for Telnet 261
Hytelnet—Finding Resources Available through Telnet 264
FTP 269

URL Format for FTP 270
Retrieving a File by Anonymous FTP 270
Method 1—View the file first 272
Method 2—Don't view the file; use Shift+click 273
Working with Different File Types 275
Finding Files Available by Anonymous FTP 282

Archie **283**
Using Archie 284
Different Types of Searches 285
Archie Servers 286
Priority 287

Gopher **287**
URL Format for Gopher 289
Finding Resources Available Through Gopher 289
Subject Trees (Directories) 289
Veronica (Searching Gopherspace) 291

Summary **296**

Exercises **298**

CHAPTER 9
Legal Issues, Ethical Issues, Privacy, and Security   303

Privacy and Civil Liberties **305**
E-Mail Privacy 305
Unwarranted Search and Seizure 307
Offensive Material and Libel 308

Intellectual Property and Copyright **310**

Access—What Type at What Cost? **311**
Getting Connected 311
Access—One-Way or Two-Way? 312
Universal or Public Access 312
Free-Net 313
National Public Telecomputing Network 313

Internet Security **313**

Summary **316**

Exercises **317**

Appendix A   Glossary   **321**
Appendix B   Netscape Navigator Options and Preferences   **328**
Appendix C   E-Mail the UNIX Way: Mailx and Pine   **336**
Appendix D   Using Eudora   **361**
Appendix E   Java: Applets and Scripts   **383**
Index   **401**

CHAPTER 1

Introduction to the World Wide Web and the Internet

Millions of people around the world use the Internet to search for and retrieve information on all sorts of topics in a wide variety of areas including the arts, business, government, humanities, news, politics, recreation, and the sciences. People communicate through electronic mail, discussion groups, and Usenet News. They share information and make commercial and business transactions. All this activity is possible because tens of thousands of networks are connected to the Internet and exchange information in the same basic ways. The World Wide Web (WWW) is a part of the Internet, but it's not a collection of networks. Rather, it is information that is connected or linked together like a web. You access this information through one interface or tool called a Web browser. The number of resources and services that are part of the World Wide Web is growing at an astounding rate. There are over 20 million users of the WWW, and more than half the information that is transferred across the Internet is accessed through the WWW. By using a computer or terminal (hardware) connected to a network that is part of the Internet, and by using a program (software) to browse and retrieve information that is part of the World Wide Web, the people connecting to the Internet and the World Wide Web have access to a wide variety of services, tools, information, and opportunities.

This book is about learning to use the World Wide Web in a way that allows you to take advantage of the resources and services it makes available. It is designed for beginning and novice users of the WWW. Prior experience with the Internet isn't necessary, but it will help you move through some of the material more quickly. The text, examples, and exercises will take you through the basics of accessing and using the World Wide Web. You'll learn how to tap the virtual cornucopia of information on the WWW and find the resources you want. You'll also learn how to create documents (called Web pages) so you can put your own information on the WWW. We'll cover how to use a variety of Internet services such as e-mail, FTP, Telnet, Gopher, and others with the World Wide Web. You'll also learn a little bit about how the Internet and the WWW work. To take advantage of the benefits of access to the Internet and the WWW, you need to become familiar with the services and tools available and know about some of the major information sources.

This chapter addresses some of the basic information and concepts you need to begin using the WWW and the Internet. The topics in this chapter include:

- The World Wide Web
- Key Terms and Concepts
- The Internet
- Explanation of Internet Domain Names and Addresses
- Your Internet Connection
- Proper Network Etiquette

This chapter contains detailed examples using a Web browser to access information on the World Wide Web. These and other examples in the book demonstrate concepts and techniques. As you read the examples and follow along, you'll get step-by-step instructions for working with the World Wide Web. Remember, though, these examples reflect the World Wide Web at the time of writing. Because some things change frequently, they may not appear to you on your screen as they do in this book. The World Wide Web and the Internet are constantly changing, but don't let that hold you back. Be persistent and use your skills to work in this important environment. Change is one of the things that makes the Internet and the World Wide Web exciting, vigorous, and useful.

Several exercises appear after the chapter summary. These exercises will help you practice using the World Wide Web and will reinforce the concepts in the chapter.

This book deals with using the WWW while you're using Microsoft Windows. We'll be using the phrase *click on* regularly. By that we mean you use a mouse to point to something and then click or press the mouse button. If your mouse has two buttons, press or click on the left button. If you're working in another window environment, such as a workstation that uses X-Windows, you'll find most of the instructions are the same.

Now, let's get started!

The World Wide Web

Whether you've worked on the Internet before or not, you'll be pleased with how easy accessing the Internet is through the WWW. It's also enticing. There are thousands of Web sites on the Internet, and you can access virtually any Internet service or resource through the programs you use to work with the WWW.

You can think of the World Wide Web as a large collection of information that's accessible through the Internet. You use hypertext and multimedia techniques to browse the Web, to find information in various forms, and when you're ready, to contribute to the WWW.

The concept behind the World Wide Web is the development of a hypertext networked information system. One of the goals was to give a uniform means of accessing all the different types of information on the Internet. Since you only need to know one way to get information, you concentrate on what you want, not how to get it. Instead of having to contact and know the addresses of many different Internet sites and having to know all the details of using different Internet services (Telnet, FTP, or Gopher, to name a few), you start a program called a Web browser that lets you access a WWW site. From there you can go to other locations on the Internet connected through the WWW to search for, browse, and retrieve information in a variety of forms. You'll be able to select items by choosing them and clicking with a mouse. The items you choose from are images, icons, or text. The text is either underlined, in bold, or highlighted. The information you retrieve or view can be text, programs, graphics, images, digitized video, or digitized sound. Using a Web browser is a relatively easy way to work with information on the WWW. You need to know different ways of using other services on the Internet, but with the WWW you have just one type of interface or way of working with the Internet.

How the WWW Works

The concept of the WWW is credited to Tim Berners-Lee of CERN, the European Laboratory for Particle Physics in Geneva, Switzerland. The Web was started to provide a single means of access to the wealth of services and resources on the Internet. You access the WWW by using a program called a Web browser. There are several browsers available; the first popular browser was Mosaic, and the most popular one is Netscape Navigator. Mosaic was developed by Marc Andreesen, Eric Bina, and others at the National Center for Supercomputer Applications (NCSA) at the University of Illinois, Urbana-Champaign. Andreesen and others left NCSA to form a company called Netscape Communications Corporation, which continues to develop and market Netscape Navigator.

Each browser provides a graphical interface. You move from place to place and item to item on the Web by using a mouse to select and click on a portion of text, icon, or region of a map or image. These items are called *hyperlinks* or *links* for short. Each link you select represents a document, an image, a video clip, or an audio clip somewhere on the Internet. You don't need to know where it is or even the way your browser follows the link. What is important is what you want, not necessarily how to get it or where it is. In order for this to work, there are standard ways of specifying the links and creating documents that can be displayed as part of the WWW. Items accessible through the WWW give hypertext access to the Internet, so you don't have to know any other techniques except how to select a title, phrase, word, or icon.

What Is Available on the WWW

All sorts of things are available on the WWW in many different formats such as data, documents, images, programs, and sound files. Essentially, if something can be put into digital format and stored in a computer, then it's available on the WWW. Tim Berners-Lee (who started the WWW project at CERN) wrote in the document *About the World Wide Web*, "The WorldWideWeb (W3) is the universe of network-accessible information, an embodiment of human knowledge." (By the way, that document is available on the WWW by using the URL **http://www.w3.org/hypertext/WWW/WWW**—we'll say more about URLs a little later.) That's a strong statement, but it's certainly true. You'll find items on all kinds of topics on the WWW. There's a wide range of materials available on subjects such as art, science, humanities, politics, law, business, education, and government information. In each of these areas you can find scientific and technical papers, financial data, stock market reports, government reports, advertisements, and publicity and news about movies and other forms of entertainment. Through the WWW you can find information about many types of products, information about health and environmental issues, government documents, and tips and advice on recreational activities such as camping, cooking, gardening, and travel. You can also conduct commercial transactions on the Web; you can make purchases, go shopping, or retrieve information about something you are thinking of buying. You can tour museums, plan a trip, make reservations, visit gardens throughout the world, and so on. Just a little bit of exploring will show you the wide range and types of information available.

When you find a document or information you want, you can save it to a file on your computer, print it, or send it by e-mail to any Internet address. Instructions for saving and printing files when you're using Netscape Navigator are given right after the end of Example 1.1. E-mail is covered in detail in Chapter 3 and Usenet in Chapter 5. You can also make your own information available on the WWW. See Chapter 7 for information about that.

To put our discussion about the WWW in context, we'll start with an example of what you're likely to see when you use Netscape Navigator to access the WWW.

Example 1.1   A First Look at Netscape Navigator and the World Wide Web

Netscape Navigator is one of the most popular programs used for accessing information or browsing the World Wide Web. Here we're assuming the program is on your computer and you have a connection (either by a network or SLIP/PPP) to the Internet. In Chapter 2 we'll mention some ways to get the program, and Appendix B deals with setting options for using it.

In going through the steps of this example, we'll start the browser, explain some of the items you'll see on your screen, and then look at one of the many directories available that give easy access to a lot of information on the WWW. We'll follow these steps:

1. Start Netscape Navigator.
2. Click the directory button titled **Net Search**.
3. Explore the WWW.
4. Exit Netscape Navigator.

This will give us a chance to take a look at Netscape Navigator and set a context for some of the concepts and terms in this and other chapters. As you work through this and other examples, the **[w⊔w]** indicates something for you to do.

1. Start Netscape Navigator.

You start Netscape Navigator by either clicking on an icon labeled **Netscape** or choosing **Netscape** from a menu. In some cases you may have to select a program group from the list of programs you can run, or you may have a shortcut to Netscape on your desktop. Suppose the Netscape icon is on your desktop.

[w⊔w]   Double-click on the Netscape icon. The icon may appear as one of the following:

Netscape

Netscape
Navigator

This will start Netscape Navigator, and a window similar to the one in Figure 1.1 will appear on your screen. (In some cases your computer may go through the steps necessary to connect to the Internet. If you use a modem to connect to the Internet, the program to use the modem will start and the modem will dial the number used to connect to the Internet.) The image or text you see in the window may be different from Figure 1.1; it depends on how Netscape Navigator has been set up or configured. (Setting options and configuration are covered in Chapter 2 and Appendix B.)

The first document you see is called the *home page*. When you're browsing the Web, it's your starting point. The term home page also has another meaning. When individuals, organizations, or companies want to have a presence on the WWW or want to make information available on the WWW, they create a home page. In that sense the home page acts as a contact point or starting point for the connection between that individual, organization, or company and the rest of the World Wide Web. We'll discuss creating home pages and other Web pages in Chapter 7. The one in Figure 1.1 is the home page for Netscape Communications Corporation. It's used to make announcements, so it changes regularly.

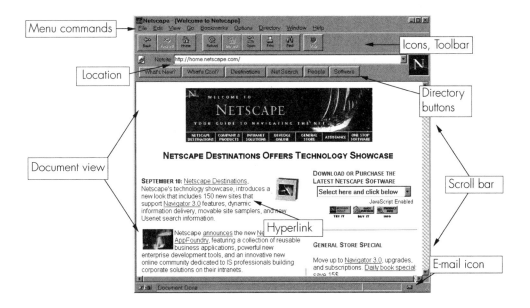

Figure 1.1   Sample Starting Window with Netscape Navigator

If you're familiar with a Windows environment, you should feel very comfortable using a Web browser. You work with many of the items in this window in the same way as any other window. You can resize the window or switch between the window and an icon representing the window. The menu commands are across the top row:

<u>F</u>ile   <u>E</u>dit   <u>V</u>iew   <u>G</u>o   <u>B</u>ookmarks   <u>O</u>ptions   <u>D</u>irectory   <u>W</u>indow   Help

The commands contain the items (such as **File**, **Edit**, and **Help**) that are common to several Windows applications. Each command represents a pull-down menu. Click on it and a menu will appear.

One of the directory buttons pointed out in Figure 1.1 will be used in this example. You select a directory button with your mouse and click on it (using the left button if your mouse has more than one button). That causes the current document or page to be replaced by another. You can get back to a previous page by pressing the icon labeled **Back**. You may have guessed that there are at least two ways to get help—use the pull-down menu item **Help** or click the directory button **Handbook**. A detailed explanation of the Menu Bar, Toolbar buttons, location, and directory buttons is in Chapter 2.

Most of the window is taken up by the view of the current document or Web page. There are several hyperlinks (we've pointed out two in Figure 1.1) on that page. The hyperlinks are part of the document, usually marked in some way so they stand out; they are either underlined, in bold, or a different color. They represent other documents or locations on the WWW. You use a mouse to move a hand or pointer to a hyperlink by clicking the mouse button, the left one if your mouse has more than one button. Click on a hyperlink and the browser tries to get the information associated with the hyperlink. Then the current document is replaced. As you move the cursor with the mouse or through a Web page, the cursor turns into a hand when it's on a hyperlink. Hyperlinks can be represented by text, icons, or images.

2. Click on the directory button **Net Search**.

There's lots of information on the WWW and it's just about impossible to keep track of it all. To help, some hyperlinks are arranged into categories to create directories. One popular, large, and well-designed directory is named **Yahoo**. You can get to that directory (and others) by clicking on the directory button labeled **Net Search**.

w^Ww   Use the mouse to point to the directory button **Net Search** and click the (left) mouse button.

Clicking the directory button causes Netscape Navigator to activate a hyperlink to a Web page that contains hyperlinks to the **Yahoo** directory and a few others. The document in Figure 1.1 will be replaced by another. A portion of it is shown in Figure 1.2. If the **Yahoo** directory doesn't appear at first, you can get to it by clicking on **Yahoo** in the short list of directories near the top or on **Yahoo!** in the longer list further down the page.

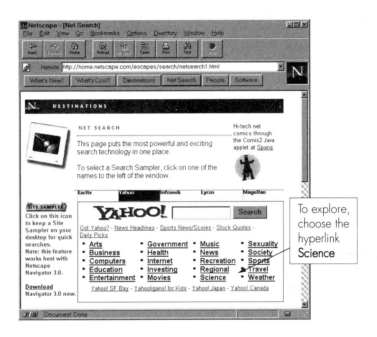

Figure 1.2   Access to Yahoo Directory from Netscape

3. Explore the WWW.

To explore the WWW, all you have to do is follow hyperlinks. Starting with a directory like this one, there's plenty of exploring to do. To be specific, click on the link **Science** as indicated in Figure 1.2. That will take you to a screen like the one shown in Figure 1.3.

Use the mouse to point to the hyperlink **Science** and click on the (left) mouse button.

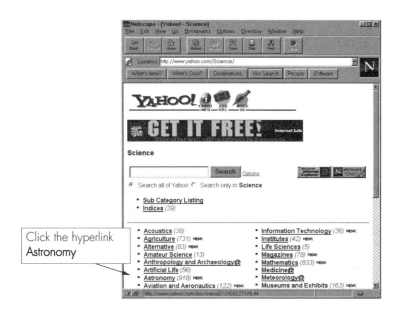

Figure 1.3   Yahoo Science

You can see there are still many topics to explore. Again, to be definite, select the hyperlink labeled **Astronomy**.

WWW   Use the mouse to point to the hyperlink **Astronomy** and click once with the (left) mouse button.

Figure 1.4 shows a portion of the document under the heading **Astronomy**. There are several items you might like to peruse.

There are lots of links to follow here, and you can follow these or any links to explore the WWW. You'll find you can move from page to page easily with a little practice. Remember to press the toolbar icon [Back] to go back through previous pages. Spend some time exploring these topics or others. When you're ready, go on to the next step.

4. Exit Netscape Navigator.

WWW   Click on **File** in the **Menu Bar** and then click on **Exit**.

The window will close and you will have ended this session with Netscape Navigator. If you're using dial-up networking (using a modem with a SLIP/PPP connection), then ending the session will probably end your connection to the Internet. If you're paying by the minute or hour for the connection and you're done working with the Internet for the time being, be sure your connection is terminated.

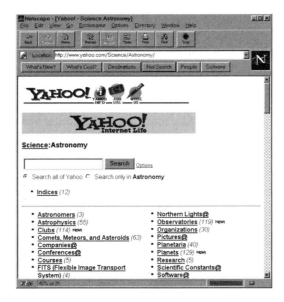

Figure 1.4   Yahoo Astronomy

Of course, you can exit Netscape Navigator in the same way you exit most other Windows applications. Click on **File** in the Menu Bar and select **Exit** or press **Alt-F** and then **X**, or double-click on the button in the upper left corner of the window.

—————————— End of Example 1.1 ——————————

Once you've been browsing on the Web you'll probably find lots of information you'd like to save or print. To *save* a document in a file while you're using Netscape, choose **File** from the Menu Bar, and then choose **Save as**. A dialog box will open. You can type in the name of the file and choose whether you want to save it as text or *HTML*. (We'll explain the difference in the next chapter.)

To *print* a document while you're using Netscape, click on the **Print** icon and a dialog box will pop up on the screen. Click on the **OK** button to print, and that's all there is, provided your printer is set up to print through any Windows application.

Key Terms and Concepts

Now that you've had a little experience with the WWW, it's a good time to mention a few key terms and concepts.

Hypertext, hypermedia, hyperlinks. When you use the WWW, you work in a *hypertext* or *hypermedia* environment. That means you move from item to item and back again without having to follow a pre-defined path. You follow *hyperlinks* according to your needs. Sometimes the items you select are part of other sentences or paragraphs; the links to other Internet resources are presented in context. The links can also be represented by icons or images, or you can select regions from a map or display.

Web browser, graphical user interface, bookmark list. A program that lets you contact a WWW site is called a *Web browser* or *browser* for short. The WWW doesn't require you to always use the same browser. Mosaic, Microsoft Internet Explorer, and Netscape Navigator work through a *graphical user interface* (GUI). They let you interact with the Internet and the information on the WWW in a multimedia setting. As you use a Web browser, you'll be able to save the locations of information or sites you find interesting, so that you'll be able to return to them anytime you use your Web browser. If you're using Netscape, they're saved in a *bookmark list.*

URL, Uniform Resource Locator. The hyperlinks are represented in a specific format called a *URL* or *Uniform Resource Locator.* The portion of the Netscape window labeled **Location:** holds the URL of the document in the window. Each Web page has a URL as its address. For example, the URL for the first of several Web pages to accompany this book is **http://www.mwc.edu/ernie/Lrn-www.html**.

Protocols, HTTP. The documents or screens are passed from a server to a client according to specific rules for exchanging information called *protocols.* Other services on the Internet operate according to specific protocols. The WWW protocol is named *HTTP,* which stands for *HyperText Transfer Protocol* because the documents, pages, or screens passed from one computer to another are in hypertext form.

HTML. The rules for creating or writing a Web page are all specified as *HTML—HyperText Mark-up Language.* This language provides the formal rules for marking text, which govern how it is displayed as part of a Web page. It would be used, for example, to mark text so it appears in boldface or italics. In order for text or an icon to represent a hyperlink, it has to be marked as a link in HTML, and the actual link itself is written as a URL. Each hyperlink you see on a Web page is represented by a URL. Chapter 7 has details about using HTML.

Client, server. Netscape Navigator is an example of a program called *client* software. While it's running it communicates with a computer known as a *server,* communicating your commands and receiving information. You work with the client and it communicates with the server. The documents or pages you see on the screen are passed to your computer (the client) from another computer (the server). You don't have to know the details to use the programs.

Hypertext and Hypermedia

The term *hypertext* is used to describe text that contains links to other text. When the "text" and links are from a variety of media (text, video, sound), as is the case in the WWW, we use the term *hypermedia.* When you're working with a screen or page, you see items in bold, underlined, or in a different color. Each one represents a link to another part of the current document, screen, page, file, image, or other Internet resource. Selecting one of these links allows you to follow or jump to the information the link represents. Also, you can return to a previous link. There's a definite starting point, but the path you take after that is your choice. It's not constrained by having to go in some sort of line; you can think of being able to go up, down, right, or left from any link. The term *hypertext* was originally coined by Ted Nelson in the mid-1960s to talk about moving through text in a nonlinear manner. WWW browsers allow the links to be represented by text, images, or digitized sound.

As an example, we'll take a look at an excerpt from a hyptertext glossary. The definitions and explanations in the glossary are connected through hypertext. The excerpt here is taken from a glossary of Internet terms to accompany the book *Learning to Use the Internet*, also by your author, and it's available on the WWW in hypertext form. To see it, use the URL **http://www.mwc.edu/ernie/glossary.html**.

Netscape Navigator. A <u>World Wide Web browser</u> (software) used for accessing information in a hypertext or hypermedia manner on the Internet. It gives the user a graphical interface (<u>GUI</u>) to Internet services and resources.

If you used your mouse to select one of the underlined words or phrases and clicked on it, you'd be taken to another part of the glossary. For example, choosing <u>GUI</u> takes you to a definition of GUI. From there you could browse the glossary following other links or return to the entry for **Netscape Navigator**. You could always follow the links back to return to where you started. The information in the glossary wouldn't change, but the way you access it and the order in which you do it would.

Many of the resources, sites, and services you access as part of the World Wide Web are accessible through several paths. The WWW allows you to browse and select those resources by letting you choose your own path within the context of Web pages and links on those pages or screens.

Uniform Resource Locator—URL

Each of the links on the World Wide Web uses a *Uniform Resource Locator* or *URL*. The URL gives a WWW browser the location and the means to get to a resource on the Internet. You need to know about URLs if you want to access something that isn't on the Web page you're working with. When someone writes about a Web page or service, they will usually give you the URL. There are references to Web pages or URLs in lots of documents you'll see on the WWW, and also in other media like newspapers, magazines, television, and radio. You've seen some examples of URLs in the figures in Example 1.1, such as **http://home.netscape.com/home/internet-search.html** in Figure 1.2, and **www.yahoo.com/Business** in Figure 1.3.

The URLs that point to Web pages or home pages all start with **http://**. That's because those are all transmitted according to the *HTTP* protocol. You'll see something different for URLs that are used to access information through other Internet services or protocols. Gopher (discussed in detail in Chapter 8) has been a popular Internet service. To access the Gopher menu you would use a URL that starts with **gopher://**. For example, MountainNet is an Internet services provider that makes information available through a Gopher and the WWW. To access the information it makes available as a Gopher menu, use the URL **gopher://Gopher.Mountain.Net**. To see the same information as a Web page, use **http://www.mountain.net/Pinnacle/amiwww/amiwww.html**.

Tip

When you have to type a URL be sure to type it exactly as it's written.

Most sites that correspond to a URL treat upper- and lowercase characters as different characters. For example, Wells Fargo Bank provides economic forecasting on the WWW through the URL **http:/ /wellsfargo.com/ftr/econ/**. If you use **http://wellsfargo.com/ftr/ECON/**, you won't get anything except an error message from your browser. So be careful when typing. Pay attention to letter case and punctuation.

You'll find it helpful to think of a URL as having the form

```
how-to-get-there://where-to-go/what-to-get
```

Its general form is

```
service://domain-name-of-site-supplying-service/full-path-name-of-item
```

where the term service stands for an Internet service or protocol such as FTP, Telnet, or HTTP. Essentially, this is like a sign pointing to something on the Internet. Starting at the far left, the portion of the URL up to the colon (:) tells the type of Internet service or protocol to use, such as FTP, Gopher, or HTTP. The Internet domain name or address of the site supplying the information comes just after the characters **://**. After the first single slash, you have the full path name of the item. All the slashes go in the same direction.

You can view files on your computer through Netscape Navigator, Mosaic, or any Web browser. To do that, use a URL of the form

```
file:///DRIVE|/name-of-file
```

You substitute the name of the disk drive that holds the file for *DRIVE|* and the name of the file for *name-of-file*. The URL for the file **goodnews.htm** on drive C, for example, is **file:///C|goodnews.htm**. Be sure to use the complete name of the file, and remember that all the slashes are the ones that look like /. For example, if the file **goodnews.htm** were in the directory **A:\mystuff\webpages**, then its URL would be **file:///a|mystuff/webpages/goodnews.htm**.

Sometimes you're going to want to go directly to a Web page without having to follow hyperlinks. You may want to do this if you find out about a URL, but don't have it as part of some other Web page. In this case you'll want to type in the URL and have the Web browser follow the URL. One way is by typing the URL in the location bar. There are other ways to give the browser a URL to use as a hyperlink. The different ways depend on which browser you're using.

If you're using **Netscape Navigator**, then you can click on the icon and type the URL, or choose **File** from the Menu Bar, then choose **Open Location**, and then type the URL.

Regardless of which method you use, you're explicitly giving the Web browser a hyperlink to follow. We'll provide more details about using URLs in Chapter 2, and a complete list of the different types of URLs in Chapter 7. For now we'll look at an example of using Netscape Navigator and going directly to a Web page by typing in a URL.

Example 1.2   Opening a Location and Typing in a URL

When you're working on the WWW you may want to visit a Web page that isn't listed as a hyperlink in the document you're browsing. To do that you give a command to open a document or location and you type the URL, rather than selecting a hyperlink. That's what we'll do in this example.

Suppose that you'll be taking a trip to Rio de Janeiro, Brazil. A friend has told you that you can find information about cities around the world by looking them up on the World Wide Web through something called **city.net**, and the URL for **city.net** is **http://www.city.net**. To test it you've got to start your Web browser and get it to use the URL. That means getting the browser to open the document or open the URL **http://www.city.net**. Then you can follow hyperlinks to get information about Brazil and Rio de Janeiro. In addition to going through the steps to open a document, we'll follow a hyperlink that's part of a map by using the mouse to point to a region of a map and click. Here are the steps to follow in this example:

1. Start Netscape Navigator.
2. Open a document or open the URL **http://www.city.net**.
3. Follow a series of hyperlinks to a map of South America.
4. Follow a hyperlink to information about Brazil by clicking on a region of a map of South America.
5. Follow hyperlinks to get to information about Rio de Janeiro.
6. Exit Netscape Navigator.

1. Start Netscape Navigator.

Click on an icon labeled **Netscape** or **Netscape Navigator**. We saw how to do that in Example 1.1.

w⁻Ww Double-click the **Netscape** icon.

This will start Netscape Navigator with the home page as it's set for your version of Netscape. Figure 1.1 showed the home page for Netscape Communications Corporation. The image or text you see in the window may be different.

2. Open a location or open the URL **http://www.city.net**.

There are several ways to open a location or URL.

1. You can select **File** from the Menu Bar and choose **Open Location**.
2. You can select the icon  from the toolbar.
3. You can change the URL listed in the location bar.

If you choose to use either of the first two methods, a dialog box will appear on the screen, then you type in the URL and press Enter. We'll use the third method here. A URL is typed in the location pane in Figure 1.5.

w⁻Ww Using the mouse, point to the location pane and click once.

Use the mouse so that the pointer is on top of the location pane and click once. The location bar will change color.

 Type **http://www.city.net** and press **Enter**.

Type the URL you want to open or follow. That will replace the URL that was present in the location pane. Press Enter. The location should look as it does in Figure 1.5.

Figure 1.5   URL Typed in Location Pane

You should see some changes around the large **N** in the upper right of the window. It looks like the **N** is in the middle of a star or meteor shower while Netscape is contacting the WWW server at city.net and retrieving the information indicated by the URL. You should see the **city.net** home page (Figure 1.6) after a short while. If things are taking too long (more than a few minutes), click on the icon labeled **Stop** to stop Netscape from trying to get information from **city.net**.

Click here to get a list of world regions covered by city.net

Figure 1.6   Home Page for city.net

3. Follow a series of hyperlinks to a map of South America.

We need to follow two more hyperlinks to get to a map of South America.

Click on the hyperlink **Regions.**

That takes you to the Web page shown in Figure 1.7 with links to various regions of the world. From there there's only one more link to follow to a map of South America.

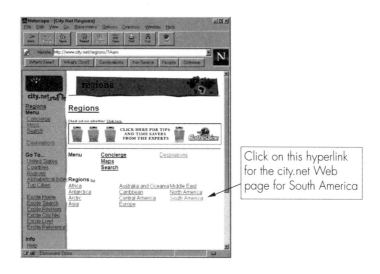

Figure 1.7   Regions Page for city.net

Two more hyperlinks need to be followed to get us to the map we want.

Click on the hyperlink of the screen labeled **"South America."**

Clicking on the phrase "South America" as noted in Figure 1.7 brings up a Web page that will take us directly to a map of South America, Figure 1.8. There are other ways to get to that map. Clicking on "Maps" in Figure 1.7 takes you to a Web page with a link to several world maps which could be followed to a map of South America. (More than one path to a specific piece of information is one of the characteristics of the World Wide Web.)

Figure 1.8   South America Page for city.net

Move the pointer to either hyperlink labeled "Maps" as shown in Figure 1.8, and click once. That will bring up a Web page with choice of maps of South America. Choose the one labeled "City.Net South America Map" as shown in Figure 1.9. Selecting that map brings up the Web page shown in Figure 1.10. You'll find it may take longer to get this page because it contains primarily images and it takes a lot of bytes to represent an image.

Click on the hyperlink labeled **City.Net South America Map**.

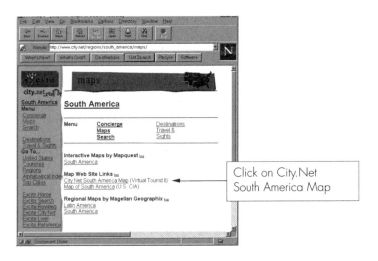

Figure 1.9   Web Page with Hyperlinks to Maps of South America

4. Follow a hyperlink to information about Brazil by clicking on a region of a map of South America.

Figure 1.10   Virtual Tourist II Web Page with Map of South America

5. Follow a series of hyperlinks to find information about Rio de Janeiro.

Now, move to some Web pages with further information about Brazil and Rio de Janeiro.

Click anywhere on the portion of the map within the borders of Brazil, as shown in Figure 1.10.

After clicking on the portion of the map for Brazil another document will appear with hyperlinks to cities in Brazil as shown in Figure 1.11.

Figure 1.11   city.net Web Page for Brazil

Click on the hyperlink **Rio de Janeiro**.

You can click on the hyperlink **Rio De Janeiro** to retrieve a Web page about Rio. One is shown in Figure 1.12.

Figure 1.12   city.net Web Page for Rio de Janeiro

You're on your own now. Follow any of the hyperlinks on this or other Web pages to get some information about Rio de Janeiro or other places.

6. Exit Netscape.

w|w|w   Click on the **File** pull-down menu, then click on **Exit.**

————————————End of Example 1.2————————————

Other chapters in this book give more details about using the WWW. We've concentrated on getting a Web browser started and then browsing the WWW.

Now on to information about the Internet!

The Internet

This section contains basic information and concepts about the Internet. The topics include:
* A Description of the Internet
* Explanation of Internet Domain Names and Addresses
* Your Internet Connection
* Proper Network Etiquette
* How the Internet Developed

A Description of the Internet

There are several ways to describe the Internet:

From a practical, recreational, or commercial point of view. The Internet is a vast collection of information that can be searched and retrieved electronically. This includes advice on all sorts of topics, data, electronic texts, government information and data, images, museum exhibits, scholarly papers, software, and access to commercial activities. Tapping into these resources requires knowing the tools and services to use.

From a technical point of view. The Internet is a network of tens of thousands of computer networks. The networks consist of over a million computer systems. These computers and networks communicate with each other by exchanging data according to the same rules, even though the individual networks and computer systems use different technologies.

From a social point of view. Millions of people throughout the world have access to the Internet. They use it to communicate with each other; they send and receive messages. An individual on the Internet can communicate with anyone else on the Internet. Since its beginnings, the Internet has been a place where people can communicate with others no matter where they are, what their status, or how great their expertise. What's important is the quality of the communication, not where or who it comes from. It's not a place where people only read or see what others have done; two-way communication is welcomed, expected, and encouraged.

Many of the people on the Internet form personal or group relationships or keep in touch with old friends. Electronic communication doesn't give the opportunity to see someone and talk face-to-face, and you might think it's impersonal. Yet there is something very personal about writing to someone through e-mail. You type a message at the keyboard with an image in your mind of the person who'll receive the message. Not all communications are personal; there's also a spirit and an expectation of sharing resources and information. It's satisfying knowing there are people around to answer questions and give help on almost any topic. It's also satisfying being able to share information you have. In some ways it's not surprising that there is so much communication and sharing on the Internet. At its technical basis the Internet is a network, and networks are created to share resources.

People communicate on the Internet in a variety of ways:

Electronic mail (e-mail). This is a basic Internet service that allows individuals to communicate. It's the foundation for the ways discussion or interest groups operate, and it can be used for access to other Internet services.

Discussions carried on in a group setting using e-mail. Some names for these groups are interest groups, discussion groups, Listserv, and mailing lists. Internet users join, contribute to, and read messages to the entire group through e-mail. Several thousand different groups exist; they're used to share opinions and experiences, ask and answer questions, or post information about a specific topic or interest.

Group discussions, asking questions, and sharing information through Usenet (also known as Internet News). The messages are called articles and are grouped into categories called newsgroups. Individuals can post articles to specific groups, reply to an article so the reply is posted to the newsgroup or sent only to the original author, or read articles. The communication here is from one computer system to another; it's available to individuals but isn't carried through their e-mail. Usenet existed before the Internet was in the form it is today, but the news (as it's called) is often carried from site to site on the Internet.

There is no organization or agency controlling activity on the Internet. Control is in the hands of individuals and local organizations, schools, or businesses. This allows for the formation of discussions, the exchange of ideas, and the spread of information in a free and open manner. The users come from a variety of countries and cultures, and this diversity, along with this open two-way communication, contribute to the Internet's utility and vigor. Some people describe the Internet as a form of anarchy, mainly because there isn't any central control. However, a number of laws apply to communications and activities on the Internet, local and regional network policies govern its use, and Internet-wide rules of etiquette and rules for acceptable behavior exist. The laws of one country or rules for one network can't be applied to everything that happens on the Internet. But, because the communications often travel across several networks going from their source to their destination, local policies and laws can apply. Individuals have been arrested, sued for libel, or otherwise censured because of messages sent on the Internet. The people using the Internet have a say in the way it's used. Inappropriate messages and practices are often met with a large number of complaints and protests, and sometimes result in the offenders losing access to the Internet. Some of these issues are discussed in detail in Chapter 9.

The number of people gaining access to the Internet is growing at an astounding rate. If the number of users increases at the same rate as in 1995, every person on Earth could have Internet access by 2003! This isn't technologically possible, and there are a few countries the Internet doesn't touch. However, the Internet is a growing, vigorous, and valuable means for communication and interaction.

From a Practical, Recreational, or Commercial Point of View. The Internet offers a staggering amount of information on a wide variety of topics. Some of it is practical; it can be used for business, research, study, or technical purposes, including access to the services and information provided by professional organizations: documents, government information, data, on-line bibliographic searches, articles, publications, and software. You can also use the Internet for commercial applications. This includes researching and using financial and economic data, marketing and buying items of all types, and making services available for a fee. Additionally, you can use your access to the Internet for personal and recreational purposes: finding information related to your interests and hobbies, getting software and other items you'll find personally useful, and even receiving advice. Other types of information include travel recommendations and news, medical and health information, weather reports, entertainment listings, library holdings, museum exhibits, and sports news. You'll be able to find people interested in and information about almost any topic. You can tap into university and other libraries throughout the world, museums, commercial publications, archives of software for many different types of computer systems, and databases of information dealing with topics such as art history, extragalactic data, literature, and molecular biology, to name a few.

Sharing information and resources is at the very heart of the Internet, so almost everything is available free of charge other than what you pay to access the Internet. However, some information and articles from magazines, newspapers, and periodicals do carry an extra charge. Carrying on secure business transactions on the Internet is becoming more commonplace.

It's easy to see how, as Internet use becomes more commonplace, one of the fastest growing sectors is in the area of commercial applications. Some are concerned that this will ultimately restrict the free-flowing sharing of information. On the other hand, a large involvement by the commercial sector will likely speed up the development of faster and more secure means of transferring information on the Internet.

You access the information or communicate with others on the Internet by using a collection of tools and services that connect you to people, information, and resources. There are three basic services:

Electronic mail (e-mail). An efficient and convenient means of user-to-user communication.

Telnet. Allows you to connect to and log into a remote computer. It appears as if there is a direct connection between your computer or terminal and the one at the remote site. You can then access any of the public services or tools at the remote site. Telnet can be used for access to libraries, databases, and other Internet services.

FTP (File Transfer Protocol). Transfers files from one computer on the Internet to another. Many systems on the Internet make archives or collections of files available to anyone on the Internet through anonymous FTP.

Newer tools and programs provide a common method to access almost everything on the Internet. Having a single way to access all the Internet services means more than having one super-duper program or exceptional tool. You need that, but you also need a standard, Internet-wide way to indicate which service to use, which site to contact, and what to do at that site. That's the idea behind the World Wide Web—provide a single means of access to virtually everything available through the Internet: services, resources, tools, and information.

From a technical point of view. The Internet is a network connecting thousands of other computer networks. Each network on the Internet has a unique address, and the computer systems making up a network have an address based on the network's address. At a basic level the addresses are numeric, a sequence of four numbers separated by periods. An example is **192.65.245.76**. You don't need to memorize numeric addresses; often they can also be specified as names, such as **www.mwc.edu**. Each piece of information passed around the Internet contains the sender's address and the delivery address. As information is passed around the Internet, each of the networks decides whether to accept it or pass it on. Once information is accepted within a network, it's the network's job to get it to a specific computer system.

The Internet is designed so the computer systems within one network can exchange information with computers on other networks. The rules that govern this form of communication are called *protocols*. Using the same protocols allows different types of networks and computer systems to communicate with each other. Each needs to have the software and hardware in place so it can deal with information in the form specified by the protocols. This means a computer system or network has to be able to transform information from its own into the form(s) designated by the protocols, transform information from the protocol's form to its own form, and send and receive information in that form. Two protocols used are *Internet Protocol* (IP) and *Transmission Control Protocol* (TCP). You'll often see these mentioned together as *TCP/IP* when dealing with the software needed to make an Internet connection.

Packets of characters (*bytes*), like envelopes holding messages, carry information on the Internet. Using the IP protocol, a message consisting of at most 1500 bytes or characters is put into a packet. Each packet has the address of the sender and the address of the destination. These addresses, mentioned above, are called IP addresses. You can think of a packet in the same way you think of a letter sent by a postal service. Using the TCP protocol, a single large message is divided into a sequence of packets, and each is put into an IP packet. The packets are passed from one network to another until they reach their destination. There, the TCP software reassembles the packets into a complete message. If packets are lost or damaged, a request is sent out to resend them. It isn't necessary for all the packets in a single message to take the same route through the Internet, or for the same message to take the same route each time it's sent. This notion of a message naturally applies to e-mail, but it's extended to apply to many of the other services on the Internet.

The Internet is a *packet-switched network*. The emphasis is on transmitting and receiving packets, rather than on connecting computer systems to each other. When Telnet, for example, is used it appears as if there is a direct connection between two computers on different parts of the Internet. However, it's a *virtual connection*; the two systems aren't directly connected to each other, it just appears that way. In reality, packets are being passed from one system to another. Passing information and implementing the Internet services with packets, instead of one long steady stream of bytes, keeps one system from tying up the networks with a connection dedicated to one program.

Most Internet services operate according to a scheme called *client/server*. A user on one computer system starts a program that contacts another remote computer system. The client is the program the user is running, and the server is running on the remote system. The user gives commands to the client, which passes them on to the server. The server interprets those commands and returns information to the client, which passes information to the user. WWW browsers operate on the same principle. When you use Netscape or another Web browser, you start a program that acts as the client, and it contacts a computer system running a WWW server. The information you see is passed from the server to the client. The commands you give are either used by the client to work with information on your system or passed from the client to the server, since any server can deal with several clients. So a single WWW server can handle requests from many client programs. A server simply responds to individual requests from clients, and the clients take care of presenting the information to the user. All of this information is passed as packets between the server and the client.

The networks on the Internet use hardware or a device called a *router* to communicate with other networks. The router on a network accepts packets addressed to it and passes on packets addressed to other networks. It's up to the individual computer systems to take care of sending and receiving packets. Each computer system with a direct connection to the Internet has to have the hardware and/or software to allow it to work with packets. This usually means either a network card with TCP/IP software is in the computer you use, or you get a direct connection by using PPP (*Point to Point Protocol*) or SLIP (*Serial Line Internet Protocol*) software and a modem. If you're using a modem, but not using PPP or SLIP, then you probably don't have a direct connection to the Internet, but you're contacting a computer that does.

Not all computer networks are part of the Internet; some use a different technology for their network operations. These can, however, exchange information with the Internet. This is done through a *gateway*, which allows different networks to communicate with each other. Systems connected through gateways can usually exchange electronic mail, but other Internet services may not be available.

Explanation of Internet Domain Names and Addresses

Networks and computer systems on the Internet exchange data and communicate with each other. An address is assigned to each network, and each computer in a network has an address based on the network's address. These addresses are made up of a sequence of four numbers separated by periods, such as 192.65.245.76. Each of the numbers is in the range of 0 through 255. Starting from the left, the numbers in the address identify a network, and the number(s) on the right identify a specific host or computer system. For example, the network portion of the address **192.65.245.76** is **192.65.245** and the host portion is **76**. On networks with more hosts, the last two or three numbers are used. An address in numeric form is called an IP address. Information sent from one site on the Internet to another is divided into packets, and each packet has the IP address of the sender and the IP address of the destination.

This numeric scheme of IP addresses works well for computer systems, but it's difficult (close to impossible) for people to remember, and type correctly, a sequence of four numbers for every Internet site they need to contact. Therefore, many Internet sites also have names; for example, **jupiter.research.wonder.com** or **cs.greatu.edu**. The name is called a *domain name*. Like the numeric address, domain names are a sequence of words separated by periods. How many words? There are at least two, with three and four being more common, but there could be more. The most specific information, usually the name of a computer system or host, is on the left and you get more general information as you move to the right. This is the opposite of the arrangement of a numeric address.

The collection of networks making up the Internet is divided into groups called domains. The domains represent either a type of organization or a geographical location. For example, a site in the domain **edu** would be an educational institution, and a site in the domain **tx.us** would be in Texas in the United States. Each IP address (numeric address) is associated with one or more domain names. An address specified as a domain name is automatically converted to the IP address. The name of a specific computer system or *host* on a network is called a *fully qualified domain name*. Here's a dissected example.

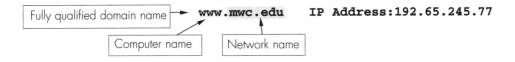

Fully qualified domain name → **www.mwc.edu**   IP Address:192.65.245.77

Computer name   Network name

Table 1.1 lists domains by type of organization.

Domain	Type of Organization	Example: Name and IP address	
com	commercial organizations	pipeline.netsurf.com	157.22.1.3
edu	educational institutions	enuxsa.eas.asu.edu	129.219.30.12
gov	government (US)	csab.larc.nasa.gov	128.155.26.10
mil	military (US)	nic.ddn.mil	192.112.36.5
net	networks	ftp.sura.net	128.167.254.179
org	nonprofit organizations	gopher.eff.org	204.253.162.4

Table 1.1   Top-Level Domains

The geographical names representing a country or state are two letters long. Here's an example:

```
Fully qualified Domain Name:    askhp.ask.uni-karlsruhe.de
Two-letter Domain Code:         de
Country:                        Germany
```

Since there are hundreds of countries throughout the world, we can't list them all here. *FAQ: International E-mail accessibility,* compiled by Olivier M.J. Crepin-Leblond, contains a list of two-letter country codes. The document is available on the WWW by using the URL **http://www.ee.ic.ac.uk/misc/country-codes.html**. (In case you're wondering, FAQ stands for Frequently Asked Questions. It's a common term on the Internet, and it's used to describe a collection of common questions about a topic. Don't worry, a FAQ contains answers as well.)

A domain name can tell you something about the site or computer system you'll be contacting. If the domain name is geographical, you can tell the country and maybe more information about the locality. Let's look at the fully qualified domain name **www.physics.utoronto.ca**. Starting from the left, **www** indicates this system is probably a WWW server, **physics** means this system is probably connected with the physics department, and **utoronto.ca** places the site at the University of Toronto, Canada. Except for knowing Canada corresponding to **ca**, all of this was guesswork. There are no hard and fast rules for local names. However, you'd be making a good guess if you got mail from **somebody@lib.umich.edu** who was connected with the library at the University of Michigan.

Your Internet Connection

You're using a computer or a computer terminal to access the Internet. You know how to turn it on and get things set up so you can tap into the Internet. That's great! The details about doing these things vary depending on the type of computer and software you're using and a number of other things. This book focuses on accessing the resources and services on the Internet through the World Wide Web after you're connected. If you need some help getting started or connected, find a local expert, get in touch with the company or organization that's providing you with Internet access, or start reading the manuals. A number of good books explain the hardware and software issues of getting connected, and there's lots of good advice about that on the Internet.

In order to use a graphical Web browser—such as Netscape Navigator—you need a computer system that can deal with graphics easily, such as one that can run Microsoft Windows, Windows 95 or X-Windows (Unix), or a Macintosh. Also, you're going to need software to enable you to use the Internet protocols (TCP/IP), and you need to have a connection to the Internet. This can be done in two ways: connecting directly to a network from your computer by having a *network card* with TCP/IP software, or using a dial-up connection where your computer uses a modem and software for SLIP or PPP to connect to a network.

Your computer is directly connected to a network. It has the hardware (usually called a network card and a cable connecting you to a network) and the software (TCP/IP) to allow it to send and receive packets with other computer on the Internet. In this case, we say you've got a *direct IP connection* to the Internet.

You use a modem to call and connect to a network. Your computer and the network you reach through the phone lines communicate with each other by using software called PPP (Point to Point Protocol) or SLIP (Serial Line Internet Protocol). Both of these allow your computer to send and receive packets just as if there were a direct and dedicated connection to a network. This is called a *dial-up IP* connection to the Internet.

With either of these types of connections you'll have to have some software and hardware installed on your computer. You'll have access to all the services and resources on the Internet, and be able to take advantage of graphical interfaces to using the Internet, as well as sometimes using only text.

Tip

Be sure you have all the information you need to connect to the Internet.

You have to have an IP address to communicate on the Internet. The IP address can be *static* (never changes) or *dynamic* and is generally assigned to you by the host or server system when you make a connection to the Internet. You'll also need to know your *domain name*, the IP address of the *router* or *gateway* (the system that communicates the information between the network and the Internet), the IP address of the *domain name server* (the system that handles translating IP addresses into numeric addresses), and the IP address or the fully qualified domain name of the servers that will provide you with e-mail (*mail or SMTP server)* and Usenet news. These have to be set when you first connect to the Internet. Find a knowledgeable person to give you this information, and be sure to get it from your Internet service provider.

Tip

Get the type of connection and service you need.

If you want to provide information from your system to the Internet, such as a home page on the WWW, then you'll need an IP address that doesn't change. This means you'll need a fully qualified domain name, and the computer you'll be using has to be running all the time. In that case, you may want a direct IP connection to the Internet. An alternative is to prepare your Web pages on one computer and then have them stored on another computer that is a server to the WWW. Check to see what the service provider's policies are toward the amount of e-mail you can receive and how much you can store. Finally, be sure you know the charges associated with use. For many personal dial-up IP connections, the user pays a flat monthly fee for a fixed number of hours and extra hours are charged at a separate rate. For example, one commercial service recently quoted charges of $15.00 per month for four hours per day access, and it charges extra hours at the rate of $1.95 per hour.

Proper Network Etiquette

The Internet connects networks throughout the world and there isn't any one agency controlling it. People from many different countries, cultures, and backgrounds use it in an effective way. All this diversity, along with no central control, could lead to disorganized anarchy, a lack of concern for the effects of using resources at other computer systems, and an indifference to the feelings, opinions, and concerns of individuals. Any of these effects would be intolerable and would detract from the utility, richness, and vigor of the Internet. It may seem too good to be true, but the users of the Internet generally behave in a way that protects individuals, fosters the sharing of information, and preserves Internet resources. This is because users realize the benefits both to individuals and to the group of maintaining the manner in which the Internet has developed and continues to grow.

Over the years organizations have developed policies, rules, and codes for acceptable behavior. We'll list a few issues here that you'll want to consider as you use the Internet:

Resources and Services. The services and resources on the Internet are generally offered in a spirit of cooperation or sharing. They need to be used in the same manner. In many cases you'll be a guest, accessing resources on a remote computer system. Be a good guest and show respect for the needs and wishes of the host. This can mean limiting the amount of time you spend using a remote system, limiting the amount of disk space or other resources you might use on a remote system, and limiting your access to nonpeak times.

Individuals. There is strong support for individual rights, feelings, and opinions on the Internet. The users represent a wide range of opinions and values. Some folks may express opinions that aren't to your liking; some things may be offensive to you. Before making an immediate reply or taking instantaneous action, take some time to consider your response. Treat others with respect and concern.

Copyrights. Material on the Internet is generally protected by copyright laws or treaties. Because something can be copied electronically and is easy to obtain, doesn't mean it can be distributed without permission. Most of the information contains a copyright statement indicating that it can be distributed electronically and used for noncommercial purposes. This applies to text, images, and other types of information.

Commercial Activities. For a relatively long time, in terms of the history of the Internet, commercial activity wasn't allowed. That's not the case now, but the Internet is still not wide open to marketing or commercial announcements. It's technologically possible to send an e-mail announcement of a product or service to thousands of people on the Internet. That type of activity is usually met with many protests, wastes a lot of resources, and generally does more harm than good. Take some time to know the culture and expectations of Internet users before attempting any commercial activities.

The Law. Generally, laws governing espionage, fraud, harassment, libel, obscenity, and theft apply to messages and other activities carried on electronic networks. Several laws have been passed in the US and other countries that apply specifically to electronic communications. There is a lot of freedom and openness on the Internet, but that doesn't mean it's beyond the rule of law.

Contribute to the Internet. The Internet is a network, and networks are created to share resources. When you have the opportunity to make something available to others on the Internet, do so. This includes helping others with questions, collecting and organizing information, or sharing your resources.

How the Internet Developed

In the late 1960s, the United States Department of Defense, through its Advanced Research Projects Agency (ARPA), funded research into the establishment of a decentralized computer network. From the beginning, some of the developers and researchers saw the advantages of a network in which computer systems of differing types could communicate. They also foresaw the development of a community among the users of this network. The network, named ARPANET, linked researchers at universities, research laboratories, and some military labs. The 1970s saw the further development of the ARPANET and the establishment of networks in other countries. There was a relatively small (less than one hundred) number of sites or hosts (computer systems) on these networks. In the early 1980s other networks around the world were established.

In the late 1980s the National Science Foundation (US) funded the development of a network (using the Internet protocols) named NSFNET to connect supercomputer centers in the United States. Many colleges and universities were encouraged to connect to that network. The number of sites increased rapidly; there were over ten thousand sites in 1987 and over one hundred thousand in 1989. Similar activity, although not on such a large scale, was taking place in other countries as well. This worldwide collection of networks and computer systems communicating according to the same protocols has come to be what's called the Internet.

Usenet, the *User's Network,* originated in 1979 and allowed people to share information in the form of articles arranged into newsgroups. Usenet was developed completely separate from the Internet, but programs and protocols for distributing articles on the Internet are readily available. A number of commercial networks and some using technologies that can't be adapted to Internet protocols were started in the 1970s and 1980s. Two examples are CompuServe, which charges users for connect time and other services, and BITNET, a network that linked many universities. Public access to the Internet has always been an issue during its development. The Cleveland Free-Net, a community-based network, was also developed in the late 1980s to give Internet access to anyone with a computer and modem. Several other community groups have started free-nets, some of which have joined to form the National Public Telecommunications Network (NPTN).

Funding for the development and operation of ARPANET, NSFNET, and several other networks throughout the world was subsidized by government funds. These networks established *acceptable use policies,* which gave rules for their use and stated what type of activities were allowed on these publicly supported networks. The policies prohibited any purely commercial activities and set the tone for a developing code of network ethics or etiquette. Commercial networks were also being developed, although they could not, under the acceptable use policies, use the transmission links of the public networks. So for some time commercial activity on the major portion of the Internet in the United States was prohibited. However, in 1988 several commercial networks reached an agreement with NSFNET to allow their e-mail to be carried on NSFNET. This enabled a user on CompuServe or someone using MCImail to send a message to someone with an Internet address at a public institution, such as a college or university. Messages could also be sent from NSFNET to these private networks, but e-mail from one user on a private service couldn't be transported over NSFNET to another user on a private service.

In 1990 ARPANET ceased to exist as an administrative entity, and the public network in the United States was turned over to NSFNET. The Internet was growing at a remarkable rate and clearly becoming bigger than the public institutions wanted to manage or support. In the early 1990s commercial networks with their own Internet exchanges or gateways were allowed to conduct business on the Internet, and in 1993 the NSF created the InterNIC to provide services, such as registration of domain names, directory and database services, and information about Internet services to the Internet community. These services were contracted to the private sector. In 1995, the NSF terminated all direct support and supervision of the Internet.

The explosive growth on the Internet and the inclusion of commercial networks and services has been accompanied by an astounding increase in the population of Internet users, including users who are not part of an academic or research community. The Internet is reaching the size and importance of an infrastructure, a necessary underpinning of society. In 25 years the Internet has grown rapidly from a research project into something that involves millions of people worldwide.

Summary

The Internet is used by millions of people around the world for communication, research, business, as a source of all sorts of information, and for recreation. One of the most popular and effective ways to tap into its resources is through the World Wide Web (WWW). The WWW is a vast collection of information that's connected like a web. There is no beginning or end; the information is accessible in a nonlinear fashion through connections called hyperlinks. You view the resources on the WWW by using a program called a Web browser. This book concentrates on the Netscape Navigator browser. You navigate through the WWW by pointing to hyperlinks (underlined or boldfaced words or phrases, icons, or images) and clicking once with the mouse. To use the WWW and the Internet effectively, you need to know how to use some of the services, tools, and programs that give access to their resources, as well as some of the sources of information.

It's possible to link information in almost any digital form on the World Wide Web. Text files, programs, charts, images, graphics files, digitized video, and sound files are all available. Not only do you find things from a variety of media, but you also get a great deal of information in many categories or topics.

When using the WWW you work in a hypertext or hypermedia environment. Items, services, and resources are specified by a Uniform Resource Locator or URL. These are used by Web browsers to specify the type of Internet service or protocol to use and the location of the item. The URL for the list of What's New on the WWW, for example, is

`http://www.ncsa.uiuc.edu/SDG/Software/Mosaic/Docs/whats-new.html`

The protocol or service in this case is **http** or hypertext transfer protocol, and a Web browser using it would contact the Internet site **www.ncsa.uiuc.edu** and access a document in **/SDG/Software/Mosaic/Docs/whats-new.html**. Hypertext documents are exchanged according to a protocol called http (hypertext transport protocol). The documents on the WWW are called Web pages. These are written and constructed using a language or rules called HyperText Markup Language (HTML).

The Internet can be described in a variety of ways. It can be viewed in terms of the people who use it and the ways they communicate with each other to share information and ideas. It's also reasonable to look at it as a vast information system on all sorts of topics. From a technical point of view, the Internet is a network of thousands of computer networks comprised of over a million computer systems. These networks and computers communicate with each other according to certain rules or protocols. The ones mentioned most frequently are the Internet protocol (IP) and the Transmission Control Protocol (TCP). You'll often see them referred to together as TCP/IP.

There are a variety of tools and services used to access the Internet. Three basic services form the foundation for other Internet services.

- Electronic mail enables users to exchange messages electronically.
- Telnet allows users on one computer to log into and access services on another (remote) computer on the Internet.
- FTP (File Transfer Protocol) allows users to copy files between computer systems on the Internet.

Users can communicate with individuals using e-mail, but there are also facilities for group discussions:

* Interest groups, Listserv, or mailing lists make it possible for users to engage in discussions focused on a specific topic by using e-mail.

* Usenet or Internet News is a system for exchanging messages called articles arranged according to specific categories called newsgroups. Here, the messages are passed from one system to another, not between individuals.

There are several other resources and services, and using a WWW browser allows you to access all of them. Using a Web browser also means that you usually don't have to learn different ways of doing things as you go from one type of service or protocol to another.

Each site on the Internet has a unique numeric address called its IP address and usually a corresponding name called the domain name. Information is passed around the Internet in packets. Each packet contains information, the address of the sender, and the address of the destination. The packets can take different paths through the Internet. It's up to the software at the destination to receive the packets and reassemble them. The emphasis is placed on the packets, not on the connections between systems. Users generally access sites by giving a domain name; the hardware and software convert a domain name to an IP address.

Many of the services operate according to a client/server model. A program called the client is started on one system and contacts a program called the server at another computer on the Internet. The commands typed or given by a user are sent to the server by the client. The server sends a reply to the client, and the client presents the information to a user.

You can access the Internet by having a direct connection from your computer to a network. In that case, you'd be using TCP/IP. Another way is by using a modem to call an Internet service provider and gaining access through a PPP (point to point protocol) or SLIP (Serial Line Internet Protocol).

The Internet developed through projects sponsored by governments in the United States and elsewhere to allow researchers to communicate with each other and share results. The initial work began in the late 1960s. There has been a tremendous growth both in the number of networks communicating according to the Internet protocols and the number of users accessing the Internet during the 1980s and 1990s. Now the Internet connects commercial, research, academic, and government networks throughout the world.

There is no central controlling agency that governs the activities on the Internet. However, a number of local laws, acceptable use policies, and codes of ethics adopted by most users help to make the Internet productive, useful, and exciting.

To use the Internet effectively you have to learn to use the services and tools described in this and the following chapters. You need to remember you're sharing a resource that's spread throughout the world. There will be times when everything doesn't work perfectly, and you'll need to practice using the Internet. In any case, be persistent and be ready to learn new things. You won't break or damage the Internet. It's a dynamic and vigorous place to learn, work, and enjoy yourself!

Exercises

Questions about your access to the Internet

1. What type of connection do you have to the Internet (TCP/IP, SLIP, PPP)? What are the charges for Internet access and who pays them?

2. Write down the steps you have to follow to access the Internet.

3. What is the domain name and IP address of the system you use to connect to the Internet?

4. What is your e-mail address?

5. What is the name, e-mail address, and phone number of someone you can contact when you have problems or questions about using the Internet?

6. What are the rules regarding proper use and behavior on the Internet in your organization or on the network you use to access the Internet?

7. What's the name of the WWW browser that you use? (Mosaic, Netscape Navigator, or ???)

Getting Information about the WWW

For this group of exercises you're going to have to get to the home page for the World Wide Web Project. Regardless of what browser you're using, you can get there by opening the location whose URL is **http://www.w3.org**. Here is another way: If you're using Netscape, press the directory button **Net Directory** (shown in Example 1.1), select the hyperlink **Computing** from the Excite Directory, select **World Wide Web**, select **TechnoWeb**, and finally select **World Wide Web Consortium**.

8. What are the first four hyperlinks on the home page for the World Wide Web Consortium? Follow one and describe what you find.

9. Select the hyperlink **About the World Wide Web and the Web Community** from the home page. What are some of the items listed? Follow the link labeled **vision**. What does that tell you about the WWW?

10. In the section **The World Wide Web and the Web Community** you'll see a hyperlink **People involved in developing the World Wide Web**. Who are each of the following: Tim Berners-Lee, Karen MacArthur, Henrik Frystyk Nielsen?

Browsing the WWW

11. Go to the home page for the WWW Consortium, select the hyperlink **The World Wide Web and the Web Community,** and then the hyperlink **World Wide Web Virtual Library.** Follow the hyperlink **Archaeology.** Describe what you find.

12. While in the **Virtual Library,** select an area that you find particularly interesting. Which is it? Describe what you found.

13. Go to the Yahoo Directory on the WWW. (It's URL is **http://www.yahoo.com** and it's also near the middle of the Netscape Net Directory Web Page. So you can access it the way we accessed city.net in Example 1.2 or the way we accessed the Excite directory in Example 1.1.) Select the hyperlink **Entertainment.** By following hyperlinks, visit three different amusement parks from three different countries. Which ones did you choose? What did you find?

14. Go to the Yahoo Directory. Let's relax a bit. Follow the hyperlink to the category **Recreation.** Bungee or Bungy is listed in the list of individual hyperlinks under the topic Recreation. Find it, note its location, and then describe what's there.

15. Go to the Yahoo Directory and select a category that you would like to browse. Write down at least three hyperlinks of documents you find interesting. Save those three documents in files in your computer and print the documents.

CHAPTER 2

Using a Web Browser

By following the examples and exercises in Chapter 1, you know that with a little practice the basics of using a Web browser are relatively easy to learn. This chapter deals with the practical issues of using a WWW browser and how to use the commands and tools to make effective use of the information and resources available on the World Wide Web.

When you start a WWW browser or follow a hyperlink, the browser (acting like a client) sends a request to a site on the Internet. That site (acting like a server) returns a file which the browser then has to display. In order for you to see or hear what's in the file, the browser has to be able to interpret its contents. This differs depending on the type of file; text, graphics and/or images may be displayed. If the file is written using HyperText Markup Language (HTML), the browser interprets the file so that graphics and images are displayed along with the text. Depending on the HTML code in the file, the text is displayed in different sizes and styles and hyperlinks are represented on the page.

What to Expect from a Web Browser

Before we get involved in all the details, let's discuss what to expect from a Web browser. Of course, you can expect to use a Web browser to look at Web pages throughout the Internet or to connect to various sites to access information, explore resources, and have fun. The Web browser will enable you to follow the hyperlinks on a Web page and also to type in a URL for it to follow. You expect the browser to have a number of other commands readily available through menus, icons, and buttons. And what about the times you need help? Your browser ought to include an easy way to get online help as well as built-in links to other resources on the Web that can give you help or answers to your questions.

You'll definitely want a way to save links to sites you've visited on the WWW so you can get back to them during other sessions. Web browsers take care of those in two ways, through a *history list*, which keeps a record of some of the Web pages you've come across in the current session, and a *bookmark list*, which you use to keep a list of WWW pages you want to access any time you use your browser. The name of the site and its URL are kept in these lists. The bookmark list is particularly important and the browser will contain tools to manage and arrange it.

34

The Web browser will include the means for you to search for information on the current page as well as search the WWW itself. You'll be able to save a Web page in a file on your computer, print a Web page on your computer, and send the contents of a Web page by e-mail to others on the Internet. Web browsers also give you access to Usenet newsgroups. Netscape Navigator has all these features, and starting with version 2, also includes the software for you to handle sending and receiving your e-mail.

World Wide Web pages can contain text and images, as well as hyperlinks to digital audio, digital video, or other types of information. Your Web browser will probably come equipped to handle many of these. But whether you can access something also depends on the software and hardware on your computer. If you don't have the programs and the hardware (a sound card and speakers) to play a sound file, then it's not reasonable to expect a Web browser will provide the means to handle sound files. However, Web browsers include ways to let you add to the list of software they use to display or play different media. If you do come across a file or hyperlink to something the Web browser isn't configured to handle, you can add what are called *helper applications* or *helpers*. These are programs that let you work with certain types of files. For example, a program called Real Audio lets you listen to certain types of sound files. A number of news broadcasts and talk shows are available in a format that you can hear using Real Audio. You first have to get the software (use your Web browser and the URL **http://www.realaudio.com/**) and then add the Real Audio Player (the helper application) to the list of other helpers. You do this by setting options or preferences for your browser. Setting options include ways to choose the font and colors used for displaying text, setting your e-mail address, and others.

To take advantage of some of the most exciting things on the World Wide Web, your browser needs to properly display and handle Web pages that contain animated or interactive items. Netscape Navigator can incorporate these features through its ability to interpret programs written in Java and Java Script. Other technologies such as Adobe Acrobat documents, Macromedia Director presentations, and a variety of other video and audio capabilities are available through the use of plug-ins. A browser should be able to work with Web pages that take advantage of these methods of presentation and involvement on the World Wide Web. See Appendix E for information about using Java and Java Script in your own Web pages. Use the URL **http://home.netscape.com/comprod/products/navigator/version_2.0/plugins/index.html** to find a list of plug-ins available for Netscape Navigator.

Quick Review and Some Tips

In this chapter we'll cover the details of using a Web browser. Before getting started, here are some terms that were introduced in the last chapter and are worth reviewing.

Home page. When you start a Web browser, the first page or document you see is called the *home page* for the browser. It's where you start on the WWW, and it's one of the options you can set. The term is also used another way. Individuals, corporations, institutions, and organizations often have a page or document on the WWW that gives information about them. This is also called a *home page*. For example, the URL for the home page for MTV is **http://www.mtv.com**, the URL for the home page for the Smithsonian Institution is **http://www.si.edu**, and the author's home page is **http://www.mwc.edu/ernie**.

URL, Uniform Resource Locator: A URL is the World Wide Web address of a page or location. For example, **http://cirrus.sprd.umich.edu/wxnet/servers.html** is the URL to use to get to a long list of sites on the WWW that give weather information. Interested in finding subway routes in any of several cities throughout the world? Use the URL **http://metro.jussieu.fr:10001/bin/cities/english**. Want the instructions in French? Use **http://metro.jussieu.fr:10001/bin/cities/french**. The first part of the URL tells the Web browser which protocol to use to contact a remote site. The ones that use the *hypertext transport protocol*, which is used to transmit Web pages across the Internet, all start with **http://**.

Page, location, document. The terms *location*, *Web page*, or *document* are used interchangeably. Each of these terms refers to the information you get from one World Wide Web address. Sometime the information fits in just one window, but when a document is more than one window long, you can scroll through it using the scroll bars on the window or keyboard commands. You use the browser to go from one page to another, from one location to another, or from one document to another.

`Tip`

Point and click.

Although the appearances and the details of using Web browsers are different, they're all used essentially the same way:

You use a mouse to move a hand or pointer to an icon, menu item, button, or underlined portion of the window and click the mouse button (the left one if your mouse has more than one button). If you've clicked on a link in the document, the browser follows that link and the current document is replaced or another window pops up. Clicking on text or icons in the border of a window pops up a menu from which you can choose an action. Clicking on an icon or button in the border may cause an action without your having to choose from a menu or dialog box.

`Tip`

Learn to help yourself.

This chapter contains the important details about the menus and options available with a WWW browser, but we won't go into all the details. There are too many to list in the space we have here, some are likely to change, and most browsers give you easy access to an online handbook and online help. If you get into the habit of looking at the help available online, you'll know how to help yourself. Also, you'll know where to get up-to-date information. Where it seems appropriate, we will refer you to the online manual or handbook for further details or explanations.

You access the Netscape Navigator Handbook by clicking on **Help** in the menu bar and then selecting **Handbook** from the pull-down menu.

Now on with Chapter 2. We'll go over details and give some examples using the Web browser Netscape Navigator. The topics we'll cover are:

* Starting and Stopping the Browser
* The Web Browser's Window
* Getting Around a Page and the World Wide Web

- Getting Help
- Saving, Printing, and Mailing Items from the World Wide Web
- Using the Web Browser with Local Files
- Bookmarks—Keeping Track of Favorite Places
- Setting Preferences and Options
- Where to Obtain a Web Browser on the Internet

Starting and Stopping the Web Browser

Starting a Session on the WWW

You need a connection to the Internet and you need to use a WWW browser. What sort of Internet connection do you have?

If your computer is directly connected to a network, you probably already have access to the Internet. You may have to start a program by giving a command or clicking on an icon to activate your connection. If you gain access to the Internet by using a modem, you probably have SLIP or PPP access to the Internet. To activate your connection, start Netscape Navigator. This will start a program that dials the correct number and then prompts you for a log-in name and password.

There are other variations, so it's a good idea to check with the folks that provide your Internet connection for the exact details. To start Netscape Navigator double-click on one of these icons:

 or

Netscape   Netscape
            Navigator

Ending a Session on the WWW

Ending a session on the WWW means stopping or exiting the browser program. You may also have to terminate your connection to the Internet. If your connection to the Internet is a SLIP or PPP modem connection and you or somebody is paying by the minute or hour, then you need to be sure to terminate the connection as well. In many cases, ending the Netscape session automatically ends the modem session.

You stop the Web browser program in the same way you end almost any other Windows program or application. Four ways to do that are:

1. Double-click on the upper left corner.
2. Click on the ☒ in the upper right corner
3. Click on **File** in the Menu Bar and then click on **Exit**.
4. Press **Alt** + F and then press X.

Here are some ways to end the modem session in case that doesn't happen automatically when Netscape ends: Click on the button **Disconnect** in the dialog box or window representing your Dial-Up Networking connection; select a command from a pull-down menu that hangs up the phone (modem); or choose an item from a menu that starts a log-out or *Bye* program. Just remember to terminate the connection so that you or someone else doesn't get an expensive bill from the company that provides your Internet services.

The Web Browser's Window

When you start a WWW browser, a window opens on your screen. It's the Web browser's job to retrieve and display a file inside the window. What is in the window will change as you go from site to site, but each window has the same format. The items that help you to work with the Web document in the window include the scroll bar, Menu Bar, and Toolbar, and they are the same every time you use the browser. The major components or parts are shown in Figure 2.1. They are:

* Menu Bar
* Toolbar
* Location
* Directory Buttons
* Content Area
* Scroll Bars
* Status Bar

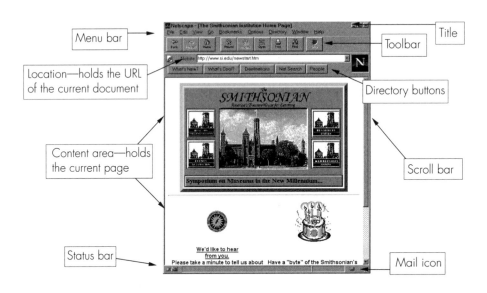

Figure 2.1   Netscape Window with Major Components Labeled

Tip

Giving commands using the keyboard—Keyboard shortcuts.

You can access all the commands for using a Web browser by pointing and clicking on a word, icon, or portion of the window, but sometimes you may want to give a command using the keyboard. To do this, use the key labeled Ctrl or the key labeled Alt along with some other key. For example, to mail a document to an Internet address, you can select Mail from a menu or use Ctrl+M. Thus Ctrl+M means hold down the key labeled Ctrl, press the key labeled M, and then release them both.

As another example, the command Alt+H will display a menu of items to select for helpful hints about using your Web browser. You hold down the key labeled Alt, press H, and then release them both. Commands given this way are called "keyboard shortcuts." We'll mention keyboard shortcuts at appropriate sections of the chapter.

Menu Bar

The Menu Bar near the top of the window consists of:

<u>F</u>ile   <u>E</u>dit   <u>V</u>iew   <u>G</u>o   <u>B</u>ookmarks   <u>O</u>ptions   <u>D</u>irectory   <u>W</u>indow   <u>H</u>elp

You choose any of these by moving the mouse pointer to the word and clicking on it. You can also activate one by using the Alt key along with the underlined letter. For example, to display the menu associated with File use $\boxed{\textbf{Alt}}$ + F.

Selecting an item from the Menu Bar gives a pull-down menu from which you select options or choices. As an example, if you click on **File** you see the display in Figure 2.2. Select any item in that menu either by clicking on it with the mouse or by pressing the underlined character in its name. (No need to press the Alt key, as when you select an item on the Menu Bar.) You select Print in Figure 2.2 to print the current document or Web page. You can select it from this menu by clicking on it with a mouse or by pressing **p** (upper-or lowercase) once the menu is in view. Some items on the menu are followed by Ctrl+ a letter, such as:

<u>N</u>ew Mail Message   Ctrl+M

in Figure 2.2. (This means you can use a keyboard shortcut or select the command from the menu.) You use this to mail a copy of the current document or Web page to someone on the Internet. Select it from this menu after the menu is in view or by pressing **Ctrl+M** at the keyboard at any time.

New <u>W</u>eb Browser	Ctrl+N
<u>N</u>ew Mail Message	Ctrl+M
<u>M</u>ail Document	
Open <u>L</u>ocation ...	Ctrl+L
Open <u>F</u>ile ...	Ctrl+O
<u>S</u>ave As ...	Ctrl+S
Pa<u>g</u>e Setup...	
<u>P</u>rint ...	
Print Pre<u>v</u>iew	
<u>C</u>lose	Ctrl+W
E<u>x</u>it	

Figure 2.2   File Pull-Down Menu

Selecting an item that's followed by ..., as in Open Location..., brings up a dialog box so you can give more information or select additional options. If, for example, you select Open Location.., you will then type in a URL and press Enter to retrieve the Web page you want to open.

The individual pull-down menus are:

File
This menu lets you print, mail, or save the current document into a file. It also lists items that let you open a new window, open a location (go directly to a URL), or open a file. **Opening** a file means viewing a file that's on your computer with the Web browser. The items related to **printing** include a way to preview a document before it's printed and an item that lets you set up a printer. Finally, this menu has items that let you close the window and/or end the WWW session.

Edit
Use this to **copy** items from the current document to other applications such as a word processor. The menu also contains an item called **Find,** which produces a dialog box that lets you search the current document for a string of words or letters. This is useful if the current document contains a long list of items and you're interested in only one or a few.

View
The items on this menu allow you to **reload** a copy of the current document in case there have been some changes to the source page since the time it was originally loaded, **refresh** the current page to its original state (this is useful if you're filling out a form on the screen and want to start over), or **load images** in case the images in a document were not immediately loaded automatically. The last two items let you view the **document source** or **document info.** Viewing the source version of the current page lets you see which HTML commands were used to create it. This is useful if you want to become familiar with ways to write your own Web pages. Selecting document info shows information about the current document, such as when it was last modified and whether it's a secure document. Secure documents are used for commercial or private transactions.

Go
These items take you to different documents or pages that you might have already viewed during the current Netscape session. Netscape keeps a list of the pages (the **history list**) you've been through to get to the current document. You can go **back** to the previous page, or **forward** to a page you've just come back from. Go to the **home page** for this session and take a look at the current **history list.** Select any item on the history list by pointing to it with the mouse and clicking on it. There is also a command **Stop Loading** to halt the connection that's attempting to bring something to the Web browser's window. You'll want to use this one if it's taking too long to load a page.

Bookmarks
Web browsers let you save links to places on the WWW you'd like to return to in this or other sessions. A **bookmark** in Netscape is just like a bookmark you might set when you're reading a book; it's a way to mark your place so you can find it later. The items in the bookmark list are URLs. Choose this menu to **add** the current URL to your bookmark list or to go to another window that lets you work with your bookmark list to choose an item from the list, arrange the items on the list, or modify the list in any way.

Options

Working with the items on this menu helps you set preferences that determine how the Web browser operates, what items will appear in the window, and how the current document will look. For example, you can set the programs that will be run to view images and play sound or video as part of a Web page. You can control what's shown on the screen and how Netscape works with your network and computer system. There's a separate item for the preferences you must set to use e-mail and Usenet news. These include the domain names or IP addresses of the mail and news servers. Some preferences and options are considered throughout the book. All are discussed in Appendix B.

Directory

This contains a list of interesting items you might want to spend some time looking at. Several of the items listed here are also available through the directory buttons, including **What's New?** (a list of new items available through the WWW) and **What's Cool!** (a list of interesting pages on the Internet). It also includes **Netscape Destinations** (an overall directory or list of places to go for information), **Internet Search** (a list of tools you can access to search the Internet), **People** (a list of tools to find e-mail addresses), and **About the Internet** (a collection of links to guides describing the Internet and its uses.)

Window

Use this open or go to other Netscape windows. You can open the Netscape Mail window to work with your e-mail or open the Netscape News window to read or write Usenet news. Other selections take you to your address book (to use with e-mail) or the bookmark or history list (explained below).

Help

This is the item to choose to get help about using the Web browser. It includes a link to frequently asked questions (FAQ) about Netscape and a useful handbook, which contains a tutorial and an explanation of the commands you use with Netscape Navigator.

Toolbar

Web browsers, like other Windows software, have a row of icons called the Toolbar. The Toolbar is just below the Menu Bar. Each icon works like a button. You press it (click on it with the mouse) and some operation or action takes place. In some cases, a dialog box pops up if the command has some options or if you need to provide information. For example, if you click on the icon to print the current document, you can select options to select a printer and you need to specify whether you want to print the whole document or a part of it. The icons give you a visual clue to the operation or action they represent. The commands they represent are all available through the items on the Menu Bar, but the icons give a direct path, a shortcut to the commands. The ones for Netscape Navigator are explained in Table 2.1.

Icon	Name	Explanation
Back / Forward	Back and Forward	These two buttons with directional arrows move between documents or Web pages you've already seen. **Back** takes you to the previous item on the history list and **Forward** can only be used if you've previously used **Back**.
Home	Home	Takes you to your home page, the one you first saw when you started Netscape.
Reload	Reload	Reloads the current document. If it didn't load completely, is disturbed in some way, or if the source has changed since you last accessed it, you may want to reload it.
Images	Images	If images are displayed automatically, then this will be on the Toolbar, but it won't be accessible to you. If images aren't displayed automatically and you'd like to see the images in the current page, click on this to see them. A setting in the **Options** menu controls whether images are displayed automatically.
Open	Open	Click on this to open a location. A dialog box will pop up on the screen, you type in the URL that represents the location, document, or Web page, and press the button labeled **Open** to access it.
Print	Print	Click here to print the current document. You'll be able to specify whether you want all or some of the pages printed along with other options about the printing.
Find	Find	Click on this to find a string (one or more words) in the current page or document. A dialog box will appear. Type the string to find and then click on **Find**. The search goes from the current position to the end of the document, but you can specify the search to go up from the current position to the beginning.
Stop	Stop	Clicking on the **Stop** sign will stop the loading of the current Web page. This is useful if it's taking a long time to contact a site or load a page.

Table 2.1   Icons in a Netscape Navigator Window

Location Bar

This box, just below the Toolbar, contains the URL for the current document displayed on the screen. If you want to go directly to a document or location on the WWW, you can type its URL here, press Enter, and the Web browser makes the connection, gets the information or file, and displays the page. Typing a URL here has the same effect as using the icon **Open**. If you're using Windows 95, the current location can be saved as a shortcut on the desktop. Move the mouse pointer to the "link" icon just to the left of the location bar, hold down the left button and move the pointer to the desktop area of your screen, and then release the button.

Directory Buttons

Netscape Navigator includes a row of directory buttons below the location pane. Each takes you to another Web page, most of which are directories of items on the WWW or ways to find items and people on the Internet. There is a button for an online handbook. Table 2.2 lists each button and gives a brief description. The items in each directory are selected by Netscape Communications.

Directory Button	Description
What's New!	A list of sites or locations that are new and innovative on the Internet.
What's Cool!	A list of interesting sites on the WWW. Includes innovative applications and Web pages—museums, animations, and audio. What's cool is decided by some folks at Netscape, so you may disagree.
Destinations	This takes you to a Web page containing links to resources and information on the World Wide Web. Some of the topics included are news, business, shopping, travel, and newsgroups.
Net Search	Click here to search the WWW for resources or information. You select which program you'll use to search, type one or more keywords, and wait for results. You'll get back a Web page that has hyperlinks to resources matching the keyword(s) you type. Searching the WWW is covered in detail in Chapter 6.
People	Click here to get to tools to help you find e-mail addresses and even mailing addresses for people.
Software	Click here to download or purchase the latest versions of software available from Netscape Communications Corporation.

Table 2.2   Directory Buttons in Netscape Navigator

Content Area or Document View

This is the portion of the window that holds the document, page, or other resource as your browser presents it. It can contain text or images. Sometimes the Content Area is divided into or consists of several independent portions called *frames*. Each frame has its own scroll bar, and you can move through one frame while staying in the same place in others. The Netscape E-mail and New Window are divided into frames as you'll see in Chapters 3 and 5.

Scroll Bars

Netscape has horizontal and vertical scroll bars. The horizontal one is at the bottom of the window and the vertical one is at the right of the window. These and their associated arrows help you move through the document. The scroll bars work the same as the ones in common Microsoft Windows applications.

Status Bar, Progress Bar, and Security Information

When you are retrieving a document, opening a location, or following a hyperlink, the bar along the bottom of the window (the status bar) holds the URL that's being used. It also lets you know whether a site is being contacted, if it's responding, and once a connection is made, the number of bytes that have yet to be transferred to complete the transmission. The bar on the far right, called the progress bar, and gives a graphical view of how much of the complete page has been received.

Information available through the World Wide Web is passed across the Internet. That means that any site on the path of the transmission can intercept the packets that make up the document or Web page. Thus, it's difficult to guarantee the security or privacy of an exchange of information (such as a credit card number) across the WWW. We all face that same problem whenever we use a portable wireless telephone. Netscape Communication Corporation provides the means to guarantee secure transmissions. This involves using specific servers and routes, and also the means to encrypt a message. If the document you're working with is secure, the key in the lower left will be blue, otherwise it looks as if the key is broken. It's not a good idea to send sensitive or valuable information through the WWW if the key isn't blue, but it's always your decision.

Mail Icon

Netscape Navigator shows a mail icon in the lower right corner of its windows. It indicates the status of your electronic mail. When you start Netscape Navigator, you'll likely see the icon with a question mark (?) to its right. That means the mail hasn't been checked. To check your e-mail, you click on the mail icon. Once it's been checked, the question mark is removed. If new e-mail arrives while Netscape is in use, an exclamation point (!) appears to the right of the mail icon.

Getting Around a Page and the World Wide Web

You've probably spent some time browsing the World Wide Web and some of the resources and information it has to offer. In this section we'll go over moving around within a page and also how to go from one page or location to another. Knowing this, you'll be able to get around the WWW effectively.

Moving Through a Page

When you start a WWW browser you see a portion of a page or document in the window. As you may remember, the starting page is called the *home page*. Many of these pages contain more information than is displayed in one window, so you need to know how to move through a document. There are several ways to do this—by using the scroll bars or the keyboard, or by searching for a specific word or phrase.

Using the Scroll Bars. You can move around or through a document by using the vertical and horizontal scroll bars on the right and bottom of the window. Use the vertical scroll bar to move up and down in the document, and use the horizontal scroll bar to move right and left. Each bar has an arrowhead on each end. You can click on these to move in the direction they indicate. Clicking on the arrowhead pointing down moves the window down one line in the document. Clicking on the up arrow has a similar effect, but the movement is up. Each scroll bar also has a scroll box within it. If you click on the scroll box, you can move very quickly in the direction it is moved. Clicking on a region of the scroll bar on one side or the other of the scroll box moves you one window in that direction.

Using the Keyboard. You can use the keyboard to move within a document. Pressing the up or down arrow will move you up or down one line. Pressing the Page Up key moves up one window length and pressing Page Down moves down one window length. Pressing Ctrl+Home takes you to the beginning of the document and pressing Ctrl+End takes you to its end.

Finding Text or Searching a Page. You can search a document for a word, portion of a word, phrase, or, more generally, any string of characters. To find a string you first have to get the dialog box labeled "Find" on the screen, as shown in Figure 2.3. There are three ways to do this—click on the icon labeled **Find** , select **Edit** from the Menu Bar, and then select **Find**, or use Ctrl+F from the keyboard.

Figure 2.3   Find Box

Once the **Find** dialog box is up, you type in a string (words or characters) and press Enter or click on the button **Find Next**. You can cancel a search by clicking on the button labeled **Cancel**. You can search in one of two directions. **Down** searches from your current position to the end of the document. Up searches from the current position to the beginning of the document. Mark the box **Match case** if you want to match the string exactly.

Moving Between Pages

As you work with and browse the World Wide Web you'll often be going from one page to another. Much of the time you do this by clicking on hyperlinks, but you can also go directly to a Web page, document, or location by typing its URL and then letting the browser retrieve it for you. You can also move between pages you've already visited by using the **Back** or **Forward** arrow icons on the Toolbar to move between pages during a session. Web browsers also let you save URLs or titles of the pages you've visited in one session so you can access them easily during that or any other later session. These are saved in lists called the *history list*—sites visited during the current session, and the *bookmark list*—names of sites saved from one session to the next.

Tip

When you can't wait—Breaking a connection or stopping a page.

Press the key labeled Esc or click on the **Stop** icon 🔘 to stop a page from being loaded into your browser or to cause Netscape to stop trying to connect to a site.

When you want to follow a link or go after a document, click on text or an icon. Watch the status bar to see if the remote site holding the information has been contacted and if it's responding. Your Web browser will try for a certain amount of time (a minute or so) to contact the remote site. If you don't want to wait that long or you don't want to wait for a complete page to be displayed by the browser, press Esc or the Stop icon. This doesn't close the browser; it just interrupts the transmission or attempted connection.

Going Directly to a Web Page. We'll describe four ways to go directly to a Web page, document, or location. In all cases you type the URL and press Enter. Netscape Navigator attempts to make the connection, and if it can retrieve the page, will bring it up on the window.

If the browser can't retrieve the page, check your typing to make sure you've got the URL right. There could be other problems as well. If the page is not available to the public, you'll see the message **403 Forbidden** in the window, or if the page doesn't exist, you'll get the message **404 Not Found**. It could also be that the site is out of service or too busy to handle your request.

One way to go directly to a Web page is to click on the pane in the window labeled **Location**. After the pane changes color, type the URL and press Enter.

After you take the action described in each of the following three ways to move to another location, a dialog box labeled **Open Location** pops up on the screen. Type the URL of the site you want to go to and press Enter. The Web browser then attempts to make the connection, and the page you've requested replaces the current one in the window.
  1. Click on the Open icon 🔲.
  2. Click on **File** in the Menu Bar and then select **Open Location**.
  3. From the keyboard press Ctrl+L.

Using Back and Forward. You can move to the previous Web page by clicking on the icon 🔲, by choosing Back from the **Go** menu in the Menu Bar, or by pressing Alt+◀ from the keyboard.

Once you've gone back, you can go forward to the previous page by clicking on the icon 🔲, by choosing Forward from the **Go** menu in the Menu Bar, or by pressing Alt+▶ from the keyboard.

You can also go forward and back by pressing the right mouse button (while the pointer is on a Web page) and then selecting **Back** or **Forward** from the menu that pops up on the screen.

As you go from page to page, Netscape Navigator keeps track of the ones you've visited, but because you can go from site to site in a hypertext manner—not in a straight line—it doesn't save a list of all the sites you've visited. And likewise, forward and back make sense only when we're talking about items we go to in a sequential manner. So you can go from a site named A to a site name B and then come back to A and then go to a site named C. Pressing **Back** takes you to A, and from there going forward takes you to C. In other words, you can't get back to B again by using **Forward** and **Back**. Here's a diagram that might help.

Once you're at **C** you can go back to **A**, and when you're at **A** if you go forward, then the only place you can go is to **C**.

Keeping Track—The History List. The Web browser keeps a record of the path you've taken to get to the current location. That path consists of a list, the *history list,* of pages opened on the way to the present location. It doesn't keep track of every location or page you've visited, just the ones that you can reach through **Forward** or **Back**. The list changes as you move around the WWW. Some things are added and others removed automatically; selecting an item from the history list doesn't change it. You'll want to use this list to go directly to a Web page that's on the list without having to go through all the pages in between.

To use the history list, bring it up on to the screen by pressing Ctrl+H from the keyboard or clicking on **Go** from the Menu Bar and selecting **View History...** from that menu. Figure 2.4 illustrates a sample history list. The highlighted item shows the title and URL of the current page. You can select and highlight any item by using the up or down arrow on the keyboard or by using the mouse. Once you've highlighted the location you want, click on the button labeled **GoTo** or double click on the highlighted item. The button labeled **Create Bookmark** will add the URL and name of the highlighted item to your bookmark list. You will want to add the name of a Web page (and its URL) to the bookmark list when you want to be able to return to it in another session on the WWW.

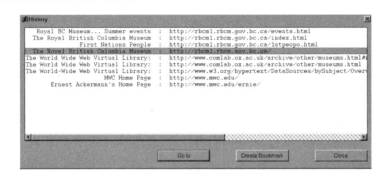

Figure 2.4   History List

Keeping Track—The Bookmark List. The bookmark list is a collection of hyperlinks to Web pages that you want to save from session to session. (The history list disappears at the end of a session.) They could be your favorite sites, ones you find useful, or ones you've looked at briefly but want to return to in the future. You see each item on the bookmark list as the title of a Web page (you don't see the URL as in the history list), but each entry is a hyperlink. The browser includes programs to let you manage and arrange the list.

To use the bookmark list to go from the current Web page to another, first bring the list into view on the screen by pressing **Ctrl+B** from the keyboard, or select the pull-down menu **Bookmarks** from the Menu Bar and then select **Go to Bookmarks**. To highlight or select an item on the list, use the up or down arrows on the keyboard or the mouse. Then press Enter or double-click on the item with the mouse. Figure 2.5 shows a portion of a bookmark list.

We'll take a break from the giving the details of using a Web browser and go through an example of how to use some of these commands to browse a section of the WWW. We'll look at the WWW Virtual Library, a directory of information available on the Internet through the World Wide Web, and investigate the section titled **Sport**. The information in the directory is arranged by subject such as Sport, Music, or Art. Each of the sections is maintained by volunteers; people like you who have the facilities and experience to collect, present, and (hopefully) keep up to date hyperlinks to information on a topic they're interested in. As with any college or public library, there are lots of topics in the Virtual Library to look through; you can spend lots of time browsing and you'll often find links to useful and interesting information. You don't find books as in a physical (real) library, but you find all sorts of information in text or other forms. It's definitely worth several visits.

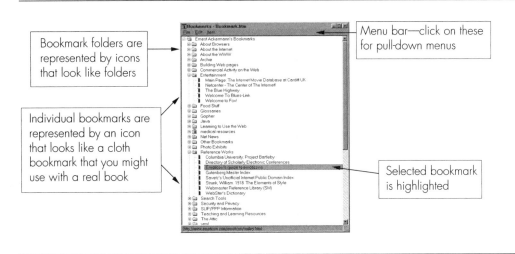

Bookmark folders are represented by icons that look like folders

Individual bookmarks are represented by an icon that looks like a cloth bookmark that you might use with a real book

Menu bar—click on these for pull-down menus

Selected bookmark is highlighted

Figure 2.5   Portion of a Bookmark List

Example 2.1   Browsing the WWW Virtual Library—Sports

This example takes us to the WWW Virtual Library arranged by subject. It's a good place to keep in your bookmark file and contains hyperlinks to information on lots of subjects from Aboriginal Studies to Zoos. Going from site to site is sometimes called *net surfing* or *surfing the Internet*. That means going from location to location finding interesting, entertaining, or useful sites and resources, regardless of the type of information you're dealing with. Just to show how easy it is to visit a number of sites, regardless of where they are located, we will look in the subject area Sport in the WWW Virtual Library for information about (water) surfing (pardon the Net pun!), take a trip to "Virtually Hawaii," and then check in on the 1996 Olympic games.

Although this example focuses pretty much on the topic of sports, you will also see hyperlinks that could easily take you to different topics if/when you choose to follow them. It's this interconnection of sites and topics that makes the term World Wide Web appropriate. Even though some of the steps can be followed by using commands from the keyboard, we'll use the mouse to point and click on the appropriate hyperlinks or items from the Menu Bar or Toolbar. As you work through this and other examples, the ⓦⓦⓦ indicates something for you to do.

Here are the steps we'll follow:
1. Start Netscape.
2. Open the location for the World Wide Web Virtual Library (WWWVL) arranged by subject.
3. Search the Virtual Library home page for the section titled **Sport**.
4. Select the hyperlink to the Sport home page.
5. Search the Sport section for items dealing with surfing.
6. Select the hyperlink to **The Blue Room** for Hawaii.

7. Browse **The Blue Room** page and select the hyperlink **Full Pictures of the Globe,** global satellite images.
8. Select the hyperlink **Virtually Hawaii** at the bottom of the page for Satellite Oceanography Laboratory.
9. Use the history list to go back to the Sport home page.
10. Get information about the Olympics.
11. End the session.

While you're going through the steps in this example, practice using the **Back** and **Forward** icons. As long as you click on **Forward** as many times as you click on **Back,** you won't lose your place.

1. Start Netscape.

The way you start Netscape Navigator depends on how it's installed on your system and the type of networking you use. You may have to start your Internet connection first—especially if you're using Dial-Up Networking. Then you need to select and double-click on the program icon for Netscape Navigator. It may be in a folder on your desktop or in the program list. If you've installed it yourself then you'll probably know where it is, otherwise you need to ask for some help or search your system for a program file whose name is Netscape.

2. Open the location for the World Wide Web Virtual Library (WWWVL) arranged by subject.

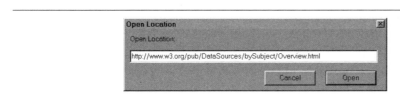 Click on the **Open** icon, type **http://www.w3.org/pub/DataSources/bySubject/ Overview.html**, and click on the button **Open**.

When you start your Web browser, your home page will appear on the screen. There just might be a hyperlink to the WWW Virtual library. Browse through your home page by either pointing to the vertical scroll bar and moving it down, by pressing the down arrow or space bar, or by pressing the Page Down key. If you don't find a hyperlink to the Virtual Library, then click on the **Open** icon and type in the URL for the WWW Virtual Library arranged by subject, **http://www.w3.org/hypertext/ DataSources/bySubject/Overview.html**, as shown in Figure 2.6.

Open Location

Open Location:

http://www.w3.org/pub/DataSources/bySubject/Overview.html

Cancel   Open

Figure 2.6   Open Location to the WWW Virtual Library by Subject: Type Its URL

3. Search the Virtual Library home page for the section titled **Sport**.

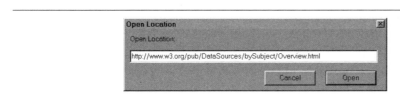 Click on the **Find** icon, type **sport**, and click on the button labeled **Find Next**.

Click on the icon **Find** from the Toolbar to search a Web page for a string of one or more text characters. A dialog box will appear on the screen. Type in the string **sport** as shown in Figure 2.7 and then click the button labeled **Find Next**. That will take you to the next occurrence of the string **sport** on the page. Sometimes you may have to use **Find** more than once. **Sport** could be part of another word (transportation, for example) on the Web page, and if that word appears before **sport** then the Find operation will take you there before you find the word you're looking for. In that case, click on **Find Next**. When you're done searching click on the button labeled **Cancel** to remove the dialog box from the screen.

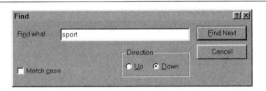

Figure 2.7   Using Find to Search for String "sport"

4. Select the hyperlink to the **Sport** home page.

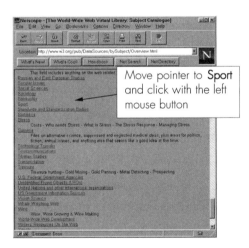 Move the mouse pointer to the hyperlink **Sport** and click with the (left) mouse button.

Figure 2.8   Sport Highlighted on WWW Virtual Library Page

Figure 2.8 shows the Web page with **sport** located. Move the mouse pointer to the word **Sport**. The pointer will turn into a hand, which tells you you're at a hyperlink. Press the left mouse button to follow it to the home page for the Sport section of the WWW Virtual Library. That's shown in Figure 2.9.

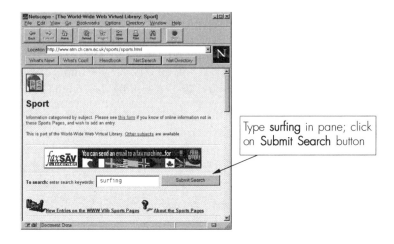

Figure 2.9 Home Page for Sport Section of WWW Virtual Library

5. Search the Sport section for items dealing with surfing.

Type **surfing** in the box alongside the button **Submit Search**, then click on the button.

You know by now you could search the home page for **sport** by clicking on the **Find** icon as in a previous step. But this page has a simple search form to fill out. Type the string **surfing** in the box and then click on the button **Submit Search**. You'll find forms like this on several Web pages. After you click on **Submit Search**, a program runs at the server that supplies this page and all the entries in related pages with a search for the word **surfing**. Figure 2.10 shows what to expect from the search.

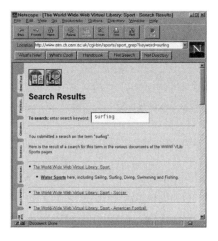

Figure 2.10 Search Results Using the Keyword Surfing

w⁴ʷ Click on the hyperlink **Water Sports**.

Click on the first hyperlink on the page. That takes you to the section of the Sport page containing information about water sports. This is shown in Figure 2.11.

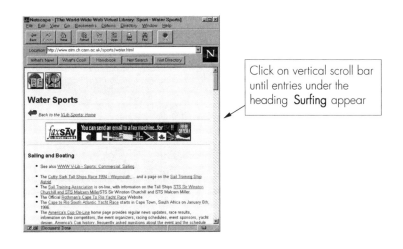

Click on vertical scroll bar until entries under the heading **Surfing** appear

Figure 2.11 Web Page for Water Sports

There's at least one entry about surfing since your search brought you here, but it's not visible in the first window. We could use the icon labeled **Find**, but instead we'll get some practice using the scroll bar. Clicking on the vertical scroll bar once or twice will bring up the section about surfing. You can also press the space bar or the Page Down key to move down the page. Figure 2.12 shows a portion of the Surfing section.

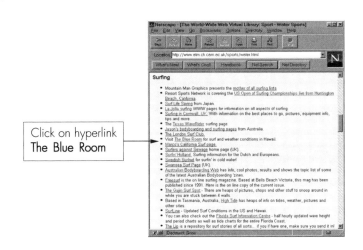

Click on hyperlink **The Blue Room**

Figure 2.12 Surfing Section of Water Sports Web Page

6. Select the hyperlink to **The Blue Room** for Hawaii.

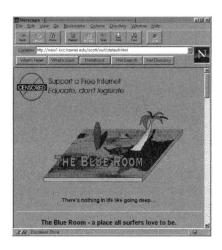 Move the mouse pointer to the hyperlink **The Blue Room** and click.

Pointing to and clicking on the hyperlink **The Blue Room** takes you to the home page for that site. Figure 2.13 shows a visit to that site.

Figure 2.13 Home Page for The Blue Room, Hawaii

7. Browse **The Blue Room** page and select the hyperlink "Full Pictures of the Globe," global satellite images.

Browse this page and feel free to follow hyperlinks to get information about surfing in Hawaii. If you go away from this page you can always get back by clicking the Back icon on the Toolbar. We're going to take a look at some global satellite images courtesy of the Satellite Oceanography Laboratory.

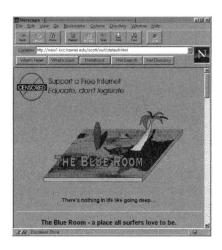 Move down The Blue Room page by pressing **PgDn** until you see the hyperlink **Full Pictures of the Globe**.

Figure 2.14 shows that link as it appears on The Blue Room Web page.

Figure 2.14 Hyperlink Full Pictures of the Globe

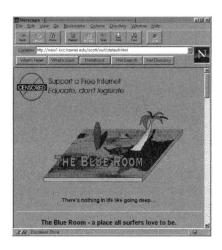 Click on the hyperlink **Full Pictures of the Globe**.

Clicking on that hyperlink brings up a Web page similar to the one shown in Figure 2.15. (If the hyperlink doesn't work, use the URL **http://satftp.soest.hawaii.edu/satlab/gms.html**.) You may have to wait a while for the images to completely transmit to your Web browser. You can tell the transmission is complete when there aren't any more stars, comets, or asteroids streaming passed the **N** in the upper right. You'll also see the message **Document Done** appear briefly in the status bar. Don't rush on to the next step. Take a little time to look at the satellite images and maybe browse some other hyperlinks on the page. You can get a larger copy of one of the images by clicking on them.

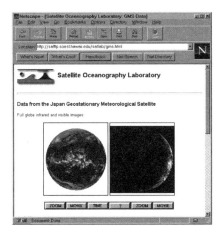

Figure 2.15 Full Globe Images from the Satellite Oceanography Laboratory

8. Select the hyperlink **Virtually Hawaii** at the bottom of the page for Satellite Oceanography Laboratory.

_W_W_ Press **Ctrl** + **End** to get to the end of the current Web page.

The hyperlink to **Virtually Hawaii** is at the bottom of this page. Pressing Ctrl+End takes you to the end of a page quickly (once the page has been completely transmitted to your site). Figure 2.16 shows the links at the end of the page.

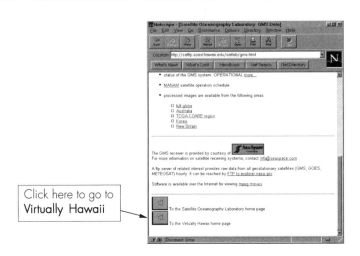

Figure 2.16 Page with Hyperlink to Virtually Hawaii

Click on the hyperlink to **Virtually Hawaii** at the bottom of the page.

Clicking on that takes us top the Web page shown in Figure 2.17. We've really done some traveling here and maybe we ought to take some time and browse around Hawaii for a while.

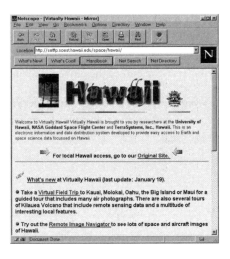

Figure 2.17 Home Page for Virtually Hawaii

It is a nice place to visit, but on to the rest of this example.

9. Use the history list and go back to the Sport home page.

We've traveled through several pages and now would like to get back to the home page for Sport in the WWW Virtual Library. Certainly one way to do that is by pressing the **Back** icon in the Toolbar until the proper page appears. But then we'd have to go through all the intervening pages. It's quicker to select the site from the history list. You can get to the list by Ctrl+H from the keyboard.

wWw Press **Ctrl**+H.

This displays the history list as shown in Figure 2.18.

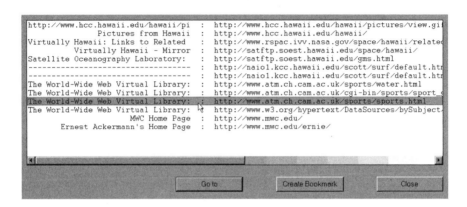

Figure 2.18 History List with Hyperlink to Sports Highlighted

wWw Using the mouse or **↓**, highlight the entry to the **Sport** section of the WWW Virtual Library.

wWw Click on the entry or the button **Go To**.

By highlighting and selecting the entry **Sport**, you'll return to the Sport home page in the WWW Virtual Library as shown in Figure 2.9. Now we'll go to a page with information about the Olympics.

10. Get information about the Olympics.

Now you are at the Sport home page. You search for information in the same way we searched for information on surfing.

wWw Type **Olympics** in the search box and press **Submit Search**.

The results of the search are shown in Figure 2.19.

Figure 2.19 Search Results Using Keyword Olympics

Several entries about the Olympics are on this page. Use the **Find** icon on the Toolbar to look them over.

Click on the **Find** icon on the Toolbar.

Type **Olympic** in the dialog box and click on the button **Find Next**.

Following the step above will take you to all the entries on the page containing the word **Olympic**. Follow the hyperlinks you'd like.

11. End the session.

You knew when we started that this had to end sometime. Now's the time.

Click on **File** on the Menu Bar.

Select **Exit** from the menu.

That's it!

————————————————End of Example 2.1————————————————

Getting Help

There are several ways to get help about using Netscape Navigator. Online help is available while you're using Netscape. There is a list of Frequently Asked Questions (FAQ) about using Netscape with answers included and several Usenet newsgroups dedicated to discussion about using a WWW browser. (Using and accessing Usenet is covered in Chapter 5.)

Online Help

You can get help online while you're using Netscape Navigator by clicking on the pull-down menu item **Help** on the Menu Bar.

Clicking on **Help** brings up a menu from which you can select one of several types of information. Choose any one for more information.

This includes:

* Information about Netscape, including how to register your copy and information about getting a newer version of Netscape Navigator.
* An online handbook, which includes tutorials and a reference section.
* Notes about known problems with the software (Release Notes).
* Frequently asked questions and information about security.
* Ways to give Netscape feedback about its products and get support.
* A list of hyperlinks to tools and instructions for creating Web pages and services.

The Handbook

Netscape Navigator, like most Web browsers, has online help available. You get to it by selecting **Handbook** from the **Help** pull-down menu from the Menu Bar or by clicking on the directory button. The Handbook is a quick and useful resource. It's available when you need it while you're using your Web browser.

The Handbook is divided into several sections, so you can select the part that's right for you at the time you need it. The sections include a quick start introduction, a complete tutorial, a reference section, and an index. When you get stuck or can't remember how to do something, look to the Handbook for help.

Frequently Asked Questions (FAQ)

Frequently Asked Questions or FAQ is a traditional way to collect common questions and provide answers on the Internet. As you browse the Internet you'll see FAQs on all sorts of topics. Some examples are health care for pets, privacy on the Internet, or questions related to specific software or products. These FAQs are usually maintained by volunteers or a specific company. Netscape maintains several FAQs about their products, and you can get to them by choosing Frequently Asked Questions from the **Help** pull-down menu from the Menu Bar or by explicitly opening a location (typing in a URL) using the URL. Two other FAQs you'll find useful are:

* World Wide Web / A Guide to Cyberspace—A good introduction to getting started on the WWW. URL **http://www.hcc.hawaii.edu/guide/www.guide.html**
* World Wide Web FAQ—This is available in English and other languages at several sites on the WWW. You should pick the one closest to you. Here's a partial list:
    * Boutell.com, Inc., western United States (North America). URL **http://www.boutell.com/faq/**
    * United States Military Academy, eastern United States. URL **http://www.usma.edu/mirror/WWW/faq/**

* Island Internet, British Columbia, Canada (North America).
  URL **http://www.island.net/help/faq/www_faq/**
* Acer Inc., Taipei, Taiwan (Asia, in Chinese). URL **http://www.acer.net/document/cwwwfaq/**
* Fraunhofer Institute for Computer Graphics, Darmstadt, Germany. URL **http://www.igd.fhg.de/www/documents/servers/mirrors/www-faq.html**

There are several (at least 15) Usenet newsgroups that host discussions about the WWW, and each maintains its own FAQ. A list of Usenet newsgroups about the WWW is available though the World Wide Web FAQ mentioned above. One direct link to the list of newsgroups is **http://www.boutell.com/faq/ngroups.htm**. You ought to check this because it has the names and descriptions of the groups, and it's likely to contain new ones as they're created. Three of them are:

comp.infosystems.www.authoring.html	For discussion of writing Web pages using HyperText Markup Language (HTML).
comp.infosystems.www.browsers.ms-windows	For discussion of Web browsers used with Microsoft Windows and NT operating systems.
comp.infosystems.www.announce	Used to announce new Web pages.

Saving, Printing, and Mailing Items from the WWW

Suppose you're working on the WWW and you come across a document, data, program, picture, sound or video clip, or anything you'd like to save. Or maybe you want to e-mail it to someone else or get a printed copy of it. A Web browser comes with the tools and commands to let you do these things. Commands are available through the pull-down menu under **File** in the Menu Bar, through some of the icons in the Toolbar, or through some keyboard shortcuts.

Much of what you find on the WWW can be saved into a file on your computer, making it easy to share and distribute information on the WWW. Making it easy to share and exchange information is one of the main reasons the WWW project (and the Internet) was started. There's also a drawback to this. This free access to information makes it difficult to control unauthorized distribution of anything that's available through the WWW. So something you make available can be copied (in fact, an exact digital copy) by anyone with a Web browser, even though it's usually illegal to make copies of works without the permission of the author or the person who owns the copyright to the material. This sort of copying is something that can be done, but in many cases, should not be done, according to copyright laws and international conventions. In many cases, the material comes with a statement explaining the rules for personal use of the material. For example, here' a quote from **http://sunsite.unc.edu/expo/vatican.exhibit/exhibit/About.html** describing limitations to use of the materials in the exhibit **Rome Reborn** offered by the Library of Congress.

The text and images in the Online Exhibit ROME REBORN: THE VATICAN LIBRARY AND RENAISSANCE CULTURE are for the personal use of students, scholars, and the public. Any commercial use or publication of them is strictly prohibited.

Remember that because something is available on the WWW doesn't necessarily mean you may make a copy of it, and in almost every case the material can't be used in any sort of commercial activity without written permission.

Saving Web Pages in a File

Any Web page can be saved in a file on your computer. When a page is saved, you get the text portion of the page. The images are not included. This is because the images and other portions of what you see really exist in files other than the one that holds the text you see on the screen. You may want to save a Web page in a file on your computer so you can get to it in the future without connecting to the Internet.

To save a page you give the command to Save to a File. A dialog box opens in which you select the format for the saved page (source or text) and give the name of the file to hold the page. If you save it in text format, you'll have only the words you see on the screen. A page saved in source format include the text along with the HTML commands or tags used to create the page. It's really useful to see how others have used HTML to create and make Web pages when you're thinking about translating your designs for Web pages into HTML.

The three examples in Figures 2.20, 2.21, and 2.22 show a portion of a Web page as it appears on the screen (using a Web browser), how it looks saved in a text file, and how it looks saved in source or HTML format.

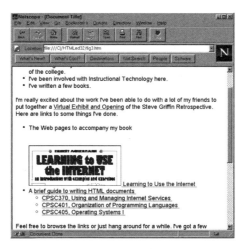

Figure 2.20   WWW Format

Here are links to some things I've done.
 * The Web pages to accompany my book
   [Image] Learning to Use the Internet
 * A brief guide to writing HTML documents
 * Web pages to accompany some courses I've taught or I'm teaching
   o CPSC370, Using and Managing Internet Services
   o CPSC401, Organization of Programming Languages
Feel free to browse the links or just hang around for a while. I've got a
few URL's in my attic you might want to look at.

Figure 2.21 Text Format

Here are links to some things I've done.
<UL>
<LI>The Web pages to accompany my book
<A HREF="http://www.mwc.edu/ernie/lrn-net.html" >
<IMG SRC="http://www.mwc.edu/ernie/smcover2.gif"> Learning to Use the
Internet
</A>
<LI>A <A HREF="http://www.mwc.edu/ernie/writhtml.html" >brief guide to
writing
HTML documents
</A>
<li>
<ul>
<LI><A HREF="http://www.mwc.edu/ernie/cpsc370.html" >CPSC370, Using
and Managing Internet Services
</a>
<LI><A HREF="http://www.mwc.edu/ernie/cpsc401.html" >CPSC401, Organization of
Programming Languages
</a>
<LI><A HREF="http://www.mwc.edu/ernie/cpsc405.html" >CPSC405, Operating
Systems I
</a>
</ul>
</UL>
<P>

```
Feel free to browse the links or just hang around for a while.
I've got a few URL's in my <a href="http://www.mwc.edu/ernie/attic.html">
attic</a>
you might want to look at.
```

Figure 2.22 Source View

Saving Items on a Page from the WWW into a File

Almost anything that has a hyperlink to it can be saved in a file. You can save items after you receive them—like saving a Web page to a file once the page is on the screen—or you can save them without seeing or hearing them beforehand. To save whatever is on the other end of a hyperlink, move the mouse pointer to the hyperlink, hold down the Shift key, and click the (left) mouse button. For example, if a hyperlink takes you to an image or graphic, then pressing Shift and clicking on the link would let you save the image in a file. Naturally, the same holds true for audio or video files. The link can point to anything on the WWW—another Web page, a document in special format (such as a document prepared with a word processor or spreadsheet), an image, a compressed archive of files, a video file, an audio file, or anything. (Who knows what you'll find on the WWW.)

You get to information by following a hyperlink. You can save the information pointed to by the hyperlink in the way we've described in this section. That saves at least one step. Sometimes, of course, you may not be aware of where the hyperlink will take you. When you click on a hyperlink and it refers to a type of file that your browser is set up to handle, you'll have the option of saving the result in a file. For example, the browser I have isn't set up to automatically handle a hyperlink that takes me to a file whose name ends with **.exe**. (Probably a good thing, because then I might be running programs on my computer that I retrieved from the WWW without checking them for viruses.) When I follow a hyperlink to a file whose name ends with **.exe**, Figure 2.23 pops up on my screen and I have the option to save it to a file. If I want to save the file, I choose **Save** and then specify a name for it. (We'll cover the option Configure a Viewer later.) Then I check it with software that examines programs for a virus.

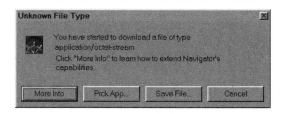

Figure 2.23 Unknown File Type Notification

Tip

Check programs from the Internet for a virus.

A computer virus, like a biological one, cannot live on its own and is spread only through programs that are run on a computer. Viruses can't be spread through text or data files. Don't use an executable file (name ends with **.exe** or **.com**) you've retrieved from the Internet or WWW without first making sure it doesn't have a virus. Have it checked by a program that detects viruses.

Printing Documents

What you see in your browser window can be printed to any printer you can access from the computer that has the Web browser running on it. When a Web page is printed, everything you see in the window—text, graphics, images—is passed on to the printer.

Giving the command to print brings up a dialog box in which you can select the printer, request several copies, and select which pages of the Web page will be printed. The phrase *pages of the Web page* may seem strange, but remember that a Web page isn't confined to a physical page. You can preview the printing by picking the preview option. That way you can get an idea of the physical layout of the printed Web page.

 Tip

Controlling the appearance of the printed copy of a page.

You can change the size or the type of font that's used to display and print Web pages. By picking a larger font you increase the size of text on the screen and also the text that's printed. Likewise, choosing a small font decreases the amount of paper needed to print a Web page. You select a font and font size by choosing the **Options** pull-down menu in the Toolbar, then selecting preferences, and finally **Font**.

Mailing a Web Page

You can mail a Web page to any Internet address. Mailing a page means sending only the text that's on the page or sending the source. The source is the text along with all the HTML statements that specifies hyperlinks, control the format of the page, and identify the source for the images and graphics on a page. In this sense, mailing a Web page is similar to saving a Web page in a file.

You give the command to mail a Web page, and a window pops up where you fill in the Internet address to send the e-mail, the subject, and anything else you'd like to write or include. Only the URL for the current Web page is automatically included in the message. You can send the page (either text or source) as an *attachment* to the e-mail (we'll say more about this in Chapter 3), or you can send it quoted (as text) in the body of the message. If you found something on a page that you wanted to share with someone else, it might be appropriate to mail them the URL. If they don't have access to a WWW browser, then it would be better to attach or quote the Web page. If it's included in the body of the message it can be edited, so you can send a portion of the page.

Using the Web Browser with Local Files

The Web browser can be used to view a file that's on a disk on your computer. You don't need the Internet to access those files, called local files. It's really convenient to use your Web browser to look at local files; sometimes easier than opening another application or program to view a file. Once you're viewing a file with the Web browser, you can work with it just like any Web page, including printing it or sending it by e-mail. This is also a convenient way to check Web pages while they're being developed.

The local file has one your browser can work with. You really can't expect it to display a spreadsheet file without a program that lets you work with spreadsheets. On the other hand, you can expect it to work well with a text file or HTML file. It will let you view graphics or images if they're stored in GIF (file name ends with **.gif**) or JPEG (file names ends with **.jpg**) format. These types of files work well because your browser is already set up or configured to work with files of these types. For other types of files, you may have to set some "helper applications" in the preferences section of your browser. When you want to view a file, Netscape starts a program called a viewer that lets you look at the contents of the file. For example, if it's a text file, it's displayed in the window just as it appears; if it's a GIF, then a viewer is started that lets you look at images; and if it's an HTML file, it's displayed by following all the HTML commands. If there is no *viewer* for your file, Netscape lets you know and gives you a chance to give the name of a viewer for the file. The term viewer means more than a program that lets you look at a file. It can also mean a program that lets you hear the sound encoded in an audio file. Naming the viewer is also called setting a helper application.

To view a local file choose **File** from the Menu Bar and then **Open**. A dialog box pops up and you type in the name of the file or browse through your files until you find the one you'd like to view. If the browser can display it, it will appear in the window. If the browser can't display the file, a dialog box will appear that lets you associate a helper application with files of that type. If you know the helper application you want to use, fill it in. If not, you may have to ask someone else for assistance. Some places to check on the WWW for helper applications are:

http://home.netscape.com/assist/helper_apps/windows_helpers.html
      maintained by Netscape Communications

http://wwwhost.cc.utexas.edu/learn/use/helper.html
      maintained by TeamWeb, University of Texas, Austin

http://ssdc.ucsd.edu/dt/helpers.html
      maintained by Doug Tower at University of California, San Diego

Bookmarks—Keeping Track of Favorite Places

You can save the links to interesting and useful Web pages you look at through your browser by adding the hyperlink to your bookmark list. That's the name Netscape gives to the collection of hyperlinks you've saved; each one is like a bookmark into the World Wide Web. Whenever you're using the browser you can call up your bookmarks and follow any of the links. The bookmarks survive from one WWW session to the next.

To add the current Web page to the bookmark list either use the keyboard shortcut Ctrl+D or:

1. Click on **Bookmarks** from the menu bar.
2. Choose **Add Bookmark** from the menu.

The item is automatically added to the bookmark list.

To jump to an item on the bookmark list, click **Bookmarks** in the Menu Bar. The list of current bookmarks is displayed. Use the mouse to highlight or select a bookmark, and Navigator will take you to that item on the WWW. If the bookmarks are arranged in folders or categories, select a category and then a bookmark.

If there are many entries in the bookmark list, you may want to search the list for an entry. You can search the list, but you have to get to the bookmark list first for searching, sorting, deleting, or any sort of task that manages or manipulates the list entries. In Netscape Navigator you can access the bookmark list three ways: click on **Bookmarks** in the Menu Bar and select **Go to Bookmarks..**, use the keyboard shotcut Ctrl+B, or click on **Window** in the Menu Bar and select **Bookmarks**. The bookmark list is displayed in its own window with a Menu Bar. Click on **Edit** and then selct **Find**. (You can also use the keyboard shortcut Ctrl+F.) A dialog box appears, type the word or phrase, and click on the button labeled **OK**.

The bookmark list is fairly important, and as you use your browser you'll find yourself adding lots of items to the list. Netscape Navigator comes with tools that let you manage the bookmark list by editing it, arranging the items into folders or categories, and even placing them on the desktop for quick access. There are lots of features available that aren't used by everybody. You'll learn how to take advantage of them after gaining experience and feeling comfortable using the bookmark list. We'll go over a few in the next example.

Example 2.2   Working with the Bookmark List

In this example we'll look at adding items to the bookmark list, and then creating a folder or category and adding some items to it. There are several others things that can be done with the bookmark list and its entries, but we don't demonstrate all of them here to conserve space. The selections in the pull-down menus in the menu bar of the window that holds the bookmarks (see Figure 2.5) are used to perform all the operations on the bookmark list. Here are a few things you can do form the pull-down menus: Have Netscape check to see if any of the bookmarks have changed since they were last visited by selecting **What's New?** from the **File** menu; **Cut**, **Copy**, **Paste**, **Delete**, or **Find** items in the list from the **Edit** menu; access the **Properties**, **Sort** bookmarks, and **Insert Bookmarks**, **Folders**, or **Separators** from the **Item** menu. As you move through the WWW you'll find items you'll want to return to or use often. You can save those items in a bookmark list, call up the bookmark list any time you're using your Web browser, and go directly to the items you've saved without having to go through the any of the intermediate Web pages you worked through to get there in the first place. Also, the bookmark list stays with you whenever you use the browser on the same computer; not just for a single WWW session.

In the example you'll see several different menus without a clear connection of how you get from one to the other. That's intentional. We want to concentrate on setting and using bookmarks. The windows that appear here could have come from one session or several sessions.

Suppose you've started your Web browser in the same way as in previous examples and you're browsing the home page for the World Wide Web Virtual Library. The URL for that site is **http://www.w3.org/pub/ DataSources/bySubject/Overview.html,** and rather than type it in or remember the path you took to get there, you can add it to your bookmark list.

Press **Ctrl**+**D** to add the current Web page to the bookmark list.

A bookmark can also be added to the list by clicking on **Bookmarks** from the Menu Bar and than selecting **Add Bookmark.**

Now suppose you're browsing the Virtual Library, you select the category **Archaeology**, and then you come upon the Web page **ArchNet: Museums and Research Facilities** (**http://spirit.lib.uconn.edu/ ArchNet/Museums/Museums.html**) as shown in Figure 2.24.

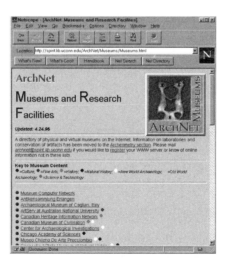

Figure 2.24 ArchNet: Museums and Research Facilities

From here you visit several museums on the list and add some to the bookmark list. If the bookmark list was empty when we started or had no categories, then the bookmarks are added one after the other. If categories already exist, the new bookmarks are added to the category that's labeled with a graphic that looks like a real bookmark Here we'll assume there weren't any categories in the bookmark list and take a look at it at this point.

To view the bookmark list click on **Window** in the Menu bar and select **Bookmarks.**

Figure 2.25 shows the current bookmark list.

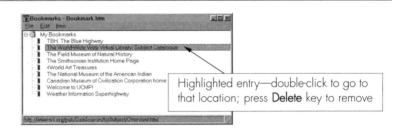

Figure 2.25 Bookmark List

Clicking on an entry once highlights it. To go to the location specified by the item, double-clicking on it. To remove an entry, highlight it and press the **Delete** key or select **Cut** from the pull-down menu under **Edit**. To change the name or other information about a bookmark item, select **Proper-ties..** from the pull-down menu under **Item**. You select or highlight several entries by highlighting one and holding down the Ctrl key as you click on others. A group can be deleted in the same way as one item. To sort the entries in alphabetic order, highlight a group and choose **Sort Bookmarks** from the pull-menu under **Item**.

You close the bookmark window by pressing Ctrl+W or clicking on the **X** in the upper right corner. But the window doesn't have to be closed; it's fine if the window is still on the screen or in the background while you're doing other things on your computer or the Internet.

More items may be added any other time you're browsing or working with information on the World Wide Web. At some point you may want to arrange your bookmarks into categories. Starting with the bookmark list shown in Figure 2.25 we'll add one folder titled **Museums** and put all the museum sites in that folder. Here are the steps to follow once the bookmark window is open:

w⁴w   Click on **Item** in the Menu Bar and select **Insert Folder...**

Clicking on **Insert Folder** brings up the window shown in Figure 2.26, except the first pane contains **New Folder** and the second larger one is empty.

w⁴w   Click on the top frame and type **Museums**. Click on the bottom frame and type **Interesting Museums on the World Wide Web**. Click **OK** when you're finished.

Figure 2.26 shows the new folder window filled in. The date added is filled in automatically by Netscape.

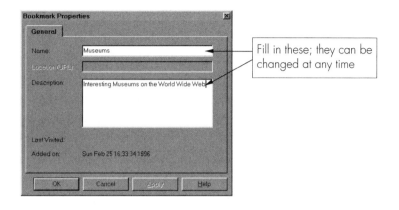

Figure 2.26 Bookmark Properties Window for a Folder

After you click **OK** the folder is added to the bookmark list as shown in Figure 2.27.

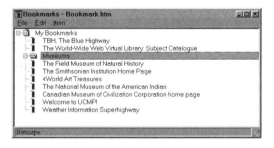

Figure 2.27 Bookmark List with Newly Added Folder "Museums"

Each of the hyperlinks or entries that represent a museum can be put into the new folder in the same way. Here's the instructions to move the item **The Field Museum of Natural History** into the folder.

Click on **The Field Museum of Natural History** and hold down the mouse button. Drag the highlighted entry to the folder **Museums** and release the button.

An item can also be moved to a folder by highlighting it, selecting **Cut** from the **Edit** menu, highlighting the folder, and selecting **Paste** from the **Edit** menu.

After all the entries for museums are placed in the folder, the bookmark list would look as shown in Figure 2.28.

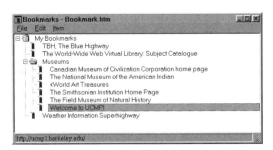

Figure 2.28 Bookmark List Showing the Entries in the Folder "Museums"

As we said earlier, there are other things you can do with the bookmark list. Some things you may want to try are: Double-click on the open folder to close it so only the name of the folder appears in the list.

Double-click again to open the folder.

Move items that aren't in the folder to the bottom of the list in the same way items were added to the folder.

Sort the items in the list by highlighting more than one and choosing **Sort Bookmarks** from the menu **Item**.

————————————End of Example 2.2————————————

Setting Preferences and Options

Your Web browser lets you set several options and preferences. This allows you to customize the Web browser to meet your needs through the options you specify. The preferences let you set items that deal with the way Web pages are displayed and the way the browser works with other programs. Some of the things you can do are to set the startup or home page, specify the way the Web browser displays pages and images, determine how your browser will deal with e-mail and Usenet newsgroups, and set other preferences for the way the browser will work with your computer system and network. Many of these options will be set for you the first time you use the browser, and we won't cover all the options here. When you have questions about some of the options, it's a good idea to ask someone about them, read the online manual included with your browser, or check some of the sections under **Help** in the Menu Bar. Experimentation is good, but be sure to write down the current settings before you change anything. You don't want to create unnecessary problems for yourself or someone else.

To set options and preferences, select **Options** from the Menu Bar. Several options are displayed in the pull-down menu, including ones that let you specify whether the window should display the Toolbar, location, or directory buttons. Clicking on any of these either removes or adds a checkmark. If the checkmark is present, the item is displayed, otherwise it is not. For example, a check mark alogside **Show Toolbar** means the Toolbar is displayed in the window, and no check mark means it's not. You can always set or reset these. The option Auto Load Images determines whether images on a Web page will automatically be retrieved and displayed. If it's taking a long time for you to retrieve pages with images, you may want to turn this off.

Selecting Preferences from the Options menu brings up another window that really lets you customize the way Web pages are displayed and the way the browser will work with your computer and network. Here is where you can set the styles, colors, and fonts for displaying Web pages, set your e-mail address and the Internet information for working with e-mail and Usenet news, and set up the helper applications that let you display, hear, or view files of certain types. You can also set options that specifically deal with the Web browser working with your Internet connection. Let's set your preferences for the home page, the colors and fonts used to display Web pages. Example 2.3 shows how to set the home page and work with Link styles.

Example 2.3   Setting the Home Page and Link Styles Preferences

Netscape Navigator allows you to set several options or preferences for the browser. Most are preset so you don't need to set a lot of options before you use the browser. In this example we'll set options or preferences that name the home page for the browser and the styles for hyperlinks. Preferences are set by first clicking on **Options** in the Toolbar, selecting a preference category (General, Mail and News, Network, Security), and then choosing a panel. All the options and preferences are discussed in Appendix B. Assuming that Netscape Navigator is already started we'll follow these steps:

1. Select **Options** from the Menu Bar.
2. Select **General Preferences**.
3. Select the panel labeled **Appearance**.
4. Set the home page.
5. Modify the Link Styles.
6. Put the new settings into effect.

Now to go through it step by step:

1. Select **Options** from the Menu Bar.

Click on **Options** on the Menu Bar.

This activates a pull-down menu. Several preferences can be set or modified.

2. Select **General Preferences**.

Click on **General Preferences** from the pull-down menu.

Clicking on **General Preferences** brings up a collection of panels. One will occupy the window (there's no telling which one). Click on the tabs to select the one to modify. A panel and tabs are shown in Figure 2.29.

3. Select the panel labeled **Appearance**.

It may be that the panel with the tab **Appearance** is in view when you completed the previous step. If it isn't then bring it into view.

w[ᵂ]w Click on the tab labeled **Appearance**.

The preferences window will appear as in Figure 2.29.

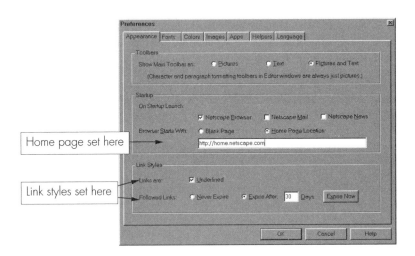

Figure 2.29   Appearance Panel in Preferences Window

You see there are several preferences that can be set here. The way things are set on the panel, we have Toolbars shown as pictures and text, Netscape browser starting when Navigator is started, a home page displayed and set to the home page for Netscape Communications, and link styles set so hyperlinks are underlined and they expire within 30 days. This last preference gives the number of days before a followed link reverts back to the color of an unfollowed link. The different colors acts as a visual clue to help you remember which links you've followed. The default is to have links expire after 30 days.

4. Set the home page.

We're going to set the home page to the home page of Franklin, Beedle & Associates. They're the folks who publish this book. Feel free to set yours to whatever you'd like. Its common to set it to your personal home page or the home page of your school, organization, or business.

Highlight the entry in the pane holding the URL of the home page by double clicking on it.

w[ᵂ]w Type **http://www.fbeedle.com** to replace the current URL.

5. Modify the Link Styles.

The links can be underlined or not and the number of days for links to expire may be changed. Here we're going to keep or select the style so hyperlinks are underlined and set the number of days to 7. You can choose any value you'd like. Making it too short doesn't give you much of a clue of where you've been, and setting it too long may not be to your liking. It is a good idea to have followed links revert to the same color as unfollowed links since things change frequently on the Web its a good idea to occasionally visit sites again. If you want to clear all the links you've followed then click on the button labeled **Expire Now**. The color of links can be set, but in a different panel. The one labeled **Colors**. We won't modify the colors here. To accomplish our task we'll follow these steps.

Click the checkbox labeled **Underlined** show a check mark appears as in Figure 2.30.

Click the radio button next to **Expire After**.

Highlight the entry in the pane holding the number of days by double clicking on it.

Type **7** into the pane holding the number of days after which links expire.

The modified appearance panel should look like the one in Figure 2.30.

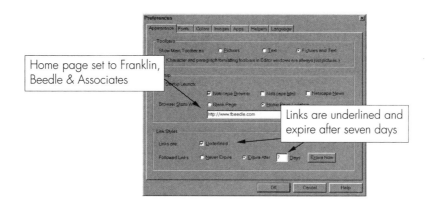

Figure 2.30   Appearance Panel with Modifications

6. Put the new settings into effect.

Click on the button labeled **OK**.

To see if the changes have taken effect, click on the icon **Home** in the Toolbar.

—————————————————End of Example 2.3—————————————————

Where to Obtain a Web Browser on the Internet

Netscape Communications Corporation developed Netscape Navigator and offers it as a commercial product. You can download a copy for evaluation purposes. However, it is free to students, faculty, and staff of educational or nonprofit organizations. Versions are available for Unix (X-Windows), Microsoft Windows, and Macintosh systems. You can retrieve a copy of Netscape Navigator by using the URL **http://home.netscape.com/comprod/mirror/index.html** or by anonymous FTP by using the URL **ftp://ftp.netscape.com**. Follow the instuctions from Netscape to install the browser.

If you already have a Web browser, why add another one? It's not so much that you need another browser as that you want to keep up to date and have the most recent version of the Web browser you're using.

Summary

A Web browser is used to access the information and resources on the World Wide Web. Whenever you start the browser or access a hyperlink, the browser—which is a computer program—sends a request to have a file transferred to it. The browser then interprets the information in the file so it can be viewed in the browser's window, or in some cases, viewed through another program. For example, if a hyperlink points to a text file, then the file is displayed in the window as ordinary text. If the hyperlink points to a document written in HyperText Markup Language (HTML), then it's displayed by the browser, or if the file is a sound file or an animation, then a program different from the browser is started so the file can be heard or seen. Most of the facilities and capabilities are built into the browser, but in some cases your computer needs to be equipped with special equipment or programs. A good example of this is where a hyperlink points to a sound file. Your computer needs to have a sound card, speakers, and the software to play the sounds.

Starting a Web browser usually means first activating your connection to the Internet and then clicking on an icon or command to start Netscape Navigator. If the cost of using the Internet depends on how much time is spent being connected, then be sure to terminate the Internet connection when the Web session is over.

The commands you use to work with the Web browser are available through the Menu Bar, the Toolbar, the directory buttons, and the keyboard. These, along with the scroll bars, stay the same regardless of what you're viewing or working with on the World Wide Web. The Menu Bar is a collection of pull-down menus that you can use for almost every operation or command. One menu (**Options**) lets you set options and preferences for the Web browser. The preferences may be personal or depend on the computer or network. Another menu (**Help**) lets you select one of several ways to help yourself learn about Netscape, including an online manual. The Toolbar has a number of icons that give quick access to some of the commands in the pull-down menu. Several commands are also available as keyboard shortcuts, meaning that you can type them directly on the keyboard instead of using a mouse. The directory buttons give quick access to the online manual, a number of directories or special listings of sites, some tools to use for searching, and Usenet newsgroups.

Once a page is in the browser's window, you can move around the page using the keyboard, scroll bars, or mouse. You can search for words in the page. Move the mouse to a hyperlink (the pointer turns to a hand) and click on it to follow it. A URL can be typed in the location bar or you can select a command or icon to open a location. In any of these cases, the browser will follow the URL you've typed or represent the hyperlink to view another Web page.

The browser keeps track of the sites you've visited within a session. It does this so you can backtrack and return to sites during a session. The backtracking is restricted to traveling in a straight line. Suppose you start at site **A**, go to **B**, and then go to **C**. If you click on the **Back** icon you'll be taken to **B**. Click on it again and you'll go to **A**. You can click on the **Forward** icon and be taken to **B** (from **A**) and click on it again and you'll go to **C**. Now, suppose you go from a site called **Base**, then go to a site named **Right**, return to **Base** (by pressing **Back**), then go to a site named Left, and then return to **Base** again. If you click on **Forward** now, you'll be taken to **Left**. The browser keeps a list, called the history list, of the sites you've visited within a session that are accessible by **Back** and **Forward**. You can collect a set of hyperlinks in a list called the bookmark list. These will be available from one session to the next. The browser contains commands to let you maintain and manage your bookmark list.

Provided you're not breaking copyright laws or conventions, information found on the World Wide Web can be saved into a file, printed, or mailed to an Internet address. You can also use the browser to view local files. When you're developing your own Web pages, you may want to use this to test them before making them available to anyone on the Internet.

There are a number of sites on the Internet from which you can retrieve the most recent copy of a Web browser, programs that work with the browser to display/view/play certain types of files, and useful information and help. The browser lets you access, retrieve, work with, and enjoy the information and resources that make up the World Wide Web. To coin a phrase—the browser is your window to the Web.

Exercises

These exercises are designed to help you become familiar with using your Web browser. They may also introduce you to some interesting sites on the WWW. As you do them, refer back to the material in this chapter and to the online manual included with Netscape.

1. Start your Web Browser.
   a. Describe what's on the home page.
   b. Go to the bottom of the home page using the scroll bar.
   c. Go to the top of the home page using a keyboard shortcut.
   d. Follow a hyperlink from the home page, then follow a hyperlink from that page. Click on the icon labeled **Back**, then click on it again. Where are you? Click on the icon labeled **Forward**. Where are you now?

2. Go to the WWW Virtual Library Arranged by Subject. **http://www.w3.org/pub/DataSources/bySubject/ Overview.html**
   a. Add it to your bookmark list.
   b. Go to the section of the Virtual Library for the subject **Music**. Who maintains this area of the Virtual Library?
   c. What resources are available from the main Music page?
   d. Follow a few hyperlinks according to your interests. What's in your history list?
   e. Go to a location in the middle of your history list by selecting it from the list, and now return to the site at the top of the history list. What sites did you visit?

3. Spend a little time browsing the section on Music in the WWW Virtual Library. Add a few of the sites you find interesting to your bookmark list. What's in your bookmark list now?

4. Go to the section **Collecting** in the WWWVL arranged by subject. Work through this to find five bookmarks related to either one thing or a collection of things you're interested in. Add them to your bookmark list.

5. Go to a site on the WWW that holds the World Wide Web FAQ. (One place to start is **http:// www.boutell.com/faq/**.)
   a. List the URLs of four different sites that hold the WWW FAQ in four different countries on three different continents.
   b. Add the one that's closest to your bookmark list.
   c. Give a summary of the answers to these questions from the section titled **Introduction to the World Wide Web**.
   What is the Web?
   What is a URL?
   Can I catch a virus from a Web page?

6. Open the location or go to the Web page for the Consumer Information Center using the URL **http:/ /www.gsa.gov/staff/pa/cic/cic.htm**. Select the section from the catalog dealing with employment. Follow the hyperlink to a pamphlet such as **Is There Another Degree in Your Future?** or **Resumes, Application Forms, Cover Letters, and Interviews**.
   a. Save a copy of the article in a file on your computer.
   b. Print a copy of the article.
   c. Send a copy of the article by e-mail to a friend who can use it.

7. For the file you saved in the previous exercise,
   a. View it as a local file using Netscape Navigator.
   b. Copy it to a floppy disk or include a portion of it in a document you can prepare using a word processor on your computer.

8. If you've done the previous exercise, you've probably collected a number of entries in your bookmark list. Using the instructions in Example 2.1 and the online manual, arrange your bookmark list so the items are arranged into at least three categories (with at least three headers).

9. Go to the home page for National Public Radio (**http://www.npr.org/**). Follow the link to **NPR Audio on the 'Net—RealAudio.**
   a. If a Real Audio Player isn't present on your computer, follow the hyperlinks and instructions to download it to your computer.
   b. Follow the instructions on the Web page **http://www.realaudio.com/hpproducts/player/index.html** (you may already have seen this when downloading the player) to install it as a helper application with your version of Netscape.
   c. Now go to **http://www.realaudio.com/contentp/npr.html**, the Real Audio page for NPR and follow hyperlinks to listen to all or a portion of a recent broadcasts from All Things Considered or ExercisesMorning Edition.

10. Do you have a QuickTime movie player configured as a helper application? If not, go to the QuickTime site at Apple Computer, **http://quicktime.apple.com/** to get one. (One source is the FTP site for Apple Computer **ftp://ftp.info.Apple.Com/Apple.Support.Area/Apple.Software.Updates.**)
    a. Download and install the player as a helper application according to the directions you find.
    b. Try it out by accessing the URL **http://www.mwc.edu/ernie/sg/45.html** and click on the hyperlink representing a movie. (The file is large—about 2 megabytes—and may take a while to be retrieved by your browser.)

CHAPTER 3

The Basics of Electronic Mail and Using Netscape E-Mail

Electronic mail, or e-mail, lets you communicate with other people on the Internet. E-mail is one of the basic Internet services, and by far the most popular. You can use it for any type of conversation; it's a way to keep in touch with friends, get information, start relationships, or express your opinion. Much of the time you'll be exchanging messages in plain text form (like the words on this page), but you can also exchange files in other formats such as spreadsheets, files for word processors, images, or programs. You can use e-mail to join discussion groups and access other Internet services, but you can get to those other services using your Web browser as well. You can send messages to anyone with an Internet address, and likewise, you can receive e-mail from anywhere on the Internet. With over 30 million people having some sort of connection to the Internet, you've got the opportunity to communicate with people nearby and around the world in a relatively quick and efficient manner.

You use a mail program on your computer to compose, send, and read e-mail. Once you compose (write) a message, it's sent in electronic form, usually passing through several other sites on the Internet. E-mail is held at its destination until the person to whom it's addressed reads it, saves it in a file, or deletes it. The recipient does not have to be logged in or using a computer for the e-mail to be delivered. When she does use her computer and checks for e-mail, it will be delivered to her.

E-mail is a very convenient way to communicate with people; it's personal, and it seems everybody likes to get mail. Because e-mail is used so often, it's worth spending some time to learn about how it works and its capabilities.

This chapter focuses on the basics of e-mail. All versions of Netscape Navigator have the capability to send e-mail (we looked at that in Chapter 2), and Netscape version 2 or later includes the programs to both send and receive e-mail. Some folks use other e-mail programs, such as Eudora, cc:Mail, Mailx, or Pine. Regardless of which you use, you'll have to understand many of the following topics:

* How E-Mail Works
* Advantages and Limitations of E-Mail
* Understanding Internet E-Mail Addresses

* Dissecting a Piece of E-Mail—Headers, Message, Signature
* Finding Someone's Internet E-Mail Address
* Sending E-Mail from the Internet to Other Networks
* E-Mail Etiquette
* Working with Nontext Files
* Working with Netscape Mail

We'll demonstrate using e-mail by working with the e-mail system that comes with Netscape Navigator. Most e-mail programs operate in basically the same way. The details of using Mailx and Pine, Eudora, and cc: Mail are covered in the appendices at the end of the book. The topics we'll cover here include:

* Setting Options in Netscape to Let You Use E-mail
* Reading E-Mail
* Saving, Deleting, and Printing Messages
* Composing and Sending E-Mail
* Replying to a Message
* Working with an Address Book

How E-Mail Works

Electronic mail lets you send and receive messages in electronic form. The person you communicate with could be any other user on the Internet, someone using the same computer system as you, or someone on a computer system thousands of miles away. The e-mail is transmitted between computer systems, which exchange messages or pass them on to other sites according to certain Internet protocols or rules for exchanging e-mail. You don't need to be concerned with many of the details; that's the computer's job. But you ought to know a little bit about the way e-mail works.

Sending e-mail is similar to sending something by a postal service. If you're sending a letter or a package to someone, you follow these steps:

1. Write the letter or make up the package.
2. Address it.
3. Put on the proper postage or pay the charges to send it.
4. Drop it off somewhere so it can be sent on its way and eventually delivered.

You don't care much about which methods are used to deliver it or what route it takes. You prepare what you want to send, address it, and hand it to the postal service or delivery company. You expect them to take care of the details of delivering the letter or package. With e-mail you follow similar steps:

1. Start an e-mail program.
2. Give the address of where to send the e-mail.
3. Compose a message using that e-mail program.
4. Give a command to send the message.

You've probably noticed that we've left out the part about adding postage and paying charges. Individual users don't pay a per message fee for e-mail in many organizations—schools and companies—that have Internet access.

You use an e-mail program to address, compose, and send the message. E-mail programs are called *mail user agents* because they act on the user's behalf. The user agent lets you prepare and send messages and also work with the mail you've received. The e-mail program acts as a go-between with you and computer systems, and the computer systems handle the details of delivering and receiving mail. Once again, you don't have anything to do with how the mail is delivered.

Messages are sent from one site to another on the Internet in this way. When you compose your message, it's all in one piece, but when it's sent out to the Internet, it's divided into several pieces called packets. The number of packets depends on the size of the message. Each of the packets contains, among other things:

* The e-mail address of the person who sent the mail, the sender.
* The e-mail address of the person to receive the mail, the recipient.
* Between 1 and 1500 characters of the message.

The packets are sent to the destination, passing through several Internet sites. Thousands of networks and millions of computers make up the Internet, and packets are passed from system to system. Each site accepts the packets addressed to it, but passes on the messages destined for another address. The packets can travel or arrive at their destination in any order, and they don't all have to take the same path. When you communicate with a remote site, you may think you have direct connection, but that's usually not the case. At the destination, the packets are collected and put in order, so the e-mail appears to be in the same form it was sent. If there are errors in the packets or if some are lost, the destination sends a request back to the source asking for the message to be resent. All of this takes place according to SMTP, *Simple Mail Transfer Protocol*, the protocol the Internet uses to transport message between computer systems. SMTP uses TCP, *Transmission Control Protocol*, which provides a reliable means of communication.

> To put it all in a nutshell:
> *A message sent by e-mail is divided into packets, and the packets are sent (possibly by different paths and passing through different sites) to the destination, where they are reassembled into the original message.*

When you use Netscape on a personal computer that's using MS-Windows or if you're using a Macintosh, your computer isn't turned on all the time, so there has to be another computer system (one that's usually in fine running condition), called an e-mail server, able to receive your mail at any time. In this case, that other system—perhaps the one at your Internet service provider or computer center—holds the e-mail addressed to you until you start Netscape on your system and check to see if you've received any new e-mail. Your computer sends e-mail to the e-mail server by SMTP, and the server system exchanges e-mail with the rest of the Internet. When you check to see if there's any new e-mail, another protocol, *Post Office Protocol* (POP), is used.

How E-Mail is Exchanged between Computer Systems

Once a message is sent, it's put out on the Internet and usually delivered in a short time—minutes or seconds. But a few things could cause problems:

* There are delays. The computer system at the destination might not be accepting messages because it's down (not working) or too busy doing other things, or there is no path on the Internet to the destination—which usually means that some computer system or network is temporarily unavailable. If a message is delayed, the program handling mail will try to send it at another time.

* The mail can't be delivered to the remote site. The system at the destination could be down for several days, or perhaps the address is wrong. Most programs handling e-mail try to deliver a message for at least three days. If it can't be delivered at the end of that time, you'll probably receive e-mail notifying you of the problem. If you type an address that doesn't exist, you'll be notified about that as well—usually pretty quickly.

* The mail is delivered to the remote site but can't be delivered to the recipient. The local part of the address might be wrong; you'll get e-mail back about that. The recipient might have no more space left in his mailbox; either a disk is full or a quota (set by the system administrator) was exceeded. In this case you, the sender, may not be notified. After all, the mail was delivered to the remote site and the address is correct.

* Other problems. The person to whom you sent the message doesn't check to see if there is any e-mail, doesn't read the e-mail you sent, or accidentally deletes it. You may never know if any of these things happens. The most you can expect from an e-mail system is for it to notify the sender if there is some reason why the recipient could not receive the e-mail.

When you read your e-mail, once again you use a program (a mail user agent) that helps you work with the messages you have waiting for you. On many systems you're told if you have e-mail when you log in, you access the system you use to contact the Internet or start your system. The e-mail messages can arrive at any time. They're added to a file, your mailbox or **Inbox**, which is part of a directory that holds all the e-mail for the system. The packets making up an e-mail message arrive at the e-mail server, they're assembled, and then added to your mailbox. It holds all the messages on the server addressed to you, and only you can read your mail. If for some reason your mailbox gets scrambled, corrupted, or is changed so you can't read your mail, get in touch with the system administrator or call your Internet service provider. On many systems, all the users share the space allocated for the directory that holds e-mail. Usually there's enough space to hold a lot of messages, but it's important that you delete old e-mail messages and messages you've read so there is space to hold everybody's e-mail.

Advantages and Limitations of E-Mail

Advantages

E-mail has a number of advantages over some other forms of communication. It's quick, convenient, and nonintrusive.

- You can communicate quickly with anyone on the Internet. E-mail usually reaches its destination in a matter of minutes or seconds.
- The cost of communication has nothing to do with distance, and in many cases, the cost doesn't depend on the size of the message. The cost is based on the number of messages, not where they're sent.
- You can send letters, notes, files, data, or reports all using the same techniques. Once you learn how to use your e-mail program, everything is sent the same way.
- You don't have to worry about interrupting someone when you send e-mail. The e-mail is sent and delivered by one computer system communicating with the Internet. Although it is put into someone's mailbox, the recipient isn't interrupted by the arrival of e-mail.
- You can deal with your e-mail at a convenient time. You don't have to be interrupted when e-mail arrives, and you can read it or work with it when you have the time. Also, you can send it at a convenient time. It doesn't have to be written or sent at a time when you know the recipient will be available.
- You don't have to play phone tag or make an appointment to communicate with someone. Once again, the e-mail is sent when it's convenient for you, and it can arrive even when the recepient isn't using her computer.
- You don't have tobe shy about using e-mail to communicate with anyone. E-mail isn't anonymous—each message carries the return address of the sender—but you can write to anyone with an Internet address. All the messages appear the same to the person who gets the e-mail. The messages are generally judged on what's in them, not where they're from.

Limitations

- E-mail isn't necessarily private. Since messages are passed from one system to another, and sometimes through several systems or networks, there are many opportunities for someone to intercept or read e-mail. Many types of computer systems have protections built in to stop users from reading others' e-mail, but it's still possible for a system administrator to read the e-mail on a system or for someone to bypass the security of a computer system. This is discussed in more detail in Chapter 9.

* It's difficult to express emotion using e-mail. The recipient doesn't have the benefit of seeing your facial expressions or hearing your voice. You have to be careful with humor or sarcasm, since it's easy for someone to take your message the wrong way and interpret your words in a manner different from how you mean them.

* You can receive too much e-mail, and you have to take the time to deal with it. You'll probably have some limit on the amount of space your e-mail can take up on the computer system you use. If you join a discussion group (as described later in this chapter), it's possible that you'll be flooded with messages that may be of little value or even offensive, since you can receive "junk" e-mail in the same way you receive other types of junk mail. Some people see e-mail as an inexpensive way to market products or advertise. In any of these cases, you may have to take active steps to delete the e-mail you receive and try to stop it from being sent to you in the first place.

* It's possible to forge e-mail. This is not common, but it is possible to forge the address of the sender. You may want to take steps to confirm the source of some e-mail you receive.

* Some e-mail systems can send or receive text files only. Even though you can send and receive images, programs, files produced by word processing programs, or multimedia messages, some folks may not be able to properly view your message.

Although there are some drawbacks to using e-mail, it's still an effective and popular way to communicate.

Understanding Internet E-Mail Addresses

An e-mail address on the Internet usually has the form:

```
local-address@domain-name
```

The local-address part is often the user's *log-in name*, the name you give to get in touch with your Internet server. That's followed by the character @, called the *at sign*. To its right is the domain name of the computer system that handles the e-mail for the user. Sometimes the domain-name portion is the name of a specific computer such as **oregano.mwc.edu**. It could be more general, such as **mwc.edu**, and in this case the systems at the site **mwc.edu** handle delivering mail to the appropriate computer. The portions or fields making up the domain name are separated by periods (the periods are called dots).

Here are two examples:

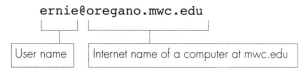

If you were going to tell someone the address, you would say **ernie at oregano dot mwc dot edu**. (Ernie and oregano are pronounced as a word, but **mwc** [em double-u see] and **edu** [e dee you] are pronounced as individual letters.)

When you know someone's e-mail address, you have an idea of their log-in name and the name of the Internet site they use. You should be able to send e-mail to **postmaster** at any Internet site. That's the address to use if you have questions about e-mail to or from a specific host or site or general questions about a site. However, you may not get a quick response, since the person designated as *postmaster* usually has lots of other duties.

Sometimes you'll see or have to use addresses in the form:

```
coco%jojovm.bitnet@brownvm.brown.edu
SMTP%jojo @great.place.com
IN%friener@more.money.us
```

In these cases, the local address is handled by a gateway through the domain name to the right of the @. A gateway is a computer system providing e-mail transfers between the Internet and another type of network.

Dissecting E-Mail—Headers, Message Body, Signature

One piece of e-mail has three main parts:

1. Headers
2. Message body
3. Signature

The *headers* are pieces of information that tell you and the e-mail system several important things about a piece of e-mail. Each header has a specific name and a specific purpose. You'll see some, but not necessarily all the headers each time you read a piece of e-mail. They're all generated and put in the proper form by the e-mail program you use, some with information from you, such as the address of the recipient, and some done automatically, such as the date.

When you read an e-mail message with Netscape, you're likely to see these headers. Here is a list of the most common headers. Figure 3.1 shows these as part of an e-mail message.

Subject:	The subject of the e-mail
Date:	When the e-mail was sent
From:	The e-mail address of the sender
To:	The e-mail address of the recipient

The *message body* is the content of the e-mail—what you send and what you receive. When you're sending e-mail to a computer system where your message will be interpreted by a computer program, you'll be given instructions to use specific words or phrases in the message body. One time you might have to follow instructions like this when you subscribe to a discussion group. (Discussion groups are covered in Chapter 4.) Here's an example:

```
TO SUBSCRIBE (UNSUBSCRIBE): Send e-mail message to:
                    Majordomo@world.std.com
The body of the message should read: Subscribe (unsubscribe) rocks-and-fossils
```

The *signature,* which is optional, isn't a signed name but a sequence of lines, usually giving some information about the person who sent the e-mail. It is made up of anything the user wants to include. Usually a signature has the full name of the sender and some information about how to contact the person by e-mail, phone, or fax. Some signatures also contain a favorite quotation or some graphics created by typing characters from the keyboard. Make sure it's not too long. The longer it is, the more bytes or characters have to be sent, and so the more traffic to be carried on the Internet. It's fun to be creative and come up with a clever signature, but try to limit it to five lines.

You don't have to type in the signature each time. E-mail programs will automatically append the contents of a specified file to each outgoing message. The name of the file depends on the program you're using for e-mail. Some common names are **signature, sig,** or **signature.pce** on computers that use Microsoft Windows as the operating system. On Unix systems the name **.sig** or **.signature** is often used. Most e-mail programs allow you to specify what file to use as a signature, but you should check with a local expert about the precise name of the signature file. With Netscape, you set the name and location of the signature file in the **Mail** and **News** sections of the **Options** pull-down menu.

Figure 3.1 shows an e-mail message dissected into its parts: headers, body, and signature.

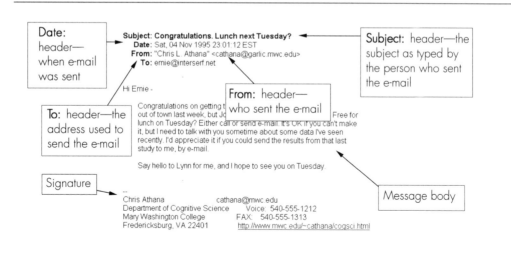

Figure 3.1 E-Mail Message Dissected

The e-mail you receive may include other headers as well as those shown in Figure 3.1. We wanted to show the major ones.

Finding Someone's Internet E-Mail Address

Once you get the bug of communicating by e-mail, you'll probably start to wonder about the e-mail addresses of your friends, and there may be other times you'll want to know someone's e-mail address. Some methods and services exist to help find e-mail addresses, but none of them are guaranteed to produce satisfactory results every time. A few of them will be covered in this section.

The problem with finding someone's e-mail address is that there is no central directory. If you were looking for someone's phone number, you'd either look in a phone book or call an information service. That approach usually works; everyone with a phone number usually receives a bill to pay for phone services, and even though there are lots of phone companies, each has up-to-date and readily available records. The situation on the Internet is much different. Many users don't pay any direct fees, and there isn't any central agency that registers each user. Users are added and deleted by individual Internet sites; the decisions are made locally. It might be advantageous to have a directory of all Internet users and their e-mail addresses, but such a directory just doesn't exist.

Here are a few ways to find someone's e-mail address:

* Ask! Call or write to ask for an e-mail address. This is usually the easiest method.
* Check for an e-mail address on a resumé, business card, stationery, or a Web page.
* Look at the return address in the **From:**, **Return-Path:**, or **Reply-To:** e-mail headers.

Send e-mail to **postmaster@domain-name.** The person designated as postmaster will get back to you when she has time.

Consult some directories for collections or lists of e-mail addresses or Web pages. Several of these are available through the item **People** in the pull-down menu **Directory** on the Menu Bar or by clicking on the directory button labeled **People.** Here's a short list of collections of names and e-mail addresses:

* Yahoo Directory: the section Reference: White Pages, **http://www.yahoo.com/Reference/White_Pages,** and the section Entertainment:People:Indices, **http://www.yahoo.com/Entertainment/People/Indices/.**
* CMC Information Sources CULTURE—People—Lists—directories, home pages **http://www.december.com/cmc/info/culture-people-lists.html.**
* People on the Internet, a listing of resources available through the Gopher server at Yale **gopher://yaleinfo.yale.edu:7700/11/Internet-People.**
* Read and use FAQ: How to Find People's E-mail Addresses, **http://www.qucis.queensu.ca/FAQs/email/finding.html,** maintained by David Alex Lamb (**dalamb@qucis.queensu.ca**). Contains lots of resources and tips for finding e-mail addresses.
* Use an automated service. Several sites run services, online information databases, and other systems that contain ways to find e-mail addresses. Here's a list of a few types:

Phone books   Several sites on the WWW provide phone book services allowing for searches of the names, e-mail addresses, and other information about users. A large collection of these is kept at the Gopher server at Notre Dame University. To get to it, open URL **gopher://gopher.nd.edu**, then click on **Non-Notre Dame Information Sources**, and finally click on **Phone Books—Other Institutions.**

Usenet-addresses

A database of the e-mail addresses of people who've posted messages to Usenet (Usenet is discussed in Chapter 5) is maintained by a computer system at **rtfm.mit.edu**. You search the database by sending e-mail to **mail-server@rtfm.mit.edu** with **send usenet-addresses/name** in the body of the message. For **name** substitute one or more words separated by spaces to represent the name of the person whose e-mail address you are seeking. (For example, try the message **send usenet-address/ernest ackermann**.) You will get a reply by e-mail. How long you have to wait, an hour or two or longer, depends on the load on the system at **rtfm.mit.edu**.

Commercial Services (Free)

Several commercial services provide free e-mail address search services. They each have unique features but also have many features in common. Type in a person's name, where they're from, or some other information, and the service returns an e-mail address, provided it can find a match in its database. Two to try are Four11, **http://www.four11.com/**, and WhoWhere?, **http://www.whowhere.com/**.

Sending E-Mail from the Internet to Other Networks

A number of other networks exchange e-mail with the Internet but aren't part of the Internet. Some of these networks use technology and protocols that aren't compatible with the Internet, and some are private commercial networks. Exchanging e-mail with people on other types of networks isn't difficult. You need to know the proper form for an address. The e-mail addresses on these other networks may follow different rules or have a form different from Internet e-mail addresses. Once you know the right form for an address and send something off, the e-mail is routed on the Internet to a gateway system. You can think of a gateway as a computer that allows for the exchange of e-mail between incompatible networks.

The most extensive list of ways to send e-mail from one network to another is **Inter-Network Mail Guide**, currently maintained by Scott Yanoff (**yanoff@csd.uwm.edu**). It's available on the WWW at **http://www.nova.edu/Inter-Links/cgi-bin/inmgq.pl.** Table 3.1 lists ways to send e-mail from the Internet to several different networks.

Network	User Name or ID	Address from the Internet
America Online	My Buddy	mybuddy@aol.com
Applelink	buddy	buddy@applelink.apple.com
BITNET	buddy@site	buddy@site.bitnet
		or use buddy%site.bitnet@cunyvm.cuny.edu
CompuServe	1234,897	1234.897@compuservecom
FidoNet	my buddy at 5:6/7.8	mybuddy@p8.f7.n6.z5fidonet.org
Genie	buddy	buddy@genie.geis.com
MCI Mail	My Buddy (123-5678)	1235678@mcimail.com
Prodigy	buddy	buddy@prodigy.com

Table 3.1   Sending Mail from the Internet to Other Networks

Note that if you're sending e-mail to a person on CompuServe, the comma in the CompuServe address is replaced by a period (.) in the address you use from the Internet. Here are two other examples. Suppose you want to send e-mail to someone who is known as Chris Athana on America Online. Use the address **chrisathana@aol.com**. Suppose a friend has a BITNET address of **cathana@abcVM.abc.edu**. Their address from the Internet would be **cathana@abcVM.abc.edu.bitnet** if your mail system can handle that correctly. You could also use an address such as the following:

```
cathana%abcVM.abc.edu.bitnet@cunyvm.cuny.edu
```

E-Mail Etiquette

Writing to someone through e-mail is communicating with another person. You need to remember that the recipient will read it without the benefit of being with you and seeing your expressions or getting your immediate and considerate reactions. You need to say what you mean in a clear, direct, and thoughtful way. Here is a list of rules you should follow when writing e-mail:

* Choose the subject heading carefully. Make it brief, descriptive, and to the point. In many cases, it's the first thing that will get a reader's attention or make the reader ignore your message.
* Be careful about spelling and punctuation. Try to follow the same rules you'd use if you were writing a letter or a memo. If you want to state something strongly, surround it with asterisks (*) or write it in uppercase, but don't take this too far. Some folks equate items in uppercase letters with shouting.
* Make your message as short as possible, but don't make it cryptic or unclear. Lots of users have to deal with disk quotas that limit the amount of e-mail they can receive. Keep the body of the message succinct. Limit a message to one or two screens.
* It's a good idea to include parts—but not all—of an original message when you are writing a reply. Include only the portions pertinent to your reply. Many e-mail programs allow you to annotate or include your remarks within the body of a message you've received. If you can't do that, summarize the original message and write a reply. For an example of this kind of correspondence, look ahead to Figure 3.16.
* Check the address when you compose a message or reply to a message you've received. Be sure it's going to the person(s) who ought to receive it. If the original message was sent to a group of people, such as a mailing list or discussion group, be sure of the address you use so the reply goes to an individual or the entire group as necessary. It's embarrassing when e-mail is sent to a group but is meant for an individual.
* Be careful when using humor and sarcasm. The person reading the mail may misinterpret your remarks, and you won't be around to immediately clear up a misunderstanding.
* Don't assume the e-mail is private. It's easy to forward e-mail, so the message you send could be shared with others.
* Take some time to consider what you will write. You can never be sure where the e-mail you write will end up. Also, if someone writes something that upsets you, don't react immediately. Perhaps you've misinterpreted the original message. You'll find you can usually give a better response if you take some time to think about it.
* Include a signature with all your e-mail. This ought to include your full name and some information about how to contact you by telephone or your mail address. Try to keep the signature to four or five lines.

Working with Nontext Files

All mail systems can send and receive text (also called ASCII) files—ones that contain only plain characters. In fact, some are designed to do only that. Other types of information such as images, sound, video, programs in the machine language of a computer, spreadsheets, compressed files, or files produced by a word processing program can't be sent or read unless the e-mail program uses some scheme to handle these types of files. In general terms, before a nontext file is sent it has to be encoded into a form the e-mail program can deal with. In order to read, view, or hear this encoded file, it has to be decoded into its original format. Many e-mail programs, including the one with Netscape, can deal with messages encoded in *Multipurpose Internet Mail Extensions* (MIME). MIME is becoming the standard way to work with nontext files as part of e-mail or Usenet articles. But there are other programs or formats for encoding and decoding. BinHex has been used on Macintosh systems and with older versions of Eudora, a popular e-mail program. The most common programs for this purpose on Unix systems (and many DOS systems) have been uuencode and uudecode. We'll be working with MIME later in this chapter along with other details of using the e-mail portion of Netscape Navigator.

The programs uuencode and uudecode are commonly used to encode (before sending) and decode (after receiving) files. To send a nontext file, first encode it with a command similar to:

```
uuencode filename filename > filename.out
```

This takes the contents of the file named **filename** and puts it in a form that can be sent by any e-mail program. The file **filename.out** has the original file in encoded form. The first line of the file **filename.out** will look something like:

```
begin 600 filename
M1G)O;2!N971W;W)K<RUR97%%U97-T0'9I<F==I;F%EA+F5D=2!&<D@3F]V(#$X
```

The line **begin 600 filename** is a giveaway that this file was constructed with uuencode and that it can be decoded by using uudecode. You may see a number different from 600; it depends on what has been encoded. If a file like this is received as part of an e-mail message, first save it to a file, say xyz, and then decode it with the command:

```
uudecode xyz
```

That will create a file whose name is the same as the name in the first line of the encoded file. Files encoded according to MIME also have a specific format and boundary or tag lines so you know that MIME is involved and something about the format of the file that's been encoded.

Figure 3.2 is an excerpt from an e-mail message encoded using MIME as it would appear to a mail program that doesn't recognize messages in that format.

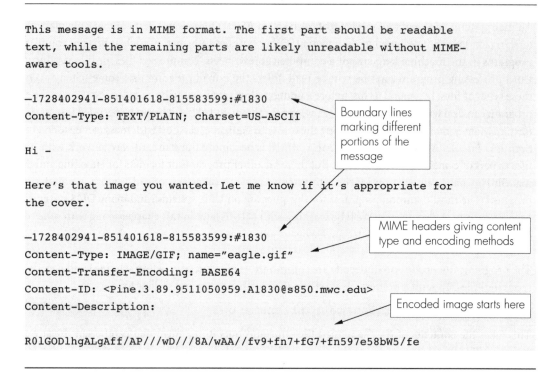

This message is in MIME format. The first part should be readable
text, while the remaining parts are likely unreadable without MIME-
aware tools.

-1728402941-851401618-815583599:#1830

Content-Type: TEXT/PLAIN; charset=US-ASCII

> Boundary lines marking different portions of the message

Hi -

Here's that image you wanted. Let me know if it's appropriate for
the cover.

-1728402941-851401618-815583599:#1830

> MIME headers giving content type and encoding methods

Content-Type: IMAGE/GIF; name="eagle.gif"

Content-Transfer-Encoding: BASE64

Content-ID: <Pine.3.89.9511050959.A1830@s850.mwc.edu>

Content-Description:

> Encoded image starts here

R0lGODlhgALgAff/AP///wD///8A/wAA//fv9+fn7+fG7+fn597e58bW5/fe

Figure 3.2   Message Encoded with MIME

When you view a message that's in uuencode or MIME format through the Netscape mailer, the attached encoded file is either displayed in original form or the mail program gives you the option of saving the encoded information in a file. In the later case, it will be decoded and saved in its original format.

Working with Netscape Mail

In this section we'll look at using the e-mail program that's included with Netscape Navigator 2.0 or later. Other popular e-mail programs are covered in the appendices. You'll find that the commands and procedures for using the Netscape Mail program is similar, but not the same, as those used with other e-mail programs.

Figure 3.3 shows a Netscape mail window that you'd use to read your e-mail. To get to this window and to start to read your e-mail, click on **Window** in the Menu Bar and then select **Netscape Mail** from the pull-down menu.

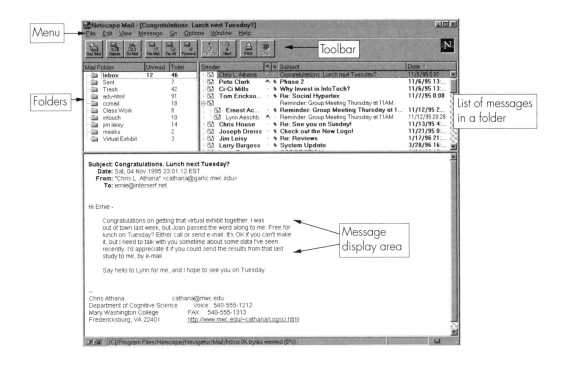

Figure 3.3   Netscape Mail Window

As in other Netscape windows, there is a Menu Bar with pull-down menus and a Toolbar with icons. The top portion (called a frame) of the window tells about your messages. It holds a list of folders on the left and the messages in the current folder on the right. The bottom frame holds the current message, the one highlighted in the frame in the upper right. Double-click on any message to read it. Double-click on any folder to open it to get another list of messages. To look at messages in another folder, click on the name of the folder. Once a message is open for reading you can print it, delete it, or save it to a different folder. You send a reply to the person who sent it to you by clicking on the icon labeled **Reply**, or forward the message to another Internet address by clicking on the icon **Forward**.

Figure 3.4 shows a window you'd use to compose a message. It too has a Menu Bar and a Toolbar. You can get to this window by typing Ctrl+N anytime, clicking on the icon labeled **New Mail** from the Netscape Mail Window, or by clicking on **File** from the Menu Bar of the Netscape browser window and then selecting **New Mail Message** from the pull-down menu. Once the window (called the Message Composition Window) is active, you can compose or write a message. Position the cursor in the bottom frame with the mouse and start typing. Fill in the address (**Send To**) and **Subject**, and send it off when you're ready. Commands to fill in and modify the panes in the window are available through the pull-down menus in the Menu Bar or by clicking on the icons in the Toolbar.

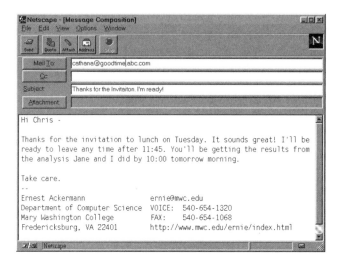

Figure 3.4   Netscape Window for Composing an E-Mail Message

The commands you can use at any stage are available through the menus and icons. Online help is always available by clicking on **Help** in the Menu Bar. The e-mail program also has MIME (Multipurpose Internet Mail Extensions), so the mail you read and send can contain information in text format and a range of other types.

The topics covered in this section include:
* Setting Crucial Netscape Mail Options
* Knowing When New Mail Has Arrived
* Getting Help
* Opening and Closing the Mail Window
* The Netscape Mail Window
* Reading E-Mail
* Saving, Printing and Deleting Messages
* Setting Other Mail Options
* Composing and Sending E-Mail
* Replying to a Message
* Forwarding E-Mail
* Working with an Address Book

Setting Crucial Mail Options in Netscape

Before you use e-mail the first time with Netscape, some mail options and preferences must be set. Many of the options are technical, but they are absolutely crucial to your being able to send or receive e-mail. These include the Internet domain name of your SMTP and POP servers. The SMTP server handles sending e-mail, and the POP server delivers it to your personal computer. You also need to set your e-mail address and name. If you don't share the computer with others, these have to be only set once. Once they are set, either by you or someone else, e-mail can be sent and received. Other options to decide on are the type of encoding to use to deal with nontext portions of e-mail, the name and location of your signature file, the way the folders are arranged, and the way the list of messages in the folders will be displayed. We'll discuss those options a little later in this chapter. It's essential that you have the correct name of your SMTP and POP servers, otherwise e-mail can't be sent or received. You get those names from a support person or group in your school or organization, your Internet service provider, or the local e-mail resident expert.

To set options and preferences for e-mail, click on the pull-down menu **Options** and select **Mail and News Preferences**. (You'll also be setting options this way to configure Usenet news.) This brings up a window similar to what's shown in Figure 3.5.

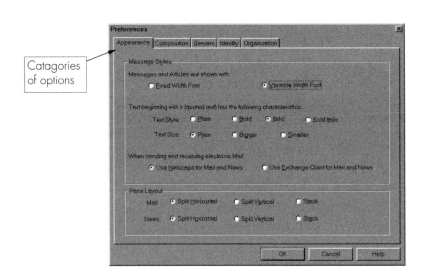

Figure 3.5   Preferences Window for Mail and News

The different categories or types of options appear as tabs across the top row. To see the options or preferences that can be set, click on the tab. Once you've set your preferences click on the button **OK** to save them or **Cancel** if you change your mind. We'll go over the categories one by one starting with the two that are the most crucial to e-mail, **Servers** and **Identity**.

Servers. The category **Servers** is where you set the Internet name of the computer systems that act as the SMTP server for e-mail and the POP server. Recall that the SMTP server is the computer system that transports the e-mail you write to the rest of the Internet, and the POP server is the system that delivers e-mail from the Internet to your personal computer. You get their names from the people in charge of the computer systems in your school or organization or your Internet service provider (ISP). E-mail can't be sent without the Internet domain name of the SMTP server, and if a POP server is involved, e-mail can't be received unless the POP server is identified. Figure 3.6 shows the e-mail portion of the **Servers** category filled in. The SMTP server is **mail.earthlink.net** and the POP server is **mail** (in this case, it's the same as the SMTP server). You get to this category by clicking on the **Servers** tab. This is also where the servers for Usenet news (Chapter 5) are set.

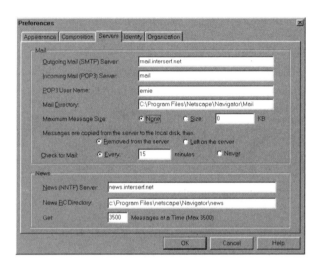

Figure 3.6   Server Category for Setting E-mail Options

The pane labeled **Mail Directory** holds the name of the directory that holds all your mail folders, including your **Inbox** or incoming e-mail. We've previously set or clicked on the radio button **Removed from the server**. Having it set this way means that when you check for new e-mail, the mail is copied from the POP server to your computer. It could be set to be left on the server. Doing it this way means that e-mail isn't transferred to your computer. It may build up on the server, and each time you check your e-mail you'll get more than one copy of the same e-mail. If you always use the same computer to check your e-mail and you're allowed to keep files on it, then you'll probably want to have it set this way. What you do will depend on your work habits and local policies.

Identity. The category **Identity** is where you give the e-mail program important information—your e-mail address so folks can reply easily to you, your name, and the location of your signature file. You need to supply your e-mail address so any messages you send out will have your e-mail address in the **From:** header. When you compose a message, the e-mail program automatically takes the information in the first three panes and makes it part of the message. When someone receives it they see whatever you've put in the pane labeled **Your Name**. In Figure 3.7 that pane holds the name Ernest Ackermann. Anything could be put there. (If you wanted folks who got e-mail from you to see that it comes from Ace Webster, then feel free to put that in the pane.) When they give a command to reply to your message, their e-mail program addresses the reply to what is in the pane labeled **Reply-To address**. In this case, it's the same as the one in the pane labeled **Your E-mail**, so someone who receives a message from this address replies to the same address. The pane labeled **Your Organization:** is used when you reply to or post an article to Usenet news. It's also used with some e-mail programs. You give the full name (directory and file) of the file holding your signature in the last pane in the category. Figure 3.7 shows the category **Identity** with all panes filled in.

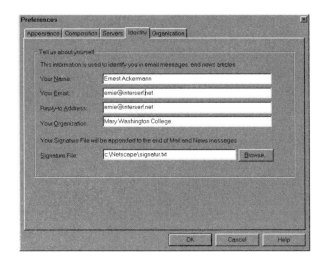

Figure 3.7   Identity Category—Who You Are, Your E-Mail Address, and Location of Signature File

Getting Help

Help for using or setting up e-mail is available in the mail window or in the browser window. Click on **Help** on the Menu Bar and then select **Handbook, Release Notes,** or **Frequently Asked Questions.** The Handbook has sections dedicated to using the e-mail system. You can also look up topics by using the index in the Handbook. It's a good idea to find out who you ought to contact at your school, organization, or company that provides your Internet services if you've got problems or questions. For information about setting options in a specific category, click on the button labeled **Help** for each category.

Knowing When New Mail Has Arrived

You can tell when new e-mail has arrived for you by looking at the small envelope in the bottom right corner of the border of a Netscape Window. When an exclamation mark (!) appears alongside the envelope, it means that new e-mail has arrived.

Opening and Closing the Mail Window

In order to read your e-mail, you have to open the mail window. You do that by clicking on the pull-down menu **Window** in the Menu Bar and then choosing **Mail Window.** If your mail is delivered through a POP server, then the first time you open the window you'll be prompted to enter your e-mail password. That's the same password (usually) that you use to access your Internet account or service. A sample mail window is shown in Figure 3.3. This is where you work with your e-mail. You can select messages to read, save to a folder, print, or delete. You can reply to messages, and messages can be forwarded to other Internet addresses. After you're finished dealing with your e-mail, you close the window by pressing Ctrl+W on the keyboard or clicking on the pull-down menu **File** and then choosing **Close.** You can keep this window on your desk top so you can go to it quickly.

The Netscape Mail Window

We've taken a quick look at the Netscape Mail Window before. Figure 3.3 shows a sample window, and here we'll take a more detailed look at it. Here we'll discuss the Menu Bar, Toolbar, and the mail window. Notice the window is divided into three frames—one for the folders list, one for the messages list, and one to display a message. Each of these can have its own scroll bar, and you can move through one independent of the others.

Menu Bar

Each entry in the Menu Bar represents a pull-down menu. Clicking on each shows the menu. Some of the items in a menu are listed with keyboard shortcuts; keys to press that immediately start an action. The first one, **File**, for example, has an item **Get New Mail Ctrl+M**. You can check for new mail from your POP server by selecting this item or pressing Ctrl+M on the keyboard at any time, without selecting the menu. We'll describe each menu item.

File   Lets you check for new mail from the POP server or deliver mail you've composed in case you've set e-mail options so e-mail isn't delivered immediately. It also contains items to let you work with your mail folders by opening a folder, creating a new folder, compressing a folder (which means to remove the messages you've deleted) or emptying (delete the messages from) the **Trash** folder. You can print the current message, the one that's displayed in the message frame. Finally, it contains items to close the mail window or exit. Exit means to end the Netscape Navigator session.

Edit   Use the items here to copy a selection from the message frame to the clipboard so it can be pasted into another application, delete a message or a folder, select a thread of messages (ones all on the same topic), or search for specific text within the current message. It also contains items to select if you want to *undo* a previous edit action.

View   These options deal with how the list of messages in a folder and individual messages are displayed. You can use the item **Sort** to arrange your messages in order by date, subject, or sender. For the message you're currently viewing in the message frame, you can select an item so that all headers are shown. Otherwise you see only the **Subject:, Date:, From:,** and **To:** headers. These are the most important and showing only headers makes it easier for you to concentrate on the text of the message. You can specify whether attachments are to be displayed inline, as in Figure 3.8 below, or shown as links to be activated by a mouse click.

Message	This menu has a number of items that let you compose a new message (New Mail Message) or forward the highlighted message in the message list to another Internet address. Once a message is displayed in the message frame, you can select items to reply (**Reply**) to the sender of that message or to everyone (**Reply to All**) listed as a recipient of the message. Also use this to mark the current or a list of messages and move or copy the current message to a folder. Moving it removes it from the current folder and copying makes a copy of it. You can also add the sender of the current message to the address book.
Go	The items here take you to the next or previous message. You can also go to the next or previous unread or marked messages. It also has an item to stop loading the current message from your server.
Options	This contains the same menu you see when you select **Options** from the browser screen. You can set options for the browser, mail, and news. You can also set whether to show all messages or only unread messages in the current folder.
Window	This is the essentially the same menu you see when selecting **Window** from the browser window. You can go to the browser, the news window, the address book, or the bookmark list.
Help	This is the same menu you see when you click on **Help** in the menu bar for any Navigator window.

Toolbar

The Toolbar is a sequence of labeled icons that you click on to perform the indicated action. We'll discuss them by listing the labels.

Get Mail	Clicking on this causes Netscape to contact your POP server to see if any new mail has arrived. If it has, it's delivered to your system.
Delete	This deletes the message that's highlighted or selected in the message list. It's moved from the current folder to the Trash folder.
To: Mail	Click here to compose, address, and send a new message.
Re: Mail	Use this to reply to the sender of a message. Clicking on this pops up the window used for composing messages. The address of the sender of the message that's displayed in the message window is automatically written into the **Mail To:** pane of the new message.
Re: All	Use this to reply to the sender and all recipients of a message. Clicking on this pops up the window used for composing messages. The address of the sender is automatically written into the **Mail To:** pane of the new message, and everyone else's address is automatically put into the **Cc:** frame.

Forward   Clicking on this sends a copy or forwards the highlighted message in the message list to another Internet address. You get the window for composing a message with the Subject: header filled in. You need to give the address of where it's going to be sent. You can also modify the outgoing message by adding something to it or editing it. The original message is sent along as an attachment.

Previous   This takes you to the previous unread message. If there is a series of unread messages and you select the middle to read, then you can use this to go to a previous one.

Next   This takes you to the next unread message.

Print   Click on this to print the message displayed in the message display area.

Stop   This stops the transmission of one or more messages from your system to the POP server.

List of Folders, List of Messages, and Message Display. The following describes these areas:

Folders—The frame in the upper left portion of the mail window holds a list of folders or directories. Each of these can hold messages. You click on **File** from the Menu Bar to create a new folder or open one that isn't listed. E-mail messages are stored in the folders. For each folder you see the number of messages it holds and the number of messages that haven't been read. To see a list of the messages in the folder, double-click on 🗀, just to the left of the folder's name. The list of messages will appear in the Messages frame to the right. You can create folders to save messages by clicking on **File** and selecting **New Folder.** This helps you organize the messages you've received if, for example, you get a number of messages on a topic or from someone. You can go through a folder replying to, deleting, printing, forwarding, etc. the messages. Putting e-mail in folders keeps you from having to deal with a hundred or more different messages that aren't organized in any way. Three folders will usually be present: **Inbox**—messages you've received but haven't put into any other folder; **Sent**—copies of the messages you've sent; and **Trash**—copies of messages you've deleted. The name of each folder is displayed along with a count of the total number of messages in the folder and the number of unread messages.

Messages—The Messages frame shows a list of the e-mail messages in the current folder. The list is arranged either by date, subject, or sender. You specify the way the list is sorted by clicking on **View** in the Menu Bar of the mail window. The headings along the top of the panel are **Sender,** a flag, a dot, **Subject,** and **Date. Sender** shows the name of the person who sent the e-mail; the flag is used to mark messages; the dot indicates whether the messages has been read—a bright ball shows it hasn't been read yet; **Subject** shows the **Subject:** header of the message; and **Date** shows the date the message was sent. Clicking on a message in the list displays it in the **Message Display Area.** A selected message can be deleted, printed, or saved to a folder. To save it to a folder, click on **Message** in the Menu Bar, choose **Move** or **Copy,** and then select the name of the folder. Clicking on the dot in the flag column marks or flags a message. You can mark a message as **Read** or **Unread** by clicking on the dot in the column. Using the vertical scroll bar in this pane lets you scroll through the list. If all the headers don't show, or the listing seem cramped, change the size of the mail window.

Message Display Area—E-mail messages are displayed in the bottom pane of the mail window in the message display area. The current message is displayed here. To see another message, click on it in the message list or use the **Next** and **Previous** icons in the Toolbar. A message is displayed with headers including **Subject:**, **Date:**, **From:**, and **To:**, followed by the body of the message. This pane has both a horizontal and vertical scroll bar to use to move through the message. You can also use the up or down arrow keys to move up or down through the message one line at a time. Netscape e-mail displays any attachments if they're images that the browser can display. It displays anything, including attached Web pages that can be viewed by the browser. If an attachment can't be viewed this way, it's displayed as an icon. Clicking on the icon either starts a program on your computer to view or play the file, provided it's a type that's listed in the browser's Helper Applications. Otherwise, it's saved to a file on your computer.

Reading E-Mail

To read your e-mail, you have to open the mail window. If this is the first time you've opened this window in this Netscape session, you'll be asked for the password for your mail system or POP server. Type it in the dialog box and press Enter. Then Netscape contacts the system that delivers mail to you. If any messages have arrived at the server since you last checked, they'll be delivered now, and the oldest of the new messages will be displayed in the message display area of the window. In any case, when you open the mail window you'll be looking at the messages in the folder **Inbox**. This is where all incoming messages are delivered by the computer. You can, however, save e-mail in other folders and use the mail system to manage and read these folders. The list of folders shows the number of unread messages and the total number of messages in each folder. The list of messages in the open folder is displayed in the **Message List** pane. You can read messages in this or any folder by clicking on the name of the folder.

Click on an entry in the message list, and the corresponding message is displayed in the message display area. You move from message to message by either selecting one from the message list and clicking on it with the mouse, clicking on the icons **Previous** and **Next** from the Toolbar, or choosing an item from the **Go** pull-down menu that takes you to another message. Using the icons labeled Previous and Next takes you through unread messages.

Example 3.1   Opening the Mail Window, Reading a Message, and Closing

You open the mail window by selecting **Netscape Mail** from the **Window** pull-down menu in the Menu Bar. If necessary, give your e-mail password; type it in the dialog box that appears on the screen. If there's e-mail waiting for you on your mail server, it will be delivered to you, and the most recent one will be displayed in the message display area or pane. If there is no new mail you can select one from the message list. Figure 3.3 shows the Netscape mail window we will use for this and the next example. We'll follow these steps:

1. Open the mail window.
2. Read the e-mail.
3. Close the mail window.

1. Open the Mail Window.

wWw Click on **Window** in the Menu Bar and then click on **Netscape Mail**.

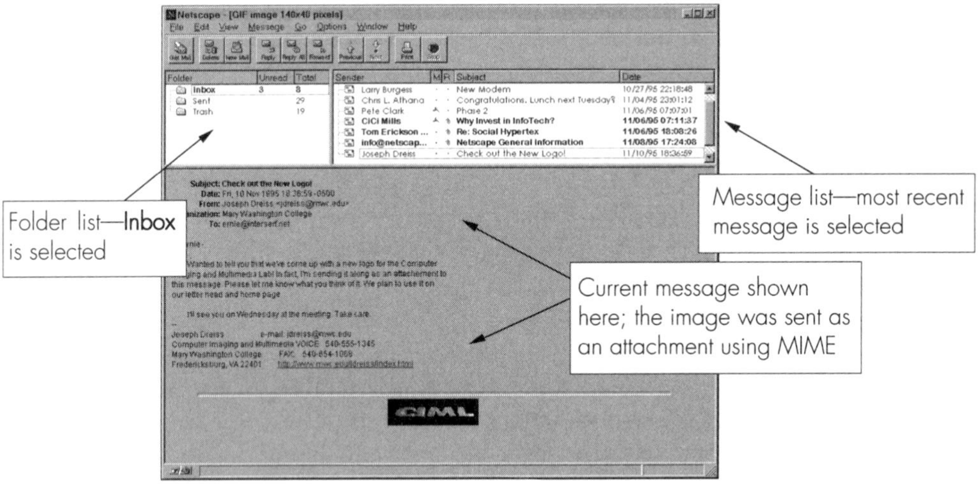

Figure 3.8   Mail Window, Reading a Message

Opening the mail window checks for new mail, lists your messages, and displays a new message. The current message, usually the oldest of the new messages, is highlighted as shown in Figure 3.8. **Inbox** is the folder that's currently open. To see the messages in another folder, click on it. (You'll see later how to save messages in folders.) The current message is displayed in the message display area. The message in Figure 3.8 includes text and an image. The image was sent as an attachment, but nothing extra had to be done to see it here. Netscape mail will automatically display images in uuencode, GIF, or JPEG sent as attachments. If a message contains a Web page in HTML format or anything in HTML as an attachment, then it's displayed just as if you were viewing it with the Netscape browser.

2. Read the E-Mail.

Open the mail window and the message list pane holds a list of messages in your folder **Inbox.** The listing for each message includes the name of the sender, the subject, and the date it was sent. Messages that haven't been read are marked with a green dot. Messages can also be flagged or marked by clicking on the dot in the column headed by a red flag. Figure 3.8 shows three unread messages and two flagged messages.

W"W   To read any message, click on its entry in the message list.

W"W   To read the next message in the list, press the down-arrow key (⬇). To read the previous message in the list, press the up-arrow key (⬆).

W"W   To read the previous or next in the list of unread messages, click on the icons ▣▣.

Viewing or reading a message shows it in the bottom pane, the message viewing area of the window. The message display area is like other windows in the sense that it has horizontal and vertical scroll bars and you can use the appropriate keys on the keyboard, for example, Page Up or Page Down, to move through the message.

As you're reading your messages, new messages might arrive for you. If they're not delivered immediately, you can check the POP server for them by clicking on the icon labeled **Get Mail**. In this case Netscape contacts the server and checks for new mail. If there is any new e-mail, it's delivered and the oldest of the new e-mail is displayed.

When you're done working with your mail, you may want to close the mail window.

3. Close the Mail Window.

W"W   Press Ctrl+W or click on **File** in the Menu bar and select **Close** to close the Mail Window.

─────────────────────────────End of Example 3.1─────────────────────────────

Saving Messages

You can save a message into a file or into a folder. To save an e-mail message in a file, go to the message list and highlight the entry for the message you want to save by clicking on it. Then click on **File** on the Menu Bar and select **Save As**, or press Ctrl+S. A **Save As..** dialog box pops up, and you type in the name of the file to hold the message. If you pick a name that already exists, you'll be asked if you really want to replace it with the message you're going to save. Saving a message to a file is useful if you're going to use the body of the message with some other program. Suppose, for example, your partner sends you a copy of a project she's working on that you'd like to include in a presentation. You might want to save it in a file and then import or copy it into the presentation.

Saving e-mail in folders is a convenient way to organize your e-mail. Since you create the folders, you may want to have some that deal with a specific topic or project and others that hold the e-mail you've received from one person. You can go through a folder replying to, deleting, printing, forwarding, etc. the messages.

To create a folder, click on **File** on the Menu Bar and select the item **New Folder....** A dialog box pops up and you type in the name of the folder.

To save a message into a folder, go to the message list and highlight the message you want to save by clicking on it. More than one message can be saved into a folder by highlighting a group of messages. Now click on **Message** on the Menu Bar, and then choose either **Move** or **Copy**. Choosing either one brings up a menu from which you choose the folder you want to hold the message(s). Moving means taking the e-mail from one folder and copying it into another. Copying means making a copy of the message and putting it into the folder you choose. (Now you have two copies of the message.)

Tip

Highlighting or selecting several messages.

To select more than one message from the message list, first select one message by clicking on it. Move the mouse pointer to another message, but don't click yet. Press Shift and click (the left button if your mouse has more than one) to select all the messages including the first one marked up to and including the message at the mouse pointer. Press Ctrl and click to select the message at the pointer and the first message highlighted. If others are highlighted, the one at the mouse pointer will be added to the group.

Printing Messages

To print a message, select it by clicking on its entry in the message list and then click on the Print icon. Printing is allowed only if one entry is highlighted. A window pops up, the same one you'd see for printing anything from Netscape. You can select a printer, set options (if necessary), and finally click on the button **OK** or **Cancel**.

Deleting Messages

Deleting messages is easy and necessary to keep the amount of e-mail in the **Inbox** and other folders under control. Highlight the entries in the message list of one or several messages and press the icon labeled **Delete** or press the Delete key on the keyboard. Deleting a message sends it to the folder **Trash**. You could go into that folder to reclaim a message, in case you delete one by mistake. Deleting a message from the folder **Trash** removes it permanently.

You can delete messages from the **Inbox** or any other folder. You probably face some limit on the amount of space you're allowed so think about deleting messages regularly. Do a little more than think about it—delete some messages.

Example 3.2   Creating a Folder; Saving and Deleting E-mail

In this example we'll save e-mail into a new folder and then delete three messages. We'll follow these steps after starting Netscape Navigator:
1. Open the mail window.
2. Create a new folder.
3. Copy two messages to the new folder.
4. Delete three messages.
5. Close the mail window.

1. Open the mail window.

 Click on **Window** in the Menu Bar and choose **Netscape Mail**.

In this example we'll be concerned most with the folder list and message list. Suppose that after we open the mail window and check for new e-mail we see the folder and message lists as shown in Figure 3.9.

Figure 3.9   Folder and Message List

2. Create a new folder.

We've got two messages from Ci-Ci Mills and we're going to save them into a folder named **cici**.

 Click on **File** in the Menu Bar and choose **New Folder....**

A dialog box pops up in which you type the name of the folder.

 Type **cici** and click on the **OK** button.

A folder named **cici** is created by Netscape Navigator and appears in the folder list as shown in Figure 3.10.

3. Copy two messages to the new folder.

Now that the folder is created we can mark two messages from Ci-Ci Mills and move them into the folder.

 Click on the entry for the first message from Ci-Ci Mills in the message list.

 Move the mouse pointer to the second entry from Ci-Ci Mills in the message list, press [Ctrl], and press the mouse button (the left one if your mouse has two buttons).

Figure 3.10 shows the messages highlighted.

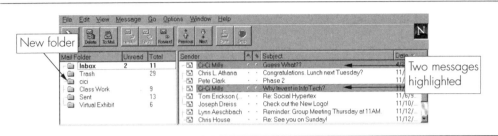

Figure 3.10 Folder and Message List after Creating New Folder and Highlighting Messages

Now we're ready to move the messages to the **cici** folder. This will take them out of **Inbox**. We can save other messages from Ci-Ci, if she ever writes to us again, in the same folder.

Click on **Message** on the Toolbar and then choose **Move**.

Another menu appears listing the names of the folders.

Click on **cici**.

The messages will be removed from the **Inbox** folder and copied to the folder named **cici**. The count of messages in both folders is adjusted. You can see that in Figure 3.11.

4. Delete three messages.

To demonstrate how to mark a range of messages and delete messages, we'll delete the three oldest messages from **Inbox**.

Click on the first entry in the message list.

Move the mouse pointer to the third message, but don't click.

Press **Shift** on the keyboard and click the left mouse button.

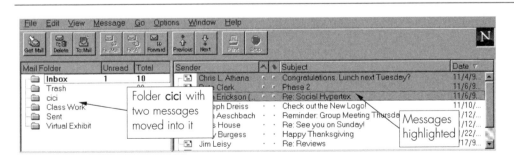

Figure 3.11 New Folder and Range of Messages Highlighted

Figure 3.11 shows the messages highlighted. To delete them we need to click on the icon labeled **Delete**.

w⁴⁴w Click on the icon labeled **Delete**.

This moves them to the folder **Trash**. At some point you'll want to delete them from **Trash** as well

5. Close the mail window.

w⁴⁴w Press **Ctrl**+W.

Closing the window ends the e-mail session, but doesn't end the Netscape Navigator session. To end the Netscape session, click on **File** on the Menu Bar and then choose **Exit**.

―――――――――――――――――――――End of Example 3.2――――――――――――――――――――――

Setting Other Mail Options

We talked about setting crucial options for e-mail earlier. In this section we'll cover setting options that control the way e-mail is displayed, the way it's sorted, how nontext e-mail is encoded and handled, and what file to use as your signature file. To set these options, click on the pull-down menu **Options** and select **Mail** and **News**. (You'll also be setting options this way to configure Usenet news.) This brings up a window similar to the one shown in Figure 3.5. You set options for any of the categories below by clicking on the tab by that name and then filling in the forms or clicking on the buttons indicated.

Appearance. Here you set options that deal with the way messages and the text within messages are displayed. You select an option by clicking on the radio buttons.

Messages and articles can be displayed in fixed width font, always the same regardless of the window size, or they can be displayed in a variable width font. Figure 3.5 has the option **Variable Width Font** selected.

The next set of options deals with the way quoted text is displayed. When you reply to an article you can include the text of the message you're replying to. This is useful to give the context to your reply. Each line of the quoted text will start with the character >. Figure 3.16 below shows an example of this. In Figure 3.5 we've selected options so the quoted text is in italic text. We can set the options to have the text appear in different styles and sizes.

Composition. Click on the tab **Composition** to bring up the window dealing with options related to composing e-mail. When you create a message to send you are composing a message.

In the first group you set the encoding method for sending messages. Choose either **allow 8-bit** or MIME. Both allow for including nontext files. You select **allow 8-bit** if you're including characters that aren't in the English alphabet or lines that are longer than 70 characters. A rule of thumb is to select MIME, and if there are problems with some characters not being transmitted, then try composing and sending messages using **allow 8-bit**.

The next set of options deals with whether copies of outgoing messages are sent to some address on the Internet or saved on your computer. You may want to do this to keep copies of the e-mail you write so you know what you've said. However, you'll occasionally want to delete some of these since they do take up space on your disk or network. You can have copies of all messages (and articles when you're using Usenet news) automatically sent to a specific e-mail address. Fill in the address in the appropriate panes. Also, you can have copies automatically saved on your system. Figure 3.12 shows a portion of the category **Composition** set so a copy of each e-mail message is sent to the address **ernie@mwc.edu** and copies are saved in **c:\netscape\navigator\mail\sent**. (Before putting an address in the **Mail Messages:** pane, make sure you have the permission of the person who'll be receiving the e-mail.)

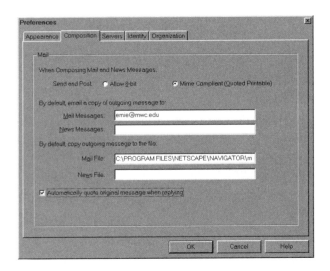

Figure 3.12   Setting Options for Copies of Outgoing E-Mail

Organization. The first item to set is whether Netscape will remember your e-mail password for you. If this isn't checked, you'll have to enter your e-mail password (usually the same as password you may need to access the Internet) the first time you check your e-mail during a Netscape Navigator session. You don't have to enter it every time, just the first. It's more convenient to have the password remembered, but if someone else is using the computer where this option is set, then they'll have access to your e-mail. Additionally, here is where you set the way you want to have the messages arranged in a folder. It's a good idea to have it set so that replies to the same message are *threaded*, or listed one after the other. You also set whether you want to see the list of your e-mail sorted by the date it was sent (**Date**), alphabetically by its subject (whatever is in the **Subject:** header), or sorted alphabetically by the name of the person who sent the e-mail (Sender). In Figure 3.13 the category **Organization** is filled in so that e-mail and Usenet news articles are threaded and sorted by date.

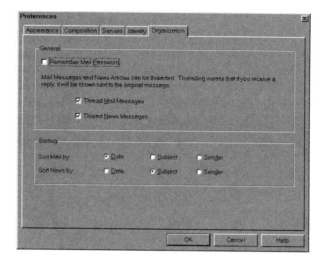

Figure 3.13   Organization—How the List of E-Mail in a Folder will be Organized and Listed

Composing and Sending E-Mail

You can send a new e-mail message from any part of Netscape, whether you're using the browser or working in the mail window or the news window. To send an e-mail message, press Ctrl+N or click on **File** on the Menu Bar and choose **New Mail Message**. If you're working in the mail window, click on the icon labeled **New Mail**. In any case, a window similar to Figure 3.14 will pop up.

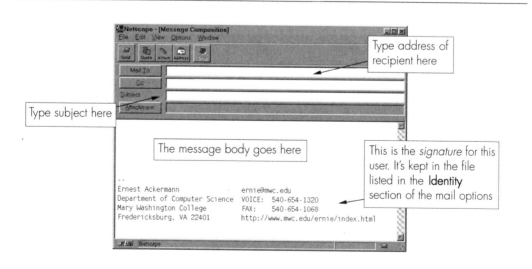

Figure 3.14 E-Mail Message Composition Window

Use the mouse to click on any of the panes or portions of the mail composition window.

The window has places for you to fill in the headers **Send To:** address(es) of primary receivers; **Cc:** address(es) where copies of the e-mail will be sent; **Subject:** what the message is about (make it brief and descriptive), and **Attachment:** name(s) of files to attach to the message. You can also move from header to header by pressing the Tab key. Separate multiple address with commas or spaces if you're sending the same e-mail to several people at the **To:** or **Cc:** headers. Use the **Attachment:** button to include files (text or nontext) with the message. You'll want to be sure the receiver can handle working with nontext files sent this way. The receiver's e-mail program has to include MIME (Multipurpose Internet Mail Extensions). Type the name of the file to include; Netscape e-mail attaches the file to the message.

There are several options you can use to choose different headers, include files, use an address book, and others. They'll be discussed later in this chapter or you can read about them in the on-line Netscape Handbook. To get a message off in a straightforward manner you need to follow these steps:
1. Open the Compose Message window (Ctrl+N).
2. Fill in the address in the pane or block next to the button **Send To:**.
3. Compose/Type the message body.
4. Send it off by clicking on the icon labeled **Send**.

Figure 3.15 shows a message ready to send. It's addressed to several people—the different addresses are separated by commas. The header **Cc:** is used to send a copy of the message to an Internet address. In this case the message is sent to four addresses. Three are listed in the **To:** header and one in the **Cc:** header. There are two attachments. The text in the message body was typed directly into the message using the keyboard. The sections below discuss composing a message and attaching files.

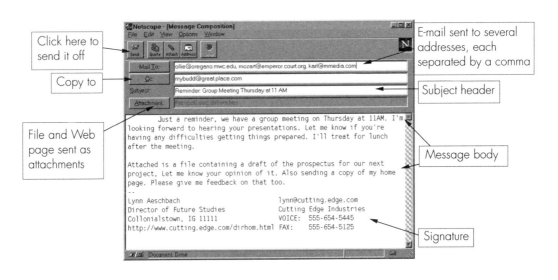

Figure 3.15 Composing E-Mail—Complete Message

Composing the Message Body. Type your message into the message body or compose the message using tools or programs with which you're comfortable. You can copy text from another Windows application or Web page. Any text on the clipboard can be pasted into the mail message. To copy/paste between applications click on **Edit** on the Menu Bar and select the appropriate action. Whether you type your message, include something from another application, or a combination of these, the e-mail program will take care of formatting the text. Type or copy the message and press Enter at the end of a paragraph. The e-mail program will handle adjusting the length of a line. You can only send plain text—no underlining, boldface, or italics—in the message body. Anything that's not in plain text format has to be sent as an attachment.

Including Attachments. Anything that's not in plain text format has to be an attachment if it's sent by e-mail. (Text files can be sent as attachments too.) Click on the icon labeled **Attachment** to attach a file to the message. A dialog box pops up. You select whether the attachment is a URL (Attach Location) or a file (Attach File). If you choose to attach a URL, then type in its URL and select whether it's to be sent in HTML format (**As Is**) or in plain text format (**Converted to Plain Text**). If you're going to attach a file, click on **Attach File**. Another window appears from which you select the file to attach or type in its name. Press the button labeled **Open** when you've got the file you want. Here you'll want to send it **As Is**. Once again, you select to send it **As is** or in text format. You can include several files and URLs as attachments.

Including a Web Page. Suppose you're viewing a Web page that contains some interesting information and you want to send a copy of it by e-mail to a friend. To send the Web page, either in HTML or text format, press Ctrl+M on the keyboard or click on **File** on the Menu Bar, and then choose **Mail Document**. The Message Composition window pops up and the URL of the current Web page is automatically included in the body of the message. You can also include the Web page as an attachment or include the text of the page in the body of the message. Here's an example. You're planning to visit the Mount Wilson Observatory near Pasadena, California, on your next trip to California but need directions to get there, and you also want to send a copy of the directions to some friends who will meet you there. You make your way to the home page for the observatory (**http://www.mtwilson.edu**) and follow the link labeled **Tourist Information** (**http://www.mtwilson.edu/tourist.html**). It's just what you were hoping to find. You send copies of the page to your friends—and yourself to be sure you have a copy— by pressing Ctrl+M, filling in the e-mail addresses in the **Send To** block, and then clicking on **File** and choosing **Include Original Text**. The text of the Web page becomes part of the body of the message.

Replying to a Message

You reply to the current message by clicking on the icon labeled **Reply**. You do this while you're reading a message or by clicking on its entry in the message list. Clicking on the **Reply** icon brings up a mail composition window just like the one for a new message (Figure 3.14), except that the **Send To**: address is automatically filled in so the reply goes to the Internet address taken from the original message. The **Subject**: will be set to **Re**: followed by the subject of the original message. If the address list in the original one includes several people you can send a reply to everyone on the **To**: or **Cc**: list by pressing the icon labeled **Reply All**. It's your choice; just be sure you don't send something to a group that you'd like to send to an individual. This can be embarrassing, especially if the reply is personal. In many situations, it's a good idea to include at least a portion of the original message so your reply can be read in context. This is particularly true if you're replying to a message that was sent to a group. Be sure to include only the relevant parts. To include the original message, click on **File** and then select **Include Original Text**. You'll have to edit the message to include the important portions.

Figure 3.16 shows what a user would see if he started a reply to everyone who received the e-mail in Figure 3.15.

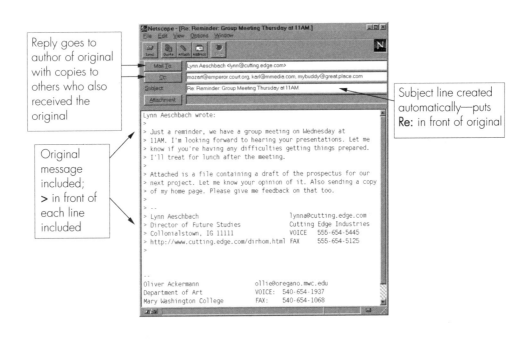

Figure 3.16 Reply to All Recipients—Include Original Message

At this point, you type/compose your reply, deleting lines from the original and including your own as you see fit. Use the arrow keys or the mouse to move the cursor to wherever you want to type. Use the mouse to highlight a portion of the text and then the items in the **Edit** menu to copy, cut, or paste a portion of the message. When it's complete, you can send it off by clicking on the icon labeled **Send**.

Forwarding E-Mail

Forwarding e-mail means passing the e-mail you've received on to another address. You can do this by highlighting one or more entries in the message list and then clicking on the icon labeled **Forward**.

When you select messages to be forwarded, a message composition window pops up like the one in Figure 3.4. The **Subject:** is filled in with [**Fwd: Subject of original message**] and the message or messages being forwarded are included as attachments. Any attachments to the original message are included with the forwarded message. You can include anything you'd like in the body of the forwarded e-mail. If you're forwarding one message, you can also include the text of the original message in the same way as including it in a reply to an e-mail message.

Working with an Address Book

Netscape e-mail includes an address book that's an integrated part of the e-mail program. You can add addresses by typing them in or having the program take them directly from a message. You give each address a nickname or short form so you can use it when you're composing or replying to a message. When you're using the mail composition window, clicking on the icon labeled **Address** opens a copy of the address book so you can select an address for the **To:**, **Cc:**, or **Bcc:** header. (**Bcc:** is like **Cc:**. A copy of the message is sent, but none of the recipients—except for the one(s) listed under **Bcc:**—know a copy is being sent.) Furthermore, several addresses can be grouped together so you can send e-mail to all members of a group or organization. It's a good idea to keep frequently used addresses in the address book. That way you don't have to remember people's addresses. Also, you won't have to save messages just because you need someone's address.

Adding Addresses. There are essentially two ways to add an address to the address book: take it from the current message, or add it by typing it into the address book.

To take an address from the current message, click on **Message** on the Menu Bar and then choose **Add to Address Book**. Netscape fills in the name and e-mail address by taking them from the appropriate headers in the message. You need to add a nickname for the address book. You can add a description or other information to the entry in the address book. Figure 3.17 shows a filled-in entry.

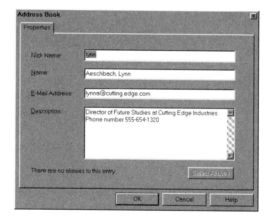

Figure 3.17 Completed Entry in an E-Mail Address Book

To add an address manually, click on **Window** on the Menu Bar and select **Address Book**. Once the address book is open click on **Item** from its menu bar and then choose **Add User**. A window similar to the one shown in Figure 3.17 will pop up. You fill in all the blanks.

After you've added the necessary information in the properties window, click on the button labeled **OK** to save it in the address book. You can change the information for an entry at any time by opening the address book, clicking once on the entry in the list, and then choosing **Properties** from the **Item** entry in the Menu Bar. Figure 3.18 shows an address book.

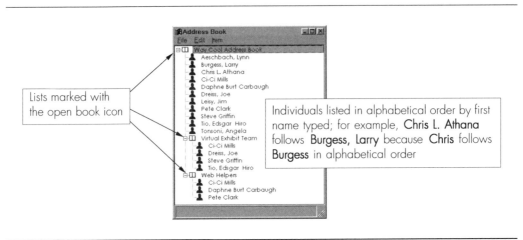

Lists marked with the open book icon

Individuals listed in alphabetical order by first name typed; for example, **Chris L. Athana** follows **Burgess, Larry** because **Chris** follows **Burgess** in alphabetical order

Figure 3.18 Address Book

Working with a Distribution List or Group Address. You can also create a distribution list, a list of addresses associated with a single nickname. That lets you send one e-mail message to a group. It's particularly useful if you regularly need to send or share e-mail with several people. To create a distribution list, first go to the address book (click on **Window** on the Menu Bar and select **Address Book**), click on **Item** in the Menu Bar, and choose **Add List**. A window pops up, similar to the one for adding an address. You type in the nickname, and in the block labeled **Name** type a name for this list. You can type a description of the list in the pane labeled **Description**. (To change any of this information at a later time, click on the folder in the address book, click on **Item** in the Menu Bar, and select **Properties...**) Figure 3.19 shows a completed entry for a group address. After you fill in the information, a book icon—with the name you typed for it—will appear in the address book. To change the information, names can be added to the list only from the group of users already in the address book. To add them, first go through the steps to add a user. Then click on the name once in the address book list, hold down the mouse button, and drag the name to the entry for the list you've added.

Deleting Addresses. Addresses can be deleted from the address book by first opening the address book, then highlighting an address (click on it once), and finally pressing the Delete key. Addresses used in distribution lists are aliases or copies of addresses from the list of individuals. Deleting one that's part of a list removes only that copy of it. Deleting a name from the list of individuals removes the name completely from the book, including all lists in which it appears.

Using Addresses. You use the nickname you've assigned to an address when you want to use an address for sending, replying to, or forwarding e-mail. Suppose, for example, we've given the list Web Helpers the nickname **webh** as shown in Figure 3.19. To send e-mail to this address, just type **webh** in the **To:** or **Cc:** field of a message you're composing. The address will be looked up in the address book. Fill in the Internet

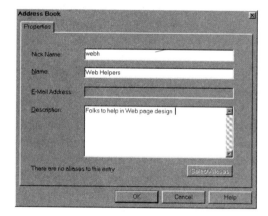

Figure 3.19   Completed Entry for a Group Address

e-mail address(es) associated with the nickname. Nicknames are useful with names you'll be using frequently. But you don't have to remember them. Whenever you're composing a message, click on the icon labeled **Address** to get the address book displayed on the screen. Then double-click on the one you want to use and you're set.

Summary

Electronic mail allows users on the Internet to communicate with each other electronically. Using the e-mail program with Netscape Navigator, you can compose messages or write and then send them to any other Internet address. You can read the messages you've received, save them to a file, print them, or delete them. You can also reply to a message or forward one to another Internet address.

An e-mail message consists of three main parts—the **headers**, which contain information about the address of the sender, the address of the recipient, when the message was sent, and other items; the **message body**, which holds the text portion of the e-mail; and an optional **signature**, which holds information about the sender such as full name, mailing address, phone number, etc. The signature ought to be limited to four or five lines, and it's put into a file so it's automatically included with each message.

In order to send e-mail, you give the Internet address of the recipient, compose or write the message, and then give a command to send it on its way. The message is broken up into *packets*, each containing the address of the sender and the address of the recipient, and the packets are routed through several sites on the Internet to the destination. The computer systems on the Internet handle the transmission and delivery of the e-mail. Once e-mail arrives at a site, it's put into a system mailbox for an individual user. She can read her mail from the system program by using an e-mail program like the one available with Netscape Navigator.

E-mail is a convenient and efficient means of communication. However, most communication is by the text of the message, so you have to be considerate and careful to communicate effectively, without misunderstandings. Since most users have a limited amount of space for their e-mail, be sure to get rid of unwanted or unnecessary e-mail and also be sure to send concise, appropriate messages to others. E-mail isn't necessarily private. Because it's transmitted electronically, there are several opportunities for someone to read your messages. It's relatively easy to forward copies of e-mail so a message sent to one person can be easily transmitted to others.

E-mail or Internet addresses usually have the form of **local-name@domain-name. Local-name** is often the log-in or user name of the person receiving the e-mail, and **domain-name** is the Internet name of the site or computer system receiving the messages. It's possible to send e-mail to addresses on networks not on the Internet. You need to know the proper form of an address to communicate with users on these networks.

Finding someone's e-mail address isn't always easy. There is no central directory keeping a list of the e-mail address for everyone on the Internet. If you want to find someone's address, one of the best things to do is to call or write that person and ask for the e-mail address. There are a number of automated services to use to search for an e-mail address. You can query a database of addresses of people who've posted articles to Usenet, and several Gopher and WWW servers provide directories for finding addresses.

The e-mail program for Netscape Navigator was discussed in this chapter. It's a full-featured e-mail program. You need to set some preferences before using it. Messages can be saved into folders, and can include text and other types (images, sound, programs, spreadsheets, word-processed documents, Web pages, etc.) of items as part of the message or as attachments. The program includes an address book. Reading and managing e-mail is carried on the Netscape mail window, and you compose e-mail in a message composition window. Online help is available.

Exercises

Questions about Your E-Mail

1. What is your e-mail address? What is the e-mail address of someone at your site to contact if you have questions or problems?

2. What is the name of the SMTP server for your e-mail? Do you use a POP server? What's its Internet address or name?

3. Is there a quota or limit on your e-mail? What is it?

Using E-Mail

4. Send e-mail to yourself with a reminder about something you need to do in the next few days.

5. Read your e-mail. Reply to at least one message. Delete two messages and forward one message.

6. Send a message, using multiple addresses, to at least three other people.

7. Using your e-mail program, save a message to a file and print the same message.

8. Create a signature for yourself and test it by sending yourself a short message.

Finding E-Mail Addresses

9. Use Four11, **http://www.four11.com/** or WhoWhere?, **http://www.whowhere.com/** to search for an e-mail address for the author of this book. Search for your own e-mail address or e-mail addresses of people with the same last name as yours. Search for the e-mail address of a friend.

10. Send e-mail to **mail-server@rtfm.mit.edu** with send usenet-addresses/name in the body of the message to try to find the e-mail address of a friend. How long did it take before you received a reply?

CHAPTER 4

Internet E-Mail Discussion Groups

You already know that electronic mail allows you to communicate with other users on the Internet. It's natural that people with a common interest should form groups to discuss issues, share information, or ask questions related to a common topic or theme. The groups go by different names—discussion lists, interest groups, Listserv, or mailing lists. In this chapter we'll use the term *discussion group* or *list* to refer to any of these types of groups.

All communication in a discussion group is carried on by e-mail. A user joins or *subscribes* to a group and then shares in the discussions of the group. A message sent to the group is usually broadcast via e-mail to all members of the group, so these discussions are public. There is an exception; some groups are *moderated* and a message sent to the group is first routed to the person serving as moderator. The moderator either sends the message on to the group or takes some other action. Some groups are very large, with thousands of subscribers, and some are very diverse, with members throughout the world. If you subscribe to an active group, you can expect many e-mail messages per day. You'll find members with all levels of experience.

Being a member of a discussion group means that you can join in discussions, ask questions, help others with questions, make announcements related to the group, or just see what others are talking about. You don't have to respond to every message; you can use your e-mail system just to read or even ignore some of the discussions. It's usually a good idea just to read messages when you first join a group so you can get an idea of the general tone and level of the discussion. Some folks use the term *lurking* to describe the behavior of observing the discussions. Lurking is just fine; it may be exactly what you want.

Discussions in the group should be carried on in a polite and civil manner. Occasionally someone gets upset about what someone else has written and sends a message to the group that insults, scolds, berates, or is downright nasty about the author of the original message. This type of message is called a *flame*. To keep things from getting out of hand, users sometimes need to be reminded to calm down or tone down their remarks. When you're ready you can send a message to the group (this is called *posting* a message), reply to the individual author of a message, or send a reply to the group. Replying to the group means your message goes to everyone on the list.

Most of the management of a list, tasks like adding new members or subscribers, removing members who choose to leave (or *unsubscribe* from) a list, and other tasks, is handled automatically by software (a collection of one or more computer programs) running on the computer that serves as the host system for the list. This software maintains the files associated with the list and responds to commands from the membership. As a member of a list you usually can retrieve archives or collections of past discussions, get a list of the current members, and ask that the list mail be sent to you in one packet, called a digest, at regular intervals instead of getting each message individually. These functions or other requests for service are handled by commands you send to an e-mail address, called the administrative address, which passes the command on to the software managing the list. Since these requests are satisfied automatically by a computer program, the requests need to be in a specific form that can be understood by the software.

When you're a member of a list, you need to know two addresses, and you need to know when to use them.

1. The address of the list, sometimes called the *list address* or *group address*. This is the address you'll use to communicate with the list. When you send e-mail to this address, the mail is delivered to all members of the list.
2. The address to request services from or give commands to the manager of the list. This address is sometimes called the *administrative address* of the list. Most lists are automatically managed by software, such as Listserv or Listproc, so the commands are executed automatically by software. Some lists are maintained and managed entirely by individuals or groups of users. These services or commands allow you to subscribe, unsubscribe, receive messages in digest form, retrieve a list of members, request archives, and so on. This administrative address is the same address you use to join or subscribe to the list.

It's easy to make a mistake and confuse the two. If you send a request to the wrong address, a member of the list will usually remind you of the correct address. If you send a message that's passed on to the managing software but was meant for the members of the list, you'll usually get a reply back indicating the message wasn't in the proper form.

The following illustration shows the relationship among you, the list or group, and the software managing the list.

In this section we'll cover the details of working with lists:

- How to Join a List
- How to Communicate with and Contribute to a List
- How to Leave a List
- Requesting Services from Software that Manages a List
- How to Find the Names and Addresses of Lists
- Proper Etiquette or Behavior in a Discussion Group
- Internet Sources of Information about Discussion Lists

Several different types of software are used to maintain discussion groups. In this chapter we'll concentrate on three: Listserv, Listproc, and Majordomo. These systems all allow the same kinds of services, and we'll mention differences between them. You can usually tell which software manages the list by looking at the administrative address, the address you use to subscribe to the list. For example, if the address is **listproc@coco.site.edu** (a fictitious address), Listproc is being used. The type of software maintaining the list is chosen when the list is created; it isn't a decision each member can make. You generally don't need to worry about which software maintains the list, but you should be aware of the differences. Some lists aren't managed by software; all functions and services are dealt with by one or more administrators. In these cases, most of the commands you'll send to the administrative address will be in ordinary prose form. You can usually get help from other members of the list, and you'll get some instructions about using the services of a list when you join.

How to Join a List

In order to join a list you need to send e-mail to the administrative address for the list. The e-mail should contain the word **SUBSCRIBE** and the name of the list. For most lists you also need to include your full name (first name, last name), unless you're subscribing to a list that's managed by Majordomo. Here are some discussion lists on the Internet. You can tell the type of software used to administer the list from the administrative or list address.

List name:	BIRDCHAT
Administrative address:	listserv@arizvm1.ccit.arizona.edu
List address:	BIRDCHAT@arizvm1.ccit.arizona.edu
Brief description:	Discussions related to birding, birding activities, and birding experiences. This list deals with wild birds; please, no messages dealing with pets.
To join:	Send e-mail to **LISTSERV@arizvm1.ccit.arizona.edu** with the message **subscribe BIRDCHAT Your Full Name** For example: **subscribe BIRDCHAT Chris Athana**

List name:	PHOTO-L
Administrative address:	listproc@csuohio.edu
List address:	PHOTO-L@csuohio.edu
Brief description:	Unmoderated open noncommercial discussion of all aspects of photography.
To join:	Send e-mail to **listproc@csuohio.edu** with the message **subscribe PHOTO-L Your Full Name** For example: **subscribe PHOTO-L Chris Athana**

List name:	F-COSTUME
Administrative address:	majordomo@world.std.com
List address:	F-COSTUME@world.std.com
Brief description:	Concentrates on design, motivation, and execution of fantasy costumes.
To join:	Send e-mail to **majordomo@world.std.com** with the message **subscribe F-COSTUME**

Note: Some versions of Majordomo software don't allow you to include your full name as part of the request to join the list. You do have the option of including your e-mail address. If you subscribe to a Majordomo list and include your full name, it may be OK. If not, you'll receive some automatically generated e-mail indicating that the version of Majordomo couldn't understand your request. Try again with a message in the form subscribe name-of-list.

Regardless of the type of list, remember you're not writing something for another person to read. You're giving a command to some software, and the command has to be in a specific form. Also, you don't have to supply your e-mail address. Since you've sent e-mail to the administrative address, your e-mail address is part of the message. The software that manages the list takes your name and address and adds them to the list of members.

What Happens Next?

You ought to receive a response from the software managing the list within a few minutes, hours, or maybe a day or two. That is, of course, provided you've used the proper address and the list still exists. If the address isn't correct, you'll probably have your mail returned as undeliverable or you'll get e-mail saying that the list doesn't exist at the site. But if you have used the proper address you'll get a response saying either you've succeeded in subscribing to the list or you've made some error in the message you sent to the administrative address. If there is some error, look up the address once more and try again.

Let's assume you've succeeded in subscribing to the list and you've received e-mail about the list. In some cases you'll be asked to confirm your request to join or subscribe, but in most cases you'll receive an immediate e-mail message welcoming you to the list. Save the welcome message! It usually contains important information about leaving or unsubscribing from the list and other commands to use to request services from the software that manages the list. It also tells you how to get more information. Once again, *save that message!* You'll probably need it in the future.

Figure 4.1 is a sample of the type of message you'll receive. It's from Listserv and it's for the fictitious list BOBOOTN. (The name was chosen just to demonstrate the message you might receive from the software managing the list.) You'll get a different but similar type of e-mail message from other list software.

```
Subject: Your subscription to list BOBOOTN
To: Chris Athana <cathana@nice.place.edu>
Reply-To: BOBOOTN-Request@listspot.coco.EDU


Dear networker,


Your subscription to list BOBOOTN (BOBO's on the Net) has been
accepted.


You may leave the list at any time by sending a "SIGNOFF BOBOOTN"
command to LISTSERV@LISTSPOT.BITNET (or LISTSERV@LISTSPOT.ABC.EDU).
Please note that this command must NOT be sent to the list address
(BOBOOTN@LISTSPOT.ABC.EDU)but to the LISTSERV address
(LISTSERV@LISTSPOT.ABC.EDU).


The amount of acknowledgment you wish to receive from this list upon
completion of a mailing operation can be changed by means of a "SET
BOBOOTN option" command, where "option" may be either "ACK" (mail
acknowledgment), "MSGACK" (interactive messages only), or "NOACK".


Contributions sent to this list are automatically archived. You can
obtain a list of the available archive files by sending an "INDEX
BOBOOTN" command to LISTSERV@LISTSPOT.BITNET (or
```

LISTSERV@LISTSPOT.ABC.EDU). These files can then be retrieved by
means of a "GET BOBOOTN filetype" command, or using the database
search facilities of LISTSERV. Send an "INFO DATABASE" command for
more information on the latter.

Please note that it is presently possible for other people to
determine that you are signed up to the list through the use of the
"REVIEW" command, which returns the network address and name of all
the subscribers. If you do not wish your name to be available to
others in this fashion, just issue a "SET BOBOOTN CONCEAL" command.

More information on LISTSERV commands can be found in the LISTSERV
reference card, which you can retrieve by sending an "INFO REFCARD"
command to LISTSERV@LISTSPOT.BITNET (or LISTSERV@LISTSPOT.ABC.EDU).

Virtually,

The LISTSERV management

Figure 4.1   Welcome Message from Listserv—Very Important!

How to Communicate with and Contribute to a List

Send e-mail to the list address if you want all the members of the list or group to receive it. Don't send e-mail meant for the members of the list to the administrative address. E-mail that's sent to the list address is either sent to all members of the list, or sent to a *moderator* who may or may not distribute the message to the rest of the group.

One other address you may need is the address of the *list owner* or *moderator*. You'll probably get that address with your "welcome to the group" e-mail. Write to the owner or moderator when you have questions about the nature of the list, if you think something is wrong with the list, or to volunteer to help the moderator.

Some lists allow you to send a message to the list only from the same address you used to join or subscribe to the list. That is a strict policy; some users access the Internet from a network of systems, and they may not always be using a system with the same address. If you have problems sending or posting a message to a list, trying posting a message from the address you used to subscribe to the list.

Sometimes you may want to reply to a message you've received from a member of the list. You can send e-mail that either goes to everyone in the group or only to the one who originated the message. The program you use for e-mail will allow you to *reply* to a message. If you reply to a message from the group, it will be sent to all the members of the group. You'll have to decide whether to reply to the list or to the individual. You shouldn't respond to the list when you mean to respond to the individual. You will likely be reminded by other members of the list that you made a mistake. If you see a message on the list that was obviously meant for an individual, you might want to send a gentle reminder to the person who made the mistake.

How can you tell if a message came from a list or from an individual? Look at the e-mail headers **Reply-To:**, **From:**, or **To:**. Each e-mail message carries with it a collection of *headers* that include information about who will receive the reply (**Reply-To:**), who sent the message (**From:**), and to whom the message was sent (**To:**). If an e-mail message has the header **Reply-To:**, the address after **Reply-To:** is the address your e-mail program uses when you choose the reply option or operation. You find the address of the person who sent the original message by looking at the header **From:**. You can also look at the header **To:** to see if the e-mail was sent to all members of the list or especially to you. Figure 4.2 shows the pertinent information.

```
Reply-To: PHOTO-L@csuohio.edu


From: cathana@right.here.edu


To: Multiple recipients of the list <photo-L@csuohio.edu>


I've been doing some reading about photography lately and came across
the term "hyperfocal distance". I'd appreciate it if someone could
tell me what that term means.


Thanks in advance,


Chris Athana
cathana@right.here.edu
```

Figure 4.2   Example Message to an Internet Group

Here are two responses. The first is the proper type of response that ought to go to either the individual sending the original message (**cathana@right.here.edu**) or to the entire list. Since the response might benefit everyone on the list, it's appropriate to reply to the list.

```
The term "hyperfocal distance" usually means the closest distance
that's in focus when the lens is focused at infinity. You can get
more information about this term and others you might be interested
in by reading Photographic Lenses FAQ or the Photographic Lenses
Tutorial. They're both available on the WWW by using the URLs http://
www.cis.ohio-state.edu/hypertext/faq/usenet/rec-photo/lenses/faq/
faq.html and http://www.cis.ohio-state.edu/hypertext/faq/usenet/rec-
photo/lenses/tutorial/faq.html.
```

The next response should be sent only to the person who sent the original message (**cathana@right.here.edu**), definitely not to the entire list. Chris may appreciate the message, but other members won't.

```
Chris,

How are you? I haven't heard from you in a while. Send me some e-mail
and I'll give you the answers to all your questions.


J. Richmond - richster@far.away.com
```

How to Leave a List

To leave or unsubscribe from a list, send e-mail to the *administrative address*. The message needs to have the name of the list you want to leave since several lists may be managed by the same software at a site. The name of the list is represented by LIST-NAME below. In most cases, you need to send the e-mail message to leave or unsubscribe from the same Internet address you used to join the list. If you have difficulty leaving a list, write to the list owner or moderator. Remember to unsubscribe or leave by sending e-mail to the administrative address, not the list address.

In the case of Listserv and Listproc, you send the message:

```
unsubscribe LIST-NAME
```

You may have to include your e-mail address when Majordomo is being used to manage a list, if you gave it when you joined the list, or if you're leaving from a different address. Send either the message:

```
unsubscribe LIST-NAME
```

or

```
unsubscribe LIST-NAME YOUR-CURRENT-E-MAIL-ADDRESS
```

Here is how to leave each of the lists mentioned before. We're assuming the Internet address was used for subscribing or joining the list.

List name:	BIRDCHAT
Send e-mail to:	listserv@arizvm1.ccit.arizona.edu
Message:	unsubscribe BIRDCHAT

List name:	PHOTO-L
Send e-mail to:	listproc@csuohio.edu
Message:	unsubscribe PHOTO-L

List name:	F-COSTUME
Send e-mail to:	majordomo@world.std.com
Message:	unsubscribe F-COSTUME
	or unsubscribe F-COSTUME cathana@right.here.edu

Requesting Services from Software that Manages a List

Lists and discussion groups generally offer a number of services to their members. In some cases, all the messages to a list are archived or saved so members can retrieve them at any time. Lists also generally allow a member to specify the way she receives mail from the group, such as one message at a time or in digest form. We'll explain some of the services a list provides as well as the commands used to get the services. All the commands are sent by e-mail to the administrative address. That way the commands may be detected by the software that manages the list. Sending a command to the list generally does nothing except to have several members of the list reply with reminders that the commands were sent to the wrong address.

Getting Help and a List of All Commands

Send a simple message:

```
HELP
```

to the administrative address and you'll receive, again by e-mail, a list of all the commands you can use with the list. This works for any type of software managing a list. Some lists also provide a reference card, really e-mail, that explains all the commands. If the managing software is Listserv send the command:

```
INFO REFCARD
```

to any system that supports Listserv. From the examples in the previous sections you could send that message to **listserv@arizvm1.ccit.arizona.edu**. Another site is **listserv@listserv.net**.

Getting a List of Subscribers

To find out who else has subscribed to a list or to check the name and e-mail address you used to subscribe to a list, send a command to the administrative address. Some lists don't allow their membership to be made public; most lists allow each member to specify whether to make her name and e-mail address available. Table 4.1 gives the commands to use to get a list of subscribers (if available). Substitute the name of the list for *LIST-NAME* and send the command to the administrative address. You'll see that almost all will understand the command **REVIEW**.

List Type	Command
Listproc	REVIEW *LIST-NAME*
	or RECIPIENTS *LIST-NAME*
Listserv	REVIEW *LIST-NAME*
Majordomo	WHO *LIST-NAME*

Table 4.1   Getting a List of Subscribers

Hiding Your Name from the List of Subscribers

You can keep your name and e-mail address from appearing on the list of subscribers if the list type is Listproc or Listserv. This is like having an unlisted telephone number. In Table 4.2 substitute the specific list name for *LIST-NAME* and send the command as e-mail to the administrative address for the list.

List Type	Command
Listproc	SET *LIST-NAME* CONCEAL YES
	SET *LIST-NAME* CONCEAL NO—use this to make your name visible again
Listserv	SET *LIST-NAME* CONCEAL
	SET *LIST-NAME* NOCONCEAL—use this to make your name visible again

Table 4.2   Hiding Your Name from the List of Subscribers

Temporarily Suspending Messages

There may be times you want to suspend receiving messages from a list, perhaps when you go on vacation or are away from the Internet for some time. You want to remain a member of the list, but you don't want any mail. (Of course you can unsubscribe to suspend messages, but then you have to join again to start receiving messages.) You substitute the specific name of the list for *LIST-NAME* in Table 4.3 and send the command to the administrative address. This service isn't supported with Majordomo.

List Type	Command
Listproc	SET *LIST-NAME* MAIL POSTPONE
	use SET *LIST-NAME* MAIL to receive messages again
Listserv	SET *LIST-NAME* NOMAIL
	use SET *LIST-NAME* MAIL to receive messages again

Table 4.3   Suspending Messages

Switching to Digest Mode

Switching to *digest mode* means you'll receive messages in a single daily or weekly mailing. Some people prefer this so they can work with messages from a group all at once, instead of receiving several messages during a day. It also helps to identify messages that come from one group. Table 4.4 shows the command(s) to use with each of the other types of lists. You substitute the name of a specific list for *LIST-NAME* and send the command by e-mail to the administrative address.

List Type	Command
Listproc	SET *LIST-NAME* MAIL DIGEST
	use SET *LIST-NAME* MAIL ACK to cancel digest mode
Listserv	SET *LIST-NAME* DIGEST
	use SET *LIST-NAME* MAIL to cancel digest mode
Majordomo	SUBSCRIBE *LIST-NAME*-DIGEST
	UNSUBSCRIBE *LIST-NAME*
	use SUBSCRIBE *LIST-NAME*
	UNSUBSCRIBE *LIST-NAME*-DIGEST to cancel digest mode.

Table 4.4   Switching to Digest Mode

Majordomo requires two commands, both included in the same message. The first subscribes to the list in digest mode. The second removes your name as a user to receive the messages as separate mailings.

Getting a List of Archived Files

Many lists are *archived*, which means that collections of past messages are kept so they can be retrieved by members. Some lists also keep collections of frequently asked questions (with answers) about the topics discussed on the list and other files useful to the group members. To get a list of the names of the files in a group's archives, send e-mail containing the command

`INDEX LIST-NAME`

to the administrative address for the list. Substitute the name of a specific list for *LIST-NAME*. For example, to get the archives for the list F-COSTUME, send the message

`INDEX F-COSTUME`

to majordomo@world.std.com.

Retrieving a File from the Archives of a List

You can retrieve any of the files in the list's archives by sending a command to the administrative address. The previous section described how to get a list of files; you might see something on the list you'd like to retrieve or someone tells you about a file that's kept in some list's archives.

You either use the command GET or the command SEND to retrieve a file from an archive (depending on the type of software that manages the list). Include the name of the list and the name of the file. Table 4.5 lists the commands to use for each type of software, and also includes an example. Substitute the specific name of a list for *LIST-NAME* and the specific name of a file for *FILE-NAME*. Remember to send your commands to the administrative address for the list.

List Type:	Listproc
Command:	GET *LIST-NAME FILE-NAME*
Example:	**GET PHOTO-L PHOTO-L.Sep-25**
List Type:	Listserv
Command:	GET *FILE-NAME FILE-TYPE LIST-NAME* F=MAIL
Example:	**GET AOU91 TXT BIRDCHAT F=MAIL**
	Listserv software also requires you to specify the type of the file, *FILE-TYPE*. This file type appears in the list of files in the archive.
List Type:	Majordomo
Command:	GET *LIST-NAME FILE-NAME*
Example:	**GET F-COSTUME TOPICS**

Table 4.5   Retrieving a File

A Summary of How to Work with Discussion Groups

Follow through these steps in working with a list or group:

1. Identify or choose a group. You'll find out about lists by reading things on the Internet, getting recommendations from friends, or searching a collection of lists.
2. Find the address used to join a group. This is usually the administrative address. For example, the address used to join the list PHOTO-L, mentioned above, is **listproc@csuohio.edu**. You'll send e-mail to this address with the body of the message having the form *subscribe list-name your-name*. (Check the section in this chapter that gives the proper form for the type of list or group you're working with.)
3. Find the address used to contribute to a group. You send e-mail to the group address, not to the administrative address, to communicate with the members of the group. The group address for PHOTO-L is **PHOTO-L@csuohio.edu**. So if you want to post a question, make a statement, or help someone out, you send e-mail to **PHOTO-L@csuohio.edu**.
4. Use services available from the list. The services available and the ways to access these services will most likely be contained in the reply you get from the administrative address when you join the list. Save that reply since you may need it later. Services include a list of members, access to archives of previous discussions, and so forth.
5. Unsubscribe or leave a group. Send e-mail to the administrative address, not to the group. In most cases, the body of the e-mail message is *signoff list-name your-name*. (Check the section in this chapter that gives the proper form to use for the type of list or group you're working with.)

How to Find the Names and Addresses of Lists

There are thousands of discussion groups or mailing lists on the Internet. How do you find lists that match your needs or interests? You're likely to hear about some lists from the folks you correspond with on the Internet; you'll also see lists mentioned if you read Usenet news (Chapter 5), or you'll see some mentioned in other things you read.

There are many ways to use the services on the Internet to find the names, addresses, and descriptions of lists. Discussion lists, Listserv, and the other types of lists existed before the Internet became as popular or available as it is today. Some of these lists existed on other networks. Over the years a number of groups and individuals have kept "lists of lists." These lists are available on the Internet and you can get any of them through e-mail or other Internet services. The addresses of these collections of lists and the services used to retrieve them are given in the section *Internet Sources of Information about Discussion Lists* below. In this section we'll talk about two ways to find the names and address of lists using Internet services: Search the names of all Listserv lists by e-mail and use tools available on the World Wide Web to search for lists.

Search the Names of All Listserv Lists by E-mail

You can search through the names of all Listserv lists by using e-mail. Sending the command

```
LISTS GLOBAL
```

to any Listserv site will return a copy of *all* Listserv lists. This is likely to be more than you want to deal with; there are thousands of entries. You can search for a key word by sending the command

```
LISTS GLOBAL /KeyWord(s)
```

To search for all lists that deal with education, for example, send the command

```
LISTS GLOBAL /education
```

in an e-mail message to **listserv@listserv.net**. You can include more than one word after the /. To search for lists dealing with agricultural education send the command:

```
LISTS GLOBAL /agricultural education
```

Note: You can send the command *lists* to other types of list management software systems as well. For example, to see the lists available through Majordomo at **world.std.com**, send e-mail to **majordomo@world.std.com** with the message **LISTS**.

Use Tools Available on the World Wide Web to Search for Lists

Here are three excellent tools on the WWW for finding information about discussion groups. Give a key word or key phrase, and the software searches a database of list names, descriptions, and associated addresses. You'll get the information you need (list name, address for joining the list, address of the list, address of the list owner or moderator, etc.) for the appropriate lists.

1. **Inter-Links.** Starting at the home page (**http://www.nova.edu/Inter-Links**), select the hyperlink **Basic Internet Services** (**http://www.nova.edu/Inter-Links/resources.html**), and then choose **Electronic Mailing Lists** (**http://www.nova.edu/Inter-Links/cgi-bin/lists**). From there you can choose **Search List of Discussion Groups** (**http://www.nova.edu/Inter-Links/listserv.html**) to search for lists.
2. **Liszt: Searchable Directory of e-Mail Discussion Groups.** The URL for the home page is **http://www.liszt.com/**.
3. **tile.net/listserv** with URL **http://tile.net/lists/**. Click on the hyperlink **Search** to search for lists. In this case the search brings back all the information you need to join a list along with hyperlinks that make it easy to subscribe.

Proper Etiquette or Behavior in a Discussion Group

Discussion groups and lists are great ways to communicate with people throughout the world or maybe even nearby. Members have discussions, post information, or ask questions. All of this is carried on within a community (the members of the list) sharing a common interest. Most communities have some rules of etiquette or behavior which may not be written down. Some things to remember about working with a list follow:

* Send messages going to the entire list to the *list address*. Send commands or requests to be interpreted by the software that manages the list to the *administrative address*. Send special requests or questions you can't resolve to the address of the list owner, administrator, or moderator.
* Spend some time getting to know the list. When you first join a list, take a little while to see the types of items discussed and the tone of the discussion. You may also find your questions are being answered.

* Write easy-to-read messages. The material you write to the list should be grammatically correct, concise, and thoughtful. It's a lot easier to read something that is well written, and many members of the list may not have the time to deal with writing that is incorrect, long-winded, and without any real point. If the posting must go on for several screens, it's a good idea to summarize it and invite others to ask you for more information.

* If you're writing a response to something from the list, include only the pertinent portions of the original message. Let's say someone starts a discussion in the group and writes something about 40 lines long. You want to respond, but only to one portion of it. Include only the portion that's relevant to your response in your follow-up message. Members of the group may not have the time or space to deal with long e-mail messages.

* When you ask a question of the members of the list, be sure to post a summary of the responses you receive. That way everyone on the list can benefit from the responses to your question. Naturally, this applies only if you get several responses and the answers to the question would be of general interest.

* Posting or sending a message to the group is a public act. Everything you write to the list may be distributed to all members of the list. If the list is moderated, your messages may be read first by the moderator(s) and then passed on to the list. If you're working with a list that isn't moderated (most aren't), your messages go directly to all the members of the list. Don't embarrass yourself. A friend, relative, or supervisor may also be a member of the list.

* The members of a list are people like yourself and need to be treated with respect and courtesy. Respond to messages as if you were talking face-to-face. A member may be from a different culture, may not be familiar with your language, and may have views and values different from yours. Don't respond too quickly to something that upsets you, and don't criticize others too hastily or without good reason. It's better to think before you write than to be sorry afterward.

* Avoid sarcasm and be careful with humor. You are communicating entirely by your words. You don't have the benefit of facial expression, body language, or tone of voice to let somebody know you're "only kidding" when you make a sarcastic remark. Members of the list will appreciate well-written, humorous pieces or responses, but be sure your writing will be interpreted that way.

* Think about whether a response to a message should go to the list or to an individual. Messages to the list should be of general interest, or a request on your part for advice, or help in solving a problem. You'll know the e-mail address of the person who made the original request, and you can send a response to that person if it's appropriate.

Internet Sources of Information about Discussion Lists

Several groups or individuals have assembled collections of information about discussion groups, Listserv, and mailing lists. Some of the collections of lists are often too large for an individual to store. But these lists can be searched on the Internet as described above. Also, some of the collections of lists are broken into smaller groups, so it may be feasible for you to retrieve some of these lists.

Before giving sources on the Internet for these lists, we'll first discuss two files you might want to retrieve. These files contain documents about using mailing lists or discussion groups and about finding sources of information about mailing lists.

❋ "How to Find an Interesting Mailing List," by Arno Wouters, identifies and describes several sources of lists and other information related to discussion groups and mailing lists. The document also contains some information about using Internet services to search for lists. The file containing the document is available by e-mail and anonymous FTP. The URL for anonymous FTP access is **ftp://vm1.nodak.edu/listarch/new-list.wouters**. To retrieve it by e-mail send the message

```
GET NEW-LIST WOUTERS F=MAIL
```

to listserv@vm1.nodak.edu.

❋ The document "Discussion Lists: Mail Server Commands," by James Milles contains information about working with discussion lists, interest groups, and mailing lists. The file is available by anonymous FTP and by e-mail. To retrieve it through your Web browser use the URL **http://lawlib.slu.edu/training/mailser.htm**. To retrieve the file by e-mail send the message

```
GET MAILSER CMD NETTRAIN F=MAIL
```

to listserv@ubvm.cc.buffalo.edu.

❋ "Publicly Available Mailing Lists," containing names, addresses, and information about lists available through the Internet. One of the best ways to access this excellent list is through the World Wide Web. Use the URL **http://www.NeoSoft.com/internet/paml/**. The Web page is copyright and maintained by Stephanie de Silva.

❋ The directory entries at Yahoo dealing with mailing lists. Using the URL **http://www.yahoo.com/text/Computers_and_Internet/Internet/Mailing_Lists/** or otherwise going to the Yahoo Directory section Computers and Internet:Internet:Mailing Lists, takes you to a collection of hyperlinks that give information about using discussion groups or mailing lists.

❋ The global list of Listserv lists. Send e-mail to any Listserv site, for example, **LISTSERV@KENTVM.KENT.EDU**, with the message

```
LISTS GLOBAL
```

to retrieve a list of Listserv groups and a short description of each.

❋ The file **interest-groups.txt**, currently maintained by Vivian Neou, is one of the oldest lists of lists on the Internet. It's large—almost 1 megabyte—and very complete. Not every user needs her own copy, but it may be suitable to have one copy available at an easily accessible site. It's available by anonymous FTP from **sri.com**. The URL for the file is **ftp://sri.com/netinfo/interest-groups**. You can search the list by using the URL **http://catalog.com/vivian/interest-group-search.html**. It can also be retrieved by sending the e-mail message

```
send interest-groups.txt
```

to **mail-server@sri.com**.

Summary

Several thousand discussion groups are available and active on the Internet. They may be called mailing lists, discussion groups, Listserv lists, or interest groups. Regardless of the name, each consists of a group of members anywhere on the Internet, and all communication is carried on by e-mail. Messages sent to the list are generally broadcast to all members of the group. This way communities or collections of people can discuss items related to a common topic, find information about the topic, make announcements to the group, or ask questions and get help from other members of the group. The large number of lists guarantees a wide range of topics. Being a member of a discussion group means you'll have access to others sharing some of your interests or your experiences. The groups are particularly useful to people who want to discuss issues with a large or diverse group. The groups extend your resources beyond a local site.

You send messages to the list by using the *list address*. Commands and requests for service are usually sent to another address called the *administrative address*. For example, the list PHOTO-L, which deals with a variety of topics related to photography, has **PHOTO-L@csuohio.edu** as the list address and **listproc@csuohio.edu** as the administrative address. Some commands and services available include *joining a list*, *leaving* or *unsubscribing from a list*, getting archived files from the lists, and getting a list of the members of the list. Be sure you use the correct address when you communicate with the group or list. Most lists also have a person designated as the *list owner*, *list administrator*, or *moderator*. That person is in charge of the list, and you send him e-mail if you have problems using the list or regarding operation of the list. Some lists are *moderated*. Messages sent to the list are first viewed by the moderator who decides whether to pass the messages on to all members of the list.

Most day-to-day operations of the list and responding to commands or requests are managed by software. Different types of software perform this function, and the exact form of the commands may be different. You can usually tell the type of software by the administrative address. For example, PHOTO-L has **listproc@csuohio.edu** as its administrative address, and it is managed by Listproc software. Commands sent to the administrative address need to be in a precise form since the commands are being interpreted by computer programs, not humans.

The lists can be thought of as communities of people sharing common interests. There are generally accepted rules of behavior or etiquette for list members. These generally deal with providing appropriate, thoughtful, and concise messages to the list, providing a summary of the responses you've received to a question you posed, and treating other members of the list (through your communications to the list) in a civil and respectful manner.

Several "lists of lists" and other documents related to using discussion groups are available on the Internet. Some of the lists can be searched using Listserv services or through the World Wide Web. The lists and documents are also available by anonymous FTP or by e-mail through commands sent to the administrative address of a list.

Exercises

Before You Begin

Several sites on the World Wide Web let you search for and find the names of discussion groups. Using the ones below come up with a list of six discussion groups along with the administrative address and list address for each. You'll use them in the following exercises, and it would be best if two were managed by Listserv, two by Listproc, and two by Majordomo.

Inter-Links	http://www.nova.edu/Inter-Links/cgi-bin/lists
Liszt: Searchable Directory of e-Mail Discussion Groups	http://www.liszt.com/
tile.net/listserv	http://tile.net/lists/
Publicly Available Mailing Lists	http://www.NeoSoft.com/internet/paml/

1. Subscribe to three lists from the group of mailing lists you found above.
   a. Make sure each list is managed by a different type of software.
   b. Compare the e-mail you get welcoming you to each list. Which was the most helpful? Why?

2. Subscribe to three lists, different from the ones you chose in Exercise 1, but from the group you found.
   a. Send the command to the administrative address to get a list of members.
   b. Send the command to the administrative address to get a list of archives or files.

3. Get the list of files or archives for a list you found that's managed by Listserv.
   a. List the names of three files you think you'd be interested in retrieving.
   b. Retrieve one of those files.

4. In the text we showed how to find names of lists available at Listserv and other sites.
   a. Find the names of the lists available through Majordomo at **world.std.com**.
   b. Subscribe to one of the lists that seems like it would be interesting to you.

5. Using techniques described in the chapter, search the list of all lists available through Listserv for the names of lists dealing with politics. Subscribe to one of those lists.

6. Use the services at Inter-Links, as described in the chapter, to search for the list WISENET mentioned above. What is the purpose or description of WISENET? Now search for information using the services at Liszt. Do you get more useful information with Liszt?

7. Again using the services available through the World Wide Web, find the names of the list owners or moderators for three of the lists in the group that you found.

8. For about a week, keep track of the e-mail from two of the groups you've joined.
   a. Write a couple of sentences describing the type of mail that came to each list.
   b. Is the mail from these groups the type of mail you expected? Explain.

9. Send or post a question to one of the lists you've joined. Think about the question before you post it and check your spelling and typing before you send it.
   a. What responses did you receive by the end of one week?
   b. Summarize the responses and post the summary to the list.

CHAPTER 5

Usenet—Reading and Writing the News

In Chapters 3 and 4 we talked about using electronic mail (e-mail) to communicate with individuals or groups. Through e-mail you're able to exchange ideas and information, participate in discussions, read what others are discussing, get questions answered, or help others with questions or problems. All of that communication takes place through your *personal mailbox*. Another popular means of exchanging information in this way is *Usenet news*; sometimes it's called *Netnews* or just *News*. You use Usenet news for the same reasons you use a discussion group—to exchange or read information dealing with specific topics. Some ways that Usenet news differs from discussion groups are:

* With Usenet you have access to many groups. Some sites carry hundreds or thousands of groups; others carry fewer groups or different ones depending on the policies and procedures of that site.
* Messages to a group aren't exchanged between individuals using e-mail; instead, messages are passed from one computer system to another.
* You use software called a *newsreader* to read and deal with the news (articles) available through Usenet, instead of using your e-mail program or sending commands to a remote site.

Usenet is similar to a *bulletin board system* (bbs), except that most bulletin boards are managed by one person and are run by one computer. There is no single person, group, or computer system in charge of Usenet. All the computers and people that are part of Usenet support it and manage it. Usenet is a community with its own generally agreed upon code of etiquette. Usenet is very large, involving thousands of computers, hundreds of thousands of messages, and millions of people. Once you get comfortable using Usenet news, you'll find it a valuable resource where you can find answers to different types of questions, get help on a variety of topics, and keep up with what's happening in the world and on the Internet. Furthermore, it's a great place to have discussions and work with a worldwide community.

Netscape Navigator includes a *newsreader* so you can use it to work with Usenet news. You'll find the ways you work with Usenet news are similar to the ways you use the e-mail part Netscape to read, write, and send e-mail. They share many of the same menus and commands and present the same interface. However, the messages in Usenet aren't organized by you or addressed to individuals or groups. They are arranged into groups by subject and distributed from one computer system, called a *news server*, to another.

This chapter concentrates on accessing and using Usenet. We'll focus on using the newsreader built into Netscape Navigator. The topics we'll cover include:

* Introduction to Usenet
* How Usenet Articles Are Organized
* Working with Usenet news
* Reading Articles
* Setting Netscape Options for News
* Saving, Mailing, and Printing Articles
* Writing to the Author of an Article
* Posting a Follow-Up to an Article
* Posting an Article
* Proper Usenet Etiquette
* Signatures, FAQs, and Finding Newsgroups
* Recommended Newsgroups and Articles

Introduction to Usenet

Usenet began in 1979 through the efforts of two people who wanted to have their computers call each other over telephone lines and exchange files. Since then it has grown to encompass thousands of computers, millions of people, and several megabytes of traffic each day. The traffic is in the form of articles passed from one system to another. There is no central control, but the news has a worldwide distribution.

It's not easy to define Usenet because it's so diverse. Instead, we'll try to describe how it works and (most importantly) how to work with it. Usenet is made up of computers and people that agree to exchange or pass on collections of files. Each file is called an *article* and belongs to one or more *newsgroups*. You can tell what types of articles you're likely to find by the name of the newsgroup. People at each site can read the articles, ignore the articles, save or print the articles, respond to an article's author through e-mail, or *post* their own articles. Posting means composing either an original article or a response to someone else's article and then passing it on to Usenet. There are thousands of computers involved, and estimates of the number of people who read Usenet news range between 5 and 30 million. So Usenet is a great way to reach a large audience, but remember that posting articles is a public act.

There are newsgroups on all sorts of topics. Some are specialized or technical groups such as **comp.protocols.tcp-ip.domains** (topics related to Internet domain style names), some deal with recreational activities such as **rec.outdoors.fishing.saltwater** (topics dealing with saltwater fishing), and one, **news.newusers.questions**, is dedicated to questions from new Usenet users. That last one is a good place to start. You'll want to participate in that group, to get answers to your questions, and to help others with questions. You've probably realized by now that Usenet news isn't necessarily news in the sense of what's printed in a newspaper or broadcast on a news report.

You may find some articles or discussions in some groups offensive. Remember, there is no overall control over Usenet. What offends you may not offend others, and it may be important to others to be able to read and discuss topics that bother you. But it's always your choice as to which articles to read and which newsgroups to look through. Some of the vitality and vigor of Usenet comes from the fact that a wide range of topics and opinions can be expressed through the News. You have the option of *subscribing* to or naming the groups that will be on your usual list of groups to read. Also, you have the option of talking with your news administrator about the appropriateness of carrying a certain group.

A Quick View of How Usenet Works

Someone posts an article to a newsgroup; using an editor or program to compose an article on his system, he creates a file and passes it on to a newsgroup. The article is passed from that person's site to another site on Usenet, possibly with other articles, at some regularly scheduled time. At that other site it is distributed to other sites, and so on. People at other Usenet sites will read the article on their systems. Someone decides she would like to respond to the original article. She either sends e-mail to the original author or posts a follow-up article. The follow-up article is distributed around Usenet with the same subject heading as the original article. Sometimes, several people at different places on Usenet respond with follow-up articles. Discussions start this way. Sometimes they stay on the same topic, but sometimes not. It's informative, it's creative, it's dynamic, it's exciting! Just a few words of warning: Using Usenet can be so appealing that you spend too much time doing it. Remember, you have a life outside of Usenet and you ought to pay attention to it. Get your other work done, take a walk, and spend some time with other human beings (assuming they're not all on Usenet).

Usenet Control Is at the Local Level

Someone at each Usenet site decides which newsgroups the site will receive or carry, which newsgroups it passes on to another site, which sites it receives news from, and which sites it will send news to. The person making the decisions about these issues is in charge of either the entire computer system or the news on its own. That person, sometimes called the *news administrator*, also decides whether users at that site can read and post articles or just read articles. Almost all control is at the local level.

When you use a personal computer to read and interact with the articles in Usenet, you decide which newsgroups to read or browse. You make up a list of newsgroups that you'll want to peruse regularly. Other newsgroups can be added at almost any time, provided they're available from your news server. The list of newsgroups and the articles themselves are (usually) kept on another computer, your news server. Some of the functions of the server are described in the next section.

How the News Is Passed Around and Stored

Each computer system that serves as a news server for Usenet runs software to receive, manage, and forward articles. The news administrator, using the software, maintains a list of newsgroups the site will carry or make available to its users and clients, a list of Usenet sites from which the computer system will receive articles, and a list of sites to which articles will be sent.

The software is set up to receive articles. Each article contains information about the newsgroup(s) it belongs to. Once an article is received, the software decides whether to accept or reject the article. It's accepted if it belongs to one of the newsgroups the site carries; otherwise it's rejected. Each article is kept in a file and is put into a directory that corresponds with or represents the newsgroup.

The administrator decides how long an article will be carried on a system and thus available to the users. At the end of a certain time—usually two weeks or less—the article *expires*. In other words, the article is removed or deleted from the system by the software managing the news.

At certain times of the day articles from one site are passed on to another site. Only new articles are passed on. If two sites, A and B, agree to exchange articles, and Site A sent article *great-one* to Site B, then *great-one* isn't sent back to Site A. But any new articles created at Site B or received by B from some other site are dispatched to site A. This way articles created at one site are passed around to other systems on Usenet.

How Usenet Articles are Organized

All articles belong to one or more newsgroups. An article is either a follow-up to another article or it's posted on a different topic. The term for posting an article to more than one newsgroup is *cross-posting*.

Threads

There may be several articles on the same topic in a single newsgroup. If each of the articles was posted as a follow-up to some original article, then the collection of these articles is called a *thread*. You'll probably want to have the articles arranged into threads. It really helps to have this sort of organization on a collection of articles in a particular group. You follow a thread by reading the articles in a thread one after the other.

Newsgroup Categories

Each newsgroup has a name that gives the topic or topics for the articles in the group. The groups are arranged or named according to a hierarchy. When you look at the name of a newsgroup, you'll see it usually consists of several words or names separated by periods. The first part of the newsgroup name is the name of the top level of the hierarchy. Moving to the right, the names become more specific. Here is a nice long name: **rec.music.makers.guitar.acoustic.**

Starting on the left, **rec**, is the name of a top-level group that includes groups that deal with artistic activities, hobbies, or recreational activities. The next name, **music,** indicates the group deals with topics related to music. The next, **makers,** tells you this group is about performing or playing music rather than another activity such as reviewing music or collecting recordings. The last two names, **guitar** and **acoustic**, pretty much nail this down as dealing with discussions or other matters related to playing or performing acoustic guitar. Here are a few other groups in the **rec.music** hierarchy to give you a feeling for this naming scheme: **rec.music.makers.piano, rec.music.makers.percussion, rec.music.marketplace, rec.music.reggae, rec.music.reviews.**

There are over fourteen thousand newsgroups and several major, top-level categories. Some of the top-level categories are given in Table 5 .1.

Name	Description
alt	**alt** stands for alternative. This includes newsgroups presenting alternative views of the world, groups dealing with bizarre topics, groups discussing unusual subjects, and other newsgroups that don't go through established channels. Two examples are **alt.aliens.visitors** and **alt.cinchilla**. (Newsgroups in this hierarchy may not be available outside the United States.)
bionet	The groups in this category deal with topics in biology, e.g., **bionet.molbio.molluscs**.
bit	The **bit** hierarchy carries groups dealing with the network BITNET. The category **bit.listserv** has newsgroups for many of the Listserv discussion groups, e.g., **bit.listserv.film-l**.
biz	The newsgroups in this hierarchy deal with discussions related to business. This is where to post and find announcements of new products or books, and also an acceptable place to market those items. An example of a newsgroup in this category is **biz.books.technical**.
comp	This hierarchy consists of hundreds of groups dealing with topics related to computers, computer systems and peripherals, computer science, and other topics related to computing. For example, the newsgroup **comp.answers** carries regular postings of FAQs (Frequently Asked Question—and answers) on a wide variety of topics in computing.
k12	Newsgroups dealing with issues related to teachers and students in grades kindergarten through 12, e.g., **k12.ed.math**.
misc	Miscellaneous topics; things that may not fit into other categories, e.g., **misc.health.diabetes**.
news	This category includes newsgroups dedicated to the use and discussion of Usenet. Two important ones you'll want to read are **news.answers**, a list of regular postings of FAQs (Frequently Asked Questions and answers) on a variety of topics in all areas, and **news.newusers.questions**, a newsgroup where beginning or novice Usenet users can ask questions and get some help.
rec	This includes newsgroups that deal with artistic activities, hobbies, or recreational activities. An example is **rec.video.production**.
sci	This hierarchy has groups that deal with scientific topics. Two such groups are **sci.med.aids** and **sci.virtual-worlds.apps**.
soc	The newsgroups in this hierarchy deal with social issues and various cultures, e.g., **soc.culture.latin-america**.
talk	This hierarchy houses newsgroups dedicated to talking or discussing. One example is **talk.politics.medicine**.

Table 5.1   Some Top-Level Newsgroup Categories

There are several other categories. Some have to do with topics of regional interest such as **ba** for the San Francisco Bay Area, **dc** for the Washington, D.C. area, and **aus** for Australia. These are useful if you live, work, or will be traveling to an area that has some newsgroups. For example, to find out about places to eat in and around Washington, D.C., read some news in the group **dc.dining**.

Working with Usenet News

This section will cover a number of topics you'll want to know about so you'll be able to work with the news and with software called a *newsreader* that enables you to read the articles that make up the news and write articles to be sent to other sites. We'll concentrate on working with a newsreader in this section. We'll also include figures and an example that deal with using the newsreader included with Netscape Navigator to work with Usenet.

What Is a Newsreader?

You use software called a *newsreader* to work with Usenet. The newsreader is the interface between a user and the news itself. It allows you to go through the newsgroups one at a time, and once you've chosen a newsgroup, it allows you to deal with the articles it contains. The newsreader keeps track of the newsgroups you read regularly as well as which articles you've read in each newsgroup. Several different newsreaders are available. Some make it easier to select newsgroups and read articles than others. Some have a character-based or text-only interface, and some have a graphical interface. The text-only newsreaders are most common in a DOS, UNIX, or VMS operating system environment. The ones with a graphical-user interface are commonly used on computers that are accessing the Internet through Microsoft Windows or on Macintosh computers.

Keeping Track of Groups and Articles—Newsrc. In addition to letting you work with the groups and articles in Usenet, a newsreader will create and maintain a file named **Newsrc**. (On some systems, particularly Unix systems, this file is named .newsrc.) If you're using Netscape to work with Usenet news, the location of this file is specified in the section **Servers** of the **Mail and News Preferences**. This important file is used to keep a list of the newsgroups that's displayed when you start the newsreader, and for each newsgroup it contains a numeric list of the articles you've read. If you haven't used News before, this file is empty until you select some newsgroups. Whenever you select a new newsgroup, the appropriate information is added to the file, and the file displays the list of articles you haven't read yet. The newsreader program changes the file **Newsrc** when you add or delete newsgroups from the list you want to read. Here's an example of an entry in **Newsrc**:

```
soc.culture.african.american: 1-3106,3108,3111,3114-3115,3117-3120
```

This is for the newsgroup **soc.culture.african.american**. The numbers after the name of the group represent articles in the group that have been read. Each article is numbered.

Subscribe or Unsubscribe? When you start a newsreader, it checks the file **Newsrc** to see which newsgroups you'd like to read. We'll call this list of newsgroups the *subscription list.* The newsreader checks this list to see if your news server has any articles belonging to these groups that you haven't read. The groups containing unread articles are listed in the newsreader window, and you can select which group to read. You can add groups to the subscription list by *subscribing* to a group. An easy way to subscribe is to display a list of all groups available from the news server and then click on the **Subscribe** check box. As you read the news you may want to unsubscribe from some groups. Perhaps you don't read the group regularly and you want to pay attention to other groups; the group or articles aren't interesting to you, or the topic or articles are offensive. It's easy to unsubscribe. Click on the **Subscribe** checkbox. After you unsubscribe, the name of the group and the numbers representing the articles you've read remain in **Newsrc**. That way, if or when you decide to subscribe again, you'll only see the articles you haven't read. There is a colon after the name of each group on your subscription list and an exclamation point after the names of the groups from which you've unsubscribed. Here are two entries from somebody's **Newsrc**. Whoever owns this **Newsrc** subscribes to **biz.books.technical** and is unsubscribed from **rec.arts.animation**.

```
biz.books.technical: 1-240
rec.arts.animation! 1-7730,7732,7735-7736,7738-7739
```

Selecting Newsgroups and Articles. Once you've started the newsreader, you'll have to go through two steps to read articles. First, choose a newsgroup by clicking on its name with the mouse. Once you've chosen a newsgroup, the available articles will be listed in a window or a portion of a window. You're at *article selection level* when you can select an article. So in these terms, a newsreader starts in group selection level, and you have to move to article selection level to read the articles themselves. If you're using Netscape Navigator for Usenet news and you're using more than one news server, then before selecting a newsgroup you'll also have to select a news server. You may want to have access to more than one server because one may offer some newsgroups that another one doesn't. Figure 5.1 shows the window for the Netscape newsreader.

Netscape News

We'll demonstrate working with Usenet by using the newsreader that's included with Netscape Navigator. There are other popular newsreaders; some are Free Agent, News Xpress, and WIN VN. To read about each of these open the URLs **http://www.forteinc.com/forte/agent/freagent.htm**, **http://www.malch.com/ nxfaq.html**, or **http://www.ksc.nasa.gov/software/winvn/winvn.html**. We're going to concentrate on the one included with Netscape Navigator. It is similar to the others, and you'll see that in many instances the same commands and concepts used for the e-mail and Web browser portions of Navigator are used with the News. You'll be selecting newsgroups and articles from a menu. The newsreader also arranges articles into threads. Having articles arranged in threads puts everyone's comments on an article in one place. You'll see it's easier to keep track of a discussion that way.

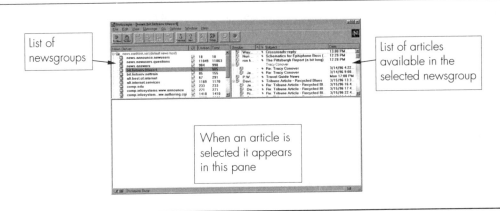

Figure 5.1   Sample Netscape News Window

Before you start using Netscape News, you have to set some of the mail and news preferences. (Click on **Options** in the Menu Bar first.) Most importantly, you have to set the Internet domain name or IP address of the system that acts as your news server. You can expect to get that from your Internet provider or some knowledgeable person in your organization. Once that's set you can start working with and enjoying Usenet. There are other preferences you can set, but working with the default settings is just fine.

Setting News Preferences. Click on **Options** in the Menu Bar, then click on **Mail and News Preferences** to bring up the window shown in Figure 5.2. This shows the **Servers** section, which is set up so you can receive e-mail. It's crucial that this is filled in correctly so you can work with Usenet news. The lower portion deals with news. The pane to the right of **News (NNTP) Server** must be filled in with the Internet domain name or IP address of a news server. The name or IP address that goes here depends on how your Internet services are provided. You should get this information from your Internet provider or someone in your organization. NNTP stands for *Network News Transport Protocol*, the protocol used to exchange Usenet news. Just below the server pane, you set the name of the directory or folder that holds **Newsrc**.

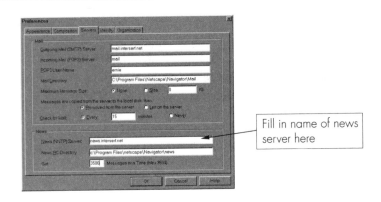

Figure 5.2   Mail and News Preferences, Servers Section

Other sections can be completed or filled in at this time. Click on the tab for each section. We'll list some of the preferences you'll likely want to set by the section in which they appear.

Appearance	Set the text style for quoted text—the text of a message that appears when you reply or post a follow-up message to an existing article. You can select plain, bold, italic, or bold italic. Decide whether you want to use Netscape or the Windows 95 Exchange Client for Mail and News. Select Netscape if you're using that for e-mail and news.
Composition	Set the way nontext portions of a posted article will be dealt with. Select **Allow 8-bit** if you will be working in a language different from English; otherwise choose **Mime**. You can set an Internet address that will receive copies of all your outgoing articles and a directory to hold copies of outgoing articles. Leaving these blank means no copies are sent or kept. These options don't affect whether something is posted, just whether you want copies. Checking the box labeled **Automatically quote original message when replying** includes a copy of the original article when you send or post a reply.
Identity	If you're using Netscape for e-mail, you've already set all the preferences in this section. You can set your name, your e-mail address, your organization, and the location of your signature file. The preferences you set here are included with your outgoing e-mail and posted articles.
Organization	Here you set the way articles are organized. Check the box **Thread News Messages** to have the articles arranged so follow-up and replies to one article are displayed one after the other. This is the recommended way of organizing articles. You also select your preferences as to whether the articles should be sorted by date, subject, or sender (who they're from).

You go through these one at a time by clicking on one tab after another. When you click on **OK**, the preferences are set and the **Options** window closes. You can always go back to change preferences.

Got all your preferences set? Did you fill in the name of the news server? Let's start working with the news!

Starting a Usenet News Session

You start the newsreader with Netscape by clicking on **Window** in the Menu Bar and selecting **Netscape News**. That opens a News window similar to the one shown in Figure 5.1. It's a lot like the mail window, and the way you work with the news is similar to working with e-mail. With news you select a newsgroup and with e-mail you select a folder; with news you select an article from a list in the newsgroup, and with e-mail you select a message from a list in the folder. The window for News, just like the window for Mail, has three panes—one for newsgroups, one for the list of articles, and one to read the articles. Figure 5.3 shows a sample window.

What to expect when a session starts. The following section explains what happens when you start a newsgroup session.

The first time you use Netscape News—You may not have subscribed to any news groups, so none will be listed in the newsgroups pane, and naturally no articles will be listed in the pane for the article list. To choose newsgroups click on **Options** in the Menu Bar and select **Show All Newsgroups**. It may take some time—perhaps a few minutes—for the list of all newsgroups to be retrieved from the server. You'll see them in the newsgroup pane as documents and folders, where the folders represent the categories in the Usenet hierarchy. Click on any folder to see a list of newsgroups and any document to see the list of articles in the group. There's lots to look through here, but you don't need to choose all your newsgroups in one sitting. Browse for a while, and when you find a newsgroup you'd like to see regularly, click on the box in the column labeled with ☑. Clicking on that box marks that newsgroup as one you've subscribed to, so each time you start News, the newsgroup will be listed in the newsgroup pane. As an example, to subscribe to the newsgroup **news.announce.newusers**, use the scroll bar in the newsgroups pane to move to the folder **news.*** and click on it to open the folder. That will list the groups and hierarchies that start with **news**. Now use the arrow keys of the scroll bar to move to the folder **news.announce.***. Click on that to open it and then select **news.announce.newusers**. The list of available articles will be displayed in the articles pane. From there you can select any article to read. Figure 5.3 shows the window you're likely to see when you've subscribed to **news.announce.newusers** and selected the first article in the list.

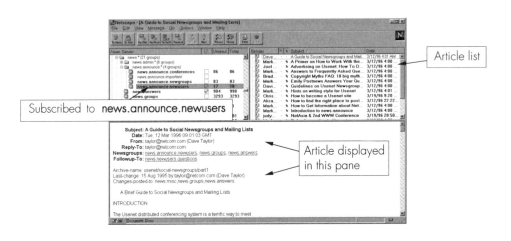

Figure 5.3   Sample News Window after Selecting a Newsgroup and Article

You've already used Netscape News—The News window opens and the list of subscribed newsgroups is in the newsgroups pane. You select a newsgroup from your subscribed list by clicking on its name in the newsgroups pane. Then the list of articles in the newsgroup is displayed in the articles pane, and clicking on an article displays it in the message pane. This is what's shown in Figure 5.4.

Figure 5.4   Article Displayed in Message Pane

Ending a Netscape News Session

Closing the News window ends the Netscape News session. Pressing Ctrl+W as a keyboard shortcut also closes the window. As long as you're still using Netscape Navigator, you can always start another news session. To terminate the Netscape Navigator, session click on **File** on the Menu Bar and then select **Exit**. Be sure to disconnect from your Internet provider if you're using dial-up access for networking.

Example 5.1   Reading an Article Using Netscape News

Before going into the details of the Netscape News window and other details of using the Netscape newsreader, it's a good idea to get a little experience in reading articles. Here we'll read an article in the newsgroup **news.answers** where many Internet FAQs are posted. We're assuming that Netscape Navigator is already started and you're working in the Web browser window.

There are only three steps to follow to read an article:
1. Open the Netscape News window.
2. Select the newsgroup **news.answers**.
3. Select an article.

Except for the choice of this newsgroup, you follow the same steps for any newsgroup moving from selecting a newsgroup to selecting an article.

1. Open the Netscape News window.

W W Click on **Window** in the Menu Bar and select **Netscape News**.

The Netscape News window will open as shown in Figure 5.1. You may have to select a news server if more than one is being used.

2. Select the Newsgroup **news.answers**.

W W Use the mouse to select and click on the newsgroup **news.answers**.

Once the Netscape News window opens, you'll see a list of newsgroups. Hopefully, **news.answers** is in the list and you can select it and move on to the next step. If it isn't, display a list of all newsgroups by clicking on **Options** then **Show All Newsgroups** on the Menu Bar. (You may have to wait a few minutes before the list of newsgroups is available on your computer.) Once the list of newsgroups has been loaded, use the scroll bar to move to the folder titled **news**. Click on it and then select the newsgroup **news.answers**. You may want to wait until all the articles are loaded before selecting one to read. Figure 5.5 shows **news.answers** selected from the newsgroup list.

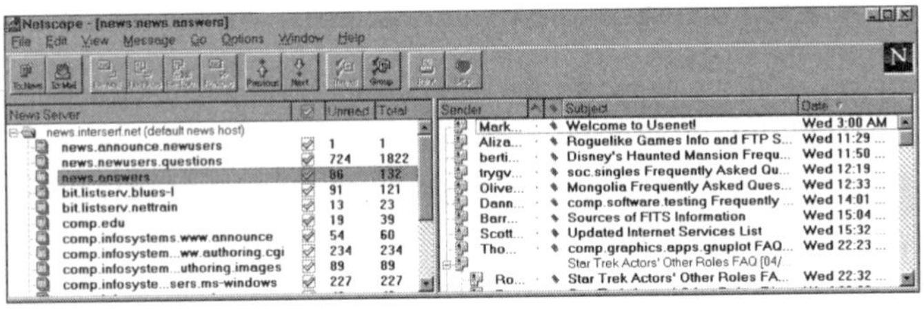

Figure 5.5   Netscape News Window with news.answers Selected

3. Select an article.

The simplest way to select an article is to click on its entry in the article list. Here we'll click on the eighth entry in the list, the article titled **Updated Internet Services List**.

W W Move the mouse pointer to **Updated Internet Services List** and click on it.

You see some headers in addition to the text of the article. The headers give the subject, sender, when it was posted, and the list of newsgroups to which it was posted.

You use the up and down arrow keys, Page Up or Page Down keys, or the scroll bar on the article pane to move through the text of the article.

You could view the next article in sequence or choose any article to read. Click anywhere in the article list pane, then use the keyboard or scroll bar in the article list pane to browse through the article list.

Clicking on the entry displays the article as shown in Figure 5.6.

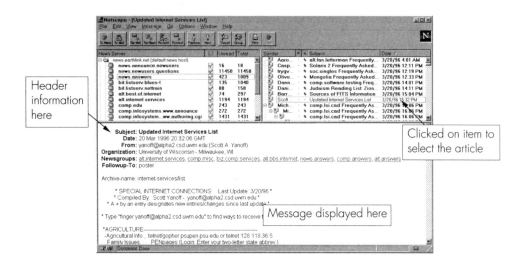

Figure 5.6   Article "Updated internet Services List" Selected and Displayed

Another way to select an article is by searching the Subject headers for key words or phrases. Use **Find** from the **Edit** pull-down menu, or the keyboard shortcut Ctrl+F. For example, suppose you've listed the articles in **news.answers** and you want to see if there's an article that deals with the topic "illustration."

Press Ctrl +F.

Type illustration in the dialog box, and click on the box labeled **OK**.

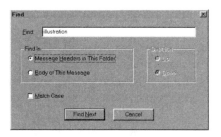

Figure 5.7   Find Dialog Box Set to Search Message Headers in the Selected Newsgroup for the Key Word "illustration"

The newsreader searches the list of newsgroups, in this case finds one that matches the search word, and displays it in the article display pane as shown in Figure 5.8.

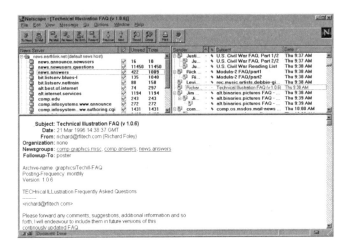

Figure 5.8   First Article Found with "illustration" in Its Subject Header or Title

When you read an article it's marked as being read. It probably won't show up the next time you select this newsgroup, but you can change that by marking it as **unread**—just click on the dot just to the left of the subject in the article list pane.

Enjoy yourself selecting and reading articles.

To move to another newsgroup, click on its name in the newsgroup list pane.

To end this news session, use the keyboard shortcut Ctrl+W, or select **Close** from the **File** pull-down menu.

————————————End Example 5.1————————————

The Netscape News Window

We've talked some about opening and closing the Netscape News window and shown examples of it in Figures 5.1, 5.3, and 5.4. We'll discuss some of the details of the window now. It's a lot like other Netscape windows. The Menu Bar is across the top clicking on an item opens a pull-down menu from which you select actions or items. Below that is the Toolbar consisting of a number of icons. Clicking on any of them causes the indicated action to take place. Below that are three panes. The one on the top left, the newsgroup pane, holds a list of newsgroups. To its right is the article list pane, which holds a list of articles in the selected newsgroup. Below both of those is the message or article pane. When you select the heading for an article from the article list, the article is displayed here. You can change the size of each of these panes. Move the cursor to one of the border lines (the cursor changes shape when you're at the right spot), press on the (left) mouse button, and drag the cursor until the pane has the desired size. Each pane also has a scroll bar you can use to move through the items or text in the window.

We'll go over the items in Menu Bar and the Toolbar and also discuss some details about the panes containing the list of newsgroups and articles.

The Menu Bar. The Menu Bar consists of the list of pull-down menus shown here.

<u>F</u>ile	<u>E</u>dit	<u>V</u>iew	<u>M</u>essage	<u>G</u>o	<u>O</u>ptions	<u>W</u>indow	<u>H</u>elp

File   The items on this menu let you open a window for a Web browser (Ctrl+N), open a window to compose an e-mail message (Ctrl+M), or open a window to compose and post an article to the currently selected newsgroup. You can connect to another news host or remove a news host from the list in the newsgroups pane. To deal with articles, you can save an article in a file on your computer, print an article, or get more articles in the selected group (in case more are available). The last two items in the menu let you close the window (Ctrl+W) or exit from Netscape Navigator.

Edit   Use the items in this menu to copy text from a displayed article, to select (highlight) all the articles in the current thread, select (highlight) all articles, or search the titles of newsgroups. You can copy a portion of an article so it can be put on the clipboard and pasted into another window. You might find this useful if you want to include a snippet from an article in an e-mail message or a document you're writing. To do that, highlight a portion of a message and then select **Copy** from the menu. Selecting a thread highlights the articles in the current thread. You can then forward all of them to an Internet e-mail address. They're put as attachments to the e-mail. Selecting **Search** pops up a dialog box in which you enter a word or phrase. The newsreader then finds the first article that contains the word or phrase in its header.

View   Select **Sort** to set the way the article headings are listed. You can choose to have articles threaded or not and sorted by date, subject, or sender. Selecting **ROT-13** scrambles or encodes the message so every letter is shifted 13 characters. Some messages are encoded this way if they contain questionable material. This way the text is scrambled so no one has to read it unless they want to. **View** is also available in the browser window, and the menu contains items that are more applicable when viewing a Web page such as **View Source** and **Refresh**.

Message   Select **Sort** to set the way the article headings are listed. You can choose to have articles threaded or not and sorted by date, subject, or sender. The option **Wrap Long Lines** is useful if lines of text don't fit in a window. Selecting this option and you won't have to use the horizontal scroll bar to view a long line. Selecting **ROT-13** scrambles or encodes the message so every letter is shifted 13 characters. Some messages are encoded this way if they contain questionable material. This way the text is scrambled so no one has to read it unless they want to. Here you also select whether to view attachments inline, as part of the message, or as links. Viewing them inline means that an image, for example, is displayed as part of the message. **View** is also available in the browser window, and the menu contains items that are more applicable when viewing a Web page such as **View Source** and **Refresh**. You can also add the sender of the current message to the address book.

Go   Use the items here to select from the **Options** pull-down menu whether to show articles to read. The first two items take you to the next or previous article. You can go to the first, next, or previous unread message, or the first, next or previous flagged message. It also has the item **Stop Loading**, which stops the loading of articles or newsgroups.

Options   The first part of this menu is the same as in other Navigator windows. You can select items to let you set general Netscape preferences or preferences for your e-mail, news, network, or security. After that you can select options dealing with which newsgroups are displayed: all newsgroups, subscribed newsgroups (whether there are unread messages or not), active newsgroups (ones you've subscribed to and have unread messages), all newsgroups, or new newsgroups (ones that have been added since you last retrieved the list of all newsgroups). If you select all newsgroups, you may have to wait a few minutes until the list is transferred to your computer. For messages (articles) you can select to have all articles in the newsgroup appear in the list of articles or only the unread ones. Articles are normally displayed only with headers showing the subject, when the article was posted, who posted it, and a list of newsgroups to which it was posted. There are other headers on an article including the path of all news servers the message took to get to your news server, the moderator of the newsgroup (if there is one), and other information.

Window   This menu is the same as other parts of Netscape Navigator. You can select items to go to the **Mail** window, the **News** window (you're already there), the address book, the bookmarks list, and a list of the open Web browser windows.

Help   This is the menu to select to get online help, and it's the same one that's available in other Netscape Navigator windows. You can go to the online handbook, the Netscape FAQ (Frequently Asked Questions—with answers), and other help facilities.

The Toolbar. The toolbar consists of the labeled icons shown here. Clicking on any of them causes an action to take place. Many of the actions deal with the current article or thread. That's the one that's highlighted in the pane holding the list of articles and displayed in the bottom pane of the window.

The first two icons are used to compose new articles or e-mail. The first is used to compose a new article to be posted to the current newsgroup, and the second is used to compose a new e-mail message.

The next four icons deal with posting or replying to articles and e-mail. The first sends a reply to the author of the current article, the second is used to compose a reply or follow-up to the selected article, the third for both, and the fourth to forward a copy of the article to an Internet e-mail address. When an article is forwarded by e-mail, the text of the current article is sent as an attachment. You set the address for the message and can add your comments when forwarding an article.

The icons **Previous** and **Next** are used to go to the previous or next article in the list.

The first icon labeled Thread deals with articles in a thread. Clicking on it marks all the articles in the current thread as read. You may want to use this after you've read one article in a thread and decided you don't want to read any more or to mark a thread as read without reading any of them. Clicking on the icon labeled Group marks all the articles in the current newsgroup as read. Sometimes this is called *catching-up*. If you only have articles displayed that haven't been read, then the next time you select the newsgroup, none of the articles you just marked will be listed.

Clicking on the icon labeled **Print** sends the text of the current article to your printer. Clicking on the last icon, the one labeled **Stop**, stops transmission of an article of list of articles from the server.

The Newsgroups Pane. The newsgroups pane holds the list of current newsgroups. From the **Options** pull-down menu, you select whether to show the subscribed groups—the ones you've subscribed to, the active groups—the ones that you've subscribed to and have unread messages, all newsgroups, or new newsgroups—ones that have been added to the list of all newsgroups. The list of newsgroups, as shown in Figure 5.5, contains the name of the newsgroup, a box indicating whether it's a subscribed group, the number of unread articles, and the total number of articles in the newsgroup. The newsgroups shown in Figure 5.5 are *active* newsgroups since they're all marked as subscribed, and each has some unread articles. You can adjust the width of each column by moving the cursor to the vertical bars in the headings. The cursor changes shape. While pressing the (left) mouse button, move it to the left or right.

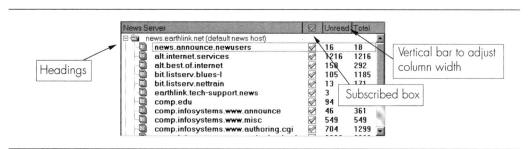

Figure 5.9   List of Active Newsgroups

Click on the name of a newsgroup to see a list of articles in the article pane.

The Articles Pane. The articles pane holds the list of articles in the current newsgroup. From the **Options** pull-down menu, you select whether to show all messages or just the unread ones—ones you haven't read yet. From the **View** menu, you select how the articles will be sorted and whether they will be threaded. The most common way to view them is sorted by date and threaded. Figure 5.6 shows a list of articles in the article pane. Each entry contains information that tells who sent or posted the article to Usenet, the title or subject of the article, whether it is subscribed to, the active groups—the ones that you've subscribed to and have unread messages—and when it was posted. The width of these columns can be changed as described above. The other two columns are used to indicate whether the article has been read or whether it's marked or flagged. To flag an article or mark it read or unread, click on the dot in the column headed with a flag or a dot. In Figure 5.10 the second and fourth items are flagged, and all except the first three are marked as unread.

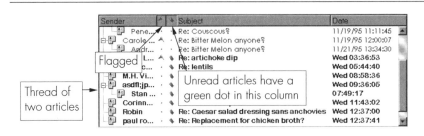

Figure 5.10 Article List in Article Pane

Clicking on an item in the article pane displays the text of the article in the pane below. It may take a few seconds for the article to be displayed since it has to be transferred or downloaded from the news server to your computer.

Reading Articles

In order to read articles you have to be in the News window, have selected a group, and have the list of available articles displayed in the article pane. Then clicking on any item in the list of article headers displays the article in the large pane taking up about the bottom two-thirds of the window. The articles will most likely be threaded. That means that articles and follow-up articles are grouped together. It's common to list only the unread articles. What does it mean to say an article is unread? It means you haven't read the article. Others may have, but remember, there is one copy of the article that everyone using the same news server can read.

Choosing an Article

Click on an item in the article list to display the article. It's as simple as that. The article will be downloaded or transferred from the server to your computer.

You go from one article to another in a variety of ways. You can select any article using the scroll bars and the mouse. You can use the icons to move to the next or previous message. You can select items from the pull-down menu **Go** to go from one article to another.

You can search the headers of the messages by using **Find** from the **Edit** pull-down menu. For example, suppose you've listed the articles in **news.newusers.questions** and you want to see if anyone has posted a question or answer about Netscape. Select **Find** from the **Edit** pull-down menu, type in **Netscape**, and click on the **OK** button. You'll be taken to the first article that contains Netscape in any of its headers (sender, subject, or date).

Reading an Article

After you click on an item in the list of articles in a newsgroup, the text of the article is displayed in the pane below the newsgroup and article panes. Figure 5.11 shows an article as it's listed. In addition to seeing the text of the article, you also see the headers that tell the subject, sender, and when it was posted.

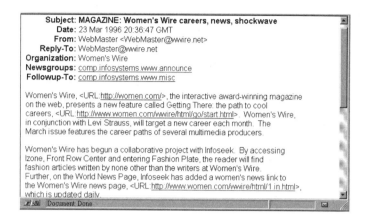

Figure 5.11 A Usenet Article

Marking an Article as Unread

When you read an article, it's marked so you won't have to read it again. Sometimes you do want to see the article again, so after you've read it you have to mark it as being **unread.** You do this in the list of articles. Use your mouse to click on the dot just to the left of the title of the article.

Saving, Mailing, and Printing Articles

There are going to be articles you will want to save. Many newsgroups have a list of frequently asked questions (FAQ) and answers for the topics they deal with, and there are lots of articles containing important information about Usenet and the Internet.

When you find something you like, you can save it to a file, send it by e-mail to any Internet address, or print the file. You can do all of these through Netscape Navigator, either by using pull-down menus or the icons on the Toolbar.

Saving an Article to a File

To save an article, click on **File** from the Menu Bar and select **Save As...** or press Ctrl+S from the keyboard. Either of these brings a **Save As** window to the screen. It's the same sort of window used for saving files, e-mail messages, or Web pages. You need to type the name of the file you want to hold the message. You probably want to save the article as a text file so select that as file type for saving. You have the option of choosing which directory or folder holds the file. It's a good idea to use the same folder or directory for saving articles when you're using Netscape. Then, at some appropriate time, copy them from that directory to others as it's necessary. That way you'll know where to find the saved news articles. You may not have the space on your disk to save every article you'd like, so be sure to delete some saved articles from time to time.

Mailing an Article

Click on the icon labeled **Forward** to send the currently selected (highlighted) article to someone via e-mail. A window to let you compose the e-mail pops up. The selected article is sent as an attachment. You can type whatever you'd like in the message body, and whatever is in your signature file is put at the bottom of the message body. Actually, more than one article can be sent—any collection of highlighted articles. It can be a thread or collection of flagged articles. Figure 5.12 shows the window that pops up to forward one or several articles. In this case it shows forwarding a thread; the pane to the right of the word **Attachments** shows a list of attachments on the same topic.

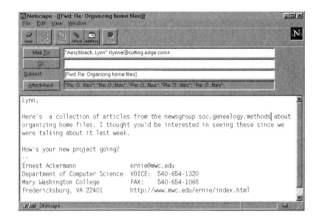

Figure 5.12 Forwarding or Mailing a Thread of Articles

To send a thread of articles, use the mouse to select (click on) and display one article in the thread. Then click on **Edit** in the Menu Bar and choose **Select Thread**. Or use Ctrl+Shift+A as a keyboard shortcut. This selects and highlights all the articles in the thread. Now click on the icon labeled **Forward** and the articles in the thread will be attachments to the e-mail message.

To send any collection of articles, first flag the articles that you want to forward or e-mail to someone else. You flag a message by clicking on the dot just to the right of the sender's name in the list of articles. After setting the flags on several messages, you need to select and highlight them; click on **Edit** in the Menu Bar and choose **Select Flagged Messages**. Now click on the icon labeled **Forward** and the articles in the thread will be attachments to the e-mail message.

Printing an Article

You can print an article when you're reading it, provided it's the only one selected. (To print a collection of articles you need to go through the steps of printing each as an individual article.) To print the article click on the icon labeled **Print**. The standard Print window pops up. Click on the button labeled **OK** to print the article without choosing any options for printing. Some of the options available include selecting a printer and selecting whether to print to a file, whether to print the entire article or a portion of it, and the number of copies to print (if your printer has that option).

Writing to the Author of an Article

Eventually you will want to respond to a statement or a question on Usenet. Here are a couple of situations that might make you want to respond to the author of an article. Somebody asks a question, you know the answer, and you want to send it. Someone makes a statement with which you strongly agree or disagree, and you want to tell your feelings and offer your opinions.

You have the choice of either posting a follow-up article, which is passed to all other Usenet sites, writing directly through e-mail to the author, or a combination of the two—posting a follow-up and sending it to the author by e-mail. You might choose this last option if you know the author isn't going to read the articles in the newsgroup frequently. In many cases it's best to write directly to the author, particularly when the original posting asks for specific information that isn't of general interest to everyone else reading the articles in the newsgroup. If your communication with the author is personal in any way, then you definitely need to send something by e-mail, not Usenet. There is a lot of traffic on Usenet; many bytes are passed around. This isn't meant to discourage you from posting a follow-up article; just think a little about how appropriate it is to post an article that gets wide distribution.

You can send a reply to an article only while you're reading an article, and you can reply to only one article. The entire article is included and you will want to make your remarks or replies within the context of that message, at the appropriate parts of the original. Be sure to delete any parts of the original message that don't have anything to do with your reply. Some tips on composing a reply are given in the section "Proper Usenet Etiquette" later in this chapter.

To reply only to the author of the article, click on the icon labeled **Re:Mail** in the group of icons related to mail messages. A window pops up, the kind used to compose e-mail messages; it's automatically addressed to the author of the article, the subject header is filled in so the author knows you're responding to her article, the article itself is included as part of the message, and your signature file is put at the end of the body of the message.

To post a follow-up and an e-mail reply, select the second (from the left) icon labeled **Re:News** from the Toolbar. A window pops up just like the windows described above except that it is addressed to the author's e-mail address, and it's set to be posted to the newsgroup.

Posting a Follow-Up to an Article

When you respond to a Usenet article, as we discussed in the section above, you can send a reply via e-mail to the author or you can post a *follow-up* article. Posting a follow-up means replying to an article and sending your reply to every Usenet site that carries the newsgroup that contained the original article. Suppose an article is posted in **rec.music.bluenote.blues** discussing the impact of Muddy Waters' music on English rock bands, and you think something important was left out. You might want to post a follow-up responding to the original. Your follow-up article is sent to any site that carries **rec.music.bluenote.blues**. You ought to post a follow-up for the same reasons you send a reply via e-mail to an author, except your reply should be interesting to enough people to be distributed to all of Usenet.

Be sure to summarize or quote from the original article in your follow-up, and read any other follow-up articles so you don't repeat an answer or comment. Since a follow-up is distributed through Usenet, take some time to compose the follow-up; don't reply without thinking about others who will read it. Be concise, be thoughtful, be considerate, and make sure the reply is grammatically correct.

To post a follow-up that goes to every Usenet site carrying the newsgroup you're reading, click on the icon labeled **Re:News** in the Toolbar. A window just like the one used to compose e-mail messages pops up. The only difference is it's not addressed to an e-mail address, it's going to be sent or posted to the newsgroup. The subject is automatically filled in and the body of the article contains the original article and the contents of your signature file.

Posting an Article

Posting an article means composing an article—a message, a question, a great discourse on some deep philosophical or extremely important political topic—and distributing it to a newsgroup. To post an article, you first choose the newsgroup. Usenet is a fairly wide-open forum. There is no central control and there are thousands of newsgroups on all sorts of topics. But some topics are not appropriate for some newsgroups. Before you post anything, read "A Primer on How to Work with the Usenet Community." You'll find it posted in **news.announce.newusers**. (If you can't find it there, click on the icon labeled **Open** on the Menu Bar of the Web browser, and use the URL **http://www.cis.ohio-state.edu/hypertext/faq/usenet/ usenet-primer/part1/faq.html**.)

Now to the *how* of posting an article:
1. Select a group by clicking on the name of the newsgroup from the newsgroup list, or if you're reading or selecting articles, your post will go to the group you're reading.
2. Click on the icon labeled **To:News** (the first one on the left).
3. A window will pop up—the same one you'd use to post a follow-up article. The name of the newsgroup will be filled automatically into the pane labeled **Newsgroup**. Type the subject of your article in the pane labeled **Subject**. Choose a subject that isn't too long and clearly states the purpose of your article. Get readers' attention with a clear and succinct subject. Read several articles in the group to see the form that others use.
4. Compose your article. Type it into the large pane of the window. If you have a signature file, its contents will be put automatically into the message. Click on the icon labeled **Quote** to include the current article in your article. You can send attachments with the article by clicking on the button labeled **Attachments**. Don't include large text or binary files (usually images) unless that sort of information is normally posted to the newsgroup.
5. Click on the icon labeled **Send** to post your article. If you don't want to post it— you've made too many typing mistakes or you change your mind—click on **File** in the Menu Bar and select **Close** or press Ctrl+W from the keyboard. You'll have one more chance to post the article, but if you don't want to send it, click the button labeled **No**.

Example 5.2   Posting an Article

In this example we'll post an article to a newsgroup using Netscape Navigator. The article is going to ask about newsgroups or FAQs dealing with allergies in humans. It's a typical question to pose to the newsgroup **news.newusers.questions.** You don't have to be a new user to post a question to that group, and not only new users read that newsgroup.

The steps we'll follow are:
1. Open the Netscape News window.
2. Select the newsgroup **news.newusers.questions**.
3. Click on the icon labeled **To:News**.
4. Type in the subject.
5. Compose the article.
6. Post it.

Except for the choice of a newsgroup, you follow the same steps for any newsgroup. We're assuming that Netscape Navigator is already started and you're working in the Web browser window.

1. Open the Netscape News window.

WW**W**   Click on **Window** in the Menu Bar and select **Netscape News**.

The Netscape News window will open, as shown in Figure 5.1. You may have to select a news server if more than one is being used.

2. Select the newsgroup **news.newusers.questions**.

WW**W**   Use the mouse to select and click on the newsgroup **news.newusers.questions**.

Once the Netscape News window opens, you'll see a list of newsgroups. Hopefully, **news.newusers.questions** is in the list and you can select it and go on to the next step.

If **news.newusers.questions** isn't listed, display a list of all newsgroups by clicking on **Options** on the Menu Bar and then selecting **Show All Newsgroups**. (You may have to wait a few minutes before the list of newsgroups is available on your computer.) Once all the list of newsgroups has been loaded, use the scroll bar to move to the folder titled **news**. Click on it and then select the newsgroup **news.newusers.questions** (Figure 5.13).

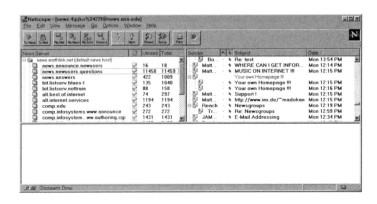

Figure 5.13 The Netscape News Window with news.newusers.questions Selected

3. Click on the icon labeled **New**.

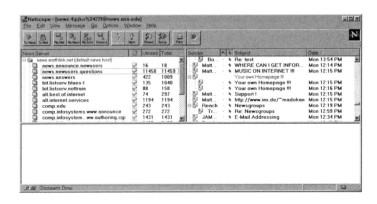 Click on the icon [🗐].

This will bring up a window that you use to give the subject of the article and type the text for the article. The window is shown in Figure 5.14.

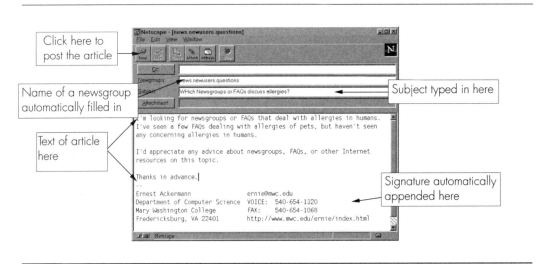

Figure 5.14   Window to Compose an Article

4. Type in the Subject.

W^⫿W Type **Which Newsgroups or FAQs discuss allergies?** in the frame labeled **Subject.**

Click on the pane labeled **Subject:** and type the subject of the article you're going to post. (The subject is the first thing most readers see about the post, so make it good.) Figure 5.14 shows the subject already typed in.

5. Compose the article.

After you type in the subject you're ready to compose or type the article. Figure 5.14 shows what it would look like when complete.

W^⫿W Move the cursor to the large pane in the bottom half of the window. Click anywhere above the beginning of your signature file and type the message.

Typing in this window is much like using other Windows 95 applications that allow you to enter text. You can use the items in the **Edit** pull-down menu in the Menu Bar for this window to rearrange text, and copy, delete, or paste text. Generally, your message doesn't have to be long or complex. Try to use correct spelling and grammar, and keep your comments focused on the subject of the article.

6. Post it.

W^⫿W Click on the button labeled **Send.**

That step is easy! The window stays around until your news server has been contacted and the article passed along to it.

You'll want to check the newsgroup regularly to see what response your article brings. You may also get some replies by e-mail.

──────────────End of Example 5.2──────────────

Before moving on to the next section, it's worth noting that the message we posted in Example 5.1 serves more than one purpose. It will likely give us some information about where to find some interesting information on the Internet, and when we see it posted in the newsgroup and get a response, we know our newsreader is working properly. Some folks post test messages—ones that say things like "If anybody can read this please write to me"—to all sorts of newsgroups. That's really inappropriate and considered bad form. The newsgroup **alt.test** exists just for that purpose. It's a place where you can post articles for testing purposes. A neat thing about that is a number of sites around the world monitor that group and automatically send a reply by e-mail. Posting a "test" message to **alt.test** is a good way to test your newsreader.

Proper Usenet Etiquette

From 5 to 30 million people throughout the world read the news through Usenet. That is a lot of people! And they're not all only reading; a lot of them post articles or respond to articles in some way. It's reasonable to think about the people who use Usenet as a community of users. With such a large and diverse community, some rules of behavior or etiquette are necessary. Many of the sites that are part of Usenet have rules, policies, and procedures that need to be followed as well. In some cases, not following the rules means you lose access to a computer system. Additionally, there are several laws governing electronic communications, and people have been sued for libel or arrested for criminal activities because of articles they've posted on the Internet.

There isn't any central control for Usenet, and there is no one except local news or system administrators to enforce rules (not laws) of behavior on Usenet. This absence of central control gives Usenet some of its vitality. It's essential that the users follow some guidelines to make using Usenet as effective, efficient, and pleasant as possible.

Over the years several documents have been developed about proper Usenet etiquette. These are regularly posted in **news.announce.newusers**, **news.answers**, or **news.newusers.questions**. Here is a list of some of them you ought to read:

- ☀ "A Primer on How to Work with the Usenet Community"
- ☀ "Emily Postnews Answers Your Questions on Netiquette"
- ☀ "Hints on Writing Style for Usenet"
- ☀ "How to Find the Right Place to Post (FAQ)"
- ☀ "Please Read Before Posting"
- ☀ "Rules for Posting to Usenet"
- ☀ "A Weekly FAQ on Test Postings"

As you look over the rules and examples of proper behavior on Usenet, you'll see they break into two categories:

1. **Rules for Using Usenet in an Effective and Efficient Manner.** These rules are based on the observation that there are many Usenet sites and participants, and most of the participants are busy. So before you post an article, a follow-up article, or a test message, think about the effect it will have on Usenet. Think about how many sites and networks will be dealing with your material. Make your postings concise and appropriate. Avoid duplication and repetition; do your own research before asking a question. Use a response by e-mail rather than a follow-up whenever you can. Use descriptive and accurate headings, since the readers can tell at a glance if they would like to read your posting. By all means attach a "signature" to your articles, but don't make it too large or difficult to understand. There are several newsgroups where you can advertise or announce products, but there are many newsgroups where this isn't appropriate. The readers will rise up against advertisements, demand an apology from the person posting an advertisement, or demand that the author of the article be banned from Usenet.

2. **Rules for Working with Other Usenet Users.** These rules are based on a desire to treat others with courtesy and respect. As you read articles and think about writing your own, remember that the folks writing and reading are humans. They make mistakes in judgment sometimes, so don't go crazy over a remark that someone has made, since they may have just made a mistake. The term *flame* refers to a message or a posting that's meant to insult someone or provoke controversy. Take the time to think before you post a flame or respond to one hastily. Also, remember that other Usenet users have feelings like yours and sometimes they're easily hurt. Don't try to be sarcastic or use subtle humor—it's really hard to do effectively in writing. The folks who read your writing won't have the benefit of seeing your face, hearing a change in your voice, or seeing your body language. Realize that your writing gets worldwide distribution, and you never know who will read it. It can be read by people whose cultural backgrounds are very different from yours. Also, consider the possibility that your postings will be read by your friends, supervisors, teachers, or parents. Be considerate, careful, and conscientious.

Signatures, FAQS, and Finding Newsgroups

Signatures

As you read articles in Usenet, you'll see a few lines at the end of most messages with the author's name, e-mail address, and sometimes a phone number, a graphic image, or a clever saying. That's called a *signature*. (You've probably guessed they don't type an elaborate signature each time they send e-mail or post an article on Usenet.) Most newsreaders and e-mail systems will append whatever is in a file called a *signature file*. With Netscape Navigator you set the location of the signature file in the **Identity** section of the **Mail and News Preferences**. You get to that by clicking on **Options** in the Menu Bar of the browser, e-mail, or News window.

You can probably make a fancy or long signature, but think twice about it. Every character in your signature is another byte. If you post a message and it goes to thousands of sites, each byte is multiplied by thousands. Each character is passed between lots of systems and stored on lots of disks. Everybody on Usenet knows you are a creative and clever person. You don't need to prove it to them through your signature. Keep the signature file simple. It's enough to put your name, e-mail address, phone number, and some mention of your company, school, or agency.

FAQs

FAQ stands for Frequently Asked Questions, a collection of common questions with answers, or a single Frequently Asked Question. Many newsgroups have volunteers who put together and maintain a collection of questions and answers. Most newsgroups have a FAQ and they're informative and useful. You can find them posted either in the newsgroup the FAQ was created for, or posted to **news.answers**. Several newsgroups hold these FAQs; you'll see them referred to as the *.**answers** newsgroups. Some of these are **alt.answers**, **comp.answers**, and **sci.answers**. Here is a short list of FAQs to give you an idea of the variety of topics:

rec.games.netrek FAQ List	Comp.Object FAQ
MINIX Frequently Asked Questions	rec.sport.hockey FAQ
HOLOCAUST FAQ: The "Leuchter Report"	FAQ: Sci.Polymers
Tolkien: Frequently Asked Questions	FAQ: rec.music.dylan
rec.martial-arts FAQ	comp.graphics.animation FAQ

This is just a small sample of the articles from **news.answers**.

Be sure to consult the FAQ for information before you post a question to a newsgroup. A newsgroup's FAQ was created to be consulted. It may be embarrassing for you if you post a question to a newsgroup and you get several replies (or follow-ups) letting you (and everyone else reading the newsgroup) know that you should read the FAQ before asking other questions. It also could be annoying to other members of the group to see questions that could be answered by a little research beforehand. The FAQ for a group will be posted regularly to the group and also posted to one of the *.**answers** groups, such as **news.answers**. If you can't find the FAQ you're looking for there, try using this URL with your browser, **ftp://rtfm.mit.edu/pub/usenet-by-group**. Many groups have a directory there that contains the FAQ for the group. For example, to find the FAQ for **rec.food.cooking**, click on the entry with that label. Another URL to use to find FAQs is **http://www.cis.ohio-state.edu/hypertext/faq/usenet-faqs/html/**. That list, maintained at Ohio State University, has the recent versions of all the FAQs found in **news.answers**. They're arranged alphabetically and by newsgroup.

Finding Newsgroups

There are thousands of newsgroups. How can you find out which to read or even which ones exist?

To find the groups that your server carries, you select **Show All Newsgroups** from the pull-down menu **Options** in the Menu Bar of the News window.

There are several lists of newsgroups available through Usenet. Keep your eye on the newsgroups **news.answers**, **news.lists**, or **news.groups** so you can read or save these listings when they appear (usually monthly).

Some sites on the WWW provide the facilities for searching for newsgroups. For the sites we'll mention, use the URL to bring up a Web page. On that page you enter a key word or phrase, click on a button labeled **Search**, and then work with the results.

❋ **Tile.Net/news—Search for Newsgroups.** URL **http://tile.net/news/search.html.** This site lets you be very flexible with the search phrase. Searching here brings up a list of newsgroups. Clicking on the name of a newsgroup takes you to a page that tells about the amount of articles that are posted daily and what percentage of Usenet sites carry the group. From there you can click on the name of the newsgroup, and if your news server carries the group you'll be taken to the Netscape News window with a list of current articles so you can select some to read.

❋ **Liszt of Newsgroups.** URL **http://www.liszt.com/cgi-bin/news.cgi.** You have to be a little more careful about the search phrase at this site, but instructions and sample search phrases are present on the page. The searching results in a list of newsgroups, each with a brief description. If you click on the name of a newsgroup and your news server carries the group, you'll be taken to the Netscape News window just as with the previous search tool.

Recommended Newsgroups and Articles

There are several newsgroups that a beginning or infrequent user should browse. These newsgroups include information about Usenet, lists of FAQs for Usenet and several newsgroups, and articles that will help you use Usenet. The newsgroups are:

news.announce.newgroups	Articles dealing with forming and announcing new newsgroups. A place to get the lists of all newsgroups.
news.announce.newusers	Explanatory and important articles for new or infrequent Usenet users.
news.answers	This is where periodic Usenet postings are put. The periodic postings are primarily FAQs. This is often the first place you should look when you have a question.
news.newusers.questions	This newsgroup is dedicated to questions from new Usenet users. There is no such thing as a "dumb question" here. You ought to browse this group to see if others have asked the same question that's been bothering you. Once you get some expertise in using Usenet, you'll want to check this group to see if you can help someone.

The articles you will want to read are posted in **news.announce.newusers.** Here's a list:

❋ "A Primer on How to Work with the Usenet Community"
❋ "Answers to Frequently Asked Questions about Usenet"
❋ "Emily Postnews Answers Your Questions on Netiquette"
❋ "Hints on Writing Style for Usenet"
❋ "How to Find the Right Place to Post (FAQ)"
❋ "Rules for Posting to Usenet"
❋ "Usenet Software: History and Sources"
❋ "Welcome to news.newusers.questions"
❋ "What is Usenet?"

Summary

Usenet news was started to share information among users of Unix computer systems. The news is a collection of messages called articles. Each one is designated as belonging to one or more newsgroups. These articles are passed from one computer system to another. An administrator at one site determines which newsgroups his site will receive and send on to another site. Users at a site can usually select any of the groups that are available and often have the capability to reply to, follow up, or post an article. Some estimates put the number of participants at over 30 million worldwide.

There isn't any central control over Usenet. A local administrator can decide which groups to receive and whether to allow articles to be passed along. There usually isn't a means to screen articles from a group or screen articles that go out. It's close to anarchy, but the independent participation gives it vibrancy and strength.

Usenet is a community of users helping each other and exchanging opinions. A code of behavior has developed. The rules can be divided into two categories: making efficient use of Usenet, and treating other Usenet users with respect. The rules are, of course, voluntary, but users are expected to get a copy of some of the articles dealing with working with Usenet and to follow the rules. Several newsgroups carry regular postings of articles meant to inform the Usenet community. These are often found in the groups **news.announce.newgroups, news.announce.newusers, and news.answers.**

There are several thousand newsgroups, arranged into categories. Some of the major categories are:

alt	Anything goes
bit	Groups also available through Listserv on BITNET
comp	Groups dealing with computing and computer science
rec	Groups that are recreational
sci	Groups dealing with topics in the sciences
soc	Groups dealing with social issues and various cultures

You use software called a newsreader to work with the articles and newsgroups in Usenet news. There are several different newsreaders available. Which one you use will depend on your preferences and what's available on the system you use to access Usenet.

Netscape Navigator comes with a built-in newsreader. Like e-mail, it has its own window you open to access Usenet. To open the News window, click on **Window** in the Menu Bar and select **Netscape News.** The window is like the Mail window. There are three panes. One holds the list of current newsgroups, another the list of articles in the newsgroup, and the third the text of the current article. You can choose to have all newsgroups listed, the newsgroups you've selected or subscribed to, or just the newsgroups you've subscribed to that contain articles you haven't read. You also have a choice of displaying all articles in a newsgroup or the articles you haven't read in a newsgroup. It's best to have the articles listed in a *threaded* fashion so that all articles on a single topic are listed together. That makes it easier to follow a discussion.

You can (obviously) use the newsreader to read the news. But it's also used to compose articles so you can post original articles or write a follow-up to an existing article. The newsreader in Netscape also gives you the means to save an article in a file, print an article, send a reply to the author by e-mail, or forward one or several articles to an e-mail address.

You'll probably find Usenet a valuable resource for information on a wide array of topics. You'll enjoy reading and participating in the discussions on Usenet. Just remember, to get your other work done and live your life outside the Internet.

Exercises

1. Find out a few things about the system you use to read Usenet news.
   a. What's the Internet domain name of the news server?
   b. Where is your signature file located?
   c. Which newsreaders are available on your system?

2. Use your newsreader to look at the articles listed in **news.announce.newusers.**
   a. Which articles are listed? (You don't have to list more than 10.)
   b. Read one of the articles that would give some guidance to a new user. What's its title? Who is the author?
   c. Using e-mail, send a copy of the file to a friend who would benefit from reading it.

3. Browse the newsgroups in the hierarchy **rec.music** (list all newsgroups, select the folder **rec,** and then select the folder [hierarchy] **rec.music**). Find one you think is interesting.
   a. What is its name?
   b. If there is a FAQ for the newsgroup, read or retrieve a copy of it. If you can't find one, post a request to **news.newusers.questions** or the newsgroup itself, asking if there is a FAQ for the newsgroup.
   c. Give a brief description of the types of articles you've found in the group.

4. Browse the articles in **news.newusers.questions.** If you find an article that poses a question you think you could answer, send the author the answer by replying to the article. If you can't find any you can answer, find one that's interesting and send e-mail to the author asking for a copy of the answer.

5. This chapter deals with Usenet. A previous chapter dealt with interest groups or mailing lists.
   a. Which one do you prefer working with? Explain.
   b. Are there some sorts of discussions or groups for which using Usenet would be preferable to using an interest group? Explain.
   c. What situations are more suited to working with interest groups rather than Usenet? Explain.

6. Suppose you could read articles from only five newsgroups. Which would they be? Why?

7. Using each of the Web sites given in the text that let you search for newsgroups,
   a. search for newsgroups that deal with horses. How do the answers compare?
   b. search for newsgroups that deal with travel in Latin-America. How do the answers compare?

8. Looking through a list of FAQs, find FAQs that deal with copyright, investments, medicinal herbs, scuba diving, and the Klingon language. Give a URL for each, the name of the author, and the date the FAQ was last updated.

CHAPTER 6

Finding Information on the Web—Directories and Searching

After spending some time surfing the Internet or browsing the WWW, people often say that there is so much information available that it must be really difficult to find anything. It would be difficult to do research, keep track of the latest changes in almost every field, or look up any sort of information without *directories* (collections of hyperlinks to the WWW and other resources) or *search engines* (programs that search WWW sites and create a database or index of all the text, titles, hyperlinks, and URLs they find) to find and organize the vast array of WWW pages and other sites on the Internet.

The hyperlinks in the directories are usually arranged according to subject headings such as News, Sports, Health, or Science. We introduced a couple of directories, Yahoo! and the World Wide Web Virtual Library, in Chapters 1 and 2. A search engine or search tool is a computer program that will search its database to find items whose text contains all or at least one of the words we give it. This chapter deals with these techniques for finding resources on the WWW.

When we list a directory or search engine, we'll give its location or URL and a summary of its features. Several examples give step-by-step instructions for using some of them. To give some focus to the discussion, we'll pick some topics to work with: financial services and investing, alternative health care, and scuba diving. You can use the techniques we show here to help you find what you're looking for.

The topics we'll cover in this chapter are:
* Directories
* Searching the World Wide Web

Some of the directories and search engines or tools were created and maintained by individuals and volunteers out of personal needs and then shared with the Internet and WWW. The popularity of the Internet and WWW has led to a number of these directories and tools being supported by commercial organizations. Most of these services are free; some companies make versions of the search tools available for a fee. The ones with a fee attached usually have more extensive databases. For most work the free services may be entirely satisfactory. But it may be worth paying for a search service if you need to find the information in a reasonable amount of time.

Directories

A directory on the WWW is a collection of hyperlinks arranged according to some scheme. The hyperlinks take you to WWW documents or other resources. They're usually arranged according to subject categories, similar to the way you'd find things arranged in a library, in a catalog, or in a phone company's yellow pages. We've already taken a look at a couple of them—World Wide Web Virtual Library and Excite. There are other types of directories. Some directories include ratings (usually supplied by users) of the sites they list, and many directories include ways to search the titles and brief descriptions of the listings. One common type of directory lists popular or cool sites, and another type lists new Web sites.

Many directories were started as personal collections of interesting and useful sites. But maintaining a comprehensive directory means checking the listings, adding new ones, and deleting others. This can grow into a job that takes full-time attention; thus, several directories now have commercial sponsors.

An easy way to access directories through Netscape is to click on the pull-down menu **Directory** or click on the directory buttons **What's New!**, **What's Cool!**, or **Net Directory**.

Clicking on **Directory** in the menu bar displays a menu that includes the same items as the directory buttons and links to information about Netscape, the Internet, and the Internet White Pages. The Internet White Pages (**http://home.netscape.com/home/internet-white-pages.html**) are a collection of tools for finding e-mail addresses of folks on the Internet.

Directories of New and Interesting Web Pages

What's New! and **What's Cool!** are both directories maintained by Netscape Communications. Each has a listing of hyperlinks and each link comes with a brief description of the Web page it represents. You use the directory the same way you'd use any Web page.

What's New! doesn't have all the new Web pages—hundreds are announced daily. It does contain hyperlinks to new resources and makes innovative use of the WWW, according to Netscape Communications. To get to it, click on the directory button What's New! or use the pull-down menu **Directory**. Several other *What's New!* lists are maintained on the WWW. There's even a section with over 30 entries within the Yahoo directory dedicated to these lists. Look in the Yahoo directory in the section "Computers and Internet:Internet:World Wide Web:Searching the Web:Indices to Web Documents:What's New" (URL **http://www.yahoo.com/Computers_and_Internet/Internet/World_Wide_Web/Searching_the_Web/Indices_to_Web_Documents/What_s_New/**).
Some *What's New* sites to consider are:

- The Scout Report (**http://rs.internic.net/scout/report**)—According to InfoScout, a listing of the best of the new sites on the Internet. A new report is usually published every week.
- What's New with NCSA Mosaic (**http://www.ncsa.uiuc.edu/SDG/Software/Mosaic/Docs/whats-new.html**)—The original "What's New!" list. A daily listing, in alphabetical order, of newly announced Web pages. Also includes a weekly pick.

* **What's New Too!** (http://newtoo.manifest.com/WhatsNewToo/index.html)—A daily listing of new sites. Hundreds of items each day.
* **What's New in the Whole Internet Catalog** (http://gnn.com/wics/nunu.new.html)—A weekly listing of items added to the Whole Internet Catalog—discussed below under general directories.
* **Yahoo What's New** (http://www.yahoo.com/new)—A daily listing of new sites, with Yahoo's Picks of the Week.

What's Cool! **http://home.netscape.com/home/whats-cool.htm**, available through the pull-down menu **Directory** or the What's Cool! directory button, lists sites that are particularly interesting or innovative, in Netscape's opinion. Several other directories are dedicated to finding and listing cool Web pages. The first one was Glenn Davis's "Cool Site of the Day" at **http://cool.infi.net**. Several others are listed in the Yahoo directory in the section "Computers and Internet:Internet:World Wide Web:Searching the Web:Indices to Web Documents" (**http://www.yahoo.com/Computers_and_Internet/Internet/World_Wide_Web/Searching_the_Web/ Indices_to_Web_Documents/**) under the headings

* Best of the Web
* Sites of the Day
* Sites of the Week

Subject-Oriented Directories

Most directories organize their lists of hyperlinks according to subject. Clicking on the directory button **Net Directory** (URL **http://home.netscape.com/home/internet-directory.html**) takes you to several we'll describe. You can get to others by using their URL or by selecting them from the Yahoo directory section "Computers and Internet:Internet:World Wide Web:Searching the Web:Directories" (**http:// www.yahoo.com/Computers_and_Internet/Internet/World_Wide_Web/Searching_the_Web/Directories/**).

Several different directories are available. They don't all have the same type of information; some are general and some very specialized; and they have different formats. Most arrange the hyperlinks into categories and you can choose any one from the list or table on the screen. After choosing a general or higher level topic, you're presented with a list of more specific topics. Many directories also include a tool for searching their collection. Searching a given directory usually results in getting a collection of hyperlinks in categories throughout the directory related to the topic you typed into the search program. Directories are fun and interesting to browse, but with a specific goal, you work your way through the topics to get to a list of Web sites that deal with your topic.

> Tip
> _____
> Take some time to learn about a directory you're using.
>
> Many directories have a Help section, a description of how to use the directory and available tools, or some information about the purpose of the directory available as a hyperlink from the main page. Take a little time to read about the directory so you'll be able to use it more effectively.
> _____

Before listing and describing a few directories, we'll show an example of working through the Yahoo directory.

Example 6.1   Finding Resources for "Financial Services. Investing" Using Yahoo

As a frugal and wise person with some money you'd like to invest, you're going to want to investigate some resources on the WWW that deal with financial services or investing. (Well, maybe you're going to have some money to invest some day, and you want to be ready.) One place to start looking is in Yahoo. Here are the steps to follow to get to yahoo and then to sections dealing with financial services and investing. If you follow this example while using a computer, you'll probably want to browse other sections as well. Feel free to browse, but don't get too distracted to follow these steps.

1. Go to the Yahoo Directory.
2. Select **Business and Economy**.
3. Select **Markets and Investments**.
4. Select **Personal Finance** and browse the listings.
5. Go back to **Markets and Investments** and then go to **Mutual Funds**.
6. When you're ready, go to your home page.

We're assuming you've started Netscape. Here are the details for the steps.

1. Go to the Yahoo Directory.

wWw   Click on the icon labeled **Open**, type **http://www.yahoo.com**, and click the button labeled **Open**.

With the instructions above, you're using an icon in the Toolbar. There are other ways to get to Yahoo: Click on the pull-down menu **File** and select **Open Location** and type the URL for Yahoo given above, or click on the directory button labeled **Net Directory** and find Yahoo! on the Netscape Internet Directory Web page. Regardless of how you do it you'll get to a page similar to the one shown in Figure 6.1.

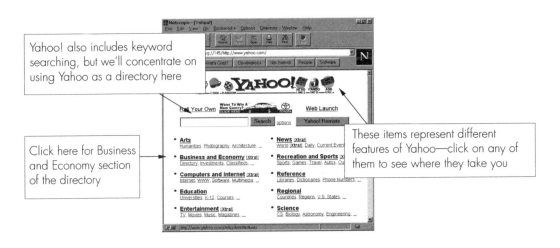

Figure 6.1   Yahoo Directory as It Appears after Clicking on Net Directory

2. Select **Business and Economy**.

W^WW Click on the hyperlink **Business and Economy**.

Once Business and Economy is selected a window similar to Figure 6.2 will appear. You see there's lots to choose from; each entry is a hyperlink.

Figure 6.2   Business and Economy

The entries that end with @ are also in other categories or sections of the directory. Clicking on **Economics@**, for example, takes you to the section **Social Science: Economics**.

3. Select **Markets and Investments**.

W^WW Click on the hyperlink **Markets and Investments**.

Selecting Markets and Investments takes us to a page with more categories and some specific sites, shown in Figure 6.3. For example, the hyperlink **Investor Web** goes to a Web page, while **Mutual Funds** goes to another category or section in the directory. Follow **Personal Finance** for the next step.

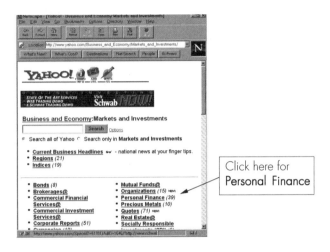

Figure 6.3   Markets and Investments

4. Select **Personal Finance** and browse the listings.

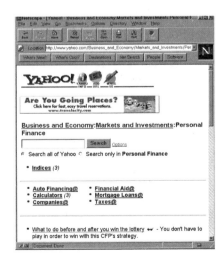 Click on the hyperlink **Personal Finance**.

Selecting **Personal Finance** takes us to a page with information about practical financial matters and hyperlinks to sites that claim to be useful to beginning and novice investors. Figure 6.4 shows a sample screen from the category.

Figure 6.4   Personal Finance

You can spend a fair amount of time browsing these topics. Instead of doing that now, why not add this to your list of bookmarks? In case you don't remember, here's how to add the current Web page to your bookmark list. Select **Bookmarks** from the Menu Bar and then click on **Add Bookmark**.

5. Go back to **Markets and Investments** and then go to **Mutual Funds**.

We're going back to the previous page to select the section **Mutual Funds**.

wW Click on the icon ▨ in the Toolbar.

That takes us back to the Markets and Investments page (Figure 6.3).

wW Click on the hyperlink **Mutual Funds**.

Figure 6.5 shows a portion of the directory section Mutual Funds. The listing contains hyperlinks to some other sections of Yahoo and several links to resources on the WWW for learning about, analyzing, and investing in mutual funds.

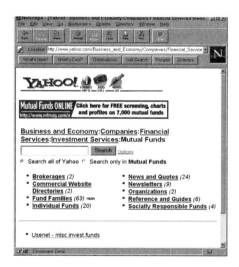

Figure 6.5   Mutual Funds

6. When you're ready, go to your home page.

wW Click on the icon ▨ from the Toolbar.

Clicking on the icon **Home** takes you to the home page for this Netscape session.

What to do now? Your choice. There's a big Web for you to explore!

————————End of Example 6.1————————

Example 6.1 showed some of the basic steps to follow when you're working with a directory. A list of selected directories is next. We'll give the name of the directory, a URL to get to it, and a description of what it contains. We're also including some examples to show some other ways of using a directory. Some of the directories are well suited to researching a topic. Some are very good at letting you quickly reach the information you want. When you find a directory you like, add it to your bookmark list.

* **Argus/ University of Michigan Clearinghouse for Subject-Oriented Internet Resource Guides,** or just *Clearinghouse,* **http://www.lib.umich.edu/chhome.html** bills itself as "The Premier Internet Research Library." Originally developed through the University of Michigan Library, Clearinghouse is a collection of Internet guides to information about specific topics, for example, Political Science or Adult Distance Learning. Many of the guides contain detailed information about interest groups related to the given topic. Anyone can submit a guide. If it's acceptable by Clearinghouse rules, it will be rated and made available. To get a good rating, a guide has to satisfy criteria set up by Clearinghouse. The rules, criteria, and rating system are available through hyperlinks from the home page. Clearinghouse is jointly sponsored by Argus Associates and University of Michigan.

* **Excite Directory,** **http://www.excite.com** provides a directory and a means to search the directory and other sites on the World Wide Web. Excite works as a guide to information on the Internet. It contains a search tool (Excite Search); a directory of Web sites (Excite Reviews); a link to City.Net; "Excite Live," a personalized list of hyperlinks to news, weather, or entertainment information; and a reference section with links to business information, maps, a dictionary, and ways to find e-mail addresses. Excite Search is easy to use and lets you search a database of Web documents, Usenet articles, or classified adds posted to Usenet. Excite Reviews has information arranged by subject. Each listing is accompanied by a written review to give you an idea of what's at a site and whether it's what you're looking for. In Example 6.2 below we show how to use the directory. The home page is shown in Figure 6.6.

Example 6.2   Using Excite to Find Resources for Alternative Health Care

Health care seems to be a topic on everyone's mind. In this example we're going to show a couple of ways to get information on health care in general and then specifically search for hyperlinks related to alternative health care. We'll use the Excite Reviews to show a directory that reviews its entries and also discuss using the search tools that are part of several directories.

First, we'll go through the directory categories to find hyperlinks that will take us to appropriate information and then search for pertinent hyperlinks using the search tool.
1. Connect to Excite home page.
2. Select **Health & Medicine.**
3. Select **Medicine.**
4. Select **Alternative Medicine.**
5. Use the search tool with the search phrase **alternative health care** to find appropriate entries.

1. Connect to Excite home page.

The Excite Directory is accessible through the URL **http://www.excite.com**.

WWW Click on the icon [Open] from the Toolbar.

WWW Type **http://www.excite.com** and press **Enter**.

You can also reach the Excite home page through a hyperlink on the Web page that you see after clicking on the Netscape directory button **Net Search**. The home page for Excite is shown in Figure 6.6.

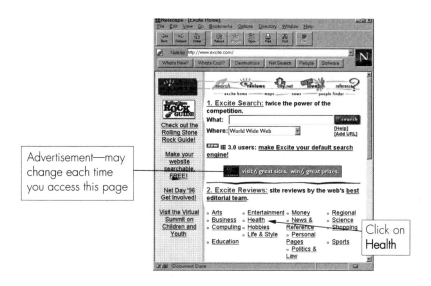

Advertisement—may change each time you access this page

Click on Health

Figure 6.6   Home Page for Excite

2. Select **Health**.

There are two primary ways to find entries in the Excite Directory. You can go through or browse the categories in Excite Reviews, or you can type a key word or phrase in the form box next to the box labeled **What:**, next to the button labeled **Search**, in Excite Search. In this example we'll first browse the categories and do a search in later steps.

WWW Click on **Health** on the home page shown in Figure 6.6.

Clicking on **Health** brings up the Web page shown in Figure 6.7.

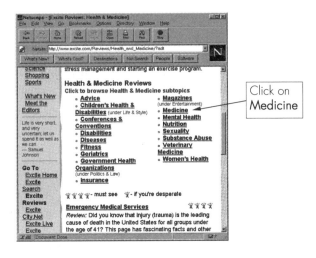

Figure 6.7   Categories in Excite Directory Under Health

3. Select **Medicine**.

The first part of the Web page for Health is likely to contain the text of an article about some health-related issue. Use the vertical scroll bar or press the Page Down key to get to the main categories or sections under **Health**. They're shown in Figure 6.7. From there we'll select the entry **Medicine**.

w⁴w   Click on **Medicine**.

Figure 6.8   Excite Directory Entries Under Medicine

4. Select **Alternative Medicine**.

Figure 6.8 shows the categories in the section **Medicine**. One of them is **Alternative Medicine**. That wasn't exactly what we were looking for, but it's probably the best bet at this point.

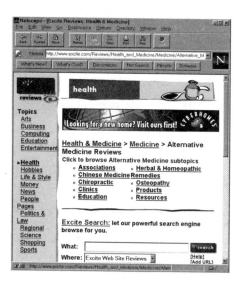 Click on **Alternative Medicine**.

After selecting **Alternative Medicine**, we get a listing of several categories dealing with the topic. Figure 6.9 shows a portion of the list of categories. From here, to get the most general listing of items, we might choose **Resources**. We'll leave the choice up to you if you want to explore this further.

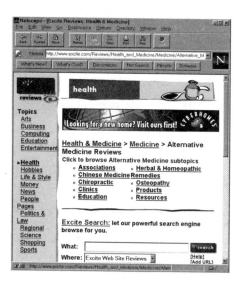

Figure 6.9   Alternative Medicine Listings

5. Use the search tool with the search phrase **alternative health care** to find appropriate entries.

By browsing the categories, we've found some items in the directory related to alternative medicine. Instead of browsing, we could search the directory. This might bring up items from more than one category. To search, type the search phrase or word into the search form as shown in Figure 6.10 and click on the button labeled **Search**.

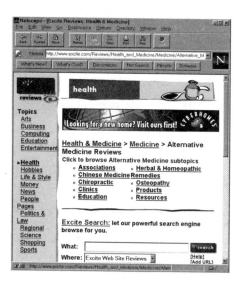 Type **alternative health care** into the search form and click on the button labeled **Search**.

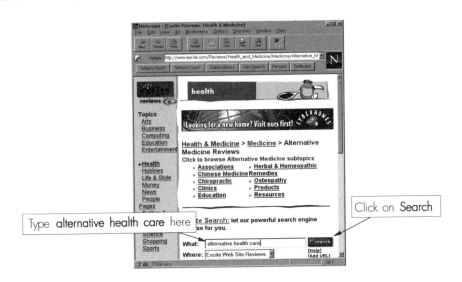

Figure 6.10   Using "alternative health care" to Search the Directory

A portion of the results is shown in Figure 6.11.

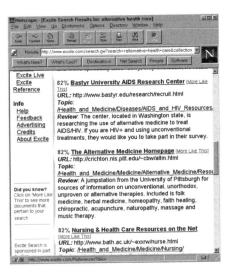

Figure 6.11   Search Results

Now you get to peruse the listings and explore. You can form more complex or sophisticated phrases for advanced searching. Click on the hyperlink "Advanced Search" at both the top and bottom of the current page for instructions on how to form those types of search phrases. For example, if you were interested in alternative health care as it related to chronic illnesses, you could type in a new search phrase alternative AND health AND care AND chronic AND illness and click on **Search**.

————————————End of Example 6.2————————————

✸ Global Network Navigator (GNN), **http://www.gnn.com**, is more than a list of World Wide Web sites. It is a gateway to a number of Internet resources and gives access to several guides for navigating through the Internet. These guides include the Whole Internet Catalog—a directory of Internet resources arranged by subject; Best of the Net—a collection of the better resources from the Whole Internet Catalog; and Netizens—a collection of Web pages written by GNN users. Also included are electronic publications on personal finance, travel, education, books, sports, and Web Review Magazine—a weekly electronic magazine, **http://webreview.com/index.html**, or *e-zine*, dealing with the World Wide Web. The main subject guide is the WebCrawlerSelect, **http://webcrawler.com/GNN/ WebQuery.html**, part of the Whole Internet Catalog.

Example 6.3   Finding WWW Resources Related to Scuba Diving Using GNN

The Global Network Navigator contains more than a directory, so there's lots of stuff to look at here, but we're going to concentrate on using the Whole Internet Catalog to find some Internet and Web resources dealing with scuba diving. Why scuba diving? Just for fun! If you'd rather find information on another topic, you'll find the techniques to use are the same as we use here. Here are the steps we'll follow:

1. Open the location to the Global Network Navigator.
2. Choose **Whole Internet Catalog Select**.
3. Select **Water Sports** from **Sports**.
4. Select hyperlinks dealing with scuba diving.

1. Open the location to the Global Network Navigator.

You've got to open the location and go to the URL **http://www.gnn.com**.

Wꟿ**W** Click on the icon 🖳 from the Toolbar.

Wꟿ**W** Type **http://gnn.com/wic** and press ⟦**Enter**⟧.

This opens the location for the home page for Whole Internet Catalog GNN. Figure 6.12 shows a portion of that page. Some of the hyperlinks are represented as text, but others—including the one we'll use—are represented as images.

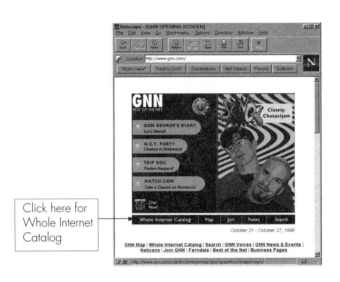

Click here for
Whole Internet
Catalog

Figure 6.12 Portion of the GNN Home Page

2. Choose **Whole Internet Catalog Select**.

We're going to access the Whole Internet Catalog, so you need to move the mouse to the image **select** or the text **WIC Select**.

Click on the image labeled **select**.

These steps take you to the page for the Whole Internet Catalog Select that contains, among other things, general subject headings.

Click on the heading **Sports**.

The Whole Internet Catalog shows its general subject headings. Figure 6.13 shows the first part of the Web page for the Whole Internet Catalog for Sports. Water Sports is one of the topics listed.

3. Select **Water Sports** from **Sports**.

Water sports , as shown in Figure 6.13, is listed under the section Sports.

Click on **Water Sports**.

Clicking on **Water Sports** takes you to the portion of the Recreation page at GNN that deals with water sports. That's shown in Figure 6.14.

Click here for directory information on water sports

Figure 6.13   Web Page for the Whole Internet Catalog Featuring Section on Sports

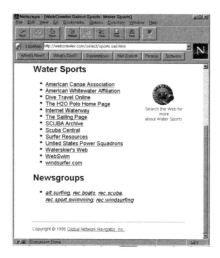

Figure 6.14   Water Sports

4. Select hyperlinks dealing with scuba diving.

Figure 6.14 shows several hyperlinks dealing with scuba diving—two Web pages and one newsgroup. Select any or all of them. We'll leave it to you to have fun following the hyperlinks.

————————————————End of Example 6.3—————————————————

❋ Information Sources—The Internet and Computer-Mediated Communication, http:// www.december.com/cmc/info/index.html. This extensive list, compiled and maintained by John December, is a list of sources focusing on resources on the Internet and using the Internet for communication and information. It's presented in three levels with the first being the most general. This very useful directory represents several years of work. December also maintains Internet Web Text, http:// www.december.com/web/text/index.html, a directory to items on the WWW.

❋ Inter-Links, http://www.nova.edu/Inter-Links/start.html, was created and is maintained by Rob Kabacoff from the Center for Psychological Studies at Nova Southeastern University in Ft. Lauderdale, Florida. It's very well designed with each topic or page usually fitting within a window of 25 lines. This keeps it from being as detailed as some directories, but it's designed to be interesting and useful. The links are chosen carefully, so the items they point to are informative, accessible, and appealing. The primary categories are Basic Internet Services, Topical Resources, Fun and Games, Guides and Tutorials, News and Weather, Library Resources, Reference Shelf, and Search the Net.

❋ Internet Services List, http://www.spectracom.com/islist/, created and maintained by Scott Yanoff, is a list of sites and services on the WWW and the Internet. The list is arranged by subject, with entries covering a wide range of areas. Some of the topics are Agriculture, FTP, History, Literature/ Books/ Languages, Mathematics, Paranormal, Software, Travel, Weather, and Women/Feminism. Yanoff started his list in 1991. He updates it monthly and continues to maintain it as a service to the users of the World Wide Web and Internet.

❋ The McKinley Internet Directory, http://www.mckinley.com/, also known as Magellan. It's available from the Netscape directory button Net Directory. The home page features a form to fill out and use for searching the directory using a key word or phrase. It can also be browsed by going through a list of categories. It contains listings of Web sites and resources available through Telnet, FTP, and Gopher as well as newsgroups and mailing lists. Not only does it contain all these items, but each is accompanied by a brief summary and the sites are rated and reviewed. This can be very helpful in selecting useful information or resources. Figure 6.15 shows the home page for Magellan with search phrase **environment policy** typed in.

Figure 6.15   Home page for McKinley Directory

* **Tradewave Galaxy**, or **Galaxy** for short, **http://galaxy.einet.net/galaxy.html**, is a comprehensive, subject-oriented directory provided as a service to the World Wide Web. Several of the areas in the directory are monitored and developed by volunteers or "guest editors." In addition to being an encyclopedic directory, it also includes a very good general search tool for finding resources on the Internet, World Wide Web, and Galaxy's Web pages.

* **World Wide Web Virtual Library Arranged by Subject**, http://www.w3.org/hypertext/DataSources/bySubject/Overview.html. This extensive directory, staffed entirely by volunteers, has existed almost since the beginning of the World Wide Web. Topics range from aboriginal studies to zoos. Each volunteer agrees to maintain a collection of hyperlink related to a specific subject. The subjects can be viewed alphabetically or according to Library of Congress standards. This is useful to both researchers and the general public.

As you get the chance to browse these directories, you may come across several others. Keep a directory or two in your bookmark list, so you'll be able to get to them quickly.

Searching the World Wide Web

You know there's lots of information available through the World Wide Web. Hundreds of new resources are added each day. When you want to research a topic or find some fact, you need to do it efficiently and quickly. A number of search tools or programs, called *search engines*, are designed to search for the information available throughout the WWW. You type in a key word or phrase, and the tools return a collection of hyperlinks to Internet or WWW resources that contain the key word(s). The search engines are relatively easy to use and they give quick results.

Directories can be used to find information, but they are most useful when you know what you're looking for and what category or heading it's under. Most directories include a search tool to look only through that directory. More general search tools, the search engines we'll be discussing in this section, help you collect and then browse information from lots of sources.

Several of the search engines were developed by individuals because they wanted a substantial tool for finding resources on the WWW. Every tool we'll discuss has no fee for using it; most are sponsored by or owned by a commercial organization. Some have more comprehensive versions, which are run as a sub-scription service for a monthly fee. Timely and worthwhile information is valuable. The ability to search resources as large as those available on the WWW quickly and comprehensively is something many corporations, news agencies, and research organizations are more than willing to pay for.

Using a Search Tool

The home page for each search tool contains a dialog box or frame where you type in a key word or phrase. Click on a button labeled **Search** or **Submit** (in the content area of the window) and the search begins. The search engine then examines a database for items that contain the key word(s). The database consists of a large collection of information the search program has gathered from the WWW. It isn't the WWW being searched, but this database or index of terms found on Web pages. The search engine then brings back the search results—a list of hyperlinks and, in some cases, a summary of the information found by clicking on each hyperlink. You use the search results in the same way as any other Web page.

The search results are arranged in order according to a score assigned by the search program that indicates how relevant the material is to your search term(s). If one item has a higher score than another, then it makes a better match to your key word or phrase. It could also be that an item with a higher score contains one or more of the key words in its title, or the key words are mentioned frequently. You may get many items in the results, so you'll want to look at the ones with higher scores.

Search Options. Search programs allow you to select options for your search. Most search tool home pages start with a form you fill out to do a simple search, without any conditions for the search, and offer a link to another Web page where you can specify options. The options differ among search programs, but the general categories are display options—specify how much detail you want to see and how many hyperlinks to list on one Web page; resources to search—some search only WWW documents, others search Gopher, Usenet, and other resources; and type of search—all words, any words, exclude some words.

For WWW resources, you can include or exclude the titles of Web pages, the URL for Web pages, or the content of Web pages (this gives the most chances for a match).

We need to talk a little about the types of searches. When you give a single key word, you get back hyperlinks to items that contain that word. When you want to search using several words or a phrase, you can be selective about getting results that match all the words or ones that match any word in the phrase. Some search tools give you even more control by allowing the use of AND, OR, and NOT. Phrases using these terms are called *Boolean phrases*. If two words are connected by AND, then they both must appear. If two words are connected with OR, then one or both will appear, and if NOT is in front of a word, then documents containing that word are excluded from the list. For example, if you wanted to search for items dealing with alcohol or drug abuse but didn't deal with crime, you could use the phrase "alcohol and abuse or drug and abuse not crime." Not every search engine allows Boolean phrases, or if one does, you may have to express the Boolean phrase in a different form.

Selected Search Tools

This section contains a list of several search tools or search programs that you can use to find information on the World Wide Web. Each one listed below is accessible through a hyperlink, directory button, or URL. We'll include a brief description of each and the URL for the home page. We list several because there isn't one universal search tool. They all have a similar interface—you type in a key word or phrase and the search program returns a list of results (hyperlinks) arranged in order from most relevant to least relevant. All have online help so you can get general information on using the program, the different ways you can formulate the key phrase you'll use for searching, and technical information about the search tool and methods used. But they're not all the same. There are differences in the algorithms to find items that make the best matches, the options for searching, and the options for displaying the results. Each has its own strengths and its own database of Web information used for the searches. The databases are updated regularly. Items are added when part of the search tool goes out to the Web and examines URLs that have been supplied by users. In this gathering phase, the search program indexes the information on a Web page associated with a URL and then follows and collects hyperlinks from there.

Examples for using the search tools are also included; unfortunately, we don't have the space to give an example of using each. The examples were chosen because they're popular, comprehensive, and relatively easy to use. Next, some URLs are given for Web pages that contain a hyperlink or interface to several search tools. Which search tools you use regularly will probably depend on the ones you find most useful for your needs. So try a few, make bookmarks to the ones you like, and always be on the lookout for the next generation of good tools.

Excite

Types of searches: All words or any words in a phrase. Boolean phrases allowed.

Sources to search: Select one of Web pages (full text), Excite Web site reviews, Usenet articles, or Classified ads from Usenet articles.

Home page URL: **http://www.excite.com**.

Excite, provided by Architext Software, works as a guide to information on the Internet. It contains a search tool (Excite Search); a directory of Web sites (Excite Reviews); a link to City.Net; "Excite Live," a personalized list of hyperlinks to news, weather, or entertainment information; and a reference section with links to business information, maps, a dictionary, and ways to find e-mail addresses. Excite Search is an easy-to-use tool that lets you search a database of Web documents, reviews of Web sites (Excite Reviews), Usenet articles, or classified adds posted to Usenet.

Excite Search is designed to understand phrases, sentences or words. It uses Intelligent Concept Extraction™, their proprietary search technology, which is designed to be fast, accurate, and precise. An effective strategy is to use descriptive phrases. Using "mental health research" is more effective that using "mental health" or "research" if you're after items that contain information about research related to mental health."

The results of a search are ranked, and they can be displayed in order of relevance—called *confidence* by Excite—grouped by site; the sites are also selected in order of relevance. Grouping them by site is good if there are several pages from the same site that match the key phrase. Figure 6.16 shows the search screen for Excite using the key phrase **mental health research**, with options set for a concept search using Excite's database of Web documents. Click on the hyperlink **Help** for more information about Excite Search. Figure 6.17 shows a partial list of the hyperlinks arranged by confidence or relevance. Click on the hyperlink **Advanced Search** for information about using Boolean phrases and other options for search phrases.

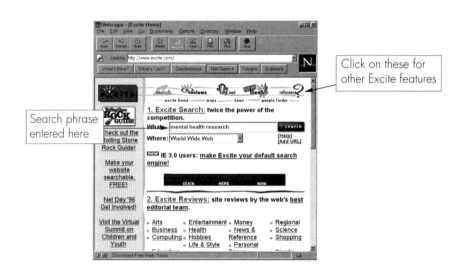

Figure 6.16   Excite Web Search Page

Galaxy

Types of searches:	All words or any word in a phrase. Boolean phrases allowed.
Sources to search:	Select one or more from Web pages (full text, titles, hyperlinks), Gopher sources, or Telnet directory.
Home page for searching URL:	**http://galaxy.einet.net/cgi-bin/wais-text-multi**.
Home page for Galaxy directory and other services URL:	**http://galaxy.einet.net/galaxy.html**.

After trying the search program, you may want to take a look at the list of hyperlinks to other search tools available through Galaxy by using the URL **http://galaxy.einet.net/search-other.html** or clicking on the hyperlink **Other Searchable Reference Materials and Directories** on the Web page for the search tool.

Galaxy, a service provided to the Internet by TradeWave, maintains a directory of WWW resources and a database of Web documents along with a search tool. The directory was described in the section in this chapter about directories. The starting page for the search tool, Searching the Galaxy, is shown in Figure 6.18. You can select matching any of the search terms all of the search terms. By clicking in the appropriate

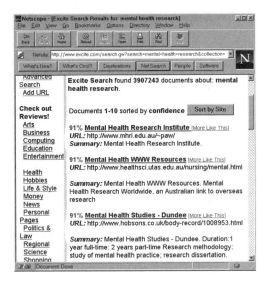

Figure 6.17 Partial List of Results from Search Using the Key Phrase "mental health research"

boxes, you can choose among searching information from the World Wide Web, the Web sites listed in the Galaxy directory, a list of Gopher sites, or Usenet sites. Galaxy lets you search two or more types of resources from this list. You can also specify that Web pages be in a certain topic area such as science, humanities, communities, and so on. The search page also has hyperlinks to get help, start the search, or display a list of other references to search.

If you're searching Web documents, you select text or content of Web pages, titles of Web pages, or hyperlinks on Web pages. These Web pages are the ones that make up the database for Searching the Galaxy. Selecting **all text** is the most comprehensive because it searches the text or content of the Web pages in the database. With this selected, you also get a choice of the type of listings: short—hyperlink only; medium— hyperlink and excerpt from the text, or long output—everything from the first two along with a list of frequently occurring words in the document and an outline of the Web page. You might want to pick **title text only** if you know about a Web page but don't know its URL. Suppose, for example, you're looking for the David Letterman home page, and you don't want to get a list of pages whose text includes the words David Letterman. Use **David Letterman** as the key phrase and click the boxes **all search terms** and **title text only**. Then click **Search** and you'll get just a few results (only two in a recent search). These are the Web pages that Galaxy has in its database whose titles contain the phrase. Selecting **link text only** lets you hone in on specific information but usually returns more items than **title text only**. Once again, using **David Letterman** as the search string and selecting **link text only**, you'll get a much longer list of matching items, hyperlinks that contain the words **David Letterman**.

It's possible to do searches in Searching the Galaxy using Boolean expressions, connecting key words with *and*, *or*, or *not*. You can't tell that from the home page for Searching the Galaxy, but you'd find out about it by reading in the help section (click on **Need Help?**). Example 6.4 goes through the steps of using a Boolean expression.

Example 6.4   Searching for "Personal Finance or Investing" with Galaxy

We're going to look for resources on the WWW dealing with personal finance or investing. Suppose you've been frugal and now you're ready to do some investing, hoping to increase your fortune. In addition to reading books or magazines on the subject (since you're frugal you'll get them from your local library), you'll want to see what information or resources are available on the Internet.

We use Galaxy in this example because we're going to use a Boolean phrase, such as **personal and finance or investing**, and Galaxy allows you to search with Boolean phrases like that one. (Not all search engines do.) We'll use this capability of the Galaxy search engine further to narrow the search by using the phrase **personal and finance or investing not stock** to exclude resources dealing with stock. (We exclude stock just to demonstrate how to exclude something rather than giving a hot investment tip!) As we go through this example we'll start using both terms in the phrase **personal finance**. Then we'll use a Boolean phrase to get information about personal finance or investing, and finally we'll narrow our search to exclude stock. We'll assume Netscape is started.

Here are the steps to follow:
1. Go to the home page for Searching the Galaxy.
2. Using the search phrase **personal finance**, set options for a search of all terms, short output, and all text of Web pages.
3. Specifically include investing in the phrase by using **personal and finance or investing**.
4. Narrow the search to exclude pages that deal with stock by using the Boolean phrase **personal and finance or investing not stock**.

1. Go to the home page for Searching the Galaxy.

W⁻W   Click on the icon **Open**, type **http://galaxy.einet.net/cgi-bin/wais-text-multi** into the dialog box, and click on the button **Open**.

Opening the location for the Searching the Galaxy page brings up a window as shown in Figure 6.18.

2. Using the search phrase **personal finance**, set options for a search of all terms, short output, and all text of Web pages.

W⁻W   Type **personal finance** in the box to the left of **Search**.

W⁻W   Click on the items all search terms, select **Short Output**, click the checkbox for **Search the Web**, and click in the circle by **all text**.

W⁻W   The search request is now filled in as shown in Figure 6.19.

Figure 6.18   Home Page for Searching the Galaxy

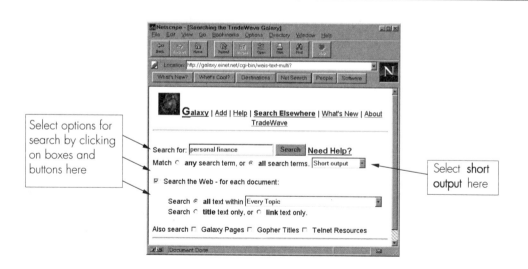

Select options for search by clicking on boxes and buttons here

Select **short output** here

Figure 6.19   Search Request Using "personal finance" Matching Both Terms

Click on **Search**.

Clicking on the **Search** button submits your request to Galaxy. In a few moments you'll get a response. A portion of a typical response in shown is Figure 6.20.

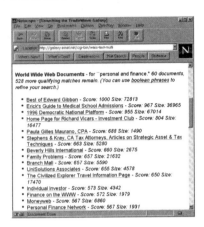

Figure 6.20   Search Results Using "personal finance" as Search String

The results are presented in order of relevance. All the results are hyperlinks and you can click on any of them.

3. Specifically include investing in the phrase by using **personal and financing or investing**.

We're going to use a Boolean phrase **personal and finance or investing** for the search now. This will get us hyperlinks to Web pages that contain both words **personal finance** or pages that contain the word **investing**. This isn't an either-or situation; we can retrieve hyperlinks to pages that contain all three. However, we won't get any that contain only the word **personal** or only the word **finance** without the other. The steps to follow are listed below.

We have to change the key phrase for the searching. It's probably easiest just to replace it at this point.

WWW   Move the mouse pointer to the text box to the right of **Search for**, highlight the current search phrase, and type **personal and finance or investing**.

You highlight the phrase by moving the pointer to the beginning of the phrase, holding down the mouse button, and then moving the pointer to the end of the phrase. Since we don't want the search program to use the words *and* or *or* as part of the key phrase, we need to select **Match any search item**.

WWW   Click on the circle immediately to the left of any search item.

Figure 6.21 shows the search screen filled in ready for this phase of the search.

Change to match any search term

Type Boolean search phrase here

Figure 6.21   Search Form Filled Out for Boolean Phrase "personal and finance or investing"

Click on the button **Search.**

Figure 6.22 shows the list of results.

Figure 6.22   Search Results Using Boolean Phrase "personal and finance or investing"

There are more results than are displayed on this page. Clicking a button at the bottom of the page titled **More search results...** will give you more results. There's a link to information about Boolean phrases that you select to get help or information on that topic.

4. Narrow the search to exclude pages that deal with stock by using the Boolean phrase **money and management or investing not stock**.

We're going to narrow our search here to exclude sites that contain information about stock. Narrowing a search means making it more restricted. One way to do this is to use the word "not" in a Boolean phrase. You may also be able to do it by dropping a word or words from the key search phrase, but that doesn't guarantee that something will be excluded. In that case, you're only saying it's not necessary to include it.

We'll use the search phrase **personal and finance or investing not stock**. This excludes pages that contain the word "stock" and other forms of it such as "stocks." Galaxy, like many search tools, uses a technique called *stemming* to search not only for a word but for similar words, ones where the original word forms the base. We'll fill out the search request as shown in Figure 6.23. Figure 6.24 shows an excerpt of the results. Make sure that the match is for any search item, as in the previous step.

   Move the mouse pointer to the text box to the right of **Search for**, press the End key to take the pointer to the end of the phrase, and type not stock.

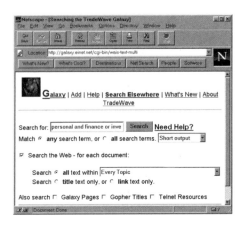

Figure 6.23   Search Form for Boolean Phrase "personal and finance or investing not stock"

   Click on the button **Search**.

Figure 6.24   Search Results Using Boolean Phrase "personal and finance or investing not stock"

Now that you've got the list of resources, you can explore them.

————————————End of Example 6.4————————————

Infoseek Guide

Types of searches: All words or any word in a phrase. Boolean phrases allowed. Can require exact match, proper names, words appearing in specified order, and words appearing near each other. For details click on the hyperlink **"click for tips"** on the Infoseek home page or use the URL **http://guide.infoseek.com/Help?sv=N1&pg=SearchHelp.html.**

Sources to search: Infoseek Guide uses a database that includes Web pages, Usenet newsgroups, and other Internet sources. For more information about the sources used for searching, click on the hyperlink **Help** on the Infoseek home page.

Home page URL: **http://www.infoseek.com.**

Infoseek is also available by clicking on the directory button **Net Search** or by clicking **Directory** in the menu bar and selecting **Internet Search**.

Infoseek is an easy-to-use search tool. It's listed prominently on the page you'll see when you click on the directory button **Net Search**. To use it from there, click on **Infoseek**. When the new page appears, type in a key word or phrase and click on the button labeled **SeekNow**. Infoseek can be used to search resources on Web pages, Usenet newsgroups, and others at no charge. Infoseek Professional includes access to other databases including wire services and business periodicals, and it's available for a monthly subscription fee. For more information about Infoseek Professional click on the hyperlink **About Infoseek** on the Infoseek home page or use the URL **http://info.infoseek.com.** Figure 6.25 shows a version of the home page for Infoseek Guide. The home page contains a search form, a list of topics much like a directory, and hyperlinks to Big Yellow—a business directory, Fast Facts—a guide to e-mail addresses, stock quotes, quotations, World News, and the Your News—a tool that lets you choose news stories by category.

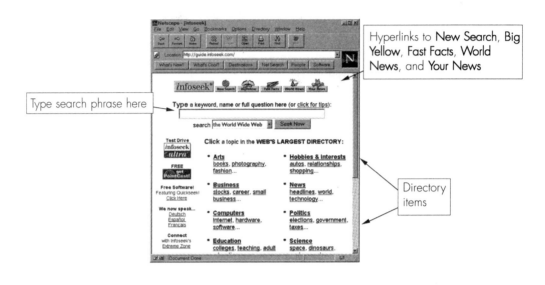

Figure 6.25   Infoseek Guide Home Page

Infoseek allows you to write search phrases that give a lot of control over what's found. You can use Boolean phrases, require that the words in the search phrase appear in a document in order or near each other, and match proper names. The rules (syntax) for writing search expressions are available by clicking on the **Help** hyperlink, and then clicking on **Quick Reference to Syntax, http://guide.infoseek.com/Help?pg=SyntaxHelp.html**. It's best to look at that Web page if you're going to use Infoseek regularly and whenever you have a question about the syntax or effective ways of searching. For example, that page tells you to use uppercase or (capital) letters when you're working with a proper name such as Earth, the planet, to keep from getting results that contain the word earth, dealing with the soil or land. Table 6.1 gives some of the rules.

To	Do	Example
Separate proper names	Type a comma between them	Robert Dole, Bill Clinton
Require that words appear next to each other	Surround them with quotes	"romantic poetry"
Require that words appear close to each other	Type a hyphen between them	alternative-health-care
Require that words appear near each other	Surround them with square brackets	[environmental hormone]

| Require that a word be included (AND) | Type a + before it | water sports +scuba |
| Exclude a word | Type a – (minus) before it | Investing –audit |

Table 6.1   Rules for Writing Search Expressions with Infoseek

Here are two other examples of using those rules:

* We want information about the NBA—National Basketball Association. We use the search phrase NBA National Basketball Association. Suppose we want to restrict the search so we see information about the NBA that includes a schedule of games. We might use the phrase **NBA+National Basketball Association+[schedule game]**.

* We want to exclude information about salaries for the players, coaches, or management. It's probably enough just to exclude the word *salary* since we don't have to be specific about whether we mean the salary for players, coaches, or management. If we've been doing these searches, we see that it's enough to include only NBA in the search phrase. So we'll use the search phrase **+NBA+[schedule game]–salary**.

When you use Infoseek, the results are listed, 10 per Web page, arranged by how relevant each is to the search phrase. The list of results includes a hyperlink to the Web page containing information that matched your search phrase and a brief excerpt form the page. Infoseek tends to work quickly and effectively.

Lycos

Types of searches:	All words (AND), any word (OR), or a number of words (2,3,..,7) in a phrase. Allows for different degrees of matching from "loose" to "strict." For details read Lycos Help Page, **http://www.lycos.com/help.html**.
Sources to search:	Database of millions of Web pages, Gopher resources, and hyperlinks. Searches titles, headings, hyperlinks, and key words.
Home page URL:	**http://www.lycos.com**

Lycos, originally developed at Carnegie Mellon University, has over 65 million Web pages indexed in its database. The Lycos robot or spider searches out and adds thousands of documents each day. A portion of the home page for Lycos is shown in Figure 6.26. The home page contains a place for you to enter a key word or phrase. It has hyperlinks to other Lycos Web pages that help you use Lycos, give information about Lycos and Lycos Inc., and add or delete URLs to the Lycos database. The Lycos home page also gives access to news stories, a directory of sites arranged by subject, Top 5% Sites—those visited most frequently, City Guide—a guide to selected US cities, links to pictures and sounds on the Web, People Find—ways to find street and e-mail addresses, Road Maps—maps of locations in the US, and Point Review, a directory that reviews and rates Web pages.

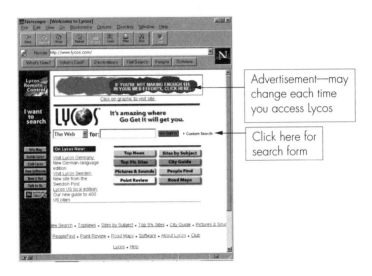

Advertisement—may change each time you access Lycos

Click here for search form

Figure 6.26   Home Page for Lycos

You get to the Web page Lycos Search Form, **http://www.lycos.com**, which lets you set options for a search by clicking on **Custom search** just to the left of the button labeled **Go Get It**, as shown in Figure 6.26. The search form is shown in Figure 6.27. Search options are set to allow a match of any word (OR), two to seven words in the search phrase, or all words (AND). The other search option lets you set the results displayed from those making a *loose* match to only showing those that make a *strong* match. The loose match option gives the most results, since it returns items with a relevance score in the range of 1.0 down to 0.1. The strong match gives results whose score is from 0.9 to 1.0, giving the most relevant resources from the database. Though loose match gives the most results to choose from, some of them (the ones with the lower scores) may not be relevant to your task. Display options can also be set from this page. You select the number of items, from 10 to 40, to be displayed per Web page. The results can be listed in summary form—hyperlinks only along with a relative score; standard form—hyperlink, score, URL, and an excerpt from the Web page pertinent to your search phrase; or detailed form—containing the information in the previous two formats along with detailed information about the Web page, including the number of links it has matched, and the URL of the Web page.

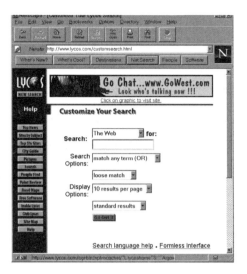

Figure 6.27   Lycos Search Form

Example 6.5 shows some of the details of using Lycos.

Example 6.5   Searching the WWW for Resources on Health Care

Health care when we're sick or injured, and taking care of ourselves when we're well is important to each of us. Alternative health care focuses on natural medicine and alternatives to currently established forms of medical practice. This example shows how to find some hyperlinks relevant to alternative health care using Lycos. You may want to do this either to satisfy your own curiosity, as a research project, or to build a collection of hyperlinks you might use regularly. After finding some resources on alternative health care, we'll also look for some information that deals with the costs of standard and alternative health care. Assuming that Netscape is already started on your computer, follow these steps to accomplish that task:

1. Go to the home page for Lycos.
2. Go to the search page for Lycos.
3. Set options to search for information related to alternative health care.
4. Modify the search to include the word **cost**.

1. Go to the home page for Lycos.

W⁴W Click on the **Open** icon. Type **http://www.lycos.com** into the dialog box. Click on the button **Open**.

The home page for Lycos is shown in Figure 6.26. We could enter search terms here and click on Search to begin searching. That's the quickest way to do a search, but it returns the most possible entries (over 15,000 when we tried). The results from this quick method match any of the words in the search phrase and the match is set to a loose match. We want to make the search more restrictive to get the more relevant items.

2. Go to the search page for Lycos.

WWW Click on **Custom Search**.

The Lycos Search Form page is shown in Figure 6.27.

3. Set options to search for information related to alternative health care.

WWW Type **alternative health care** in the second box on the page.

WWW Select Search Options to **match all terms (AND)** and choose a **good match**.

WWW Set Display Options for **10 results per page** and **standard results**.

Figure 6.28 shows the search form filled out this way.

Figure 6.28   Lycos Search Form Completed

WWW Click the button **Go Get It**.

Clicking on the button **Go Get It** gets the search under way. In a relatively short time—provided the servers at Lycos aren't too busy or your network connection isn't overloaded—you'll get a Web page with results. Figure 6.29 shows an excerpt. Since we used the **standard results** display option, for each item we have a hyperlink, an outline (if there's some text other than hyperlinks of the page), and an abstract of what's on the page.

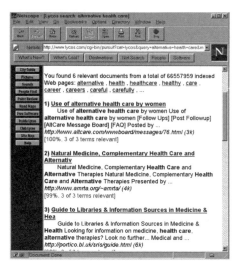

Figure 6.29   Excerpt of Search Results

Now it's time for you to explore, learn about, or analyze the search results. You can visit the sites by clicking on the hyperlinks to see what's available at the sites listed and what's available through hyperlinks at those sites. Reading the abstracts gives an indication of what's available at these sites and helps you decide which you'll visit first.

Any of these hyperlinks can be added to your bookmark list. To do that, first click on the hyperlink. Once your browser has displayed the new page, click on the pull-down menu item **Bookmarks** and then select **Add Bookmark**.

Looking at the results here we see that the phrase *complementary health care* is also used to describe our topic. You might want to include the term in the search to see if you get other relevant resources. To do that go back to the search page and modify the search string and search options to match those in Figure 6.30. We changed to **match 3 terms** to get listings of items that matched either alternative or complementary health care.

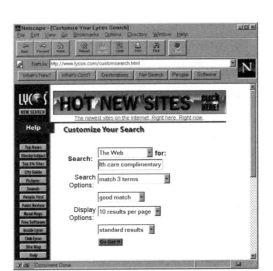

Figure 6.30   Search Options Modified to Include Complementary Health Care

W³W Click on the icon **Back**.

W³W Click on the entry in the Search box, press **End** on the keyboard, and type **complementary**.

W³W Click on the entry in **Search Options** to **match 3 terms**.

W³W Click on **Go Get It**.

Does this yield any other results? We'll leave it to you to find out. If you want to expand the search, you can also change the Search option from **good match** to **loose match**.

4. Modify the search to include the word **cost**.

Now we'll add the word **cost** to our search phrase. We're going to use the phrase **alternative health care cost** with a search option of matching any three words. Why not match all four? That might be too restrictive. It's appropriate at this point to see what we might find that matches **health care cost** or **alternative care cost**. (The order of the words in the search phrase doesn't matter.) The appropriate parts of the search request page is shown in Figure 6.31.

W³W Click on the icon **Back**.

W³W Click on the entry in the search box to modify the search phrase so it reads **alternative health care cost**.

Figure 6.31 Summary Results "alternative health care cost" Match Any Three Words

wthw Click on the entry in Search Options to **match 3 terms**.

wthw Click on the entry in Display Options to display **summary results**.

wthw Click on **Go Get It**.

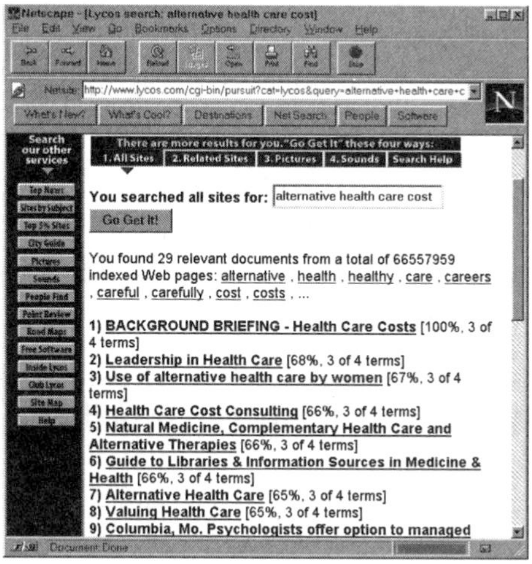

Figure 6.32 Excerpt from Results Page Using Search Phrase "alternative health care cost"

Choosing **summary results** puts only hyperlinks on the results page. This gives a quick way to identify some new links that we'd like to explore or consider. Looking at Figure 6.32, we see that 29 documents were found. The first has a rating of 100%, the highest possible. Changing the Search Option to **close** or **strong** match wouldn't give us any new Web resources; it would only limit the items shown to only the first one. You may also want to try clicking on the hyperlinks **Related Sites**, **Sounds**, or **Pictures** to get a list of hyperlinks—Web sites, sound files, images—related to the current topic.

It's up to you to determine which, if any, of these resources is appropriate for your task. Happy surfing and researching!

―――――――――――――――――End of Example 6.5―――――――――――――――――

Open Text Index

Types of searches:	Three types of searches: Simple Search—all words or any word in a phrase; Power Search—full Boolean phrases along with ways to specify order and nearness of terms; Weighted Search—gives some terms more weight or importance than others. For details, click on **Help** hyperlink or **Hints for Getting Better Results** at **http://index.opentext.net/help/help.html**.
Sources to search:	Database of resources from the WWW and resources available through Usenet, FTP, and Gopher. Words in search phrase may be matched to full text, the title, a summary, or the first URL of a document. Includes WWW pages. Details available through the OpenText FAQ (**http://index.opentext.net/main/faq.html**).
Search page URL:	**http://index.opentext.com**

Open Text is a free, full-featured search tool. It has several distinctive features. There are two types of searches—simple and power. You can view the word or words matched within the context of the document, and Open Text will automatically search for documents similar to any one listed as a result of a search. The simple search uses a single word or phrase with matches made on all or any words in the phrase. The power search lets you use Boolean expressions, selects matches based on the nearness and order of the terms in a phrase and the portion of page (title, whole page, summary) to search. It also allows for searches of current events, newsgroups (using Deja News), and e-mail addresses. We won't go through all the options and methods for searching. The Help pages that come with Open Text and the Frequently Asked Questions (FAQ) give several clear examples on using Open Text. We'll show an example that deals with refining a search or improving the results.

―――――――――――――――――――――――――――――――――――――

Example 6.6   Searching with Open Text—Hiking and Camping in Canada

Ready to search for sites on the Web that tell about hiking and camping in Canada? Canada is a great country, and it has some wonderful natural places.

We'll start the search with the key phrase **Hiking camping Canada** and request that all the words be matched. (By the way, we tried a search with **hiking and camping in Canada** and got no matches. The search engine evidently takes those requests literally and didn't find any pages that contained it exactly as it was typed.) As in the other examples, we'll assume you've started Netscape. Instead of starting with the page for simple searching using Open text, we'll start with the search form that allows for "power" searches.

1. Open the URL for the Home page for Open Text Index Web page for "power" searches.
2. Fill out the search form and submit it.
3. Improve the search.
4. Browse results.

1. Open the URL for the Open Text Index Web page for "power" searches.

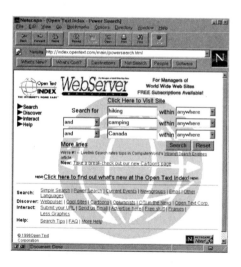 Click on the **Open** icon, type **http://index.opentext.com/main/powersearch.html** into the frame in the dialog box.

That takes you to the first home page for an Open Text power search. Figure 6.33 shows it filled out for the search we'll be doing in this example.

2. Fill out the search form and submit it.

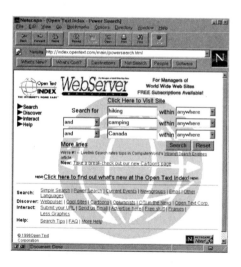 Type **hiking**, **camping**, and **Canada** in the three frames as shown in Figure 6.33.

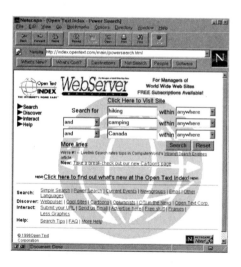 Click on the button labeled **Search**.

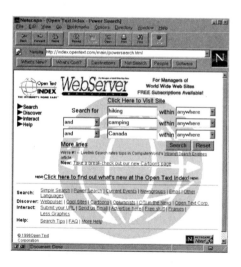

Figure 6.33   Search Form for Open Text

After you follow these two steps, the form should look like the one in Figure 6.33. If you want to get some help as you're formulating a search, click on the hyperlink **Help**. Now we're ready to start the search.

Click on the **Search** button.

3. Improve the search.

Soon after submitting the search we'll get the first page of results. An excerpt of the results page is shown in Figure 6.34. You see that Open Text found 644 pages to match the words in the search phrase. That's too many to browse easily. We'll improve the search; in other words, make the search more restricted.

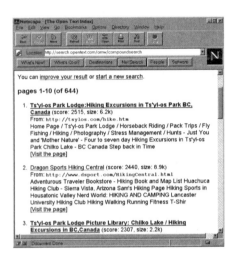

Figure 6.34   Excerpt of Search Results from Open Text

Before moving on you ought to note that for each resource found Open Text gives a URL, relative score, size, and summary. A hyperlink to an item, the hyperlink **Visit the page**, and the URL accompany each resource.

  Click on the hyperlink **improve your result**.

We're going to restrict the search by stating that the terms ought to appear near *Canada* in the text, and we're going to exclude anything that has a reference to United States in the Summary—keep it purely Canadian. Figure 6.35 shows the form to use for this search.

The terms in the pane labeled **Within:** and the one to the right of it are selected from a list of choices. You see the list by clicking on the box. You don't type them in.

Figure 6.35   Search Form for Improved Search

In the second line, select **Followed By** to replace **And**.

At the end of the third line, select **But not**.

Type **United States** into the leftmost pane on the line and select **Summary** for the pane labeled **Within:**.

Click on the **Search** button.

4. Browse results.

Submitting the search form in Figure 6.34 gives far fewer results (30 when we last tried it). This focuses the search, but some resources that would be useful may be lost. We can't always have it both ways. With lots of time, every source could be checked, but time seems to slip away on the Web. Figure 6.36 shows an excerpt from the results page.

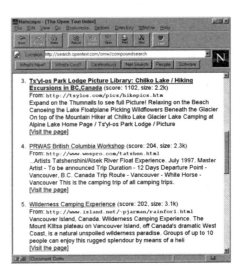

Figure 6.36   Search Results from Open Text

─────────────────End of Example 6.6─────────────────

WebCrawler

Types of searches: All words or any word in a phrase. You can limit the number of results from the search form. Help with searching is available through the hyperlink **Help, http://webcrawler.com/WebCrawler/Help/Help.html** from the home page.

Sources to Search: Database includes WWW pages. Information about WebCrawler is available by clicking on the hyperlink **Help** from the home page, and then selecting items that describe WebCrawler, its features and how it works.

Home page URL: **http://webcrawler.com**

WebCrawler was started by Brian Pinkerton as a research project at the University of Washington. It has since been moved to America Online. WebCrawler is free to anyone on the Internet, it works quickly, and it gives useful results. It also contains a good description of how it and other search engines work as well as useful information about using the WWW and the Internet. Click on the hyperlink **Help, http://webcrawler.com/WebCrawler/Help/Help.html,** to start looking through this information. WebCrawler is good to use for quick results, and it does allow for Boolean phrases using AND, OR, and NOT, as well as ADJ (to search where terms are adjacent or next to each other) and other ways of specifying search terms.

Suppose we wanted to use WebCrawler to search for information on scuba diving. We'd go to the home page and then fill in the search form as shown in Figure 6.37.

Figure 6.37   Search Form Using "Scuba Diving" with WebCrawler

Then click on **Search** and see the results. An excerpt of some results is shown in Figure 6.38. They're all hyperlinks that can be explored by clicking on them with a mouse.

Figure 6.38   Search Results Using "Scuba Diving" with WebCrawler

General Search Lists. You've seen there are several different search engines in use on the WWW. We've shown the strengths and differences of some search engines, but new ones are bound to be created. One way to keep up with what's going on with search tools on the WWW is to look at some of the Web pages dedicated to listing and working with several search engines. The ones listed here also let you choose a search engine to use.

* All-in-One Search Page, **http://www.albany.net/allinone/**

  This service lists several different categories of resources for searching including Word Wide Web, General Internet, People, Technical Reports, and several others. After selecting a category, you submit your request to any of the listed search tools. The search form is a simple frame allowing for a phrase for each tool, so there's an easy-to-use interface. This service was developed and is supported by William D. Cross.

* CUSI, **http://pubweb.nexor.co.uk/public/cusi/doc/list.html**
CUSI is an acronym for Configurable Unified Search Index. The idea behind CUSI is to give a uniform interface to a variety of search engines. The user specifies the search phrase and then selects a search engine or tool to use. The URL above is the home base for these types of services; no searching is done at that Web page. All the CUSI sites throughout the world are listed as hyperlinks. Click on one near you, fill in the search form, and select a search engine or tool. You might also want to add the hyperlink to your bookmark list. The CUSI project was started by Martijn Koster in 1993 at Nexor in the U.K.

* Internet Sleuth, **http://www.isleuth.com**
Internet Sleuth lists several general-purpose search engines, and also gives a directory to search tools for specific categories. Selecting **Employment**, for example, brings up a page with listings of several job banks available on the WWW and also gives search forms so they can be searched. The Internet Sleuth is a service offered through the Internet Business Connection, **http://www.intbc.com**.

* Savvy Search, **http://www.cs.colostate.edu/~dreiling/smartform.html**
Savvy Search takes your search phrase and submits it to several WWW search engines. It gives a simple, quick interface to several search tools concurrently. Savvy Search was developed by Daniel Dreilinger at Colorado State University.

Summary

With all the information available on the Internet and the World Wide Web (over 10 million Web pages), it's difficult to find what you want, unless the information is organized or you use a tool to search for it. Fortunately for all of us, there are people who collect, classify, and organize hyperlinks and put them into directories, and there are also people who have created tools (programs) for searching the WWW.

The hyperlinks in the directories are usually arranged by categories and the categories are in alphabetical order, like an encyclopedia or phone directory. Some categories you'd likely find in a directory are News, Health, Recreation, or Science. You start by selecting one of these general topics by clicking on its name. Then another Web page appears that has listings related to the topic. The listings are either hyperlinks to specific resources or a hyperlink to another page of listings in the directory. For example, to get information on hiking the Appalachian Trail, you may have to first choose Recreation, then Outdoors, then Hiking, then Trails, and finally Appalachian Trail. Some directories include services to help you find appropriate information. Some have ways to search the directory. You type in a word or phrase to describe what you're looking for, and you get back a list of hyperlinks to relevant directory entries. Being able to search the directory makes it easier to find what you want. Some directories include a description and rating of each item. You can read about what you're likely to find at a site before following the hyperlink. The chapter contains the URL for several directories. Clicking on the button **Net Directory** takes you to several of these, so they're easy to get to from Netscape Navigator.

The search tools, called search engines, examine Web pages throughout the Internet and then create databases or indexes based on the URLs of the pages, the titles of the pages, and the pages' contents. When you want to find something using these search engines, you type in a word or phrase, set some options, and then click on a button to start the search. The program brings back a list of results in order according to how relevant they are to the word or phrase you gave. Part of what the search engine does is to find items in its database that match your request and then to determine, by various algorithms, whether your word or phrase plays an important part in the item. A document whose title is "Scuba Diving" and lists several hyperlinks to information about scuba diving, or one whose text describes scuba diving in Boynton Beach, Florida (**http://www.flinet.com/gulfstream/scuba.html**), would be considered more relevant than one that contains the phrase scuba diving once or twice in a list of activities available at a resort.

The search engines described allow you several options. In most cases you can specify the number of results per Web page, how detailed the results list will be, and how to work with a phrase you give. The search engines will match either all the words in a phrase or any of the words in the phrase. Other terms for this are AND when all words are matched and OR when any words are matched. The phrase "hiking camping Canada" when all of the words have to be matched, for example, will give results that contain the words hiking and camping and Canada. Using the same phrase when any of the words can be matched will bring back results where one, two, or three of the words are present, pages that contain hiking or camping or Canada. Some search engines let users use the words or symbols for *and*, *or*, or *not* to form what are called Boolean phrases. If you want to exclude items that contain the term Alaska from the results but include information about hiking or about camping in Canada, you'd use a phrase like **hiking and Canada or camping and Canada not Alaska**. The exact form or syntax for expressions like this may be different from one search tool to another.

Several of the search engines described in this chapter are accessible from the Web page you'll see when you click on the **Net Search** button from Netscape. There are also several Web pages that contain links and/or an easy interface to several different search tools.

Directories are good to use for browsing or for looking for items that you can define easily—like scuba diving, which you'd expect to find under a category such as Recreation or Sports. Using a search engine sometimes lets you cover more categories than a directory and it's also good to use when you're not sure of the category to hold the items you're searching for. Using a search tool also gives you the opportunity to describe what you're looking for with a plain or Boolean phrase. The directories and search engines you use will depend on what suits you and your tasks the best.

Exercises

This set of exercises deals with using directories. For these exercises use directories; please, no search tools.

1. Using the directories Yahoo, Whole Internet Catalog Select, or Internet Services List, find two hyperlinks or URLs for each of the following topics:
    Photography
    Amusement parks
    Genealogy
    Hang gliding
    Recipes

2. Using the directories Inter-Links, the World Wide Web Virtual Library, or Tradewave Galaxy, find two hyperlinks or URLs for each of the following topics:
    Feminism
    Shareware
    Science Museum
    Nonprofit organizations on the Internet
    Places where you can get a local weather report
    Software related to Windows 95

3. Using a directory you haven't used for the previous exercises, find a hyperlink to the Internet Movie Database.

4. Using a directory (your choice), find a Web page or pages that tell what the major broadcast and cable networks will be showing on TV tomorrow in your locality. Follow the hyperlink and see if you can get a printout of the TV listings for tomorrow.

5. Using any directories, but no search tools, find at least one Web page that has links to software you can download and evaluate before buying (shareware) on each of these topics Windows 95, Internet, and World Wide Web.

6. Using any directories, find at least three resources for each of these topics.
    Migration
    Cryptography or encryption
    Dictionaries
    Historic documents, specifically the Magna Carta
    Symbolic mathematical computations

7. After using several directories, pick two you liked using and explain why. Pick one you didn't like using and explain why.

For these exercises use search engines, not directories please.

8. For each of the topics below and using two search engines, list the three top items from the results.
Compact disc
Comic books to trade
Women's studies
Personality analysis, but not stress analysis
International trade agreements
Economic impact of deforestation of tropical rain forests

9. Use search tools to answer each of the following:
   a. Who is Douglas Engelbart?
   b. What else can you discover about Theodore Holm Nelson, other than that he was often called Ted and is involved in a project named Xanadu?
   c. Who are Naguib Mahfouz and Kenzaburo Oe? What do they have in common?
   d. Who are Judy Kay, Karen Sparck Jones, and Ingrid Zuckerman, and what do they have in common?

10. Find a definition or explanation of each of the following and print out an image of each.
Hertzsprung-Russell diagram
Periodic table of the elements
Mass spectrograph
Chromatic tuner
Julia and Mandelbrot sets

11. Using two of the search engines described in this chapter, search for resources related to each of the following. In each case, write down the top three results returned by each search engine. How many were the same?
Hiking and camping in Europe
Outdoor or indoor recreation, but not sports
Investing in oil futures
Places to buy CDs (music)
Places to buy CDs for computers

12. a. You have been assigned to write a paper on the ways political parties are using the Internet for organizing and the ways they're using it for campaigning. What are some sources of information on these topics on the World Wide Web?
   b. You're going to write an article about the ways volunteer and nonprofit organizations have been using the Internet. List five of the best resources on the Web for this project. Find sources on the Web that deal with social responsibility: helping others, making positive contributions to society.

13. After using search engines, pick two you liked using and explain why. Pick one you didn't like using and explain why.

14. Using directories, search engines, or both come up with a list of 10 relevant hyperlinks on any of the following topics:
    Favorite entertainment sites
    Getting started on a career
    Glossaries
    Government information
    History of the Internet
    Shareware for your computer

Writing Your Own Web Pages

In this chapter we'll talk about the basics of creating Web pages. You've seen lots of different Web pages as you've been browsing and searching the World Wide Web, and you may have been curious about how they're made. You'll see that it's a straightforward process to design and put together a basic Web page. A Web page is fundamentally an ordinary text or ASCII file, so special tools or programs aren't necessary. We'll go over the material you need to get started and also discuss proper style, how to get your pages on the Web, how to publicize your pages, and resources that can help you do more.

What turns an ordinary text file into a Web page? Two things: a Web browser and instructions or tags written in HTML (HyperText Markup Language). To better understand this, let's review the way your browser works with Web pages. The Web browser is a client program that sends requests to a server program. Whether you click on a hyperlink or type in a URL (open a location), your browser, the client, sends a request to a computer that's running the server program. The request is in the form of a URL. The server sends back a file to your computer, which passes it on to the browser. That file contains text, links to images, and hyperlinks. The format of the text on the page, the images you see on a page, and the hyperlinks are specified using HTML. The browser interprets the HTML and displays the page. If the HTML says to display a word or phrase in the file in bold font, for example, the browser does it. If the HTML tags say to display an image (and the image can be anywhere on the Web), the browser takes care of that as well. If the tag says that what follows is a hyperlink to some other page, the browser displays the text as a hyperlink and associates it with the specified URL. Links on a page can be to other pages or other types of files, such as sound or video files, images, and even some interactive programs. Even if the Web page is a local file, a file on your computer, it has the same format and it's interpreted by the browser in the same way as a Web page anywhere on the Internet.

To summarize: *Web pages are text or ASCII files in which HTML (HyperText Markup Language) is used to specify the format of the Web page, images to be displayed, hyperlinks, and possibly other elements. A Web browser interprets the HTML in the file and then displays the Web page.*

Since Web pages are text files we don't necessarily need any special tools or editors to create them. You'll find it's easier to create more complicated Web pages using editors designed for that purpose, but you can get along with any word processor or editor that can create text files, ones whose names end with **.txt**. (If you're using Microsoft Windows, then Notepad, available through Applications, is sufficient.) You'll also find that you can see the way HTML is used to put together any Web page by first selecting **View** from the Menu Bar and then choosing **Document Source**.

Now let's go on to the details. We'll include figures and examples, and create some Web pages as we go along. The Web pages will be saved in local files and viewed with the Web browser. We'll cover the following topics:

* Description of a Web Page
* Viewing the Source Version of a Web Page
* Introduction to HTML
* Tools to Help Create Web Pages
* Style Guides—How to Do It Right, How to Do It for Impact, and How to Make It Portable
* Putting Your Information on the WWW
* Resources for More Information about Creating Web Pages

Description of a Web Page

A Web page is a text file that contains HTML codes or tags. A text file is a file that contains plain printable characters. The HTML tags give the browser information about how to display or represent information in the file. The text file is also called the *source* for the Web page. You saw an excerpt of the source for a Web page in Figure 2.22 of Chapter 2.

The name of the source file has to end with the extension **.htm** or **.html**. Some examples are **resources.htm**, **mvtool12.htm**, **index.html**, and **weather.html**. If the name doesn't have that form, any HTML tags are ignored. It is possible for a Web page to contain no HTML tags; in that case, the text is displayed in plain form and there's no title on the Web page.

Figures 7.1 and 7.2 show the source for a Web page and the Web page as it's displayed by the browser. Several items have been labeled so you can see the relationship between the HTML tags and what's displayed by the browser. You can learn a few things about using HTML from looking at the source (Figure 7.1) and how it's displayed by the browser (Figure 7.2). Here are a few things to notice:

* The HTML tags are contained in angle brackets < >; for example, <**TITLE**> and <**IMG SRC="file:///C|/ inetbk/cover.gif"**>.
* Many HTML tags come in pairs. The matching tag uses a slash (/), such as <I> and </I> or <H1> and </H1>. The first example tells the browser to start (<I>) and stop (</I>) displaying the text between them in italic font.
* To write comments or notes in a document that don't show up in the window, surround the comments with <!-- and -->.

❋ Looking at the page displayed by the browser, you can see that carriage returns and spaces are generally ignored by the browser. You can use the HTML tag <P> to indicate the start of a new paragraph.

❋ <A HREF="URL"> ... text ... </A> is an HTML tag for a hyperlink. Any URL may be used between the quotation marks.

❋ <IMG SRC="file name"> is an HTML tag for an image. Put the name of the file or a hyperlink to a file containing the image between the quotation marks.

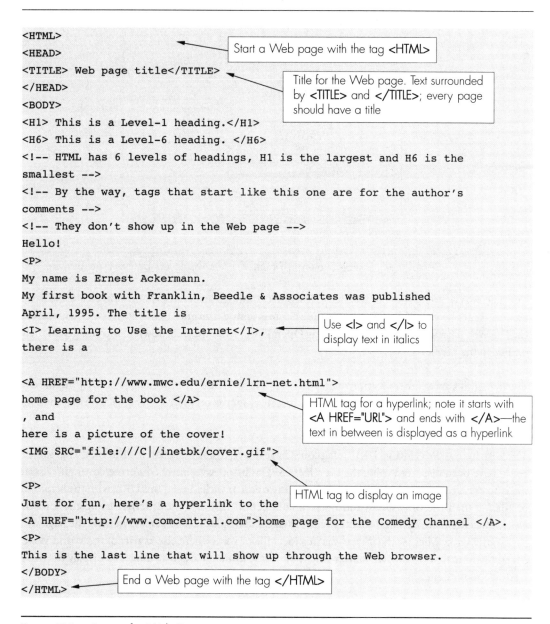

```
<HTML>
<HEAD>
<TITLE> Web page title</TITLE>
</HEAD>
<BODY>
<H1> This is a Level-1 heading.</H1>
<H6> This is a Level-6 heading. </H6>
<!-- HTML has 6 levels of headings, H1 is the largest and H6 is the
smallest -->
<!-- By the way, tags that start like this one are for the author's
comments -->
<!-- They don't show up in the Web page -->
Hello!
<P>
My name is Ernest Ackermann.
My first book with Franklin, Beedle & Associates was published
April, 1995. The title is
<I> Learning to Use the Internet</I>,
there is a


<A HREF="http://www.mwc.edu/ernie/lrn-net.html">
home page for the book </A>
, and
here is a picture of the cover!
<IMG SRC="file:///C|/inetbk/cover.gif">


<P>
Just for fun, here's a hyperlink to the
<A HREF="http://www.comcentral.com">home page for the Comedy Channel </A>.
<P>
This is the last line that will show up through the Web browser.
</BODY>
</HTML>
```

Callouts in the figure:

- Start a Web page with the tag <HTML>
- Title for the Web page. Text surrounded by <TITLE> and </TITLE>; every page should have a title
- Use <I> and </I> to display text in italics
- HTML tag for a hyperlink; note it starts with <A HREF="URL"> and ends with </A>—the text in between is displayed as a hyperlink
- HTML tag to display an image
- End a Web page with the tag </HTML>

Figure 7.1   Source for Web Page

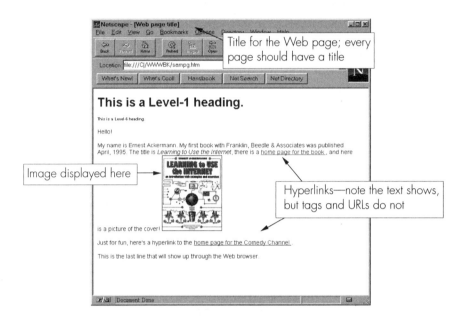

Figure 7.2   Web Page, Source Shown in Figure 7.1, as Displayed by the Web Browser

The page was written using the accessory Notebook, although any editor that would create and save a text file could have been used. In this case the file's name is **sampg.htm** and it's in the directory **wwwbk** on drive C:. The Web page was displayed by selecting **Open File ...** from the pull-down menu you get after clicking on **File** in the Menu Bar.

The hyperlinks are at other location on the Internet. The URL used for the image **file:///C|/inetbk/cover.gif** means that it's in a file named **cover.gif** in the directory **inetbk** on drive C:. The URL format for a file uses the vertical bar | after C, C|, to represent C:.

The URL in the <**IMG SRC="URL"**> tag could have linked to any image on the Internet. That same image could have been displayed using the tag <**IMG SRC="http://www.mwc.edu/ernie/cover.gif"**>, since the file is accessible through the Web server at **www.mwc.edu**. If we had used this URL, with the **http://** instead of **file:///**, then the browser would make a connection through the Internet using the URL **http://www.mwc.edu/ernie/cover.gif** to retrieve the image and display it. The person viewing the page wouldn't necessarily know whether the image was in a local file or somewhere else as part of the World Wide Web. The only thing that would give it away might be that it would take a little longer to display the image if it were at a remote site.

Figures 7.1 and 7.2 give you a basic idea of what a Web page contains, what HTML tags look like, and how HTML tags can be used. Regardless of how advanced or complex a Web page can be, remember that it contains the text you see on a page, HTML tags, and other items called elements. The elements can be images, links to audio files, links to files on your computer, links to other parts of the document, hyperlinks to other portions of the Web, or interactive programs, scripts, and inline plug-ins.

Viewing the Source Version of a Web Page

You can view the source version of any Web page. This lets you see the HTML used to create the page. It is also a straightforward process. Click on **View** from the Menu Bar and then choose **Document Source**. Figure 7.3 shows what you'd see if you chose to view the source of the Web page shown in Figure 7.2.

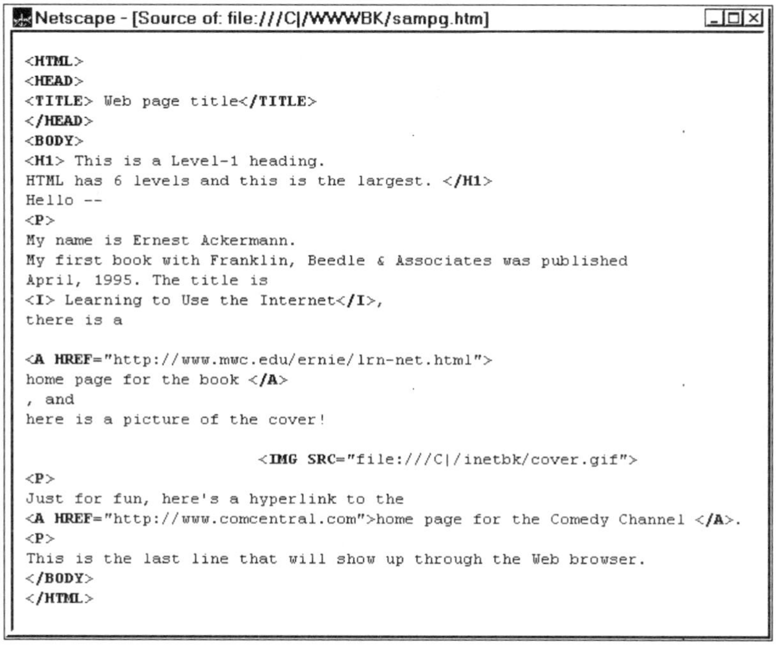

```
Netscape - [Source of: file:///C|/WWWBK/sampg.htm]                    _ □ ×

<HTML>
<HEAD>
<TITLE> Web page title</TITLE>
</HEAD>
<BODY>
<H1> This is a Level-1 heading.
HTML has 6 levels and this is the largest. </H1>
Hello --
<P>
My name is Ernest Ackermann.
My first book with Franklin, Beedle & Associates was published
April, 1995. The title is
<I> Learning to Use the Internet</I>,
there is a

<A HREF="http://www.mwc.edu/ernie/lrn-net.html">
home page for the book </A>
, and
here is a picture of the cover!

                        <IMG SRC="file:///C|/inetbk/cover.gif">
<P>
Just for fun, here's a hyperlink to the
<A HREF="http://www.comcentral.com">home page for the Comedy Channel </A>.
<P>
This is the last line that will show up through the Web browser.
</BODY>
</HTML>
```

Figure 7.3   View Document Source Window for the Web Page in Figure 7.2

Figure 7.3 shows the same text as Figure 7.1, but in a different format. Viewing the document source with Netscape shows the HTML tags and URLs in a different font and color, making them easy to pick out.

Viewing the source is a good way to see how a Web page is constructed and to learn from the work of others. It's not intended to be used for copying someone else's work. A Web page belongs to the author just like anything else, like a book or tape that someone has created and developed. If you see something you like, view the source, study how it was done, and then adapt the techniques you see to your own work.

Introduction to HTML

Web pages are written using HTML (HyperText Markup Language). HTML consists of a collection of instructions, called tags, that the Web browser interprets to display a Web page. The commands or instructions are written in HTML, but the effect isn't seen until a Web browser or some program interprets the HTML. For example, the tags <B> and </B> placed around text indicate that the enclosed text is to be displayed in bold format. So if

```
Be sure to follow the <B>Yellow Brick Road</B> to get to Oz.
```

were part of a Web page, it would be displayed as

> Be sure to follow the **Yellow Brick Road** to get to Oz.

Other examples of HTML are shown in the previous two sections of this chapter.

The commands and the way browsers interpret HTML have more to do with the organization of a document rather than with its format. A number of commands can control the way text is displayed but HTML emphasizes the hypermedia aspects of the World Wide Web—extra spaces, tabs, and line length, for example, are generally ignored by HTML; the text is made to fit within the size of the browser's window.

HTML does contain the commands or tags to create links from one part of a Web page to another part of the same page and to create hyperlinks to other Web pages or resources on the Internet. In other words, these links are embedded into or become part of the Web page. URLs are used to create the hyperlinks. The same process of embedding hyperlinks in a document is used to embed images. The text, images, and hyperlinks are called *elements* of a Web page.

Web pages are stored in plain text files; they contain ordinary printable characters. A number of tools and Web page editors to help create and write Web pages are listed in the Yahoo directory section "Computers and Internet:Internet:World Wide Web:HTML Editors" (**http://www.yahoo.com/Computers_and_Internet/ Internet/World_Wide_Web/HTML_Editors/**). These can be useful, but they're not necessary. The pages can be written using any word processor or editor that can save information as a text file. When the file is saved it ought to be put into a file whose name ends with **.htm** or **.html**.

We'll write the HTML and Web page using a simple text editor, save the file as a text file, and then view it with the Netscape Web browser. This way we'll be able to concentrate on the basics. You'll find HTML is not difficult. Organizing a body of material and developing an effective design are the harder tasks. We'll give some pointers about style and list some resources to style guides on the Web in a following section.

In this section we'll concentrate on the HTML commands to do basic formatting, create lists, include hyperlinks to other Web pages and resources, and include images in Web pages. After you understand the basics and have some confidence, you'll be ready to go forward on your own.

Some aspects of HTML not covered here include Web page elements such as tables, image maps, forms, Java scripts and programs, or inline plug-ins. They're best covered in a book that deals primarily with HTML. When you're ready to use them, consult some of the Web guides to HTML listed on pages 252.

General Form of HTML Tags

Almost all HTML tags begin with the character < (right angle bracket) and end with the character > (left angle bracket). The exceptions are the tags that represent special individual characters, such as the right or left angle bracket. Some of the tags come in pairs; they surround or enclose text. The second tag is like the first except that there's a slash / after the <. The text between is treated some special way. For example, the text between the tags <I> and </I> is displayed in italic font. You can see this in Figures 7.1 and 7.2. Some tags occur singly and cause an action. In Figures 7.1 and 7.2 we see that <P>, which causes a new paragraph to start, acts that way. We've written the tags in uppercase, but HTML ignores the case of the letters in a tag. Remember, though, that in a URL, it's very important to use the proper case for names of files.

To summarize: *Most HTML tags are enclosed between < and >. Some tags occur in pairs. The second is like the first except a slash is used after the < to indicate it's the matching tag; for example, <I> and </I>. Other tags occur as single entities, such as <P>. Tags can be written using upper- or lowercase letters; HTML ignores the case of letters in a tag. In URLs you have to pay strict attention to the case of the letters.*

Structure of a Web Page—Head and Body

Each Web page ought to start with the tag <HTML> and end with </HTML>. Between those tags, a Web page has two distinct parts: the head or heading, which gives some information about the Web page, and the body, which contains the elements or content of the Web page. The title of the Web page, for example, goes in the heading section. The other information that may be put in the heading section concerns issues that are more advanced than we're dealing with here. Use the tags <HEAD> and </HEAD> to denote the heading of the Web page, and use <BODY> and </BODY> to mark off the body of the page. The items in the heading section aren't normally displayed as part of the Web page. Figures 7.1 and 7.3 show the proper use of the tags to declare the document as being written in HTML and to denote the heading and body sections. Figure 7.4 gives a brief outline.

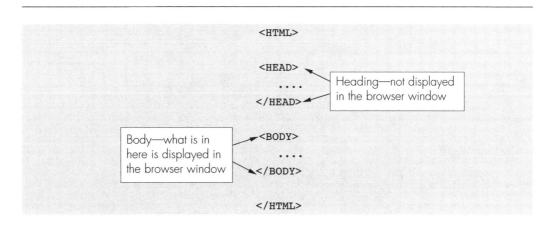

Figure 7.4   Outline of Head and Body Sections of a Web Page

Title

Every Web page needs a title. The title doesn't appear as part of the Web page, but it is visible at the very top of the Netscape Navigator window, as shown in Figure 7.2. It's important to give a page an appropriate title, because the title is the name that appears in a bookmark list, the title is the name that appears when someone uses a search engine to find the page, and the title is significant when a searching program looks for pages that are relevant to a search word or phrase. The title is put between the tags <TITLE> and </TITLE>, in the heading section of a Web page, as shown in Figure 7.1.

Author's Comments

The author of a Web page can include comments that are part of the source for the page but aren't displayed when the browser is displaying the page. Comments are useful as notes about how the page was constructed or what might need to be changed in the future. Comments serve as reminders not only to the person writing the page but also to anyone who might have to modify the page. Professional computer programmers learn early in their training that they need to include comments as part of computer program so the next person who has to perform some maintenance on the program can understand the purpose and methods of the program. The same holds true for Web pages. Comments need to be surrounded by <! -- and -->, as shown in Figures 7.1 and 7.3.

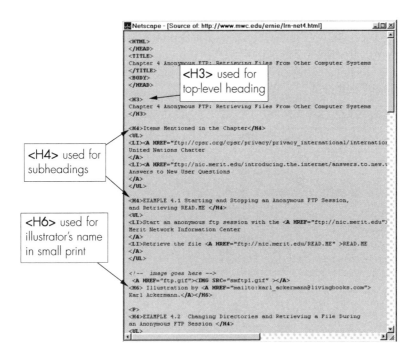

Figure 7.5   Source for Web Page in Figure 7.6

Headings

Web pages can be given a rigid structure. You can start with a top-level heading and then have several levels of subheadings. One rule used for constructing a Web page is to restate the title at the top of the body section as a level-1 heading using the tags <H1> and </H1>, then give a second-level heading using <H2> and </H2>, then a third-level heading, and so on. There are six levels of headings using the tags <H1>, <H2>,<H3>, and on through <H6>. The different levels of headings also control the size of the characters displayed. In Figure 7.2 we used <H1> and <H6>, and you can see the difference in Figure 7.2. Figure 7.5 shows a portion of the source for the Web page shown in Figure 7.6. Here the title was restated as a level-3 heading, <H4> was used for the subheadings, and <H6> was for the small lettering for the name of the illustrator.

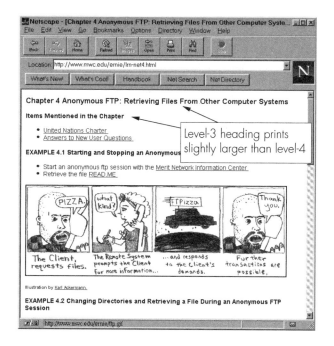

Figure 7.6   Web Page with Source in Figure 7.5

Paragraphs, Line Breaks, Shadow Lines

Blank spaces on a line and blank lines in a source document don't show up when an HTML document is displayed by a Web browser; they're ignored. The source documents in Figures 7.1 and 7.5 contain blank spaces and lines that don't appear in the Web pages as shown in Figures 7.2 and 7.6. The advantage to this is that lines are adjusted or formatted by the browser so they fit nicely within the window. There's also a disadvantage: You need to use an HTML tag to specifically mark the beginning of a paragraph or the end of a line.

Use <P> to mark the beginning of a paragraph. When the browser interprets this tag, a blank line is displayed, and the text following the <P> is displayed starting on a new line. <P> has been used in all the examples shown above. Another way to think about this is that <P> is used to separate paragraphs.

Use <BR> to separate lines. The text following the tag <BR> is placed at the beginning of the next line.

The tag <HR> puts a line, called a shadow line, on the Web page. Like <BR>, it can be used to separate lines. Often it's used to separate sections of a Web page. The length of the shadow line is automatically adjusted so it's always the width of the window.

Figures 7.7 and 7.8 show the document source and the browser view of a Web page that uses <BR>, <P>, and <HR>. These tags can be placed anywhere on a line or between lines. Neither of the tags has a matching tag.

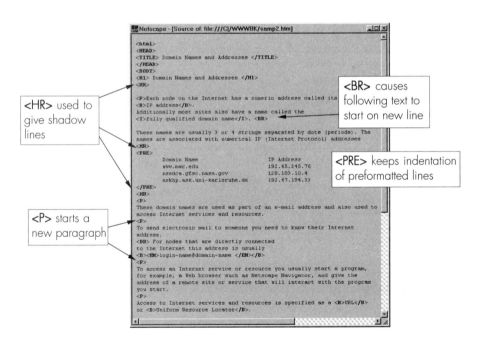

Figure 7.7   Source for Web Page Using <B>, <P>, and <HR>

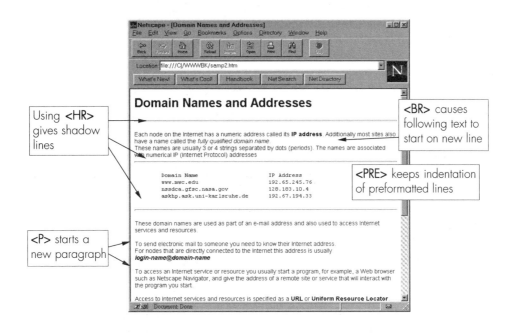

Figure 7.8   Web Page of Source in Figure 7.7

Character Formatting—Italic, Bold, Emphasized

HTML tags can be used to display parts of the text in bold or italic font. To display text in bold font surround it with the tags <B> and </B>. To display text in italic font use the tags <I> and </I>. Both of these are used in the source document shown in Figure 7.7. The tags <EM> and </EM> are also used to display text in italic font. The portion of the source in Figure 7.7,

<B><EM>login-name@domain-name</EM></B>

displays the enclosed text in bold and italic font.

Why use <EM> and <I> for italic font? Some browsers don't display text in italic font, and some people think it's better to use the tag <EM> to let the browser determine how the text will be displayed. <EM> means *emphasize* to a browser and many browsers will display the text in italics. If a browser can't display text in italic font, it will use some other font to emphasize the text. There are other tags that behave this way; <STRONG> and <B> can usually be used in place of each other.

Preformatted Text

Blank spaces on a line (except for the one necessary for proper punctuation) and blank lines are ignored when an HTML source document is displayed as a Web page. That way the text can be automatically adjusted by the browser so it looks good in different size windows. Sometimes, though, you want to have certain spacing or indenting. Use the HTML tag <PRE> to tell the browser not to automatically rearrange or format the text. Putting <PRE> and </PRE> around text indicates that it's preformatted, and the browser shouldn't change the way it's to be displayed. Text within the tags is displayed in fixed-width font, usually courier, and looks different from other text displayed by the browser. Figure 7.7 shows the use of the tags <PRE> and </PRE>, and Figure 7.8 shows how Netscape displays the text.

Quoted Text

Use the HTML tags <BLOCKQUOTE> and </BLOCKQUOTE> to display quoted text in the Web browser. Figure 7.9 shows a portion of a source document for the Web page shown in Figure 7.10.

```
Civil disobedience is certainly not a new notion, and there's a long
tradition of times when history has shown it to be necessary and reasonable.
The authors of the <I>Declaration of Independence</I> stated conditions
under which they felt civil disobedience is justified.
<BLOCKQUOTE>

"Prudence, indeed, will dictate that Governments long established
should not be changed for light and transient causes; and
accordingly all experience hath shown that mankind are more
disposed to suffer, while evils are sufferable than to right themselves
by abolishing the forms to which they are accustomed. But when a
long train of abuses and usurpations, pursuing invariably the same
object, evinces a design to reduce them under absolute Despotism,
it is their right, it is their duty, to throw off such Government, and to
provide new Guards for their future security."
 - Declaration of Independence
</BLOCKQUOTE>

References to other sources justifying civil disobedience are given
at the end of this chapter.
```

Figure 7.9 Source Code Showing Use of <BLOCKQUOTE> and </BLOCKQUOTE>

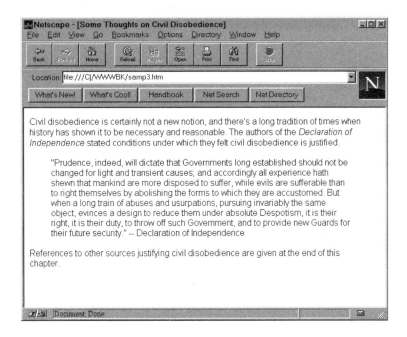

Figure 7.10 Web Page Showing Effect of <BLOCKQUOTE> and </BLOCKQUOTE>

Special Characters

Here's a question for you. If a Web browser interprets the character < as the beginning of a HTML tag, then how can we display < on a Web page? Turns out HTML has ways of representing that and other special characters. Use

&lt;	to represent	<
&gt;	to represent	>
&amp;	to represent	&
&quot;	to represent	"

There are lots of other of special characters that can be represented with HTML. These are part of standards for sets of codes which are set by the International Standards Organization (ISO). Two references for a complete list of ways to represent special characters in HTML are "Martin Ramsch - iso8859-1 table" (http://www.uni-passau.de/~ramsch/iso8859-1.html) and "ISO8859-1/HTML Stuff" (http://ppewww.ph.gla.ac.uk/~flavell/iso8859/).

Lists

HTML has the tags for several different types of lists—a sequence of items, each of which is on its own line. Additionally, the lists can be nested so one type of list is inside another. The types of lists supported by HTML are:

* Ordered (numbered) lists
* Unordered lists
* Descriptive lists

Hey! We just used an unordered list to show the types of lists you can represent with HTML.

Ordered or Numbered Lists. Ordered lists are lists in which each item is numbered. You don't do the numbering, the Web browser does. The first item on the list is numbered **1**. If you change the list and add items, the browser takes care of renumbering them. It's no surprise that these lists are also called numbered lists.

The rules for using HTML to construct ordered lists are:

1. An ordered list starts with the tag <OL> and ends with the tag </OL>.
2. Each item in the list starts with <LI>.

Figure 7.11 shows a simple example of using these rules, and Figure 7.12 shows how it would be displayed.

```
What is the Internet?
We'll look at it from these points of view.
<OL>
<LI> From a social point of view.
<LI> From a practical point of view emphasizing resources.
<LI> From a technical point of view.
</OL>
```

Figure 7.11 Example of Using HTML to Produce an Ordered List

Figure 7.12 Ordered List on Web Page

Unordered Lists (Bulleted Lists). Each item in an unordered list is marked with a dot called a "bullet." The term *unordered* means the items aren't numbered, but they do appear in the order given in the source document. These lists also go by the names *unnumbered* lists or *bulleted* lists.

The rules for using HTML to construct unordered lists are:
1. An unordered list starts with the tag <UL> and ends with the tag </UL>.
2. Each item in the list starts with <LI>.

Figure 7.13 shows a simple example of using these rules, and Figure 7.14 shows how it would be displayed.

```
This is an example of an <B>unordered list</B>.
<P>
What is the Internet?
We'll look at it from these points of view.
<UL>
<LI> From a social point of view.
<LI> From a practical point of view emphasizing resources.
<LI>From a technical point of view.
</UL>
```

Figure 7.13 Example of Using HTML to Produce an Unordered List

Figure 7.14 Unordered List on Web Page

Descriptive Lists (Indenting). Each item in a descriptive list has a title and then an indented description of the title. The items aren't marked with numbers or dots (bullets) as are ordered or unordered lists. These lists also go by the names unnumbered lists or bulleted lists.

The rules for using HTML to construct descriptive lists are:
1. A descriptive list starts with the tag <DL> and ends with the tag </DL>.
2. The descriptive title for each item starts with the tag <DT>.
3. The indented description for a title is marked with <DD>.

Take a look at Figures 7.15 and 7.16 to see an example of a descriptive list.

```
This is an example of a <B>descriptive list</B>.
<P>
What is the Internet?
We'll look at it from these points of view.
<DL>
<DT> From a social point of view.
<DD> Consider the Internet in terms of individuals and groups of users.
We'll focus on using the Internet for communication
and the virtual communities that have arisen in recent times.
<DT> From a practical point of view emphasizing resources.
<DD>Consider the Internet as a vast storehouse of information. We'll
also stress the fact that the information isn't only "on the shelf", but
that there are lots of people to answer questions and give support.
<DT>From a technical point of view.
<DD> Here's where we give an introduction to some of the technical
details and issues. We'll look at the Internet as a network of
networks, explain how the networks can communicate, and cover some
details about connecting to the Internet.
</DL>
```

Figure 7.15 Example of Using HTML to Produce a Descriptive List

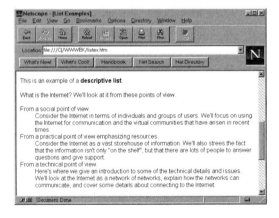

Figure 7.16 Web Page Using a Descriptive List

You can also use descriptive lists to write bibliographies in HTML. Figure 7.17 shows the source code for the bibliography shown in Figure 7.18.

```
<H3>Bibliography</H3>

<DL>
<DT>Ackermann, Ernest C. (1995).
<DD><I>Learning to Use the Internet</I>,
Wilsonville, OR: Franklin, Beedle &amp; Associates.

<DT> Comer,Douglas
<DD><I>The Internet Book: Everything You Need to
Know about Computer Networking and
How the Internet Works</I>,
Englewood Cliffs NJ: Prentice-Hall

<DT>Groves, Dawn(1995).
<DD><I>The Web Page Workbook</I>,
Wilsonville, OR: Franklin, Beedle &amp; Associates.

<DT>Liu, C., Peek, J., Jones, R., Buus, B, and Nye, A. (1994)
<DD><I> Managing Internet Information Services:
World Wide Web, Gopher, FTP, and More</I>,
Sebastopol, CA: O'Reilly &amp; Associates
```

Figure 7.17 Source HTML for Bibliography

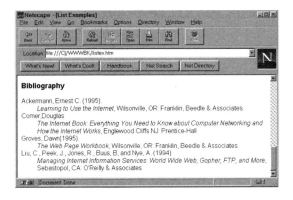

Figure 7.18 Web Page Bibliography

Nested Lists. Any of the types of lists mentioned can be nested; that is, one put inside another. You'll notice that the symbol used to mark items in unordered lists changes shape when these lists are nested. Here's an example taken from the home page (URL **http://www.mwc.edu/ernie/lrn-net.html**) for *Learning to Use the Internet*, listed in the bibliography above. Figure 7.19 shows the source and Figure 7.20 the portion of the Web page shown in the source. The part shown here has one ordered (numbered) list with several unordered lists nested inside it. We've marked the first nested list in Figure 7.19.

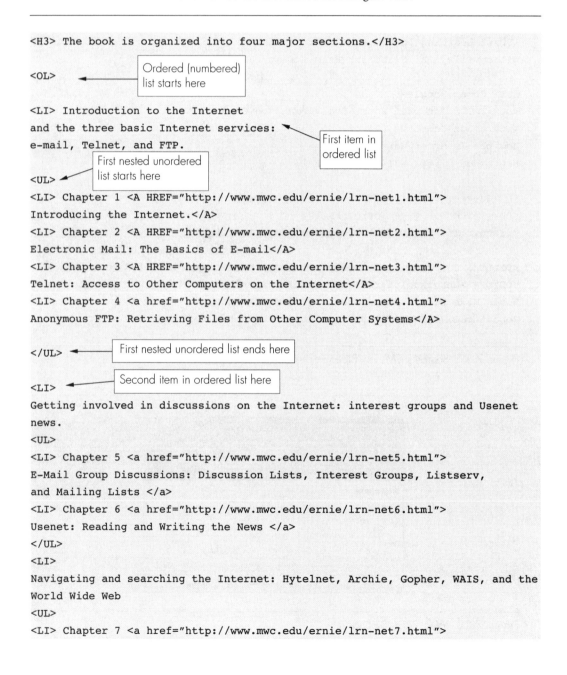

```
<H3> The book is organized into four major sections.</H3>

<OL>                    Ordered (numbered)
                        list starts here

<LI> Introduction to the Internet
and the three basic Internet services:          First item in
e-mail, Telnet, and FTP.                        ordered list
                    First nested unordered
<UL>                list starts here
<LI> Chapter 1 <A HREF="http://www.mwc.edu/ernie/lrn-net1.html">
Introducing the Internet.</A>
<LI> Chapter 2 <A HREF="http://www.mwc.edu/ernie/lrn-net2.html">
Electronic Mail: The Basics of E-mail</A>
<LI> Chapter 3 <A HREF="http://www.mwc.edu/ernie/lrn-net3.html">
Telnet: Access to Other Computers on the Internet</A>
<LI> Chapter 4 <a href="http://www.mwc.edu/ernie/lrn-net4.html">
Anonymous FTP: Retrieving Files from Other Computer Systems</A>

</UL>         First nested unordered list ends here

              Second item in ordered list here
<LI>
Getting involved in discussions on the Internet: interest groups and Usenet
news.
<UL>
<LI> Chapter 5 <a href="http://www.mwc.edu/ernie/lrn-net5.html">
E-Mail Group Discussions: Discussion Lists, Interest Groups, Listserv,
and Mailing Lists </a>
<LI> Chapter 6 <a href="http://www.mwc.edu/ernie/lrn-net6.html">
Usenet: Reading and Writing the News </a>
</UL>
<LI>
Navigating and searching the Internet: Hytelnet, Archie, Gopher, WAIS, and the
World Wide Web
<UL>
<LI> Chapter 7 <a href="http://www.mwc.edu/ernie/lrn-net7.html">
```

```
Hytelnet: Working on the Internet Using Telnet </a>
<LI> Chapter 8 <a href="http://www.mwc.edu/ernie/lrn-net8.html">
Archie: Locating Files to Retrieve by Anonymous FTP </a>
<LI> Chapter 9 <a href="http://www.mwc.edu/ernie/lrn-net9.html">
Gopher: Burrowing through the Internet </a>
<LI> Chapter 10 <a href="http://www.mwc.edu/ernie/lrn-net10.html">
WAIS: Searching Databases on the Internet </a>
<LI> Chapter 11 <a href="http://www.mwc.edu/ernie/lrn-net11.html">
World Wide Web: Lynx, Mosaic, and Netscape </a>
</UL>
<LI>
Ethical, legal, security and social issues related to the Internet.
<UL>
<LI> Chapter 12 <A HREF="http://www.mwc.edu/ernie/lrn-net12.html" >
Issues: Ethical, Legal, Security and Social</a>
</UL>
</OL>
<P>
```

Figure 7.19 Source for Web Page in Figure 7.20

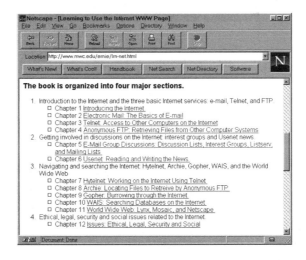

Figure 7.20 Web Page Using Nested Lists

Links

HTML was designed to allow for the construction of hypertext, hypermedia documents or Web pages. One of its strong points is that we can create links from one part of a Web page to another Web page or from a resource on the World Wide Web or to another part of the same Web page. We'll cover both of these types of tags in this section.

Hyperlinks to Other Resources on the WWW. To use HTML to represent a hyperlink to a resource on the WWW, you use two tags, with text or an image between them. The first tag starts with <**A HREF="** and includes the URL or link for the resource. The matching tag is </**A**>. As you've already seen, many HTML tags appear in pairs. We'll look at an example before giving the rules for these types of tags.

Here's an example of the HTML tags for a hyperlink:

```
The home page for <A HREF="http://www.mwc.edu/ernie/index.html">
Ernest Ackermann</A> has a link to materials for workshops and tutorials.
```

A Web browser would display that HTML as:

The home page for <u>Ernest Ackermann</u> has a link to materials for workshops and tutorials.

If someone clicked on <u>Ernest Ackermann</u> in the browser's window, the browser would open the location and go to the resource given by the URL.

The HTML rules for creating hyperlinks are generalizations of the example above.
* The first tag has the form <**A HREF="***URL***">**. An actual URL is substituted for *URL* between the pair of quotation marks (").
* The matching tag is </**A**>.
* The tags don't appear on the Web page.
* The text between the two tags appears on the Web page as underlined or highlighted text.
* If there's an image between the two tags, its border is highlighted.
* Clicking on the text or image opens the location or takes the user to the Web resources given by the URL.

Figures 7.21 and 7.22 show the use of HTML tags for hyperlinks from a Web page to other resources on the Web. Figure 7.21 shows the HTML source, and Figure 7.22 shows the Web page. There are links to sites at more than one location—a Web page can contain links to many different locations and resources. Near the bottom page an image is used within the tags for a hyperlink, otherwise the hyperlinks all appear as text. We'll discuss displaying images in the next section. You'll notice that this uses some HTML tags we've discussed before. Try to predict what the page will look like before looking at Figure 7.22.

```
<b>Got a question? Want to make a comment? </b>
<UL>
 <LI><a href="http://www.digicool.com/arttalk/main">
    Please use the Guest Book</a>
</UL>
<HR>
<A HREF="http://www.mwc.edu/ernie/sg/sgswebacc.html">
 Statistics </A>
about visitors from the WWW.
<HR>
Steve Griffin Retrospective <BR>
September 29 - November 5  <BR>
duPont Gallery, duPont Hall <BR>
<A HREF="http://www.mwc.edu/index.html">
 Mary Washington College </A>
Galleries <BR>
Fredericksburg, VA 22401
<P>
Opening Reception (in real space) <BR>
Thursday, September 28 <BR>
5:00 - 7:00 PM
<HR>
<A HREF="http://www.mwc.edu/ernie/sg/credits.html">
 Credit Where Credit's Due</A>
<HR>
<P><EM>Steve Griffin Retrospective Home Page <BR>
Mary Washington College Galleries <BR>
Fredericksburg, VA 22401 <BR>
URL:http://www.mwc.e[
<P>
For more information
<A HREF="mailto:ernie@mwc.edu"> ernie@mwc.edu</A>
<P>
<A HREF="http://www.mwc.edu/ernie/sg/virtual.html">
<IMG ALIGN=LEFT SRC="http://www.mwc.edu/ernie/sg/return.gif">
</A>
Go to Home Page for Steve Griffin Retrospective Virtual Exhi[
<A HREF="http://www.mwc.edu/ernie/sg/virtual.html">
 http://www.mwc.edu/ernie/sg/virtual.html</A>
```

Some of the hyperlinks are represented here as text

An image is used here as a hyperlink—the graphic is in the file given by the URL http://www.mwc.edu/ernie/sg/return.gif; click on it and go to the location given by the URL http://www.mwc.edu/ernie/sg/virtual.html

This hyperlink takes the user to the same Web page as the one that uses the image, except the hyperlink here is represented as text

Figure 7.21 Source for Hyperlinks Example

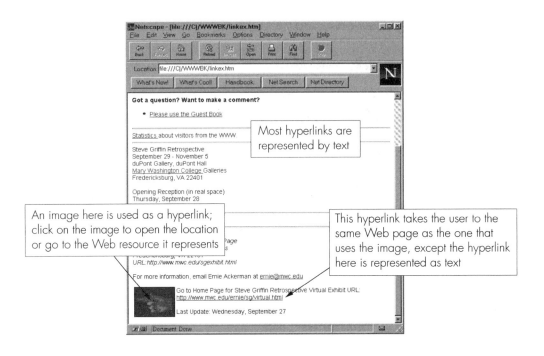

Figure 7.22 Web Page Produced by Source in Figure 7.21

Tip

The name of the file tells the browser the type of resource.

In the preceding figures you've seen hyperlinks to several resources. If the name of the file holding the resource ended with **.html** or **.htm**, the browser displays it as a Web page. If the name ends with **.gif**, it's displayed as an image. In order to have the browser display or play (if the resource is an audio or video file) correctly, the file needs to be named properly. The proper name depends on the file extension, the characters after the dot (.) near the end of its name. Here's a list of file types with the proper extensions. You or your audience will need the proper viewers—helper files—to deal with the resources. You may need additional helper programs to work with the file types marked with an asterisk (*).

Extension	Type of Resource
.au	AU audio File
.aiff	AIFF audio file
.wav	WAV audio file *
.ra, .ram	Real Audio audio file *
.gif	GIF image file
.jpg	JPEG image file

.tif	TIF image file *
.xbm	XBM bitmap image
.txt, .text	Plain text
.htm, .html	HTML document, Web page
.pdf	Adobe Acrobat format
.ps	Postscript *
.mpg, .mpeg	MPEG movie *
.mov	QuickTime movie *

Links to Other Parts of the Web Page. HTML can also be used to create links between several parts of the same document. This is very useful when dealing with a long document. Links from a table of contents or list of sections can take the reader to specific parts of the document. Links within a document are also appropriate when constructing a glossary—a list of terms and definitions —to allow the reader to consider some items in context.

Making a link from one part of the document involves link tags and an anchor tag. The anchor marks a spot within the document, and the link tags are ties to that specific anchor. Figure 7.23 shows an example of the source for these types of links, and Figure 7.24 shows how they would be displayed by a Web browser.

```
<B><A NAME="anonymousftp">Anonymous FTP</A>:</B> A means of using
<A HREF="#ftp" >FTP</A> (File Transfer Protocol) in which a user
starts an ftp session with a remote host, gives the log-in or user name
&quot;anonymous&quot;, and the <A HREF="#email">e-mail</A> address as a
password.
```

> Defines the anchor named **anonymousftp** to be tied to the text **Anonymous FTP**

> Link to the anchor **email** defined elsewhere

```
<P>
<B>Archie:</B> An information service which helps to locate a
file which can then be retrieved by <A HREF="#anonymousftp">anonymous ftp
</A>.
```

> Link to the anchor **anonymousftp** defined above

Figure 7.23 Source for Links Within a Document

```
Anonymous FTP: A means of using FTP (File Transfer Protocol) in which a user
starts an ftp session with a remote host, gives the log-in or user name
"anonymous", and the e-mail address as a password.

Archie: An information service which helps to locate a file which can then be
retrieved by anonymous ftp .
```

Figure 7.24 Web Browser Display of Source in Figure 7.23

Clicking on a hyperlink in Figure 7.24 takes the user to a portion of the document marked by anchor tags. Looking at the example in Figure 7.23 you see:

* Anchor tags have the form <A NAME="*word*"> portion-of-document </A> where *word* is some term that's used in the link tags. When the link is selected the page is displayed starting here.
* Links to portions of a document have the form <A HREF="#*word*"> text or image </A>. Selecting the hyperlink takes the user to the portion of the document where the anchor *word* is defined.

It's the # character that identifies the link as going to a portion of a document. The links we've shown here are within one document or Web page. You can use the same idea to set up links to portions of other documents, provided the document has anchors defined in it. The material in Figure 7.23 was taken from the Web page whose URL is **http://www.mwc.edu/ernie/glossary.html**. If we wanted to make a hyperlink from another Web page to the portion of the glossary that gives the definition of anonymous FTP we'd use the URL **http://www.mwc.edu/ernie/glossary.html#anonymousftp** in a link, as shown below.

```
Before 1990, you needed to learn how to use
<A HREF="http://www.mwc.edu/ernie/glossary.html#anonymousftp">
anonymous ftp </A>to access most of the material on the Internet.
```

Images

A Web browser is capable of displaying images as part of a Web page. The basic HTML tag to use for an image has the form <IMG SRC="*URL*"> or <IMG SRC="*file-name*"> where *URL* is the URL of a file or *file-name* is the name of a file on your computer that contains the image. Most browsers can display images that are in GIF or JPEG format. The browser determines the format only by the name of the file. If the image is in GIF format, store it in a file whose name ends with **.gif**. For an image in JPEG format, store it in a file whose name ends with **.jpg**.

We've used HTML tags for images as part of Web pages in some of the previous figures:

* (Figure 7.1) <IMG SRC="http://www.mwc.edu/ernie/cover.gif">
* (Figure 7.5) <A HREF="ftp.gif"><IMG SRC="smftp1.gif"></A>
* (Figure 7.21) <IMG ALIGN=LEFT SRC="http://www.mwc.edu/ernie/sg/return.gif">

The first and third URLs use complete fully qualified domain names. The second uses a relative name in place of the URL. An advantage to using a relative URL is that it's easier to type in. A disadvantage is that the image has to be in the same directory as the Web page. That restricts the location of pages and images. If you're working with a few images and Web pages, this isn't too hard to deal with, but it can get difficult to manage for complex designs. To read more about using relative names versus fully qualified names, look at the section of "Composing Good HTML" by Eric Tilton dealing with this subject using the URL **http://www.cs.cmu.edu/~tilt/cgh/**.

Tip

Make sure others can find your images and hyperlinks.

Try to avoid using a URL or file name that references a local file in terms of its location on your computer without giving the Internet address of the computer. An example of this would be the HTML tag <**IMG SRC="file:///C|mypics/greatpic.gif**">.

That tag instructs the browser to display the file mentioned where the file is on the computer that's being used to run the Web browser. That means if readers aren't using the computer that holds the file, they won't be able to see it! Hyperlinks to resources that start with **file://** and don't give the Internet domain name will have the same problem. If you want the image or the hyperlink to be accessible from other computers on the Internet you need to use a URL that includes the domain name of the system that's running the Web server. If the image was to be displayed as part of a Web page whose URL was **http://www.circlea.com/nicestuf/coolpage.html**, for example, put the image in the same directory or folder as the Web page and make its tag <**IMG SRC="http://www.circlea.com/nicestuf/greatpic.gif**">.

You can also give directions to the browser as to where the accompanying text will be displayed relative to the image. It can be displayed aligned with the top, middle, or bottom of an image. It's usually displayed to the left of the image. Use **ALIGN=TOP, ALIGN=MIDDLE,** or **ALIGN=BOTTOM** within the tag <IMG SRC="..">; for example, <**IMG ALIGN=TOP SRC="http://www.mwc.edu/ernie/cover.gif**">. With these types of alignments only one line is displayed in the specified position and the remaining text (if there is any) is displayed beginning under the image. It's also possible to align text with the entire image, starting at the top, using **ALIGN=LEFT** or **ALIGN=RIGHT.** This puts the image to the left or to the right of the text.

The method of alignment is easier to think about when you see some examples, and we'll show some as part of a Web page. The page we'll look at is accessible through the URL **http://www.mwc.edu/ernie/wwwbk/demoalign.html**. (Remember how to go to the page given by the URL? Click on the icon labeled **Open**, type the URL in the dialog box, and then click on the button labeled **Open**.)

Figure 7.25 shows the effect of using these three tags along with some accompanying text:

```
<IMG ALIGN=TOP SRC="http://www.mwc.edu/ernie/wwwbk/fleethum.gif">
<IMG ALIGN=MIDDLE SRC="http://www.mwc.edu/ernie/wwwbk/fleethum.gif">
<IMG ALIGN=BOTTOM SRC="http://www.mwc.edu/ernie/wwwbk/fleethum.gif">
```

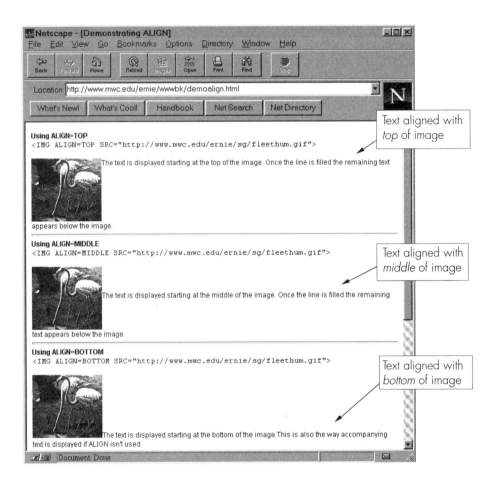

Figure 7.25 Alignment at Top, Middle, and Bottom of Image

Note that if the size of the font or window were changed, the results would be different. What we see here depends on those items as well as the resolution (number of pixels) of the screen.

Figure 7.26 demonstrates the use of left and right alignment using the following tags:

```
<IMG ALIGN=LEFT SRC="http://www.mwc.edu/ernie/wwwbk/fleethum.gif">
<IMG ALIGN=RIGHT SRC="http://www.mwc.edu/ernie/wwwbk/fleethum.gif">
```

Figure 7.26 Demonstrating ALIGN=LEFT and ALIGN=RIGHT

Table of HTML Tags

Table 7.1 lists the tags we've mentioned above.

Tag	Purpose
<BODY>,</BODY>	Marks the body of the document; what is displayed.
<HEAD>,</HEAD>	Marks heading section; contains description of the document.
<HTML>,</HTML>	Marks HTML portion; first and last tags in the file.
<TITLE>,</TITLE>	Document title is put between these tags.
<! -- .. -->	Contains comments about the document; nothing is displayed.
<H1>,</H1>	Level-1 headings in the body section; largest font for heading. There are six levels of headings: <H1> ... <H6>, each one displayed smaller than the previous one with **H6** being the smallest.
<P>	Starts a new paragraph.
 	Starts a new line.
<HR>	Shadow line; looks like a divider between sections or items on the page.
<I>,</I>	Italic text.
<EM>,</EM>	Emphasized text, often displayed as italic.
<B>,</B>	Bold text.
<BLOCKQUOTE>, </BLOCKQUOTE>	Extended quotation.

<PRE>,</PRE>	Preformatted text.
<, >, &	Represent the special characters <, >, and &.
<OL>,</OL>	Ordered or numbered list.
<UL>,</UL>	Unordered or bulleted list.
<LI>	Marks a list element in an ordered or unordered list.
<DL>,</DL>	Descriptive or indented list.
<DT>	Marks an item in a descriptive list.
<DD>	Describes an element in a descriptive list.
<A HREF="*URL*">,</A>	Used to create a hyperlink. The text or image between the tags is represented as the hyperlink on the Web page. When it's selected the actual URL given in place of *URL* is used to access a resource on the Web.
<IMG SRC="*URL*">	Used to display an image as part of a Web page. The actual URL given in place of *URL* represents an image file.

Table 7.1   HTML Tags

URL Formats

When you're writing Web pages you'll probably want to include hyperlinks to other resources on the World Wide Web. You saw in the section above on hyperlinks that you do that by using a tag in the form <A HREF="*URL*"> where a specific URL is substituted for *URL*. Here we'll give the formats for URLs for different services and types of resources on the Web.

Before going into the different formats for URLs, here's a quick review of the concept and general format of a URL. The purpose of a URL is to give the location and the means to get to a resource on the Internet. The Web browser uses it to access items, and it's becoming common to see it used as a way to let people know about a resource, source of information, or advertisement. You'll find it helpful to think of a URL as having the form

```
how-to-get-there://where-to-go/what-to-get
```

Its general form is

```
service://domain-name-of-site-supplying-service/full-path-name-of-item
```

Essentially this is like a sign pointing to something on the Internet. Starting at the far left, the portion of the URL up to the colon (:) tells what type of Internet service to use. The Internet domain name or address of the site supplying the information comes just after the characters ://. After the first single slash, you have the full path name of the item. One of the key items of a URL is the type of service or resource it represents.

Now for a list of different types of URLs. You may not have come across some of these services or resource types before; each is covered in this book. For more information, look in the chapter where a service or resource is discussed.

Resource or Service	URL Begins with	Example
Web Pages	http://	http://www.nmaa.si.edu/artdir/treasures.html Selections from the permanent collection of the National Museum of American Art.
FTP (Chapter 8)	ftp://	ftp://ftp.jpl.nasa.gov/pub/images/browse/ A directory of images from NASA Jet Propulsion Laboratory's public information FTP archive.
Gopher (Chapter 8)	gopher://	gopher://chet.ocs.union.edu:70/11/library/virtual Virtual Reference Desk at Union College Library.
Telnet (Chapter 8)	telnet://	telnet://locis.loc.gov Search holdings of Library of Congress telnet://psupen.psu.edu Pen pages. Use the log-in name **world** once you're connected. telnet://culine.colorado.edu:860 Schedule for National Hockey League. **860** is a port number.

Two other services—e-mail and Usenet news—have URLs, but they're in slightly different form. They include the ://.

E-mail (Chapter 3)	mailto:	mailto:ernie@mwc.edu Send an e-mail message to the address **ernie@mwc.edu**.
Usenet news (Chapter 5)	news:	news:rec.food.cooking URL to read articles in the news group rec.food.cooking.

Example 7.1   Writing a Web Page

Now that we know something about HTML, HTML tags, and URLs we'll put together a Web page. This Web page could be called a personal home page because it gives information about an individual. Lots of folks—probably thousands—have personal home pages. It's a way of letting others on the Internet know about you. An example of an excellent personal home page is "Jan's Home Page" (**http://www.tile.net/jan**, created by Jan Hanford.

Tip

Finding Personal Web Pages.

There are several collections of personal Web pages on the WWW. Most allow you to list or register your personal Web page. Some of the collections are

- Personal pages WorldWide, **http://www.utexas.edu/world/personal/index.html**
- WWW Virtual Library: Home Pages, **http://www.city.ac.uk/citylive/vl_pages.html**
- Netizens, Alphabet City, **http://bin-1.gnn.com/gnn/netizens/alphabet.html**

Two directory listings of places to find personal Web pages are:

* Yahoo—Entertainment:People, **http://www.yahoo.com/Entertainment/People/**
* CULTURE—People—Lists—directories, home pages, **http://www.december.com/cmc/info/culturer-people-lists.html**

An interesting article on the reasons people create personal Web pages is "The World Wide Web as Social Hypertext," by Tom Erickson (**http://www.atg.apple.com/personal/Tom_Erickson/SocialHypertext.html**).

In this example we'll create a Web page that gives some personal and work-related information. We'll break it up into three sections:

1. Name, e-mail address, work address and phone number, and description of the type of work one does.
2. List of personal interests with hyperlinks to some appropriate Web sites.
3. List of some interesting or favorite Web sites.

We'll include an image file (a photo). At the end of the page we'll include the name and e-mail address of the person who created the page, an e-mail address to use if readers have any questions about the Web page, and the date the Web page was last modified or changed.

You create the Web page by typing the HTML tags and text into a file on your computer using an editor or word processor. No matter what software you use to create the page, your work is saved in a text or ASCII file. The name of the file ends with the extension **.htm**. The image used here was created by starting with a photograph and putting it into a scanner, which created an image file. It's a picture of the author. He's not that good looking, but if you wanted a copy of it to use for practice go to his home page, **http://www.mwc.edu/ernie**, put the mouse pointer on his picture and Shift+click (press Shift and click with the left button on the mouse), and you'll be able to save it in a file on your computer.

We're going to write the page in stages; write HTML statements, save them to a file, and use the Web browser to view what we've done so far. We'll use the editor Notepad, which is part of the basic accessories for a Microsoft Windows system. Use whatever editor or word processor you'd like.

The steps we'll follow for this example are:

1. Start the editor or word processor program.
2. Type the HTML for the heading section and the HTML and text for the items in section A.
3. Save the work into a file named **webpage1.htm**.
4. Use the Web browser to view the page.
5. Repeat the previous three steps for sections B and C.
6. Add the image near the top of the page and other information at the end of the page.

Now carry through with the steps.

1. Start the editor or word processor program.

You start Notepad by selecting or clicking on its icon in the **Accessories** section of Microsoft Windows. If you're using Windows 95, click on the **Start** button, move the pointer to **Programs**, then move the pointer to **Accessories** and click on **Notepad**. If you're using a previous version of Windows, double-click on the icon **Accessories** and then double-click on the icon for **Notepad**.

Once Notepad starts you'll see a window similar to the one in Figure 7.27, except there won't be any text in the window.

2. Type the HTML for the heading section and the HTML and text for the items in section A.

Just start typing the HTML and tags necessary for the items in section A. Figure 7.27 shows the HTML tags and text necessary to have the items we mentioned in section A displayed by a viewer.

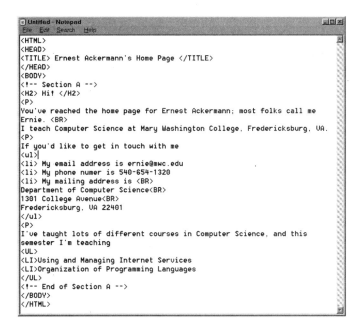

Figure 7.27 Initial Text and HTML tags for Web Page.

3. Save the work into a file named **webpage1.htm**.

To look at what's been done so far with a Web browser, you need to save the work to a file. To save a file while using Notepad, click on **File** in the menu bar, choose **Save As**, and then give a file name. You'll want to be sure of two things:
1. The name of the file ends with **.htm** or **.html**, such as **webpage1.htm**.
2. You know the name of the directory or folder that holds the file so you can find it later.

If you have the opportunity, be sure to select an appropriate folder to hold the file. You might want to create a folder named **WebPages** to hold your work. Just to be specific for this example, the work will be saved in a file named **webpage1.htm** in a folder (directory) named **WebPages**.

Suppose we're going to save the file in a folder or directory named **WebPages**. (First create the folder or directory. You can do this through Windows Explorer if you're using Windows 95 or through the File Manager if you're using a previous version of Windows.) After you select **Save As** a dialog box will appear on the screen. Type **C:\WebPages\webpage1.htm** in the portion of the dialog box labeled **File name**. A dialog box is shown in Figure 7.28.

4. Use the Web browser to view the page.

First be sure the Web browser is started. You don't necessarily have to connect to the Internet to view the file holding the Web page, because it's a local file.

Click on **File** in the Menu Bar and then select **Open File**.

A dialog box will appear on the screen. It may not be set to the folder (directory) **WebPages**, which holds the file we want to view. If that's the case, type **C:\WebPages** in the open spot labeled **File name** and press Enter. After that you'll see a dialog box similar to the one in Figure 7.28.

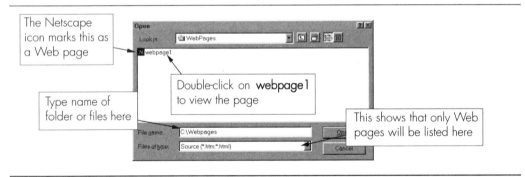

Figure 7.28 Dialog Box

Double-click on the file name **Webpage1**.

Clicking twice on the file name **Webpage1** brings the Web page you've written to the Web browser. It's shown in Figure 7.29.

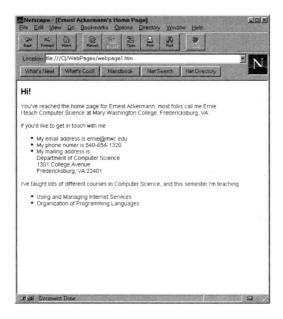

Figure 7.29 Web Browser View of Webpage1.htm

How do you like it? It's not bad, but we're going to change it just a little by adding some hyperlinks. Since the college has a home page, we'll add a hyperlink to that through the College's name and we'll also add a hyperlink so folks can send e-mail by clicking on the e-mail address on the screen. To do that we have to:

1. Use the editor or word processor to edit or change the file holding the Web page.
2. Save the changes.
3. View the Web page with Netscape again.

If both the editor and Netscape are still on the screen, you have to click on the appropriate windows to use them. Otherwise, you need to start them.

As you make changes to **webpage1.htm**, it's a good idea to keep viewing it with Netscape. Make changes, save the changes, and then click on the icon labeled **Reload** from the Netscape Toolbar. It's really useful to be able to make changes and see what they look like almost immediately, particularly when we're trying new things.

Figure 7.30 shows the portion of **webpage1.htm** with the hyperlinks added. We've pointed out the tags to add. Figure 7.31 shows the Web page as displayed by Netscape.

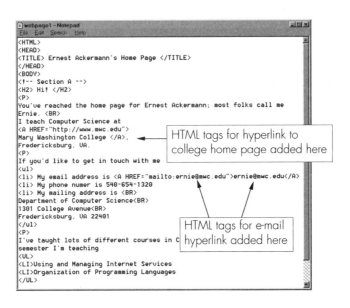

Figure 7.30 webpage1.htm Modified to Add Hyperlinks

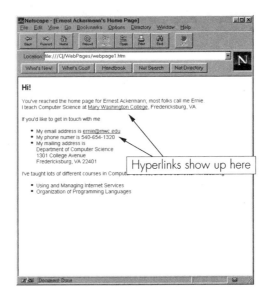

Figure 7.31 Viewing webpage1.htm After Saving Changes and Reloading

5. Repeat the previous three steps for sections B and C.

Now we need to add the information for sections B and C. In each case, you've got to add the text and HTML tags to the file **webpage1.htm** by using the editor or word processor to type in the changes. Be sure you save the changes to the file. After each change you may want to view your work as we did above by clicking on the icon labeled **Reload** in the Netscape Toolbar. Copies of Web pages that you have recently viewed through Netscape are kept in an area on the disk called the *cache* (there's likely to be a directory by that name in the folder that holds the Netscape program). When you ask to view a Web page, Netscape checks to see if it's in the cache and uses that copy instead of going out on the Internet to get a new copy. This makes for faster display of some pages, but doesn't always give you the most recent version of a page. Clicking on **Reload** goes to the source for the page and brings in a new copy.

Figure 7.32 shows the HTML tags and text we've added for sections B and C of the Web page. Figure 7.33 shows the view through Netscape.

Figure 7.32 Sections B and C

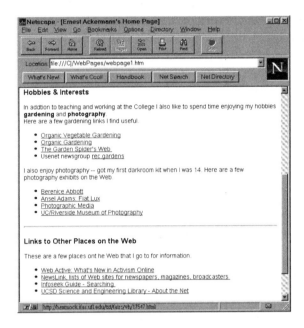

Figure 7.33 View of Web Page

6. Add the image near the top of the page and other information at the end of the page.

We're going to add a picture at the top of the page and some information at the end. The picture is in a file in GIF format and we'll use an IMG SRC tag to display it. The information at the end includes an e-mail address to use if readers have questions about the Web page, the name and e-mail address of the person who created the page (it's always a good idea to sign your work), and the date the Web page was last modified or changed.

To add the image, we'll include the HTML tag for the image between the lines

```
<P>
You've reached the home page for Ernest Ackermann; most folks call me
Ernie. <BR>
```

in the source. With this addition the source now contains

```
<P>
<IMG ALIGN=RIGHT SRC="picture.gif">
You've reached the home page for Ernest Ackermann; most folks call me
Ernie. <BR>
```

Using SRC="**picture.gif**" implies the image is in the same directory as the Web page. We've made sure that's the case, so the Web page now looks like the one shown in Figure 7.34.

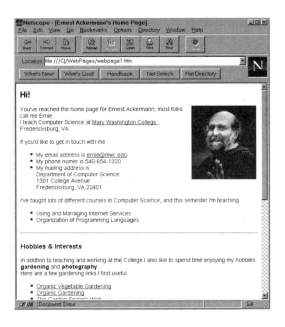

Figure 7.34 Web Page with an Image Added

To add the material at the end of the page, we'll go to the line before

```
</BODY>
```

and add

```
<HR>
Please send any questions or comments about this page to
<A HREF="mailto:ernie@mwc.edu">ernie@mwc.edu </A> <BR>
Web page written and developed by Ernest Ackermann.<BR>
Last time anything was changed here: Saturday, May 4, 1996.<BR>
Thanks for visiting!
```

Figure 7.35 shows the end of the Web page after that material has been added to **webpage1.htm**.

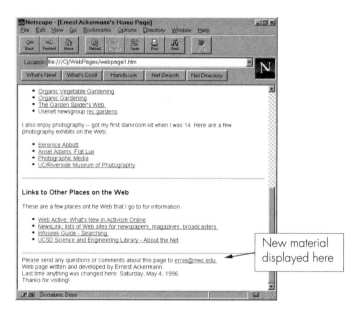

Figure 7.35

———————————————End of Example 7.1———————————————

Example 7.1 showed just one possibility for a Web page design. A page to represent a business or organization needs to concentrate more on presenting an image of the organization, the services offered, and a means to get the reader involved in requesting information, services, or products. A page that focuses on a theme (such as guitars) or an event (such as an art exhibit) needs to present information, provide a means for folks to participate, and include links to related resources or Web pages. Some pages are pure whimsy, entertainment, or playful. No matter what type of Web page you're constructing, think carefully about its purpose and design before writing and search for Web pages with a similar topic or purpose. We can learn a lot from looking at each other's work.

Tools to Help Create Web Pages

You saw in the previous section that to create Web pages you need an editor or word processor that lets you save your work in text or ASCII format. In fact, that's all you need to create relatively simple pages. When you have to create lots of pages or pages with lots of HTML, you'll want to use something easier.

There are several programs that can help you create Web pages. Working with them is like working with a word processor. Many of the programs have a menu bar and toolbar that let you create the page as you'd see it through a Web browser. The tags are often inserted automatically. For example, to create a hyperlink, you highlight text, click on the icon to create a link, and type the URL for the link in a dialog box. Several of the programs are shareware or make evaluation copies available on the World Wide Web. Netscape has recently announced the availability of Netscape Gold, which includes a Web page editor built into the Web browser. Several popular word processor programs have software, often available free on the Web, that makes it easy not only to create Web pages, but also to convert a document from the word processor format to HTML. These are useful for situations in which a number of documents have to be converted or when documents have to be produced in two formats—for the printed page and for the Web.

To see lists of sites that provide tools for creating Web documents take a look at:

- Developer Tools section of the Netscape document "Creating Web Sites" (**http://home.netscape.com/home/how-to-create-web-services.html**)
- HTML Writers Guild Tools and Utilities, **http://www2.best.com/~wooldri/tools/tools.html**
- The INTERNET Store/HTML, **http://www.internetstore.com/home/html.html**
- Web Developer's Virtual Library: HTML Editors, **http://www.stars.com/Vlib/Providers/HTML_Editors.html**
- Yahoo Directory Section Computers and Internet:Internet:World Wide Web:HTML Editors, **http://www.yahoo.com/Computers/World_Wide_Web/HTML_Editors/**

These two programs are used to create HTML using WordPerfect and Microsoft Word. Each is available without charge on the Internet:

- Internet Assistant for Microsoft Word,
  http://www.microsoft.com/msoffice/freestuf/msword/download/ia/default.htm
- Internet Publisher for WordPerfect, **http://wp.novell.com/elecpub/inttoc.htm**

Style Guides—How to Do It Right, How to Do It for Impact, and How to Make It Portable

Now that you've learned the basics of creating a Web page, you ought to consider issues of style. That means thinking about how to create a Web page that is enjoyable to look at, easy to read, and effective. Creating an effective Web page deals with issues of content, HTML, and design skills, because the page has text, hyperlinks, and images. The two primary components are effective language and two dimensional design or layout skills. You'll also need an understanding of the technical issues involved in creating and viewing Web pages—a good understanding of HTML and knowing the characteristics and limitations of Web browsers.

One difficulty with designing a Web page is that a number of technical conditions that affect the way a page looks can't be controlled—size and type of font set by the user, number of colors displayed on a monitor, and screen resolution of a monitor. Options can be set on a Web browser controlling the type and size of font used to display text, so text that looks "just right" in terms of size, and placement may appear differently to different users. There's no control over the type of monitor or display used to view a Web page. Some monitors will be set to display 16 colors, some 256 colors, and some millions of colors. An image that looks great on a display capable of displaying lots of colors may not look very good when fewer colors are available. The screen resolution or number of pixels in the viewing window affects the way the Web page appears. Images and text have their dimensions ultimately specified in terms of pixels regardless of what's being used to view them. The greater the number of pixels, the finer the resolution. An image on a screen with a resolution of 1024 by 768 pixels will generally look better, and be sharper than an image on a screen with a resolution of 800 by 600 pixels or 640 by 480 pixels. So an image that's 300 by 400 pixels, say, will appear much smaller on a screen whose resolution is 1024 by 768 pixels than it would appear on a screen with a resolution of 640 by 480 pixels. Furthermore, the size of the browser window can be changed by the user. So as you design a page you need to think about what it will look like on different types of monitors and with different user configurations. A middle-of-the-road approach would be to design a Web page so it looks good on a monitor that displays at least 256 colors and has a resolution of 800 by 600 pixels. Compromises have to be made, because it's impossible to predict the type of monitor used and the way the Web browser options are set.

There are also a number of style elements that you can control to create appealing and effective Web pages.

* Use HTML that most browsers can deal with.

The HTML presented in this chapter can be interpreted by most browsers, but other HTML tags such as those for centering text, creating tables, and background colors, aren't interpreted correctly by all Web browsers. So the HTML you use in a Web page ought to be chosen to give the page the format you'd like and be viewable in that format by most Web browsers; not everyone will be using Netscape Navigator. Try viewing a Web page with different browsers to learn what works best.

At the time of this writing, there is no agreement on all aspects of HTML among the different Web browsers. What works in one browser may not work in another. You've probably seen comments on some pages that say the page is "optimized for Netscape" or "works best with Netscape." That's because some tags are used that the Netscape browser understands, while other browsers don't. Likewise there are HTML tags that some browsers interpret while the Netscape browser doesn't. (That's one of the reasons we're concentrating on basic HTML, tags that most browsers recognize, in this section.) Why do we have these differences? The features that one browser can support and others cannot distinguish one browser from another. At the present time there are several companies that want to establish themselves as the leader in the field of providing Web browsers. Currently, Netscape has that position. Its move to give its browser the capabilities to interpret interactive elements and elements with animation, such as Java scripts and programs and inline plug-ins, was meant to allow it to keep that position. Microsoft with its browser, Internet Explorer, soon followed Netscape's lead. Most browsers support the tags in HTML version 2.0, and there is an international effort to get HTML 3.0 adopted by the primary Web browsers. To read more about this look at "HyperText Markup Language (HTML)" by using the URL **http://www.w3.org/pub/WWW/MarkUp/**.

* Use relatively small images and limit the number of images in a Web page.

It usually takes lots of bytes to represent an image. That means it may take a relatively long time for someone to view a Web page that has a number of images or a large image. We'll calculate how long it would take to display an image whose size is 54K bytes being received on a computer that's using a 28.8K (bits per second) modem to connect to the Internet. The modem can receive information at a rate of roughly 28,800 bits per second. Since each byte consists of 8 bits, the modem can receive information at 28,800/8 = 3,600 bytes per second. Since the size of the file holding the image is approximately 54,000 bytes, it take

54,000/3,600 = 15 seconds to deliver the image to the browser. Notice we're also ignoring any delay due to Internet traffic. Some, but not all, folks might be willing to wait that long for the image. If several images that size are on the page, the wait becomes unreasonable. One thing to do is to represent the image on the page by a small version called a thumbnail. Another possibility is to reduce the number of colors in the image (this is also called reducing the color depth) so the image can be represented with fewer bytes. Either can be made into a hyperlink to the full image. This gives access to the image in all its glory, but doesn't necessarily delay viewing the entire Web page.

❋ Use proper grammar and spelling.

You want your page to be effective and well received. Grammatical or spelling errors don't give a good impression of you and can turn off a reader pretty quickly.

❋ Use proper spacing and emphasis.

Let the spacing reflect the organization of the text and content of the Web page. If the page has several distinct sections, separate them with a shaded bar (<**HR**>) or blank spaces. Use bold or italic font appropriately. Section headings ought to be emphasized as well as important subsections or words. On the other hand, you need not overdo the use of spacing, shaded bars, and emphasized text. Because something can be done, doesn't mean it has to be done.

❋ Include an e-mail address for comments, the name of the author/designer/producer, the URL for the page, and the date the Web page was last modified.

These items are usually placed at the end of the Web page. The e-mail address is there in case someone reading the page has a question or suggestions about the Web page or its content. You can use the **mailto** URL to give the e-mail address a hyperlink; clicking on it will bring up a window to create an e-mail message. Web pages ought to contain the name(s) of the person(s) responsible for developing the Web page. It gives credit and responsibility where they are due. The URL for the page is included so that someone reading it will know how to reach it on the Web in case the page is printed or reproduced in some other manner. Knowing when something was changed last is helpful for readers to keep track of the most recent version of a document, and it also gives an indication of how timely the content of the Web page is. When you give the date, it's a good idea to spell out or abbreviate the month since 5/4/99 means May 4, 1999 in the United States but April 5, 1999 in Europe.

❋ Rather than create long documents, create a collection of shorter ones with a table of contents.

The difficulty with long documents is that they may take a long time to transfer before they can be viewed, and it's more time consuming to scroll or page through to find appropriate information. It's generally better to divide a long Web page into several smaller ones, and provide a contents page, making the items in the table of contents hyperlinks to the appropriate sections.

❋ Think about what you're going to write, and think about the layout before writing the HTML.

There's no substitute for planning and design. Take the time to think about what you want to do and how you can accomplish it.

Here's a list of selected HTML style guides available on the World Wide Web:

- "About the Artist" (**http://www.ankiewicz.com/artist/WebRant.html**) K. Ankiewicz. Information and opinion about using images.

- "Composing Good HTML" (**http://www.cs.cmu.edu/~tilt/cgh/**) E. Tilton. The author says this doesn't "purport" to be a style guide, but it contains lots of excellent information on topics such as "Common Errors" and "Things to Avoid."

- "Do's and Don'ts of Web Design" (**http://millkern.com/do-dont.html**) K. Signell. A brief, straightforward discussion of what works and what doesn't on a Web page. Be sure to read "Reading a Web Page" by the sane author.

- "Elements of HTML Style" (**http://www.book.uci.edu/Staff/StyleGuide.html**) by J. K. Cohen. Gives the basic rules for HTML style. Also contains links to other style documents.

- "Reading a Web Page" (**http://millkern.com/garuda/style.html**) K. Signell. A critical look at some noteworthy pages. Companion piece to "Do's and Don'ts of Web Design" listed above.

- "Style Guide for Online Hypertext" (**http://www.w3.org/hypertext/WWW/Provider/Style/Overview.html**) T. Berners-Lee. Complete guide to style by the originator of the World Wide Web.

- "The Web Developer's Virtual Library" (**http://www.charm.net/~web/Vlib**) has a section titled "Style," (**http://www.charm.net/~web/Vlib/Providers/Style.html**) containing an annotated list of these and several other HTML style guides.

- "Web Style Manual" (**http://info.med.yale.edu/caim/StyleManual_Top.HTML**) P. J. Lynch. The most complete and authoritative style manual available on the Web. A must to put into the bookmark list of every Web author.

- "Why the Web Sucks III" (**http://www.spies.com/~ceej/Words/rant.web.html**) C. J. Silverio. Silverio doesn't mince words, and his opinions are sound. Includes hyperlinks to examples of good and bad Web pages.

Putting Your Information on the WWW

To make your Web pages available to everyone else on the Internet, the Web page and all supporting files have to be placed on a computer that's acting as a Web server. That computer is running the software and has the Internet connections so that information on it can be retrieved by using a URL that starts with **http://**. Most Internet service providers provide this service to their customers, either for an extra fee or for free. If you're at an educational institution or commercial organization, there are likely to be specific procedures and policies you follow to make your Web page available to the rest of the WWW. You'll have to check the policies and procedures for your situation.

Once you put your page(s) on a Web server, you're a (Web) published author! One of the great things about the Internet is that it's almost as easy to be an information provider as it is to be an information consumer. There are a number of ways to publicize your Web page. If your Web page is a personal page, you can list it at any site mentioned in the TIP box above.

If the Web page is the home page for a business, organization, event, or anything else then it's not appropriate to use those services. There are lots of other services to use and other ways to publicize a Web page.

You can announce your page by submitting it to several special locations on the World Wide Web: What's New Web pages, Web directories, and search engines. These services give you forms to fill out telling the URL for your page, your name and e-mail address, and some descriptive information about the Web page. Depending on the workload, it may take a service several days or weeks to list your Web page. There's generally no charge to have a Web page listed by these services. Some services are selective about what's listed and may not list the page. "Netscape What's New," (**http://home.netscape.com/home/whats-new.html**) lists only selected sites, ones which they consider are advancing the technology of the Web. This contrasts with "NCSA What's New Page," (**http://www.ncsa.uiuc.edu/SDG/Software/Mosaic/Docs/whats-new.html**) which lists any announcement that's sent. All the directories we've mentioned in Chapter 6 accept submissions of URLs, and Yahoo makes a daily list available of recently added Web pages, **http://www.yahoo.com/new/**. When you submit a request to be listed in a directory you'll also have to pick the category that has the page listing. To choose the appropriate category, find pages on the same or similar topic within the directory and use the same category. You can also submit an announcement of your page to a mailing list and to Usenet newsgroups.

In addition to the individual services and sites, there are Web pages that can be used to submit a URL to several at once. Three of these are:

- Pointers to Pointers, **http://www.homecom.com/global/pointers.html**
- Promote-It! **http://www.cam.org/~psarena/promote-it.html**
- Submit It! **http://www.submit-it.com/**

Most directories have sections devoted to sites you can use to announce or publicize a Web page. Two of these are:

- The section "Computing/Authoring/Tell the World" in the Excite directory, **http://www.excite.com/Subject/Computing/Authoring/Tell_The_World/s-index.h.html**
- The section "Computers and Internet:Internet:World Wide Web:Announcement Services" in the Yahoo directory, **http://www.yahoo.com/Computers_and_Internet/Internet/World_Wide_Web/Announcement_Services/**

Two documents that give a comprehensive list of services and sites to use for announcing a Web page are:

- "FAQ: How to Announce Your New Web Site" (**http://ep.com/faq/webannounce.html**)
- "Pointers to Pointers" (**http://www.homecom.com/global/pointers.html**)

Getting your Web page announced properly can take some work, but people are going to have to know about it in order to find it among the millions on the World Wide Web.

Resources for More Information on Creating Web Pages

There's lots of help on the World Wide Web for creating Web pages and using HTML. Most of the major directories (such as Yahoo or Excite) have sections on the topic, several discussion groups and newsgroups deal with HTML and authoring at basic and advanced levels, and there are several tutorials you can use with a Web browser to help you learn. We'll give some more detail about each of those areas below. In addition to what follows, you can find a list of books on this topic by using the URL **http://www.yahoo.com/ Business_and_Economy/Companies/Books/Titles/Internet/World_Wide_Web/Web_Page_Design**. (We recommend *The Web Page Workbook,* also published by Franklin Beedle & Associates, if you're looking for a book to give you more information.)

* Listings in Directories—look at these sections of directories for information about HTML:

    eXcite, General / Computing / Authoring : Topics, **http://www.excite.com/Subject/Computing/ Authoring/s-index.h.html**

    Yahoo, Computers and Internet:Software:Data Formats:HTML, **http://www.yahoo.com/ Computers_and_Internet/Software/Data_Formats/HTML/**

    WWW Virtual Library, World Wide Web Development, **http://www.stars.com/Vlib/**
* Discussion Groups:

    HTML-LIST, HTML Authoring Mailing List. To subscribe send e-mail to **LISTSERV@NETCENTRAL.NET** with the body of the message being

    SUBSCRIBE HTML-LIST your-full-name.

    ADV-HTML, Advanced HTML Discussion List. To subscribe send e-mail to **LISTSERV@UA1VM.UA.EDU** with the body of the message being

    SUBSCRIBE ADV-HTML your-full-name

    A list of other discussions groups is kept in the document World Wide Web Mail Addresses at **http://www.w3.org/pub/WWW/Mail/**
* Newsgroups—There are several newsgroups that deal with the issues of authoring Web pages.

    comp.infosystems.www.authoring.html—discussion of issues related to HTML in terms of usage, standards, etc.

    comp.infosystems.www.authoring.images—discussion of issues related to the use of images within Web pages.

    comp.infosystems.www.authoring.misc—discussion on any topics related to writing Web pages.
* Tutorials and Guides—There are several very good guides and tutorials for creating Web pages.

    Click on **Help** from the Menu Bar, then choose **How to Create Web Services**.

    "A Beginner's Guide to URLs" (**http://www.sils.umich.edu/~fprefect/primers/url-primer.html**) is a useful guide to different URL formats.

    "HTML Guides and Other Useful Documents" (**http://www.vmedia.com/vvc/onlcomp/hpim/ resource.html**) is a good place to start for finding general resources, tutorials, and FAQs related to HTML and authoring.

    "NCSA—A Beginner's Guide to HTML" (**http://www.ncsa.uiuc.edu/demoweb/url-primer.html**) is an excellent tutorial to take you through the basics of using HTML.

Summary

Web pages are text or ASCII files in which HTML, HyperText Markup Language, is used to specify the format of the Web page, images to be displayed, hyperlinks, and possibly other elements. A Web browser interprets the HTML in the file, called the source file, and then displays the Web page. So one part of the task of writing Web pages is learning how to use HTML to design and implement appropriate and effective pages.

The source file for a Web page consists of text, URLs, and other elements along with tags or directives written according to the rules of HTML. Most HTML tags are enclosed between < and >. Some tags occur in pairs with the second being like the first, except a slash is used after the < to indicate it's the matching tag; for example, <I> and </I>. Other tags occur as single entities, such as <P>. Tags can be written using upper- or lowercase letters; HTML ignores the case of letters in a tag. In URLs you have to pay strict attention to the case of the letters. An HTML document ought to have two parts, a heading and a body. The heading contains the title for the Web page, and the body holds the content—what will be displayed on the Web page. HTML tags can be used for some control over vertical spacing, such as ending lines and starting paragraphs, but otherwise most horizontal and vertical spacing within a source file is ignored. The browser takes care of fitting the page within its window. HTML tags are also used to specify up to six levels of headings in a document, and control whether text is displayed in bold, italic, or plain font. Lists— numbered, with bullets, or descriptive—can be specified with HTML tags. HTML is also used to create and specify hyperlinks and place images within a Web page. The hyperlinks start with a tag of the form <A HREF="*URL*"> (where you substitute an actual URL for *URL*),followed by text or a tag for an image, and then terminated with </A>. The following:

```
It appears that <A HREF="http://www.mwc.edu/ernie/index.html">
Ernest Ackermann</A> is the culprit!
```

would appear on a Web page as

```
It appears that Ernest Ackermann is the culprit!
```

Clicking, in the Web page, on Ernest Ackermann would cause the browser to open the location associated with **http://www.mwc.edu/ernie/index.html**. Images are put into Web pages using a tag of the form <IMG SRC="*URL*"> where the URL of an image is put in for *URL*. The image needs to be either in GIF or JPEG format to be displayed by the Web browser. Text can be aligned with an image, either at the top, middle, or bottom. Images can be placed to the left or right of text. HTML does have lots of other tags; we've covered the basic ones in this chapter.

Since a source file is in text format, it can be created with any editor or word processor that allows you to save a file in text or ASCII form. No special program to create a Web page is necessary, but when there's lots to do or you have to convert from another format to a Web document, it's useful to have a program designed to create Web pages. Some are available as shareware, some free, and some must be purchased before using them. Several directory lists of these programs are given.

Learning HTML is one part of being able to create interesting and effective Web pages. you also need to be concerned with the content and the layout of the content. Two dimensional design skills are as important as technical skills. There are a number of technical items over which the Web page designer or author has no control such as the resolution and number of colors available on the monitor used to view the Web page. A number of tips for good style are listed along with a list of style guides available on the Web.

Putting a page on the World Wide Web means that the file(s) that make up the text, images, and other elements on the page have to be placed on a computer that's acting as a Web server. You need to check with your organization, school, business, or Internet service provider to find out the policies and procedures for your situation. Once the page is accessible through the World Wide Web or Internet and you know its URL, you can start announcing or publicizing it. A list of several different ways to announce a Web page is given.

Designing, creating, or writing a Web page is generally very satisfying. You create something and then let millions of folks around the world see it. Before making the page available to the world, you can develop it on your computer and view it with your Web browser. When you need help or want to pursue the topic further there are a number of resources, guides, newsgroups and mailing lists on the Web to give help in creating or authoring Web pages. What fun!

Exercises

1. a. Does your organization, school, company, or Internet service provider have a home page? What's the URL?
   b. Take a look at the source view for the Web page in part a. What's in the heading section?
   c. To whom do you send e-mail for suggestions or comments?
   d. When was the page last modified?

2. Suppose you've created a personal home page.
   a. Find out the steps necessary to get the page on the World Wide Web.
   b. What are the rules for the page's content? Can you put *anything* at all on the page?

3. Make some modifications to the Web page in Example 7.1.
   a. Replace the items in section A so it describes what you do professionally or the classes you're taking.
   b. Replace the items in sections B and C to reflect your interests.
   c. If you've got a picture or image in digital form, replace the image that was used in the text.

4. Suppose the file named **bobo.gif** holds an image in GIF format, and it's in the folder or directory named **c:\exercise**. To answer the following questions, supply the HTML tags to accomplish the task described.

   a. Write the HTML necessary and sufficient to display the image as part of a Web page.

   b. Write the HTML necessary and sufficient so the image appears on the page as a hyperlink without any attached text. When someone clicks on it, the current Web page is replaced by a page consisting only of the image.

   c. Write the HTML necessary and sufficient so the image appears as part of a Web page. Next to the image are the words "enter at your own risk." The words function as a hyperlink to **http:// www.mwc.edu/~ernie/funhouse.html**, but clicking on the picture does nothing.

5. Write the HTML necessary to display the list

   Dave
   Marsha
   John
   Rita
   Ernie

   a. as
   1. Dave
   2. Marsha
   3. John
   4. Rita
   5. Ernie

   b. as
   - Dave
   - Marsha
   - John
   - Rita
   - Ernie

   c. as
   1. Dave
   2. Marsha
      - John
      - Rita
   3. Ernie

6. Create a Web page that's
   a. a personal Web page for your instructor, spouse, or boss.
   b. a Web page for a small business.
   c. a Web page for a major entertainment or sports figure.
   d. a Web page for a candidate for political office.

7. Retrieve the document "Do's and Don'ts of Web Design."
   a. Each item listed as a Don't has a hyperlink to serve as an example. Follow the link and explain why you think this is an example of a Web design Don't. (Feel free to find another Web page that serves as an example.)
   b. Do the same for the items listed as Do's.

8. The HTML tag <**BODY BACKGROUND="***URL*"**>, where *URL* is the URL of an image file, makes that file the background for the Web page. That's the way some folks put a colorful background on their Web pages. Take a look at the source for the Web page at **http://www.mwc.edu/jblair** for an example of the use of a background color.
   a. Using a Web page you've written change the tag <**BODY**> to <**BODY BACKGROUND="http://www.mwc.edu/ernie/purp.gif"**> and view the resulting Web page.
   b. You may want to use other backgrounds. A collection of backgrounds is available at Texture Land, **http://www.meat.com/textures/**. Go to that site, retrieve a texture, and use it in one of your Web pages.

9. A service on the World Wide Web named CRAYON (**http://crayon.net**), which stands for CReAte Your Own Newspaper, lets you create a newspaper by automatically constructing a Web page based on your choices of news sources.
   a. Using CRAYON, create a Web "newspaper" for yourself. Print a copy of the source document.
   b. Without using CRAYON, create a Web "newspaper" for yourself.
   c. Create a newsletter that carries information about a specific topic. For example, you might want to create one about health, bicycling, a specific sport, a specific type of music, or stock market prices.

10. Create a Web page that tells the reader about a subject you're interested in or a hobby you have. Make it interesting and informative. Include links to some of the most important Web pages and WWW resources related to the subject or hobby.

11. Suppose you're in the business of creating Web pages for others. Design and build a Web page that describes your services and shows your work.

CHAPTER 8

Telnet, FTP, and Gopher

As we've seen, there's lots of information and resources available on the World Wide Web. But remember that the popularity of the World Wide Web is a fairly recent development. Mosaic, the first graphical Web browser made available to the public, was released in November, 1993, and people were using the Internet for 20 years before that. Information was and is still shared on the Internet through the services or protocols *Telnet*, *FTP*, and *Gopher*. *Telnet* allows log-in access to another computer on the Internet. It's used to execute programs (like database searches) on remote computers. *FTP*, which stands for File Transfer Protocol, is the basic means of copying a file from one computer system to another. **Gopher**, made available in 1991, became an extremely popular service because it gave access to information and services on the Internet through a relatively easy-to-use menu system.

All of these protocols can be used with a Web browser. *Protocols* are the rules through which clients and servers on the Internet exchange information. Each service has different protocols. You can tell the protocol being used by looking at the URL for a resource. You would use the URL **http://lcweb.loc.gov**, for example, to go to the home page for the Library of Congress. The protocol here, **http**, brings a Web page, with images and formatted text, to your browser. The Library of Congress also provides access to its resources through:

Telnet: Use the URL **telnet://locis.loc.gov** to connect to a remote computer and search the library's holdings.

FTP: Use the URL **ftp://lcweb.loc.gov** to copy files without viewing them first.

Gopher: Use the URL **gopher://lcweb.loc.gov** for a menu-oriented (little text and no images) interface to basically the same information available as on a Web page.

You'll find that other sites provide access through these different protocols. In this chapter we'll look at using Telnet, FTP, and Gopher with your Web browser. We'll discuss why the services and protocols are used, when and why you'd want to use them, and ways to search the Internet with them. The topics are:

* Telnet
* Hytelnet—Finding Resources Available through Telnet
* FTP

* Archie
* Gopher

Telnet

When you are working on a computer connected to the Internet, you are part of a system of networks composed of over one million computers. Networks are often designed to allow users on one computer in the network to access information or run programs on another computer on the network. The Internet allows for that possibility through the service named Telnet. The service was created so that an Internet user at one site (the local site) could access facilities, software, or data at another site (the remote site). When you use Telnet on your computer to contact another computer system on the Internet, it's as if you are directly connected to the remote system. Naturally, you have to have permission to use the remote system. Some sites require a log-in name and a password, while others don't. There are thousands of sites on the Internet that allow almost anyone access to their computers through Telnet.

When and Why to Use Telnet

Some resources on the Internet are only available through Telnet. This is especially true of the programs that search some types of databases, like library catalogs. Telnet also gives access to several bulletin boards and community network systems. When you use Telnet you're going to log in to another computer system, and you will have to use the commands for that systems. Sometimes that takes you into unfamiliar territory. You'll also find that the response from the remote system may not seem smooth or may be very slow. Some of that has to do with the fact that you're communicating with the remote system over the Internet. What you type and the response from the remote system is transmitted as a collection of packets that have to be sent, received, and assembled. Because of these limitations, you may want to use Telnet only when the resource isn't available any other way. Many of the services that used to be available only through Telnet are now available as Web pages and are generally easier to use that way.

Here are some examples of resources available through Telnet:

Library of Congress:
telnet://locis.loc.gov
Search for materials available at the Library of Congress. No log-in name or password is required.

PENpages:
telnet://penpages.psu.edu
Search and retrieve information from agricultural, health, teaching, and other databases. This service is provided by the College of Agriculture of the Pennsylvania State University and the Pennsylvania Department of Education. You type the word **world** when you see the prompt **Username:**.

Med Help BBS:
telnet://medhlp.netusa.net
A nonprofit organization of medical professionals providing information written in nontechnical terms.

Sports Schedules for National Hockey League:
telnet://culine.colorado.edu:860

Look up schedules for teams in the National Hockey League.

The Form of a URL for Telnet

You can see from these examples that the URL for a Telnet resource starts with the word **telnet**, a colon (:), and two slashes (//), as in **telnet://**. That's followed by the domain name or IP address of the computer system that provides the service available through Telnet. In some cases the domain name is followed by a colon (:) and a number, as in **telnet://culine.colorado.edu:860**, the URL for the sports schedules for the National Hockey League. That number at the end is called a *port number*. This form is used at some remote sites so an Internet user doesn't have to give a log-in name. The remote site automatically starts a program or service when your Telnet client makes the connection. You need to know this form if you're going to open the location and type in the URL yourself. In many cases, however, you'll probably use Telnet by clicking on a hyperlink in a Web document.

Configuring Your Browser for Telnet

In order to use Telnet with your Web browser, you need a Telnet program on your computer with the proper option so the browser knows the name of the file to use for Telnet applications. To see if your computer is set for Telnet use, start the browser, click on the icon labeled **Open**, and type in one of the URLs listed above. If you get connected, then all is well. If you get the message "Unable to find application," then Telnet isn't available. In that case, you or some helpful person should find a Telnet client program for you to use and set the proper preferences in Netscape.

There may be a copy of Telnet on your computer. First, ask whether Telnet is on your computer or if it came with the software you received from your Internet provider. The standard installation of Windows 95 puts a Telnet program in the directory or folder **Windows**. If that doesn't help, see if you can find a Telnet program already on the computer. Use the tools for searching directories and folders for a program or application whose name starts with Telnet. If you're using Windows 95, select **Windows Explorer** from the Start Menu, click on **Tools** from the Menu Bar, then select **Find** and then **Files or Folders**. Type **telnet*** for the name of the file to find. This may tell you if a copy of a Telnet client is on your computer. (A Telnet program could be on the computer under a different name.) If you find a copy, note its location so you'll be all set when we get to the section describing how to configure Netscape Navigator to use Telnet.

If there is no copy of Telnet on your computer, you might want to retrieve one from the Internet. There are several available; some are shareware and some are freeware. If the program is shareware, you're encouraged to copy it to your computer, try it for a while, and then send the author a fee for a full-fledged version of the program. If the program is freeware, you can copy it to your computer and use it without any cost.

These steps tell you how to get a copy of Telnet from the Internet, install it, and set the proper Netscape Navigator preference so you can use it. If you already have a copy of Telnet on your computer go to step 4.

1. Find a location on the Internet that has Telnet programs to fit into your environment.

   If you're working in a Windows environment, you can find a collection of programs that work well at the Telnet section of the site maintained by the Chicago Computer Society. Use the URL http://www.ccs.org/winsock/telnet.html for information about several Telnet programs. (There's also lots of information about other types of programs at **http://www.ccs.org/winsock**, and it's definitely worth a visit to the home page for the Chicago Computer Society at **http://www.ccs.org**.)

For other sources, use the keyword **telnet** with a program that searches the World Wide Web. Click on the directory button **Net Search** to access one. For more information on searching, look at Chapter 6.

2. Retrieve a Telnet program.
There are likely to be several Telnet programs listed at one site. How to decide which to choose? Be sure you pick a program that will work in your environment—for example, don't select a program designed for a Macintosh computer to use with Windows 95. You'll also want to be sure to select one that emulates or mimics a **vt100** terminal. A number of resources available through Telnet require vt100 emulation. Other things that might affect your choice are the program's features and its cost. We'll work here with the shareware program Net Term. It works well and is inexpensive. It's available at several places on the Internet. Try one of the following URLs to retrieve it: **ftp://www.neosoft.com/ pub/users/z/zkrr01/neterm28.zip** or **ftp://papa.indstate.edu/winsock-1/telnet/neterm28.zip**.

After you retrieve shareware you can take your time evaluating the program. If you decide to use it regularly, register the program and send payment to the author.

Regardless of which Telnet package you choose, retrieve the program. If it's a hyperlink on a Web page, click on it to bring it to your computer. You could also retrieve it by clicking on the icon **Open** and then typing in one of the URLs above. After giving the URL or clicking on a hyperlink, you might get a message "No Viewer Configured for File Type: application/x-zip-compressed" from Netscape Navigator. That's because if you selected one of the URLs above, the file is stored in compressed format using a program named PKZIP or WinZip, and your Web browser doesn't have those programs installed as "helper" programs to uncompress automatically the file after it's been transmitted. That's just fine; select the option that lets you **Save File...** A **Save As..** dialog box pops up for you to specify the folder to use to store the file. Working with compressed files is discussed in the section in this chapter on FTP. If PKZIP and/or WINZIP aren't on your computer or network, you'll have to retrieve one of them from the Internet as well. A URL for PKZIP is **ftp://ftp.ccs.org/ccs/ tools/pkz204g.exe**, and a URL for WinZip is **http://www.winzip.com/winzip/download.html**. Try the URL **http://www.pkware.com** to read the documentation that comes with PKZIP, and use the URL **http://www.winzip.com/winzip/** to go to the WinZip home page.

3. Uncompress and install the Telnet program.
After retrieving the program you'll have to uncompress it and then install the software. Let's say you've retrieved **neterm28.zip** from **http://starbase.neosoft.com/~zkrr01/ntdl.html**. Since it's in *zipped* format, you need to *unzip* it. Exactly how you do that depends on which compression program you're

using and how the Windows system has been set up on the computer you're using. It could be that by clicking on the name **neterm28.zip**, the program is automatically unzipped. If that's not the case, then create two folders or directories, one name **tempcrt** and the other named **netterm**. Copy **neterm28.zip** to the folder/directory **tempcrt**. If you' have WinZip installed, click on **neterm28.zip** and extract the files to the directory **tempcrt**. One of the new files is named **setup.exe**; click on it. The setup program takes care of everything and should install the program NetTerm. You can now safely delete the directory **c:\tempcrt**. If you don't have WinZip installed or this seems too difficult for you, then ask for help from a friend or local expert.

4. Set the Netscape Navigator Preferences.
   Click on **Options** on the Menu Bar and select **General Preferences.** Click on the section labeled **Apps.** You'll see a display similar to what's shown in Figure 8.1. Here you type in the path name for the Telnet program you want Netscape to know about. You type **c:\Netterm\netterm.exe** or whatever the name and location of the Telnet program is into the pane labeled **Telnet Application** as shown in Figure 8.1. If you're going to use the Telnet that's included with Windows 95, you'd type **c:\windows\telnet.exe** instead.

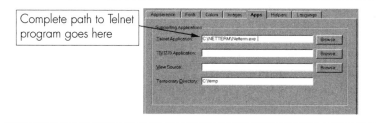

Figure 8.1   Apps Section of Netscape General Preferences Filled in to Use NETTERM as the Telnet Application

After it's typed in click on the button labeled **OK** (not shown). That makes Netscape aware of the program you'll be using for Telnet.

If you find these steps too difficult, ask for some help from a friend or local expert.

After you've set up Telnet it's ready to be used when necessary. Suppose you were perusing the home page for the Library of Congress (**http://lcweb.loc.gov**), you saw the entry for LOCIS (the Library of Congress Information Systems), and you wanted to search for books by a particular author or search for the titles of books on a specific subject. If you click on the hyperlink shown in Figure 8.2, you'll go to a Web page that has a hyperlink to LOCIS as well as some tips about using LOCIS and using Telnet from a Web browser.

From there you'll be able to search information held by the Library of Congress by using Telnet.

Figure 8.2   Home Page for Library of Congress

Here's another scenario. A friend tells you how you can look up the schedules of teams in the National Hockey League by using Telnet to **culine.coloradu.edu** at port 860. You click on the icon **Open**, type in **telnet://culine.colorado.edu:860**, click on **Open**, and away you go. Figure 8.3 show the Open Location dialog box filled in with the URL for NHL schedules.

Figure 8.3   Open a Location Dialog Box Filled in with URL for NHL Schedules

Hytelnet—Finding Resources Available through Telnet

There are literally thousands of Telnet sites. There are so many interesting resources available that you need a guide to help find what you want. *Hytelnet* is a tool for working with Telnet. Hytelnet, created by Peter Scott and others at the University of Saskatchewan, makes it relatively easy to look through and use an organized list of Telnet sites. You browse the collection using a hypertext interface; that's why it's called Hytelnet. The sites are arranged in categories by the type of service, such as library catalog, database, bulletin board, electronic book, or network information. Hytelnet also comes with a glossary of network terms and other information about Telnet, Hytelnet itself, and software used on various library systems. Hytelnet also includes "webCATS"—a collection of library resources available as Web pages. Hytelnet is available on the World Wide Web by using the URL **http://library.usask.ca/hytelnet.**

When you use Hytelnet, you move from one item to another through a hypertext interface. When you get to the pages that describe individual Telnet sites or resources, Hytelnet includes information about how to log in and log out. The Hytelnet pages are like other Web pages. In this case, you click on the name of a service or site and your Telnet program starts and makes the connection. Then you may have to type in a log-in name and password. When you use Hytelnet this way, the instructions about the site you're contacting are on the screen in the Web browser window, and the Telnet session is in the Telnet window. You need to select a library, database, bulletin board, or some other type of resource. We'll demonstrate how you might use Hytelnet in the next example.

Example 8.1   Using Hytelnet

Hytelnet is an excellent tool to guide you to Telnet resources on the Internet. Using Hytelnet, you can access library catalogs throughout the world, access a number of government and private databases, connect to various bulletin board systems, and access some resources that don't fall in any of those categories.

In this example we're going to connect to the America's Job Bank. It is a network of several thousand state employment offices. We won't give the details of using the services because that's not really pertinent to talking about Hytelnet. We'll leave that to you to explore. Assuming that Netscape Navigator is already started, here are the steps to follow:

1. Open the location **http://library.usask.ca/hytelnet/** to connect to the Hytelnet home page at the University of Saskatchewan.
2. Select the hyperlink **Other Resources.**
3. Select the hyperlink **Miscellaneous Resources.**
4. Select the hyperlink for **America's Job Bank.**
5. Log in.

> 1. Open the location **http://library.usask.ca/hytelnet/** to connect to the Hytelnet home page at the University of Saskatchewan.

W⁴W Click on the icon labeled **Open.**

W⁴W Type in **http://library.usask.ca/hytelnet/.**

W⁴W Click on the button labeled **Open.**

Opening the location for Hytelnet brings up a Web page like the one in Figure 8.4. We've labeled some of the parts to explain it.

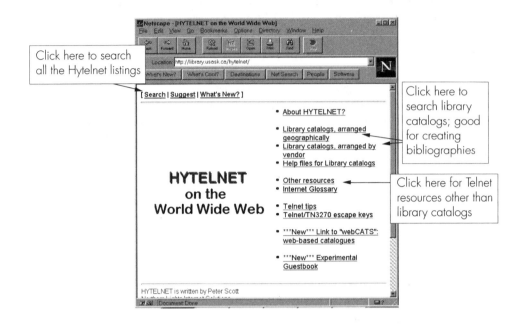

Figure 8.4   Home Page for Hytelnet at University of Saskatchewan

Following any of the links here would be interesting. We won't take a look at the library systems, but you ought to take the time to look at some of them. All types of libraries are listed—research libraries, community libraries, library consortia, specialized libraries such as law and medical libraries, and public libraries. All of these have a connection to the Internet, and through Telnet, will let you search their collections.

2. Select the hyperlink **Other Resources**.

wWw Click on the hyperlink **Other Resources**.

Selecting **Other Resources** takes you to the Web page shown in Figure 8.5. It has links to several categories of resources available through Telnet.

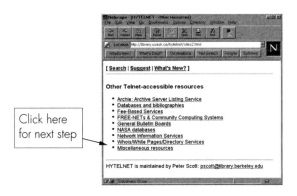

Click here
for next step

Figure 8.5   Other Telnet Resources Page from Hytelnet

3. Select the hyperlink **Miscellaneous Resources**.

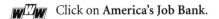 Click on **Miscellaneous Resources**.

Selecting the hyperlink **Miscellaneous Resources** takes you to a Web page that's shown in Figure 8.6. It lists lots of sites; there's probably something to catch anyone's interest.

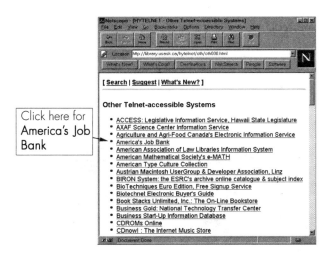

Click here for
America's Job
Bank

Figure 8.6   Other Telnet-Accessible Systems from Hytelnet

4. Select the hyperlink for **America's Job Bank**.

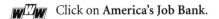 Click on **America's Job Bank**.

The Web page that comes up next, shown in Figure 8.7, isn't a list of links or categories. It contains a hyperlink to the site through Telnet along with a description of the information available at the site and instructions for accessing the resources there.

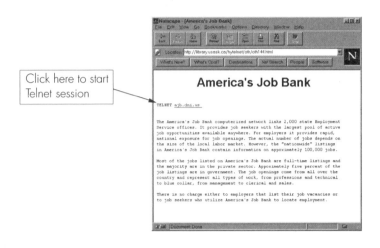

Figure 8.7   Information Page for America's Job Bank

5. Log in.

Click on the hyperlink **ajb.dni.us.**

That starts the Telnet program you're using with your browser. The Telnet program will attempt to contact the site **ajb.dni.us,** and in a relatively short period of time you ought to see a screen similar to the one in Figure 8.8.

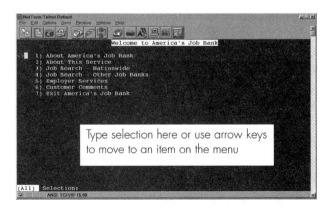

Figure 8.8   Beginning Screen at America's Job Bank

Now that you're connected to America's Job Bank, you can choose an item from the menu. Type the number of an item and press Enter, or use the up and down arrow keys to select. Typing h and pressing Enter brings some help information to the screen. Take some time to browse the menus. On each screen you will have the chance to come back to the starting menu. When you are ready to leave, return to this menu and select **Exit America's Job Bank**. If you get stuck, you can break the connection by closing the Telnet window or by choosing **File** from the menu bar and selecting **Disconnect**.

At some sites you're asked to enter the type of terminal. The remote system needs to know how your terminal or software treats the special characters the remote system will have to send to let you work with menus or other features in the Telnet window. You ought to have your Telnet program set so that it's emulating or mimicking a **vt100** terminal. That's what most sites expect. If you have some time, explore other Telnet sites accessible through Hytelnet.

————————————————End of Example 8.1————————————————

FTP

FTP, which stands for *file transfer protocol*, is one of the basic Internet services. It's designed to copy files from one computer system to another. A primary reason for creating the Internet was to allow researchers to exchange ideas and results of their work. FTP allows that sharing of information, data, or any sort of file.

In this section we'll look at using *anonymous FTP* to retrieve copies of files from another site on the Internet. The term *anonymous* means anyone on the Internet can copy files from a computer system without being a registered user of that system. In that way it's just like displaying or saving a Web page from some other site on the World Wide Web. A big difference between HTTP, the protocol used on the World Wide Web, and FTP is that FTP was created at a time when most Internet users had a fair amount of experience using computers, so it doesn't provide very much in the way of a user-friendly interface. But it's an efficient way to copy files. Anonymous FTP allows you to retrieve files that are publicly available from another computer system on the Internet. Systems that allow anonymous FTP sessions are called *anonymous FTP sites*, and the collection of files they make available are called *FTP archives*.

Before HTTP and Gopher, FTP was about the only way to copy files on the Internet. You can send a file as part of an e-mail message, but that's not really the same thing. If I want to retrieve a file at your site and it's coming to me by e-mail, I have to send e-mail to your site to request the file and the file has to be packaged up as part of a message and then sent to me. With anonymous FTP, a group of files is made available to the general public. Anyone can contact the computer system, request a file, and have it sent to them. The length of time it takes to transfer depends on the size of the file and the speed of the Internet connection or modem at the sender's and receiver's site, but is as fast as retrieving a comparable sized Web page.

In this section we'll look at:
* URL Format for FTP
* Retrieving a File by Anonymous FTP
* Working with Different File Types
* Finding Files Available by Anonymous FTP

URL Format for FTP

FTP is most effective when you know the URL for the file. The URL includes the exact location—file name, directory name, and Internet name of the remote computer system—of a file. The general form of a URL for anonymous FTP is **ftp://name-of-ftp-site/directory-name/file-name**

1. The URL for anonymous FTP starts with **ftp://**.
2. The name of the FTP site follows the three characters **://**.
3. The name of the directory starts with the first single **/** and goes up to but not including the last **/**.
4. The name of the file follows the last **/**.

All the slashes (/) go in the same direction and slant the way they would under the Unix operating system.

Suppose a friend tells you, "I found this great picture of Mars with great detail and colors. You can get it by anonymous FTP at the FTP site for the Jet Propulsion Laboratory, **ftp.jpl.nasa.gov**. You'll want to get the file **marglobe.gif**. It's in the directory **pub/images/browse**. There are also some animations at the same site in **pub/images/anim**." You'd like to view the image, and she's told you everything you need to retrieve it. The URL for that file is **ftp://ftp.jpl.nasa.gov/pub/images/browse/marglobe.gif.**

Matching this to the general form, we have the following:

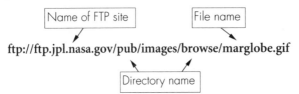

You can also use a URL to refer to a directory by putting a / as the last character in a URL. For example, if you use the URL:

> **ftp://ftp.jpl.nasa.gov/pub/images/browse/**

the Web browser displays a list of all the files or subdirectories in the directory /**pub/images/browse**. Each file or subdirectory is represented as a hyperlink and you can retrieve it by clicking on it.

Retrieving a File by Anonymous FTP

You can retrieve a file, that is, copy it from a remote site to the computer you're using, in one of two ways.

1. Typing in a URL (Open a Location).
    If you type the URL for the file (open a location) or if you click on a hyperlink without pressing the Shift key, the file is also transferred to the Web browser, rather than put directly into a file you've named. This is useful if you want to view the file before you save it to a file. If the browser is configured to display or play a file of that type, you'll see/hear the contents of the file in the Web browser window. Some examples of files of this type are text files, Web pages that are text files with HTML commands, or GIF or JPEG image files. The file may also be displayed through a widow created by another program called a "helper application." Otherwise, a message box pops up with "No Viewer Configured for File Type:." If the file is displayed in the browser window, select **Save as..** from the pull-down menu **File** in the Menu Bar. This opens a "Save As .." dialog box on the screen. Set the directory or folder name and then click on the button labeled Save. If the file comes up in the window for another appli-

cation, save it through the commands for that application. An example of this is retrieving a file in MS-Word format. See the tip below to deal with a file type that doesn't match any your browser can work with.

2. Shift and Click on a Hyperlink.
You use this if you're working in the Web browser window and a hyperlink to the file is present. To retrieve the file and save it use Shift+click on the hyperlink, hold down the Shift key, click on the hyperlink, and release the Shift key. This opens a **Save As..** dialog box on the screen. Set the directory or folder name and then click on the button labeled Save. The file will be transferred from the FTP archive site to the file you've specified on your computer.

Tip

What to do when No Viewer Configured for File Type: **pops up.**

The message **No Viewer Configured for File Type** means you've come across a file type that your browser doesn't know what to do with at the present time. Select the option that lets you **Save to Disk.** A **Save As..** dialog box pops up in which you specify the folder where you want to store the file. If you do want to see/hear the file, then be sure you have the hardware and/or software you need to uncompress, display, or play the file after it's been transmitted. There are lots of variations and possibilities for the necessary equipment and programs, so we can't cover all that here. But, if you do have everything you need, you may want to configure the browser so it knows what to do with files of that type in the future. Instructions on letting Netscape know about a particular helper application are in the Netscape Handbook (click on the directory button **Handbook**) in the section Applications: General|Helpers (select **A** from the **Index**). The URL for that section is **http://home.netscape.com/eng/mozilla/3.0/handbook/docs/panels.html#C5.**

Example 8.2   Retrieving a File by Anonymous FTP

In this example we'll retrieve the file containing an image of Mars that we mentioned previously. We're assuming that Netscape Navigator has been started and we're using the Web browser window. We will retrieve the file in the two ways mentioned above.

First we'll retrieve it by typing the URL **ftp://ftp.jpl.nasa.gov/pub/images/browse/marglobe.gif.** Web browsers can display files of this type. It will be displayed, but it isn't saved into a file that we can use again until we select **Save As..** from the pull-down menu **File** in the Menu Bar and set the folder and file name for it. In this case, we view the contents of the file before saving it.

Then we'll save the same file by opening the URL for the directory that contains the file (**ftp://ftp.jpl.nasa.gov/pub/images/browse/**), finding the hyperlink for the file, and using Shift+click to retrieve it. Retrieving a file this way is quicker because the browser doesn't have to display it first.

Method 1—View the file first

Open the location ftp://ftp.jpl.nasa.gov/pub/images/browse/marglobe.gif.

WWW Click on the icon **Open**.

WWW Type the URL **ftp://ftp.jpl.nasa.gov/pub/images/browse/marglobe.gif**.

WWW Click on the button labeled **Open** or press **Enter**.

The image is displayed by your viewer as shown in Figure 8.9.

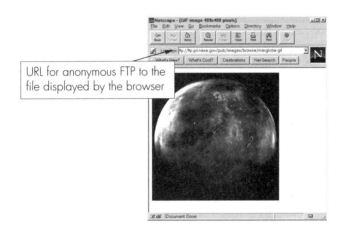

URL for anonymous FTP to the file displayed by the browser

Figure 8.9   Image of Mars Retrieved by Anonymous FTP

To save this in a file on the computer you're using, follow these steps:

WWW Click on **File** in the Menu Bar.

WWW Select **Save as ...**

Clicking on **File** gives a pull-down menu. Select the option to save what is being displayed by the browser into a file. A **Save As..** dialog box appears.

Store the file in the appropriate folder or directory.

You can save the file in the current folder. Alternately, you could select or create another folder to hold the image. Figure 8.10 shows the file being stored in a folder named **images**. Store the file wherever you'd like. It is a good idea to have one folder for all items of a similar type or a collection of files related to a project. That way it's easier for you to find the file the next time you want it.

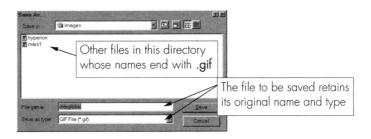

Figure 8.10   Save As.. Dialog Box for Saving marglobe.gif

Once the appropriate folder is chosen:

[www]   Click on the button labeled **Save**.

Method 2—Don't view the file; use Shift+click

Open the location **ftp://ftp.jpl.nasa.gov/pub/images/browse/**.

[www]   Click on the icon **Open**.

[www]   Type the URL **ftp://ftp.jpl.nasa.gov/pub/images/browse/**.

[www]   Click on the button labeled **Open** or press **Enter**.

This connects you by anonymous FTP to the archive server at **ftp.jpl.nasa.gov** and displays the listing of the directory **/pub/images/browse** as shown in Figure 8.11.

Figure 8.11   Initial Window for Anonymous FTP Session with ftp.jpl.nasa.gov

This initial window for anonymous FTP includes messages about key files to read if you have questions about the site. One is named **readme.txt**. It's common to find a file with a similar name (sometimes it's **READ.ME** or **readme**) at an anonymous FTP archive. When you go to an unfamiliar FTP site, it's a good idea to take the time to look at **readme** files. To read any of them, wait until you see the name listed as a hyperlink and then click on the name. This window also contains information about the items in the archive.

Now we need to find the file named **marglobe.gif**. You recall from previous chapters that there are several ways to do this. Make sure you're at the Web page for **ftp://ftp.jpl.nasa.gov/pub/images/browse/**.

Move through the listing by repeatedly pressing the down-arrow key, the Page Down key, or the space bar to move one window at a time, or use the vertical scroll bar to move through the file. Using the scroll bar is the quickest way to move through the listing, but use the method that's best for you.

W⁴W   Press **Ctrl**+F or click on the icon **Find**, type the name of the file to retrieve, and then click on the button labeled **Find Next**.

Regardless of which method you choose, you'll eventually get to the portion of the listing shown in Figure 8.12.

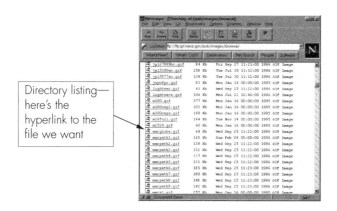

Directory listing—here's the hyperlink to the file we want

Figure 8.12   Directory Listing Showing Hyperlinks

The listing in Figure 8.12 contains an icon for each file. The icons here indicate the file is an image. It also contains the size of each file followed by the date it was last modified, and an annotation describing the type of the file.

To retrieve the file:

W⁴W   Move the cursor or mouse pointer to the name **marglobe.gif**. The cursor turns into a hand when it's sitting on a hyperlink.

w Press **Shift**+click.

At that point a **Save As..** dialog box, as shown in Figure 8.10, appears. Select the proper folder or directory for the file and click on the button labeled **Save.** A box labeled **Saving Location** appears on the screen. That box keeps you updated about the progress of the transfer from the remote site to the computer you're using.

Congratulations! You've successfully retrieved a file by anonymous FTP. You can use the file for your personal use. Before using it for any commercial purposes, be sure to obtain permission. You can retrieve files by anonymous FTP at no cost, but having retrieved a file doesn't give you the right to use it any way you'd like. The information in these files needs to be treated in the same way as information that's part of a book, newspaper, audio recording, or video recording.

─────────────End of Example 8.2─────────────

Working with Different File Types

Text files are files that contain plain printable characters, like the ones you see on this page. They're also called ASCII (rhymes with pass key) files. The source for a Web page is also a text file. It's written using HTML, made up entirely with characters you can read or print. You may know that we can think of the information stored in a computer as a string of 1s or 0s. A sequence of eight 1s or 0s is called a **byte**, and a file is a collection of bytes. In an ASCII or text file, each byte represents a character that we can view as text—letters, numerals, punctuation, and spaces. Other types of information such as images, sound, video, programs in the machine language of a computer, spreadsheets, compressed files, or files produced by a word processing program aren't text files. The information they contain isn't meant to be directly interpreted or read by a human. Files like these are called binary files because they are made up of 1s, and 0s aren't interpreted as characters or letters. They have to be given to another program or device so that we can view, hear, or see them printed on paper. You can think of all files as being divided into these two types, text and binary.

Any type of file, text or binary, can be retrieved by anonymous FTP. You'll find your browser is already configured or set up to deal with the text files and some of the binary files. There are many different types of binary files, and we'll discuss some ways to deal with them in this section.

Sometimes you can tell the file type by its name. The letters at the end of a file name following a dot (.) are called the *file extension* portion of the file name. Files whose names end with **.txt** or **.text** are almost always text files. There is more variation for binary files. Files with the extension **.arc**, **.exe**, **.gz**, **.jpeg**, **.lzh**, **.sit**, **.Z**, **.zip**, or **.zoo** are compressed files or archives (collections) of files. You need a program to uncompress these files to work with them. Look at the section "Compressed Files" below for more information. The files with extension **.gif**, **.jpg**, **.jpeg**, **.tif**, **.tiff**, and **.bmp** contain images. Netscape is set to display files whose names end in **.gif**, **.jpg**, or **.jpeg**.. Multimedia, video, animations, and sounds are often in files whose names end with **.mov**, **.mpg**, **.avi**, **.fli**, **.wav**, or **.au**. You may have to get a separate program to view or play them, although Netscape comes with a program that can deal with some of them. Here are some examples of URLs for binary files. The first three are compressed files or archives, and the last is an animation.

* ftp://garbo.uwasa.fi/windows/bitmaps/earth.zip
* ftp://ftp.oleane.net/pub/mirrors/doc/faq/sports/skating/inline-faq/part1.gz
* ftp://crl.nmsu.edu/CLR/multiling/chinese/Dictionary/ecd.exe
* ftp://ftp.jpl.nasa.gov/pub/images/browse/mars1.gif
* ftp://ftp.luth.se/pub/misc/anim/anim/museum1.mpg

You use the same methods to retrieve either type of file while using your Web browser; it doesn't matter whether it's a text or a binary file. Two ways of retrieving files were discussed in the previous section: typing the URL (open a location) and using Shift+click.

Compressed Files. Some files are stored in compressed form. Compressing or archiving can reduce the space (number of bytes) needed to store the file; compressing can cut the size by 50% or more. This also makes it quicker to transfer files. So you see why it would be beneficial to compress a file or a collection of files that is going to be shared through FTP. (Some programs such as PKZIP, used on MS-DOS and MS Windows systems or StuffIt, used on Macintosh systems, allow for the grouping or archiving of a collection of files, compressing the entire collection.) Once you get the files to your system you have to use a program that expands them for use.

You need to know the proper program to run to undo the compression. Usually the last character or last few characters of the file name indicate the program used to construct the compressed file or archive. The letters at the end of a file name following a dot (.) are called the *file extension* portion of the file name. In the file named **mrcry20.zip**, zip is the file extension. If the name of the file ends with **.zip**, then some form of the program PKZIP was used to create it. The program you use to return the file to its original form depends on what type of computer system you're using. On a Unix system you'd use the program unzip, on a DOS system you'd use PKUNZIP, on a Windows systems you'd use PKUNZIP or WINZIP, and on a Macintosh system you'd use ZipIt. (To get both PKZIP and PKUNZIP retrieve the program **pkz204g.exe** from an anonymous FTP archive. For information about these programs use the URL **http://www.pkware.com**. There are lots of anonymous FTP archives on the Internet you can use to retrieve the program; one location is **ftp://ftp.mwc.edu/pub/pc/pkz204g.exe**. A location for information about WinZip is **http://www.winzip.com**.)

Some tips for dealing with compressed files are:
* The last few letters of a file name are often the clue that the file is in compressed form.
* Find someone locally who can help you with compressed files.
* Use anonymous FTP to get copies of these files to read about the compression formats used.
  ftp://rtfm.mit.edu/pub/usenet-by-group/news.answers/ftp-list/faq
  ftp://uiarchive.cso.uiuc.edu/pub/doc/pcnet/compression

There are many different compression schemes, and each has a corresponding program to compress a file or undo the compression. One good source of information on this topic is the file **compression** maintained by David Lemson, available by anonymous FTP from **uiarchive.cso.uiuc.edu** in the directory **/pub/doc/pcnet**. The file contains a table including the name of a compression scheme, the extension attached to the name of a compressed file (you use this to know the program to use to uncompress it), and the names of the compression programs for several different types of computer systems. It also gives sources on the Internet for the compression programs. Two anonymous FTP sources for many of the compression programs are **uiarchive.cso.uiuc.edu** (University of Illinois, Urbana-Champaign) and **garbo.uwasa.fi** (University of Wasa, Helsinki, Finland). At **uiarchive.cso.uiuc.edu** look in the directory **/pub/systems** for programs that will work with a variety of computer systems, such as **linux, mac,** and **pc**. Going to any of these directories gives a list of folders representing some of the major FTP archives on the Internet. The directory **pc** (**ftp://uiarchive.cso.uiuc.edu/pub/systems/pc**), for example, contains folders representing FTP archives for DOS or Windows systems including the archives **cica, garbo, simtelnet, uiuc,** and **winsite**. Ones for working with compressed files are **/pub/systems/pc/simtelnet/msdos/arcers, /pub/systems/pc/simtelnet/win3/compress,** and **/pub/systems/pc/simtelnet/win95/compress**. Each of these directories contains a file named **00_index.txt**, which contains a synopsis of each of the programs in the directory. At **garbo.uwasa.fi**, the directories **mac/arcers, pc/arcers,** and **unix/arcers** are good places to look for information and sources dealing with compression.

Example 8.3   Retrieving a Shareware Program and a Compression Program

There are lots of shareware programs available by anonymous FTP. In this example we'll go to an anonymous FTP site and retrieve a shareware genealogy program. You can use it to build a family tree or create a database for keeping records about your heritage. Like many archives or programs available by anonymous FTP, this one is in compressed form. We'll also retrieve a program for uncompressing it. The ones we'll retrieve are meant to be used with MS-Windows computer systems. The programs are also shareware. That means you're free to use them on a trial basis, and the authors expect to be paid if you think the programs are useful.

We'll go by anonymous FTP to the archive at the Swedish University Network (**ftp://ftp.sunet.se**). The programs we'll be considering are in the directory for programs classified as home entertainment, **/pub/simtelnet/win3/genealgy**. Simtel, the coast-to-coast software repository, is a large archive of shareware and freeware for MS-DOS, MS-Windows, Windows 95, WindowsNT, and OS/2 computer systems. The software in this archive is checked for viruses before it's made available to the public.

We'll be looking into the directory **win3**, which contains programs for Windows systems. (Other directories with programs for other systems are in **mdos, win95, nt,** and **os2**.) This directory holds genealogy programs. Their names end with **.zip**. You recognize by the name that the file is compressed, and from reading the preceding section you know that you need a copy of PKUNZIP or WinZip. We'll retrieve a copy of WinZip suitable for use with Windows 95 using the URL **ftp://uiarchive.cso.uiuc.edu/pub/systems/pc/winsite/win95/miscutil/winzip95.exe**.

We'll assume Netscape Navigator is started and we're working in a Web browser window. The steps to follow are:

1. Start an anonymous FTP session with **ftp.sunet.se** and connect to directory **/pub/simtelnet/win3/genealgy**.
2. Retrieve one of the genealogy programs.
3. FTP to the directory at **uiarchive.cso.uiuc.edu** holding the archive for WinZip.
4. Retrieve **winzip95.exe**.
5. Install WinZip95 and the genealogy program.
6. Get the compression program ready to run.
7. Install the genealogy program.
8. Work with the uncompressed file.

1. Start an anonymous FTP session with **ftp.sunet.se** and connect to directory /pub/simtelnet/win3/genealgy.

WWW   Click on the icon **Open** from the Toolbar.

WWW   Type ftp://ftp.sunet.se/pub/simtelnet/win3/genealgy.

WWW   Click on the button labeled **Open**.

Figure 8.13 shows what you're likely to see in your Web browser window.

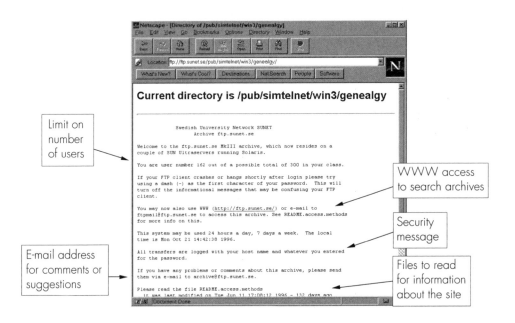

Figure 8.13   Welcome message from ftp.sunet.se

Figure 8.13 shows the first portion of the Web page that lists the files in the directory **/pub/simtelnet/ win3/genealgy**. This Web page also contains several items worth noting. Some deal with issues of general interest for anonymous FTP. You can see them all by scrolling down through the page.

* **Limit on number of users.** This site, like many others, limits the number of anonymous FTP sessions. If a site is at its limit and you try to connect, you'll get a message saying the service isn't available, asking you to try later or giving some alternative sites to try.

* **Security message.** Many sites keep a log of every FTP session.

* **E-mail address for comments or suggestions.** Feel free to write to this address if you have questions or comments about the FTP site. Don't write to this address with questions about the programs you retrieve. Use the address that comes with the programs.

* **Files to read for information.** Many sites have one or more files describing the FTP archive.

* **Hyperlink to parent directory.** The list of hyperlinks on the page includes one to the next higher level or parent directory. Clicking here would take you to **/pub/simtelnet/win3**.

* **Directory index.** Most directories contain a file, named **00_index.txt** in this case, that describes the programs in the directory. Click on the hyperlink to get a description of the files.

2. Retrieve one of the genealogy programs.

This directory contains several compressed archives, each of which is a shareware program. Two are genealogy programs, **kk302.zip** and **pan104.zip**. All the programs are suitable for use with Microsoft Windows. If you're interested in finding a program to organize your family tree you might want to try either one. here we'll retrieve just one, **kk302.zip**. The archives aren't shown in Figure 8.13; you'll have to use the scroll bar or press Page Down on your keyboard to see a listing of them.

w*W* Move the mouse pointer or cursor to the hyperlink **kk302.zip**.

w*W* Press **Shift**+click.

When you press Shift+click, a dialog box labeled **Save As..** pops up, similar to the one in Figure 8.10. You can select any folder or directory to hold the program; you may even want to create a new folder titled **genealgy** to hold the archive. That way you're likely to remember where to find the zip (compressed) file for this program. You can always delete the file or the directory when you're done with them.

w*W* Click on the button labeled **Save** when you're ready to save the file.

When you click on Save, a window titled **Saving Location** pops up. This shows you the progress made during the file transfer. Figure 8.14 shows a Saving Location window with 26% of the file having been transferred. By looking at this you'll get an idea of how long it will take to transfer the file. To stop transmission, click on the button labeled **Cancel**.

Figure 8.14   Saving Location Window

3. FTP to the directory at **uiarchive.cso.uiuc.edu** holding the archive for WinZip.

Click on the icon **Open** from the Toolbar.

Type ftp://uiarchive.cso.uiuc.edu/pub/systems/pc/winsite/win95/miscutil/.

Click on the button labeled **Open**.

4. Retrieve **winzip95.exe**.

Move the cursor to the hyperlink for **winzip95.exe**.

Press **Shift**+click.

Save the file in an appropriate directory.

As before, you'll want to select a good folder or directory to hold this file. As a suggestion, why not put it in a folder named **archiver**?

5. Install Winzip95 and the genealogy program.

The next few steps provide an example of how to make the files you've retrieved usable.

6. Get the compression program ready to run.

The file **winzip95.exe** can be run directly on your computer while you're using Windows because its name ends with .exe. If you saved it in the directory **archiver**, then use the Windows Explorer (or File Manager if you're not using Windows 95) to bring the directory into view and then click on the name of the file. You'll see that this is a self-extracting archive—as the program executes it will uncompress and create the necessary programs. The program will eventually be installed in the directory named **WINZIP**, but first needs to be extracted to a different directory. The program will extract itself to the directory named **TEMP**. You can change any of these names during the installation.

7. Install the genealogy program.

Once again, using Windows Explorer, locate the file **kk302.zip**. Click on its name and WinZip will take over. A WinZip window will pop up. Click on the icon labeled **Extract** to extract the program and associated files. You'll have to specify a directory or folder to hold the program. Follow the instructions from WinZip.

8. Work with the uncompressed files.

It's a good idea to first read any file that contains a user guide or other documentation. After that you can run the program by clicking on an application file or program file in the appropriate directory. If there's an application named **setup** or **install**, you will probably have to run that before using the program.

———————————End of Example 8.3———————————

Archived Files. Sometimes files are collected in an archive format. This is useful when several related files need to be treated as a unit. The compression program WinZip from Example 8.3 does exactly that. Other popular programs are BinHex and Stuffit for Macintosh systems, shar and tar for Unix systems, and pkzipand gzip for Unix, MS-DOS, and Macintosh systems.

Common File Extensions. Table 8.1 explains some common file extensions and notes where the compression is for specific computer systems.

Extension	Explanation
.arc	The file is in compressed mode. It may also be a collection of files in an archive. It's usually from a DOS system. Use a version of **arc** or **WinZip** to unarchive the file(s).
.au, .wav	These are sound files. They can be played by the helper application **naplayer** that is distributed with Netscape Navigator.
.gif or .jpg	The file contains an image. You can view it through the Web browser.
.gz	The file is in compressed mode using **gzip**. You need **gzip** or **WinZip** to extract it.
.Hqx	The file is in compressed or archived mode for a Macintosh. Use **BinHex** to uncompress.
.lzh	The file is in compressed mode using some variation of the **LHarc** compression scheme.
.mov	QuickTime movie file. It contains images, sound, and motion video. You need QuickTime player for Windows to view these files.
.ps	The file is in PostScript form, to be viewed or printed. You'll need a separate program to view PostScript and not every printer can print PostScript files. The program **rops** can be used to work with PostScript files.
.shar	This is a shell archive, usually from a Unix system. Use **sh** to unpack the files.

.tar, .taz, .tgz	This is a collection of files archived with the program tar, often found on Unix systems. Use **tar xvf file-name** to unarchive **file-name.tar** on a Unix system. Taz and tgz indicate archives that have been compressed. WinZip will extract these.
.txt or .text	The file is in text format.
.uue	This is in ASCII or text format so it can be sent as e-mail. It contains information that isn't in text form. You need **uudecode** to convert to proper form.
.Z	This was compressed using the Unix program named compress. You can use versions of compress or uncompress for various types of systems.
.zip	This was compressed and archived using **pkzip** or some variation. It's often used on DOS systems. Could also contain a collection of files.

Table 8.1   Common File Extensions

Finding Files Available by Anonymous FTP

There are millions of files available to anyone on the Internet who uses the service anonymous FTP. With all those files available, you need a tool or service to find their locations so you can retrieve them. Some search engines return information about resources accessible by anonymous FTP, but they concentrate on Web sources. FTP has been around longer than the World Wide Web and its primary protocol HTTP, and a tool to search databases of the contents of anonymous FTP archives was developed even before the WWW existed. The name of that tool is *Archie*. Archie is an information service that helps you locate a file to be retrieved by FTP. You use it by giving the name of a file or a portion of the name to one of several specific computers (called Archie servers) on the Internet. The Archie server looks through a database or archive of file names and returns the Internet location of the file. The location is the domain name of an anonymous FTP site and the directory that holds the file. Then you can use anonymous FTP to retrieve the file. Using Archie with a Web browser returns a Web page that has hyperlinks on it to the file(s) being sought. An Archie server will also tell you about directories whose names correspond to the name you send it.

In the next section we discuss how to use Archie. In this section we'll take a brief look at the search engine at **uiarchive.cso.uiuc.edu**, mentioned in Example 8.3, and at one of several sources of a WWW interface to Archie for finding resources available through anonymous FTP. In addition to these search tools there is a list, the "Monster FTP Sites List," of anonymous FTP sites. This list is huge; in uncompressed form it's broken up into over 20 58-kilobit files. Use the URL **http://hoohoo.ncsa.uiuc.edu/ftp/intro.html** to read about different ways of retrieving the list. If that's not accessible, you can go to the list by using the URL **ftp://rtfm.mit.edu/pub/usenet/news.answers/ftp-list/sitelist/**.

The University of Illinois at Urbana-Champaign is one of a few major FTP archive sites in the world. One thing that currently sets it apart from others is the way in which it's arranged for access to other FTP archives and the search tools it provides to find files in FTP archives. Figure 8.15 shows the Web page "Search the UI Archive."

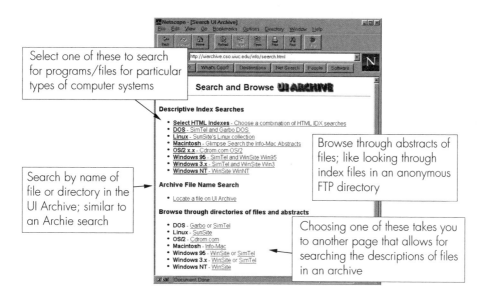

Select one of these to search for programs/files for particular types of computer systems

Browse through abstracts of files; like looking through index files in an anonymous FTP directory

Search by name of file or directory in the UI Archive; similar to an Archie search

Choosing one of these takes you to another page that allows for searching the descriptions of files in an archive

Figure 8.15 Search the UI Archive, URL: http://uiarchive.cso.uiuc.edu/info/search.html

Take the time to work through some of these hyperlinks. They're all straightforward and efficient, and a good way to find programs/software to use with your computer.

Archie

The term *Archie* is just a shortened form of the word *archive*. Archie was designed to deliver information about items available in FTP archives. (It wasn't named after the comic book character.) Archie was conceived and implemented by Alan Emtage, Peter Deutsch, and Bill Heelan of McGill University, Quebec, Canada.

The Archie home page is accessible by using the URL **http://services.bunyip.com:8000/products/archie/archie.html**, and the URL for the "Archie Information Page" is **http://services.bunyip.com:8000/products/archie/info.html**. Take a look at both of these home pages for information about Archie from the developers.

This is how Archie works. You give a file name to an Archie server and it tells you where to find the file. This is the simplest way to use Archie. You can also give some commands to tailor your search. The commands allow you to ask for an exact match, use the name you give as a substring of names of files and directories so you don't have to know the exact name of what you'd like to retrieve, and request that the results be sorted in any one of several ways. An Archie server will accept your request by e-mail, Telnet (running an Archie client program on your computer), or through a WWW form. We'll concentrate on the last method—

using the Web browser to get the form, submit it when we've filled in the pertinent information, and then display the list of hyperlinks for the files or directories. The other ways to use Archie are discussed in detail in Chapter 8 of *Learning to Use the Internet*, by Ernest Ackermann.

Note that Archie servers are generally busy. It may take several minutes or longer to get a response through a Web page.

Here is an example of one part of what you might expect from an Archie search. The search here was done giving the server the string *zambia:*

> **ftp.sunet.se**
>> File **zambia_healthnet.txt**
>> Size: 27016 bytes (27K) Bytes
>> Last Changed: 1994 Jan 14 10:00:00 GMT
>> Location: **/pub/global-net/**

The items in bold are hyperlinks.

There are several types of forms to use for Archie servers on the Internet, and the results they yield have different formats. This shouldn't be a problem since it's the hyperlinks, not how they're presented, that's important. Most formats include the name of the file or directory, the date it was last modified, and the size of the file (size may or may not be given for a directory).

Using Archie

You use Archie to locate files to retrieve and directories to browse through anonymous FTP. The steps in this process are:

1. You type a URL (open a location) to an Archie request form at an Archie server.
2. You give a word (a string of characters) to the server. You can select options that control the type of match (exact or substring), the priority for your search, and the order in which the items will be displayed.
3. The server searches a database to find the names of files and directories that match—either exactly or partially—the string you gave it.
4. The server displays the list of the items found. That list contains the name of an anonymous FTP site, the location of the file or directory you're searching for, and the name of a file or directory that matches the string you sent. The list is displayed as a list of hyperlinks.

That's it. Since you're using a Web browser the items are returned as a list of hyperlinks.

One URL for a form at an Archie server that's easy to use is **http://www-ns.rutgers.edu/htbin/archie**. It's shown in Figure 8.16. Several of the items are explained in the following sections. A list of Archie servers throughout the world is accessible through the URL **http://www.earn.net/gnrt/archie.html**. You can also use that URL for other information about using Archie.

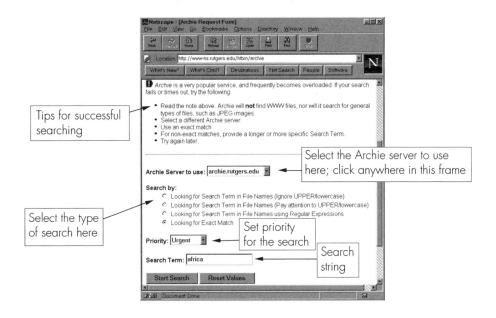

Figure 8.16   Archie Request Form http://www-ns.rutgers.edu/htbin/archie

Different Types of Searches

When you contact an Archie server, you give it a string of characters that represents the name or part of the name of a file or directory. The server searches its database using that string and returns the locations of anonymous FTP sites that have a file or directory whose name exactly or partially matches that string. The commands you send can specify the type of search. You can ask for the following types of matches:

Exact match. The server returns information on files and directories whose names exactly match the string you gave it. This is the fastest search.

Subcase match. Pay attention to upper/lowercase, case sensitive. The server returns information on files and directories whose names contain the string you gave as a substring. It pays attention to the case of the letters. For example, if you ask for a subcase match with the string *music*, Archie will match the string with *musical* or *music*, but won't match with *Music*.

Substring match. Ignore upper/lowercase, case insensitive. This is the most general of the three. It's like a subcase match, except that Archie treats all letters the same. So an Archie search with a substring match with the string *music* will match with *musical, music,* or *Music.*

Regular expression. This is the most general of all. Unfortunately, the rules for forming regular expressions are lengthy and complicated. A good source of information about regular expressions is available through the URL **http://www.wednet.edu/wednet/regex.html**. Some characters have special meanings in regular expressions. For example, the expression ^af.*xt$ matches names that begin with **af** and end with **xt**, such as **africa.text** or **african_networking.text**. This takes the most time of all.

Here are some concrete examples. The string or name we give to the server is *africa.*

⁂ **Exact match.** You ask Archie to search for files or directories with the name *africa.*

> **sun.rz.tu-clausthal.de**
> File **africa**
> Size: 1448 bytes (1K) Bytes
> Last Changed: 1985 Nov 19 23:00:00 GMT
> Location: **/pub/docs/songs/toto/**

⁂ **Subcase match.** You ask Archie to search for the names of files and directories whose names contain the string *africa.* You'll get a list containing some of the items from the exact match and others such as:

> **relay.cs.toronto.edu**
> File **south_africa**
> Size: 3879 bytes (3K) Bytes
> Last Changed: 1995 Apr 27 23:00:00 GMT
> Location: **/pub/acs/marksmanship/cdn-firearms/Laws/**
> Directory **/pub/usenet/news.answers/african-faq**
> Last Changed: 1995 Apr 05 23:00:00 GMT

⁂ **Substring match.** You ask Archie to search, disregarding the case of the letters, for files and directories whose names contain the string *africa.* The list Archie produces will include some of the items from the previous two types of searches along with other items such as*:*

> **relay.cs.toronto.edu**
> File **South_Africa.Z**
> Size: 6996 bytes (6K) Bytes
> Last Changed: 1991 Mar 31 00:00:00 GMT
> Location: **/doc/geography/world/**
> File **Central_African_Republic.Z**
> Size: 4966 bytes (4K) Bytes
> Last Changed: 1991 Mar 31 00:00:00 GMT
> Location: **/doc/geography/world/**

We gave an example of using a regular expression above. Either the substring or subcase match can be useful for browsing for sources. For example, if you do a subcase search and use the string medic, you can turn up information that would match medic, medicinal, medicine, medical, and so on.

Archie Servers

Archie servers are distributed around the world. Proper etiquette dictates that you contact one geographically close to you. Sometimes, though, it makes sense to contact one in a different time zone. For example, at 2 P.M. in New York you can be fairly sure that the servers in North America are busy. At that time the servers in Europe and Asia may not be very busy, so it may make sense to contact one of those servers. You will find the results you get may depend on which server you use. If you want Archie to search a database that includes anonymous FTP sites in a certain region, you'll want to select a host from that region. To be sure of searching a good sampling of sites in Asia, for example, you may want to use a server from that continent. However, first you ought to try to contact a local server and then go elsewhere if it's necessary. A list of Archie servers available as part of the World Wide Web is provided as a public service by NEXOR. Use the URL **http://pubweb.nexor.co.uk/public/archie/servers.html** to access the list.

Priority

You can select the priority for the search. This has an impact on others using the same Archie server. Using the form from Rutgers (Figure 8.16), the priority can be set at urgent, standard, medium, or low. Lowering the priority usually increases the time to wait for results. Archie forms at other sites sometimes list the priority in terms of the impact on others—not nice at all, nice, nicer, very nice, etc.

Gopher

Like the WWW, Gopher puts the focus on the information, not on learning a number of different techniques. A Gopher server provides a menu to represent the information and resources it has available. You work with one or more menus, choosing items that are documents (files), directories, links to other Internet sites, tools to help you find information, or other Internet services. You don't have to know many techniques to use Gopher; most of the time you only need to be able to choose items from a menu. Eventually, you come to a menu item representing a text document, image, or other type of file.

Two sources for more information about Gopher are the Web page "About Gopher and Gopher Resources" written by LoriLee Sadler, available through the resources in the Electronic Collections or Worldwide Communications sections of the Web site at Indiana University—Purdue University Indianapolis Library at **http://www-lib.iupui.edu/ecollects/gopherhelp.html**, and Gopher Frequently Asked Questions, **http://www.inf.utfsm.cl/~gopher/faq/faq.html**.

About Gopher. The software for Gopher was created and developed at the University of Minnesota to allow users to browse and retrieve documents in a campus environment. The gopher is the mascot of the University of Minnesota; that may be connected to how the software got its name. You can also think of the software working, tunneling, or burrowing its way through the Internet, in the same way a gopher tunnels through the earth.

Using Gopher. When you're using a Web browser to access a Gopher site, the items on the menu are hyperlinks. The items are represented by text with icons indicating the type of the Internet service or resource available by following the link. When you come to a link that represents a file (rather than another menu), you can view it, save it to a file, or print it by the same methods as for any other file accessible with your Web browser. Figure 8.17 shows a Gopher menu in the Web browser window.

A folder indicates a link represents another menu

Binoculars indicate the link represents a search tool

A terminal indicates the link represents a Telnet session

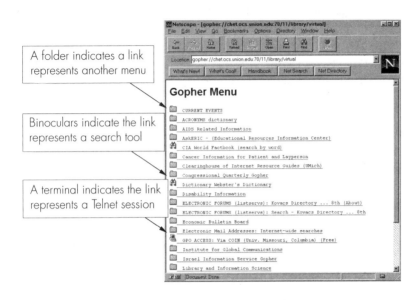

Figure 8.17 Virtual Reference Desk at Union College,
URL: gopher://chet.ocs.union.edu:70/11/library/virtual

The WWW has become more popular than Gopher, and the information on the WWW is presented in a more effective manner. Gopher sites can only display text menus. When you use the WWW, you work in a hypertext or hypermedia environment. Sometimes the items you select are part of other sentences or paragraphs. These links to other Internet resources are presented in context, rather than as a list or menu. Gopher also hides many of the details of making connections to different Internet sites and using Internet services. However, when you use Gopher you're always dealing with menus, so you have to work according to the ways the menus are defined. The entries on menus can't be very long, which means they may not be descriptive; you sometimes end up choosing a menu item that doesn't represent the type of information you wanted. Some sites are discontinuing their Gopher servers to concentrate on providing information as Web pages.

Why bother with Gopher? Here are a few reasons:

* There are several important resources on the Internet that are available through Gopher. There are thousands of Gopher servers, and a tool to search Gopher menus, Veronica, is readily available.
* Using Gopher through a Web browser is the same as accessing any Web page; you really don't have to learn anything new to use Gopher.
* It's usually faster to access Gopher menus than other Web pages because they contain only text and icons to give a clue about the resource each item represents. There is not a lot of text and there are no large images.

URL Format for Gopher

A URL for a Gopher site begins with **gopher://** followed by the Internet domain name of the site. For example, **gopher://gopher.tc.umn.edu/** is the URL for the Gopher server at the University of Minnesota. The URL in the form **gopher://internet-site-name/** takes you to the home Gopher menu for a site. URLs for Gopher items can be rather complex because many items are several menus removed from the home menu. The URL, for example, for the menu that lists Gopher servers in the United States is **gopher://gopher.tc.umn.edu:70/11/Other%20Gopher%20and%20Information%20Servers/North%20America/USA.**

Finding Resources Available Through Gopher

An extensive list of sites accessible through Gopher is accessible through the Gopher server at University of Minnesota (URL **gopher://gopher.tc.umn.edu**), and a variety of other Gopher servers contain entries for many of the Gopher servers in the world. You need to look for a menu entry with a title similar to "Other Gopher and Information Servers." The entry for a specific site can be found by going through several menus. The first menu gives you the choice of looking through a list of servers or to search for a specific server by supplying a search string consisting of some terms that describe the site or location you'd like to find.

For example, to find the Gopher server at the World Data Center on Microorganisms in Riken, Japan, you could choose to search using the words microorganisms, riken, or japan. To take an alternate approach, to find the Gopher servers in Montana, you might choose the item titled North America, choose USA from the next menu, and then choose Montana.

The term *gopherspace* refers to the collection of Gopher sites and the information you can access through those sites. In the remainder of this section we'll discuss two ways of finding resources in gopherspace: subject trees (directories) and Veronica (search engine). These are the same concepts, directories and search engines, we used for finding resources on the WWW in Chapter 6. However, we use different directories and search tools with Gopher.

Subject Trees (Directories)

There are several excellent collections of information available through Gopher. These collections are often called *subject trees*; they're like the WWW directories discussed in Chapter 6. A list of several subject trees is maintained at Tradewave Galaxy, **http://galaxy.einet.net/GJ/subject-trees.html.** A few other places to look, in case Galaxy isn't available, are AMI—A Friendly Public Interface, **gopher://Gopher.Mountain.Net/;** the English Server at Carnegie Mellon University, **gopher://english-server.hss.cmu.edu/;** and the University of Michigan Library's Gopher server, **gopher://gopher.lib.umich.edu/.**

To show what you might expect to find at a site with a subject tree, look at the next three figures. Figure 8.18 shows the Gopher menu at the University of Michigan Library's Gopher, Figure 8.19 shows the menu we'd find after clicking on the item Social Sciences Resources, and in Figure 8.20 we show the items listed under Social Sciences Resources.

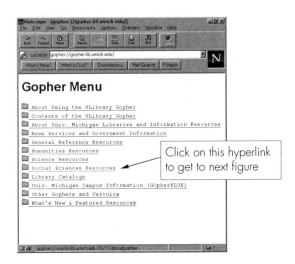

Figure 8.18   Menu Displayed by University of Michigan Library's Gopher Server

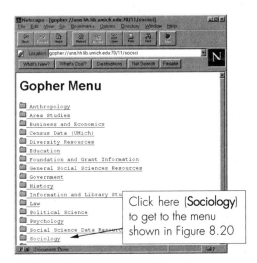

Figure 8.19   Social Sciences Resources

Figure 8.20   Sociology Menu

Veronica (Searching Gopherspace)

There are thousands of Gopher servers throughout the world. That gives us a lot of opportunities to find the information we want, but the sheer number of Gopher servers means it's necessary to have a tool to search Gopher directories and titles. An effective and popular tool to do just that is Veronica. Performing a veronica search means that you supply a word or string of words to the Veronica service, and it returns a Gopher-style menu of items containing the word(s) you provided. (It's said that Veronica is an acronym formed from Very Easy Rodent-Oriented Netwide Index to Computerized Archives, but it's hard to miss the connection with Archie, the tool you use to find files available by anonymous FTP. Veronica, a tool to search and find things in gopherspace, is similar to Archie. Furthermore, who is Archie's girlfriend in the comics? Veronica, of course!) After Veronica completes a search, you get a menu of items that is in fact a Gopher menu.

In what follows you'll see a mention of a Jughead server. Jughead is like Veronica except Veronica searches Gopher sites throughout the Internet while Jughead is usually set up to search Gopher menus at a single site. (It's no coincidence that Jughead is also a character in the Archie comics.)

You initiate a Veronica search by choosing Veronica on a Gopher menu and then selecting one of several sites providing the Veronica service. The remote site then displays a form in the browser window where you supply a keyword or keywords for Veronica to use in the search. Gopher servers are searched, and you receive a menu of topics that contain your keyword. The menu contains a collection of Gopher menu entries from gopherspace. It's a "live menu"; you use it as you would use any Gopher menu. The menu generally consists of any of the types of entries found on Gopher menus, but in some cases you can have the Veronica service return only directory names. You'll see how it works in Example 8.4.

Several Gopher sites contain lists of Veronica servers. One site at the University of Nevada, Reno (URL **gopher://gopher.scs.unr.edu/11/veronica**) has a menu that contains tips on using Veronica, two hyperlinks that allow for a Veronica search and automatically select a server for the search, and a list of 10 Veronica servers throughout the world. At times, a specific Veronica server may be too busy to satisfy your request for a search. You'll get a message if the server is too busy. Either try the same server later or try another. Selecting the items that automatically select a server may help here because this service tries Veronica servers until it finds one that's not busy, and you don't have to try a number of different servers. You may need to be persistent to find a Veronica site that will meet your needs. As an alternative, plan your search for a time of day outside of normal working hours. You'll probably have a choice of servers throughout the world, so there is always somewhere where the local time is not peak working time.

You give Veronica either a single word or a series of words, called the search string, to use in the search. When you use more than one word as the search string, you can enclose the words in quotes to ensure that entries returned will contain the words in the same order. Using **commercial use**, for example, will return entries that have both words in the order specified, such as **Commercial use of the Internet**.

Not including the words in quotes will return entries that have the words in any order or just one or a few of the words. An example of an item found using the string **commercial use** is: Sec. 788. Use of commercial standards.

Several Gopher sites list entries that can give you complete information about using Veronica. The Gopher at the University of Nevada, Reno, mentioned above, is the source for the documents "Frequently Asked Questions (FAQ) About Veronica" (**gopher://gopher.scs.unr.edu:70/hh/veronica/About/vfaq%28html%29**) and "How to Compose Veronica Queries" (**gopher://gopher.scs.unr.edu:70/hh/veronica/About/how-to-query-veronica%28html%29**).

Example 8.4   Searching Gopherspace with Veronica

You use Veronica to search gopherspace or to search for Gopher directory (menu) titles. The search of gopherspace is more general; you'll retrieve entries that are both directories and files. To start a Veronica search you need to select a Veronica server. That's a site (on a Gopher menu) that will perform the search once you supply it with the word(s) to use. In this case we'll use the Veronica directory at the University of Nevada, Reno. We're going to search for Gopher entries that contain the word "biodiversity." You use the same techniques to search for any word or phrase. This example shows how to use Veronica and also shows some of the resources available through Gopher.

We'll assume Netscape Navigator is started and we're in the Web browser window. Here are the steps to follow:

1. Type the URL (open a location) for the Gopher server at the University of Nevada, Reno.
2. Follow the hyperlink for the Veronica directory.
3. Choose the item **Search GopherSpace by Title word(s) (via NYSERNet)**.
4. Search gopherspace using the word **biodiversity**.

After that, the rest is up to you. You may want to explore some entries. If they look useful you may want to add them to your bookmark list.

1. Type the URL (open a location) for the Gopher server at the University of Nevada, Reno.

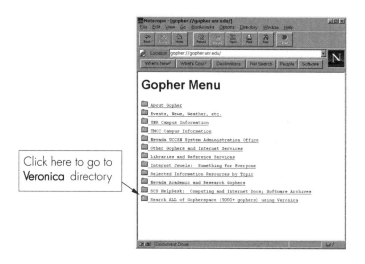 Click on the icon **Open** from the Toolbar.

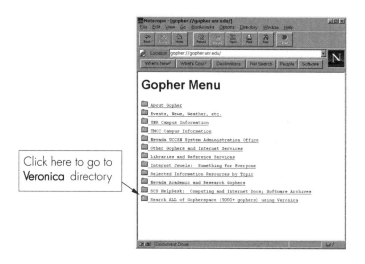 Type **gopher://gopher.unr.edu.**

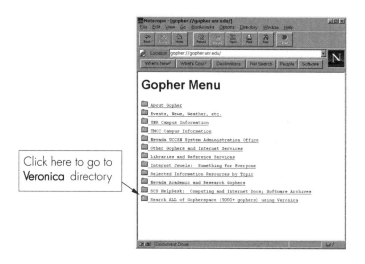 Click on the button labeled **Open.**

You'll see the window in Figure 8.21. It shows the variety of information available through this Gopher server.

Figure 8.21   Gopher Home Menu at University of Nevada, Reno

2. Follow the hyperlink for the Veronica directory.

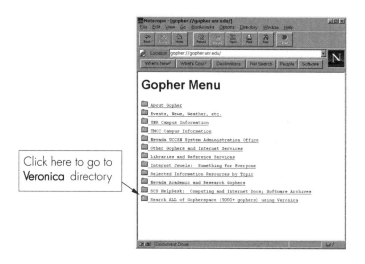 Click on the hyperlink **Search ALL of Gopherspace (5000+ gophers) using Veronica.**

Selecting that hyperlink takes you to the window shown in Figure 8.22. It has hyperlinks for the files containing information about Veronica, FAQ and Composing Veronica Entries, and a list of other Veronica servers.

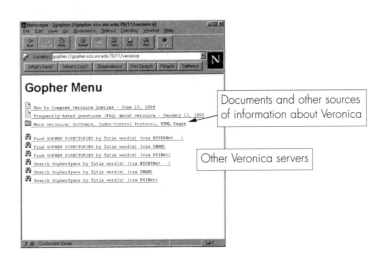

Figure 8.22   Veronica Directory at University of Nevada, Reno

We're going to use the Veronica server at NYSERnet but any would do for this example.

3. Choose the item Search GopherSpace by Title word(s) (via NYSERNet).

w**W**w   Click on the hyperlink **Search GopherSpace by Title word(s) (via NYSERNet)**.

Picking the hyperlink for a Veronica search via NYSERnet takes us to a window like the one in Figure 8.23. The window contains a form or pane in which you type the search phrase; the form is filled in in Figure 8.23.

4. Search gopherspace using the word **biodiversity**.

w**W**w   Move the mouse pointer or cursor inside the frame labeled **Enter search keywords**.

w**W**w   Type **biodiversity** and press **Enter**.

Search keyword filled in here

Figure 8.23 Search Form for Veronica

Once you press Enter, Veronica starts the search. When Veronica completes the search, you'll get a menu of items whose titles contain the word(s) you supplied for the search. Figure 8.24 shows what was returned in this case. You can see, right under **Gopher Menu**, that several sites were tried before a Veronica server was found for the search. When you try this you'll see that over 200 items are found.

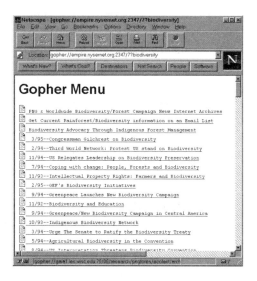

Figure 8.24 Results of Veronica Search

The rest is up to you. You can retrieve information, explore the menus, and add items to your bookmark list.

End of Example 8.4

Summary

This chapter discussed three established protocols used to share information on the Internet—Telnet, FTP, and Gopher. These servers were used before the WWW was developed, and they're still used in situations where they are most effective or appropriate. They can be used by selecting hyperlinks in the Web browser window or typing a URL to start them.

Telnet was created so that a person at one computer on the Internet could log into and use the programs and services of another computer on the Internet. There are several applications where this is useful, such as searching databases or library catalogs. The Telnet connection between two computer systems is a virtual connection; packets representing the portions of a session are passed between the two systems. This sometimes makes the session slow or seem choppy. It's best to use Telnet when that's the only way to access a resource; many Telnet services are being converted over to be accessible as Web pages.

A URL for a resource accessible through Telnet has the form **telnet://internet-site-name**
   Example: **telnet://locis.loc.gov**

or **telnet://internet-site-name:port-number**
   Example: **telnet//culine.colorado.edu:860**

Some Telnet sites require you to supply a log-in name and perhaps a password; others use a port-number. You can start a Telnet session by typing the URL or clicking on a hyperlink, but Telnet doesn't run inside a Web browser window, and it isn't always included with Netscape Navigator. You may have to retrieve a shareware or freeware version of Telnet and then configure Netscape Navigator.

Telnet gives you acces to lots of resources such as library catalogs, bulletin board systems, regional free-nets, and various databases on the Internet. A good way to find them is to use Hytelnet. It's available in several formats, but the Web version at **http://library.usask.ca/hytelnet/** is convenient to use. Each site can be selected as a hyperlink from a menu on a Web page. Each of these hyperlinks leads to a Web page that includes a hyperlink to the Telnet site and instructions for logging in, using the services, and quitting or logging out at the remote Telnet site.

FTP stands for File Transfer Protocol. Along with Telnet and e-mail, it is one of the three basic services on the Internet. It's used to share files or copy files from one site on the Internet to another. It's most effective when the name of the remote site, the directory, and the name of a file are known; FTP isn't designed for browsing. Anonymous FTP is the term used when a file can be copied from one computer to another without giving a log-in name or a password. Collections of files available by anonymous FTP are called anonymous FTP archives. One major FTP archive is at the University of Illinois, Urbana-Champaign, URL **ftp://uiarchive.cso.uiuc.edu**, and the contents of several other archives are available.

To retrieve a file by anonymous FTP, use a URL in the form **ftp://name-of-ftp-site/directory-name/file-name**, for example, **ftp://ftp.jpl.nasa.gov/pub/images/browse/marglobe.gif.** To look through a directory use a URL in the form **ftp://name-of-ftp-site/directory-name/**. For example, **ftp://ftp.jpl.nasa.gov/pub/images/**. When you use FTP with a Web browser and you give the URL for a file, the browser attempts to display the file and then you can save it into a file. If you give the URL for a directory, the files and subdirectories of that directory are displayed as hyperlinks. If you move the cursor or mouse pointer to the name of the file, hold down the Shift key, and click with the mouse, the file is copied to your computer without first being displayed by the browser. Files available by anonymous FTP are classified as being text (ASCII) files or binary files. Text files contain only printable, readable characters, like the ones on this page. Binary files contain information that's meant to be processed by a computer such as programs, compressed files, archives or collections of files, or files that can be viewed or heard such as images, video, or audio. When you're using a Web browser, you retrieve both types of files in the same way, as described above.

There are literally trillions of bytes of information, programs, and resources available by anonymous FTP. Archie, one of the first Internet search programs, is a tool to use to search anonymous FTP archives. You supply a keyword and specify whether that word is matched exactly or as a substring with items in the archives. Additionally, the search can pay attention to or ignore the case of the letters in the keyword. If, for example, the search word was *africa* and a substring match was requested that ignored the case of letters, then resources such as **African.txt, africa_travel, africa, pub/maps/africa** might be found. There are several Web sites throughout the world that provide Archie search services. Using a Web browser you supply the search word and the Archie server returns a list of matching items displayed as hyperlinks.

The Gopher system was designed to deliver documents in an academic environment. It was developed at the University of Minnesota and is available on a wide variety of computer systems. You work with a menu system to retrieve information. The menus are available through the Web browser once you follow a hyperlink to a Gopher server or give the URL for a Gopher server on the Internet. The items on the menu are hyperlinks, and thus can be one of a variety of types—file, directory, BinHexed Macintosh file, DOS binary archive, uuencoded file, Telnet session, image file, Web page, or index-search server. Gopher was developed before the WWW. It allows access to a variety of services and resources on the Internet in much the same way as Web browsers do, except that with Gopher you're always dealing with a menu. With a Web browser you deal with hypertext and hypermedia, so presenting, delivering, and discovering information is more effective on the WWW than it could be in gopherspace (the collection of material available through Gopher menus).

The basic form of a URL for Gopher is **gopher://gopher-server-name**. For example, **gopher://gopher.tc.umn.edu**. Since you trace through menus to get to items, the URLs for some items available through Gopher can be complex.

You can search Gopher sites for file or directory entries by using Veronica. There are thousands of Gopher sites throughout the world, and Veronica helps you find files or directories by searching the menu entries on these servers. To use Veronica, you choose a Veronica server, a computer system that will do the searching for you, from a Gopher menu. You'll be prompted to enter a word or sequence of words, called a search string, which Veronica will use for the search. After you enter the search string, Veronica will search Gopher servers and return a menu of items that contain the search string. You work with this menu in the same way you'd work with any Gopher menu.

Gopher is relatively easy to use. It gives you the capability to find and retrieve information by working with a series of menus. All you need to do is select an item from a menu and you can search directories, retrieve files, use several different types of Internet services, and connect to sites throughout the Internet. These capabilities, along with the large number and diversity of Gopher servers, make Gopher an effective and popular tool for working on the Internet. When you use Gopher, you can concentrate on what you need to do without having to learn a variety of specialized techniques or skills.

Exercises

Telnet

1. Find the subway route you need to follow to get from a given location to another in Paris. Do the same thing for a subway route in Boston. Impossible? Not if you use Telnet to contact the Subway Navigator. To do that, use **telnet://metro.jussieu.fr:10000**. Once you're connected, choose either French or English as the language used for the menus.
    a. Choose France/Paris as the city and find the subway route from Notre-Dame de Lorette to Champs Elysees. Which lines (trains) should you take? Which stops will you pass through? Where do you change trains? How long will it take?
    b. Now answer the same questions for the route from the airport to the Fenway area in USA/Boston.

2. The sports schedules for the National Basketball Association (NBA), National Hockey League (NHL), and Major League Baseball (MLB) are available online through Telnet. To find the schedule for the NBA, use **telnet://culine.colorado.edu:859**. For the NHL, use **telnet://culine.colorado.edu:860**. For MLB, use **telnet://culine.colorado.edu:862**. Use Telnet to answer these questions:
    a. What are the next three scheduled games for the Houston Rockets? (Basketball)
    b. What are the next three scheduled games for the Montreal Canadiens? (Hockey)
    c. What are the next three scheduled games for the New York Yankees? (Baseball)

3. Connect to America's Job Bank as shown in Example 8.1. Explore the area titled "Job Search—Nationwide" and describe what's available.

4. Exercise 1 in this group had you look up subway routes using Telnet. Did you notice that service is also available as a Web page? Use the URL for the Subway Navigator (**http://metro.jussieu.fr:10001**) and look up the same routes as in Exercise 1. Describe the benefits of using the Web interface rather than the Telnet interface.

5. Free-Nets are community-based organizations that provide free or low-cost access to the Internet. Look at the ones listed under **FREE-NETs & Community Computing Systems** in the section **Other resources of Hytelnet**. Find one located in or near where you live. Use Telnet to connect to that Free-Net. Describe the services and resources available.

Using Telnet to Search Libraries and Databases

6. You've got to do some research on Beethoven's works. Your challenge is to come up with a list of five or more references—author, title, and call number—that deal with Beethoven's chamber music. Probably any book about Beethoven will contain the topic, but the references you find ought to be specific to chamber music. Luckily, the Beethoven Bibliography Database is accessible by Telnet. Here's how to reach it. First use Telnet to **sjsulib1.sjsu.edu**. Use lib if you're prompted for a log-in name; select O on the main menu, and then select Beethoven Bibliography Database. You'll want to do a search by subject, a search by keyword, or perhaps a search by genre.

7. Start Hytelnet and select **Library catalogs, arranged geographically** and then select **Europe/Middle East**. You'll see the names of several countries listed. Some library catalogs have menus only in the language of the country; others provide an interface in more than one language. (English is a common alternative.)

   a. List at least three libraries that have search menus in a language you can read.

   b. Search one or more of those library catalogs and come up with a list of three items that have something to do with science.

8. The National Institutes of Health Library in Bethesda, Maryland, makes its catalog available through Telnet; use **telnet:// nih-library.nih.gov**. No password is required to log in. Once you're connected, select the NIH Library Catalog and you'll see a menu such as:

   A > AUTHOR
   T > TITLE
   S > SUBJECT
   C > CALL #
   W > WORDS in the title
   V > VIEW your circulation record
   I > Library INFORMATION
   D > DISCONNECT

   a. Search the catalog for books or journals whose author has the same last name as yours. If nothing meets that criterion, search for items by an author whose name is close to yours. The catalog system will let you know what is close. Write down the title, author, and call number of three items whose author's name matches these criteria.

   b. Suppose you need to do some research on the topic of AIDS. Do a subject search and report the title, author, and call number of five items.

   c. Do a word search on the topic of AIDS and report back the title, author, and call number of five items different from the ones you reported in part b.

FTP

Retrieving files containing information for FTP users

1. This exercise gives you the chance to retrieve the Readme or other introductory files at a few sites and see a sampling of what's available on the Internet.

   Retrieve and read each of the following files:
   a. /pub/README at ftp.loc.gov
      URL ftp://ftp.loc.gov/pub/README
   b. /pub/READ.ME at nic.meritedu
      URL ftp://nic.merit.edu/READ.ME
   c. /pub/etext/gutenberg/NEWUSER.GUT at uiarchive.cso.uiuc.edu
      URL ftp://uiarchive.cso.uiuc.edu/pub/etext/gutenberg/NEWUSER.GUT
   d. /pc/TODAY.TIP at garbo.uwasa.fi
      URL ftp://garbo.uwasa.fi/pc/TODAY.TIP

2. A source for the Anonymous FTP Frequently Asked Questions (FAQ) List, URL **ftp://rtfm.mit.edu/ pub/usenet-by-group/news.answers/ftp-list/faq**. Retrieve a copy of that document and put it in your bookmark list.
   a. The FAQ contains an answer to "What types of FTP information are available?" Write a summary of the answer.
   b. The FAQ also contains "URLs of the interesting things mentioned in this text." List a few of those URLs, use your Web browser to discover or verify what's at those locations, and write a brief synopsis of what you find.
   c. Give a brief synopsis or summary of the copyright notice you see when you connect by anonymous FTP to the **directory /pub/usenet-by-group** at **rtfm.mit.edu**.

3. a. Retrieve the file **rfc1855.txt** from **ds.internic.net** in the directory **/rfc**.
   b. What does that document have to say about FTP? (Hint: Look in section 4.1.)

Finding Files and Directories

4. a. Write down the steps necessary to retrieve the file named **health-care.Z** from the directory **/usenet/ news.answers/dogs-faq** at **ftp.uu.net**.
   b. Retrieve the file. It is compressed. If you have a program that can uncompress it, do so now. You can get a version of it in uncompressed form from either **rtfm.mit.edu** in the directory **/pub/ usenet-by-group/news.answers/dogs-faq**, from **ltp.univ-lyon.fr** in the directory **/pub/faq/dog-faq**, or from **mrcnext.cso.uiuc.edu** in the directory **/pub/faq/usenet-by-group/news.answers/dogs-faq**.
   c. A similar file, dealing with health care for cats, exists. Can you find it?

5. The search tool at **uiarchive**, (URL **http://uiarchive.cso.uiuc.edu/info/search.html**) lets you search for files in a number of FTP archives—Garbo, SimTel, SunSite and WinSite. Visit each of these and write a brief description of the purpose of each archive and what you're likely to find at those sites.

6. Retrieve a copy of the file, **ftp://nic.merit.edu/introducing.the.internet/answers.to.new.user.questions**. Using that file write a one- or two-sentence answer to each of the following questions:
   a. What is the difference between the Internet and an internet?
   b. What is an advantage of the domain name system (DNS)?
   c. What is Archie?
   d. How is Archie different from FTP?
   e. What is Gopher?

7. Start an anonymous FTP session with **gatekeeper.dec.com** and go to the directory **/pub/recipes**.
   a. Retrieve or set bookmarks to all the files whose names start with **choc**.
   b. Retrieve or set bookmarks to only those files whose names contain the string **rice**, but don't retrieve any files whose names indicate that the recipe has to do with **pecans** or **gumbo**.
   c. Create a menu for a dinner using the recipes in this directory. Using HTML, write it as a Web page.

Archie

8. Using any of the ways to access an Archie server, do the following. Contact three servers, each on a different continent, and request an Archie search with an exact match using the string *planet*.
   a. Which server gave the most results?
   b. Which server gave the results that would be most useful to you?

9. In this exercise you'll use Archie to help search for information about museums.
   a. Do an Archie search using the word *museum*, and be sure you request an exact match. If the server reports that there were no matches, use another server. What did you find?
   b. Now do an Archie search using the word *museums*. Again, be sure you're asking for an exact match and if there are no matches, use another server. What did you find this time?
   c. Now do an Archie search with a subcase match using the word *museum*. The results of this search should include the results of the searches you did in part a and part b. What did you find that's different?
   d. Finally, do an Archie search with a substring match using the word *museums*. How do the results in this case compare with the ones you got in part c?

10. Using the images available through URL **ftp://ftp.jpl.nasa.gov/pub/images/browse**, collect the URLs for images of all the planets in the solar system. Use your skills at creating a Web page to construct one that has hyperlinks to these images.

Gopher

1. Use the URL **gopher://gopher-server.cwis.uci.edu** to contact the Gopher server at the University of California, Irvine. Follow the hyperlink labeled **Library** and then select the hyperlink **Virtual Reference Desk.**
   a. What are the names of the hyperlinks that start with the letter P?
   b. Describe what you can find by following those hyperlinks.
   c. Find the item titled U.S. House of Representatives Gopher on the Politics and Government menu. Describe what you find in that section.
   d. What is CARL Uncover?

2. Use the URL **gopher://nmnhgoph.si.edu**, the Gopher server for the Smithsonian Institution's Natural History Gopher. Choose the item titled "About the Smithsonian Institution's Natural History Gopher."
   a. View the contents of the document.
   b. What's new at the Natural History Museum?
   c. Select the hyperlink **Related Gopher and Information Servers** and then choose **Other Biological Information Servers.** What hyperlinks can you find to servers in Japan?

3. Select one of the Gopher subject trees listed at URL **http://galaxy.einet.net/GJ/subject-trees.html**, as mentioned in the text. By saving hyperlinks in the bookmark list and/or creating a Web page, put together your own subject tree. The tree doesn't have to be elaborate or too complex. Pick five areas or subjects that interest you and collect at least three hyperlinks in each area.

4. Use the URL **gopher://english-server.hss.cmu.edu/** to connect to the English Server at Carnegie Mellon University.
   a. Look at the file **READ_ME.** It describes the purpose of the English Server. Browse through some of the directories/folders at that site. Is the statement of purpose you read accurate? Explain your answer.
   b. Describe what is in the directory/folder **Film and Television.**

Searching Gopher Menus and Using Veronica

5. Point to a Gopher server that permits Veronica searches of gopherspace. Perform a Veronica search using each of the following as a search string—*museum*, *art museum*, and *art museums*.
   a. Save at least three items from each search in your bookmark list.
   b. Write a few sentences describing the differing results obtained when you use *art museum* and *art museums* as the search strings.
   c. On any of the Veronica searches you'll see files that are images or pictures. If you can't find any at the first menu that appears, look through the menus until you find some. Save in your bookmark list or create a Web page of an exhibit of five or more images.
   d. Choose a different Veronica server and perform a Veronica search using *art museums* as the search string. You might want to pick a Veronica server in a country different from the first. Do you get the same results? Why do think that is the case?

CHAPTER 9

Legal Issues, Ethical Issues, Privacy, and Security

It's easy to get excited about using the Internet and the World Wide Web. They're vivacious, interesting, and important places to work, learn, do business, and just have fun. The World Wide Web always seems to have something new. You find not only new resources, but better services and programs, making the WWW and the Internet easier to use and more powerful. There's also a great deal of diversity; different cultures, nations, and outlooks are represented on the WWW. All these things make for an exciting environment, but as the Internet and the World Wide Web become more popular and the number of users increases, it's reasonable to expect rules, regulations, and laws governing their use. You also have to consider the effect the Internet has on our lives, our communities, and society as its use becomes more widespread. In this chapter we'll discuss a few of these issues associated with using the Internet and the World Wide Web. The issues we'll cover include:

- Privacy and Civil Liberties
- Intellectual Property and Copyright
- Access—What Type at What Cost?
- Internet Security

It's useful to take a brief look at the history of the Internet, which is related to some of these issues. In the late 1960s the United States Department of Defense, through its Advanced Research Projects Agency (ARPA), funded research into the establishment of a decentralized computer network. Some of the researchers saw the advantages of having a network in which computer systems of differing types and operating systems could communicate. They also foresaw the development of a community among the users of this national and international network. The network, named ARPANET, linked researchers at universities and research laboratories. Throughout the 1970s, ARPANET was developed further and connections were established with networks in other countries. Usenet originated in 1979, and in the early 1980s other networks in the United States and elsewhere were established. The number of sites or hosts on these networks was still relatively small, less than one thousand. In the late 1980s, the National Science Foundation funded the development of a network (using the Internet protocols) that would connect supercomputer centers in the United States. That network, called NSFNET, allowed colleges and universities to become connected. The number of sites or hosts increased rapidly, passing 10,000 in 1987. In 1989 there were over one hundred thousand hosts on NSFNET. The 1980s also saw the development of the Cleveland Free-Net, a community-based network, and the use of NSFNET to relay e-mail from a commercial network.

The funding for the development and operation of ARPANET, NSFNET, and several other networks throughout the world was heavily subsidized by the government. These networks established acceptable use policies, which gave rules for their use, stating what type of activities were allowed on these publicly supported networks. The policies prohibited any purely commercial activities and set the tone for a developing code of network ethics or etiquette. Commercial networks were also being developed, although they could not, under the acceptable use policies, use the transmission links of the public networks. So for some time commercial activity on the major portion of the Internet in the United States was prohibited. However, in 1988 some of these commercial networks reached an agreement with NSFNET to allow e-mail from commercial networks to be carried on NSFNET. That way a user on CompuServe or MCImail could send a message to someone with an Internet address at a public institution such as a college or university. Likewise, messages could be sent from NSFNET to these private networks, but e-mail from one user on a private service couldn't be transported over NSFNET to another user on a private service.

In 1990 ARPANET ceased to exist as an administrative entity, and the public network in the United States was turned over to NSFNET. The Internet was growing at a remarkable rate and clearly becoming bigger than the public institutions wanted to manage or support. In fact, they never had planned to support it forever. In the early 1990s commercial networks with their own Internet exchanges or gateways were allowed to conduct business on the Internet, and in 1993 the NSF created the InterNIC to provide services such as registration of domain names, directory and database services, and information about Internet services. These services are contracted to the private sector.

The notions behind the World Wide Web were developed in the early 1990s and Mosaic, the first graphical Web browser, was released to the public in the latter part of 1993. Web browsers and the availability of Internet connections through modems made the Internet much more accessible. These developments have led to an unprecedented growth in the number of individuals, businesses, and organizations that are using the Internet for communication, information, and commerce.

This explosive growth of the World Wide Web and the inclusion of commercial networks and services into the Internet has been accompanied by an astounding increase in the population of Internet users. Many of the new users feel that networks and computers, like a public utility, should be available anywhere, reliable, and easy to use. As the Internet becomes available to a much wider portion of the population, older modes of behavior on the Internet have changed. Commercial activity and advertising are in the process of being established at some sites and newsgroups. Businesses are determining effective and secure ways of engaging in commerce on the Internet. As the use of the Internet becomes more widespread in the areas of education, research, business, and recreation, issues of security, reliability, ownership, and liability become more important. Many local laws and international agreements are directly applicable to Internet activities. On the other hand, this is a rather new medium using technology that came into existence after many applicable laws were written. New laws and agreements recognizing these changes and differences are being established.

The Internet and the World Wide Web have grown rapidly from a research project into something that involves millions of people worldwide. Much of the Internet's usefulness comes from the fact that users and service providers depend on each other and need to support each other. Hopefully, that sort of sharing and respect will continue. Your behavior, your expectations of others, and your activities will make the difference.

Privacy and Civil Liberties

What's reasonable to expect in terms of privacy and civil liberties as they relate to use of the Internet? Your initial response might be that you expect the same protection of your privacy and the same civil liberties—such as freedom of expression, safeguards against the arbitrary exercise of authority, and protection from abusive or offensive actions—on the Internet as you have in your dealings in society. Codes of behavior or rules of etiquette have developed on the Internet over the years. In some cases laws have been adopted to provide the same level of protection of privacy and guarantees of civil liberties for working with electronic media as with any other media. An important point is that privacy and civil liberties are often defined in terms of their expression or environment. The laws in the United States dealing with privacy and expression in printed form, on paper, needed to be changed to suit electronic communications. Laws need to be modified to take into account new media and new means of transmitting information. Furthermore, the people who develop, act on, and enforce laws need to be informed of the impact of technological changes. We'll cover a few of the important issues related to privacy and civil liberties-e-mail privacy, unwarranted search and seizure, and offensive messages and libel.

E-Mail Privacy

When you send a message by e-mail, the message is broken into packets and the packets are sent out over the Internet. The number of packets depends on the size of the message. Each message has the Internet address of the sender (your address) and the address of the recipient. Packets from a single message may take different routes to the destination, or may take different routes at different times. This works well for the Internet and for you. Since packets are generally sent through the best path, depending on the traffic load on the Internet, the path doesn't depend on certain systems being in operation, and all you have to give is the address of the destination.

The packets making up an e-mail message may pass through several different systems before reaching their destination. This means there may be some places between you and the destination where the packets could be intercepted and examined. Since all the systems have to be able to look at the address of the destination, each system could be able to examine the contents of the message. If you're using a computer system shared by others or if the system at the destination is shared by others, there is usually someone (a system administrator) capable of examining all the messages. So, in the absence of codes of ethics or without the protection of law, e-mail could be very public. Needless to say, you shouldn't be reading someone else's e-mail. Most system administrators adopt a code of ethics under which they will not examine e-mail unless they feel it's important to support the system(s) they administer. The truth of the matter is they are generally too busy to bother reading other people's mail.

Electronic Communications Privacy Act. One example of a law to ensure the privacy of e-mail is the Electronic Communications Privacy Act (ECPA) passed in 1986 by Congress. It prohibits anyone from intentionally intercepting, using, and/or disclosing e-mail messages without the sender's permission. The ECPA was passed to protect individuals from having their private messages accessed by government officers or others without legal permission. That bill extended the protections that existed for voice communications to nonvoice communications conveyed through wires or over the airwaves. You can, of course, give your permission for someone to access your e-mail. However, law enforcement officials or others cannot access your e-mail in stored form (on a disk or tape) without a warrant, and electronic transmission of your e-mail can't be intercepted or "tapped" without a court order. The ECPA does allow a system administrator to access users' e-mail on a computer system if it's necessary for the operation or security of the system. The ECPA then gives the system administrator the responsibility to allow no access to e-mail passing within or through a system without a court order or warrant. She can and indeed should refuse any requests to examine e-mail unless the proper legal steps are followed.

Encryption. When you send a message by e-mail it's often transmitted in the same form you've typed it. Even though it's unethical and illegal for someone else to read it, the message is in a form that's easy to read. This is similar to sending a message written on a postcard through the postal service. One way to avoid this is to use encryption to put a message into an unreadable form. The characters in the message can be changed by substitution or scrambling, usually based on some secret code. The message can't be read unless the code and method of encryption are known. The code is called a key. Many messages are encoded by a method called public key encryption. If you encrypt a message and send it on to someone, that person has to know the key to decode your message. If the key is also sent by e-mail, it might be easy to intercept the key and decode the encrypted message.

With public key encryption there are two keys, one public and the other private. The public key needs to be known. To send a message to a friend, you use her or his public key to encrypt the message. Your friend then uses her or his private key to decode the message after receiving it. Suppose you want to send an encrypted message to your friend Milo. He tells you his public key; in fact, there's no harm if he tells everybody. You write the message and then encrypt it using Milo's public key. He receives the message and then uses his private key to decode it. It doesn't matter who sent the message to Milo as long as it was encrypted with his public key. Also, even if the message is intercepted, it can't be read without knowing Milo's private key. It's up to him to keep that secret. Likewise, if he wanted to respond, he would use your public key to encrypt the message. You would use your private key to decode it.

You can obtain a version of public key encryption software called PGP, for Pretty Good Privacy. It's freely available to individuals and may be purchased for commercial use. There are some licensing restrictions on the use of the commercial versions in the United States and Canada. Furthermore, United States State Department regulations prohibit the export of some versions of this program to other countries. In fact, current restrictions in the United States prohibit the export of most encryption methods, while other countries allow the export of encryption methods and algorithms. Some people feel strongly that these policies should be changed for the sake of sharing information and for the sake of allowing common encryption of sensitive and business messages, but others don't agree. To read more about PGP, look at "Peter's PGP Page" (**http://www.gildea.com/pgp/**) or "Frequently Asked Questions for Pretty Good Privacy" (**http://www.prairienet.org/~jalicqui/pgpfaq.txt**). See "Where To Get The Pretty Good Privacy Program (PGP) FAQ" (**ftp://ftp.csn.net/mpj/getpgp.asc**) for a complete account of acquiring PGP.

One issue that needs to be resolved is whether it should be possible for law enforcement or other government officials to decode encrypted messages. Some argue that because of the need to detect criminal action or in the interests of national security, the means to decode any messages should be available to the appropriate authorities. Others argue that individuals have the right to privacy in their communications. In the United States, the issue has been decided in favor of government access in the case of digital telephone communications. The issue hasn't been settled yet for e-mail or other forms of electronic communications.

A complete and excellent resource for information about electronic privacy is "EPIC Online Guide to Privacy Resources," URL **http://www.epic.org/privacy/privacy_resources_faq.html**, maintained by the Electronic Privacy Information Center (EPIC). Two other places you may want to look are "The Privacy Pages," URL **http://www.2020tech.com/maildrop/privacy.html**, and "Readings on Encryption and National Security," URL **http://swissnet.ai.mit.edu/6095/**, a Web page listing required and recommended readings associated with the course Ethics and Law on the Electronic Frontier offered at MIT.

Unwarranted Search and Seizure

Suppose a person is suspected of having illegal items on a computer system, such as pirated software, credit card numbers, telephone access codes, stolen documents, or proprietary information, and law enforcement officials obtain a court order or warrant to search or confiscate the materials. What are reasonable actions?

- Is it reasonable to confiscate all the disks connected to or networked to the suspect's computer system?
- Is it reasonable to confiscate all the suspect's computer equipment including the main computer, printers, modems, and telephones?
- If the items are removed from the premises for searching, how much time should pass before they are returned?
- If the suspect's system is part of a bulletin board or e-mail system with messages for other, presumably innocent persons, should those messages be delivered to the innocent parties?

The answers to these and some related questions depend on the laws governing permissible searches and seizures. The actions taken in cases such as these also depend on how well the technology is understood by the courts and law enforcement officials. For example, the Fourth Amendment to the United States Constitution guards against unreasonable searches and seizures of property. In 1990, all the computer equipment and files of one company, Steve Jackson Games, were confiscated and searched by the United States Secret Service. The warrant application released later showed that the company was not suspected of any crime. However, the law enforcement officials, in their fervor to deal with "computer crime," appeared to disregard accepted civil liberties. Some of this was undoubtedly because they were unfamiliar with the technology at that time. A printer or modem, for example, can't store anything once the power is turned off, so there is no need to confiscate those items if one is searching for what might be illegal information. These actions and the related court cases point out the need to keep the officers of the legal system informed and educated regarding the uses and capabilities of technology.

The Electronic Frontier Foundation (EFF) was formed in 1990 to, among other things, bring issues dealing with civil liberties related to computing and telecommunications technology to the attention of the public at large, legislators, and court and law enforcement officials. As a nonprofit public interest organization, EFF maintains collections of files and documents. Use the URL **http://www.eff.org** to access the home page of the EFF and **http://www.eff.org/pub/** to view their FTP library. EFF also produces a number of publications and other materials, many of which are available on the Internet. They have also provided legal services and opinions in cases similar to the one described above.

Offensive Material and Libel

Offensive and Abusive E-Mail. Virtually all codes of etiquette, ethics, and policies for acceptable use of networked computer facilities include statements that prohibit sending offensive or abusive messages by e-mail. This is, naturally, similar to the codes of behavior and laws we adhere to in everyday communications. One difference between dealing with this sort of behavior on the Internet and other forms of communication, such as the telephone or postal service, is that no one is in charge of the Internet—it is a cooperative organization. If you have a problem with someone at your site, talk with your supervisor, their supervisor, your system administrator, or Internet service provider about it. If the problem comes from another site, send e-mail to the address **postmaster@the.other.site**, and talk with the system administrator at your site or your supervisor about it. (You substitute the Internet domain name of the site in question for **the.other.site**.) Individuals have been arrested and prosecuted for making threatening remarks by e-mail. Civil suits and charges have been filed against individuals in cases of harassment, abuse, and stalking.

Sexually Explicit Material and Pornography. Some material available on the Internet may be classified as erotic, sexually explicit, or pornographic. It's not surprising since there's a large number of people using the World Wide Web and the Internet with varying preferences, interests, and cultural perspectives. Also, as with other media, there is a market for it. In the past most of this material was available through Usenet newsgroups whose names clearly identified the content, for example, **alt.binaries.nude.celebrities**. With the increase in popularity of the WWW, several commercial Web sites that traffic in explicit videos, phone sex, and items with sexually explicit themes have been set up. Most of these sites have a home page warning that the related pages contain material some might find offensive or inappropriate. The home page often contains a form where the user states that she/he is 18 or 21 years of age. It's not difficult to find this material on the Internet, but in almost every case it has to be sought out; people using the Internet aren't coerced or tricked into viewing it. The focus of the debate about this so-called "cyberporn" has been whether it's appropriate for the material to be readily available to children and whether it's appropriate to pass laws that restrict the content of the Internet. There are a number of programs that can be installed on a computer to restrict the material that can be accessed on the World Wide Web. The programs work with lists of Web pages and ways of describing the content of Web pages to filter material. One source of information about these programs and related topics is "PEDINFO Parental Control of Internet Access" (**http://www.lhl.uab.edu/pedinfo/Control.html**). The culture of the Internet has fostered personal rights and liberties, so some argue its content should not be restricted or censored. There are laws banning or restricting pornography; some countries have more stringent laws than others, and some laws restrict the distribution of the material. Private networks such as CompuServe, AOL, and Prodigy enact their own rules regarding content. Recently CompuServe removed access to several hundred newsgroups at the request of German court officials because suspected illegal (by German laws) pornographic material may be distributed through those newsgroups. In that case the laws of one country affected users throughout the world. (That story made the front page of the *New York Times* and other newspapers.) Another online service filtered out messages that contained the word "breast," but rescinded that action due to complaints form users who found information and discussions relating to breast cancer very valuable.

It seems that the current debate regarding pornography and civil liberties on the Internet will be continued for some time. The President of the United States and Congress enacted legislation that make it illegal to transmit certain materials on the Internet. The term used in the legislation is "indecent" material. This legislation presents some problems—monitoring the Internet would greatly increase the expense and complexity of maintaining current networks; the term "indecent" is open to many interpretations. It's difficult to see how this legislation could be uniformly enforced or interpreted. As this book goes to press, the Federal Court is reviewing the impact of the Telecommunications Act of 1996 on rights guaranteed by U.S. Constitution. For more material on these topics, see "Cyberporn Debate" (**http://www2000.ogsm.vanderbilt.edu/cyberporn.debate.cgi**) and "Internet Censorship" (**http://epic.org/free_speech/censorship/**).

Inappropriate Business Practices. Portions of the Internet throughout the world were often started as national or military networks. Much of the startup costs were paid by the government. In that environment, advertising was generally prohibited. In the United States, it wasn't until the late 1980s that any commercial traffic was allowed on the primary portion of the Internet in the United States. Because of a relatively recent history of little or no advertising and marketing, efforts in this direction have been met with opposition on some services of the Internet and Usenet. However, it has become common to find advertising, marketing, and commercial activities readily available on the World Wide Web.

One particularly offensive means of advertising is called *spamming*. When used in this way, the term means sending a message to many unrelated newsgroups or interest groups. It's not too hard to do, but it almost always is met with great opposition and feelings of hatred. One way to deal with it is to send a copy of the message and a complaint to **postmaster@the.other.site**. In one case, a company that spammed virtually every Usenet newsgroup eventually lost its Internet access. It wasn't banned from the Internet, but the organization providing Internet access to the company received so many complaints that they withdrew Internet services from the company.

On some newsgroups it is permissible to advertise. Advertising and commerce is allowed on the Internet, but most users prefer that it be done in clearly identified newsgroups or Internet locations.

Libel. Some libel suits have been filed based on postings to Usenet or some other network. One person or company feels that another has slandered them or falsely attempted to damage their reputation. Once again, you would expect the same laws or rules for libel in the society at large to be applied to network communications. That's generally the case, but an interesting issue comes up, centering around whether the company or organization that maintains a computer telecommunication system is responsible for libelous or even illegal messages posted there. In the United States the courts have generally drawn an analogy between these systems and a bookstore. The owner of a bookstore is not responsible for the contents of all the books in the store, and likewise, the management of commercial networked systems on the

Internet have not been held responsible for all messages on their systems. On the other hand, some commercial network systems claim to screen all messages before they're posted. In that case they may be held accountable for libelous messages. Also, consider that telephone companies aren't held responsible for the speech on their equipment since they fall into the category of a "common carrier." However, television and radio stations are responsible for the content of their broadcasts.

Intellectual Property and Copyright

You know there is a wealth of files, documents, images, and other types of items available on the Internet. They can be viewed, copied, printed, downloaded, saved in a file, or passed on to others. Just because we can copy or duplicate information we find on the Internet, is it legal or ethical to do so? Many, if not most, of these items don't exist in a physical form, so perhaps the issues about ownership that depend on something having a physical form don't make sense. The notion of ownership of something, whether it has a physical form, does still make sense as intellectual property. There are a number of laws and agreements throughout the world to protect intellectual property rights. The right to copy or duplicate materials can be granted only by the owners of the information. This is called the copyright. Many documents on the Internet contain a statement asserting the document is copyrighted and giving permission for distributing the document in an electronic form, provided it isn't sold or made part of some commercial venture. Even items that don't contain these statements are generally protected by the copyright laws of the United States, the Universal Copyright Convention, or the Berne Union. Most copyright conventions or statutes include a provision so that individuals may make copies of portions of a document for short-term use. If information is obtainable on the Internet and there is no charge to access the information, it often can be shared in an electronic form. That certainly doesn't mean you can copy images or documents and make them available on the Internet, or make copies and share them in a printed form with others. Quite naturally, many people who create or provide material available on the Internet expect to get credit and be paid for their work.

One issue that may need to be resolved is the physical nature of information on the Internet. In most cases, it exists on one disk and is viewed in an electronic form. It has no tangible, physical form when it's transmitted. The copyright law in the United States states that copyright protection begins once the work is in "fixed form," so the original portion of these works is protected by copyright. The notion of fixed form is much easier to determine with more traditional works that exist in a physical form, such as books, poems, stories, sound recordings, or motion pictures. Naturally, it seems reasonable to say a work is in fixed form when stored on a disk, but can we say the same about material being transmitted through several networks? If the work only existed on a disk, if that was the only way to obtain the work, then it's clear when the work is being copied and who may be copying the disk. On the other hand, if the information can be accessed through the Internet, one may not know if it is being copied and stored. Current laws and conventions were written for works that exist in some definite physical form, and the nature of that form may make it difficult or time consuming to make unauthorized copies. But information transmitted on the Internet or other networks is very easy to copy. When you copy something in digital form, you make an exact duplicate. Each copy is as good as the original. The ease with which works can be copied and distributed may require a law different from current copyright statutes.

Not all cultures have the same attitudes about ownership of information. Some cultures have a long tradition of sharing information and works created by individuals. Other groups feel all information should be free, and so they think it's appropriate to make works available only if there is no charge for the use of the works. The worldwide nature of the Internet and other networks requires addressing these cultural differences. When the United States deals with some countries, it may withhold a certain level of trading status if they don't abide by international copyright conventions.

Access—What Type at What Cost?

In this section we discuss two concepts involved in access to the Internet. One is the ability to become connected to the Internet and access the WWW. The other is the nature of the access—one-way, only receiving information, or two-way so everyone can be an information receiver and provider. We'll also cover the topics of providing universal access, Internet connections for everyone through Free-Nets, community-based networks, and the formation of a National Public Telecomputing Network.

Getting Connected

Getting connected to the Internet is an economic and technical issue. If you're lucky, you're part of an organization that foots the bill for the connection, but in this case you're probably paying tuition or student fees; or the overhead costs could find their way to your salary.

If you aren't already connected, you or your organization must make arrangements with an Internet service provider—a company that provides connection to the Internet at a cost. Many considerations go into the choice of a provider. Naturally, you're interested in the cost of the service, but the type of service needs to be specified, as it usually determines the cost. This is where technical issues come into play. Items to consider are the speed at which you access the Internet, the types of services provided, the fee structure, and associated costs for access. In some cases access at 9600 bits per second or less is appropriate; this is true if access is text-only. With this type of access you generally get a Unix shell account, which means you have a log-in name on a computer that uses the Unix operating system.

If you're going to use Netscape Navigator or some other graphical WWW browser, you'll need a full Internet connection, called an IP connection, to be able to run Internet application programs on your computer system. You'll probably want the connection to be at a higher speed, such as 14.4K, 28.8K, or 56K bits per second or greater. (Here K represents one thousand.) With an IP connection, the computer you use contains a network card with a cable connected to it, or your computer has SLIP or PPP access. (See Chapters 1 and 2.) These types of connections may be more expensive than Unix shell accounts, but are often worth the cost. They allow you to work in a graphical environment more efficiently, since you can run Internet applications on your computer.

Fee structures vary, and you need to choose what best fits your needs. Some providers charge a flat monthly or yearly fee regardless of how much the connection is used. Others charge a base rate for a certain number of hours per month, and then you pay extra if you're connected for a longer period of time. Some sites also allow a fixed amount of storage for files at the flat rate, and then charge extra if more is used. Finally, you need to consider any associated costs such as a start-up fee and communication charges-phone calls, modems, cable access fees, etc. What may turn out to be the most important item is support, someone to provide help and guidance when you or the users on your system need it.

Access—One-Way or Two-Way?

One thing that's made the Internet so lively and engaging is that it is a two-way connection. Anyone can be an information receiver or consumer, and just as importantly, anyone can be an information provider or producer. Furthermore, there is no central control. It's more like control through cooperation. These facts have political and economic consequences; political because of the freedom it gives-freedom of expression and freedom of discussion. At the present time there is no central control of the Internet, so the topics discussed and ideas expressed range through a variety of subjects. Some of the topics are politically popular and some are not; some support actions of local governments, and others are critical of those actions. But the primary point is that the discussions go on. A network such as the Internet allows the people who use it to organize for or against national or international issues. Issues can be discussed and calls for action disseminated. If the Internet were run or designed in the same way as radio or television—essentially a one-way communication medium—it wouldn't be such a vigorous, interesting medium. The economic implications are that it allows for the startup of businesses whose services include providing information; they can gather, analyze, and provide data. Anyone can be an information provider. Because the business is accessed through the Internet, its customers can be located throughout the world. The most important aspects of the business are the services it provides and the means customers use to access the services. In physical terms, the business doesn't have to be very large. It's the virtual nature of the business that dominates. It's not too far-fetched to think of these as storefront businesses with the Internet as their Main Street.

There are, of course, down sides to this two-way access without central control. This type of access has been used to offend and abuse others and for uncontrolled marketing. The previous section on "Offensive Messages and Libel" gives some details about this. Remember, the Internet is a cooperative venture—people sharing resources, services, and ideas. There are appropriate places for discussions on all sorts of topics and for both commercial and noncommercial activities.

Universal or Public Access

As the Internet grows in both the number of users and the physical structures needed to support it, it reaches a size sufficient to be called an infrastructure. An infrastructure is a basic service or facility necessary to support a community or society. If it is important to society, then it seems reasonable that everyone should have access to it. This is the case in some parts of the world where access to the Internet is part of a national public utility. Many more nations deal with access to a voice network, the telephone network, in much the same way. As more persons learn about and use the Internet and World Wide Web in schools and their work, it's reasonable to provide Internet access to them when they leave those environments. So it may be reasonable to view the Internet, National Information Infrastructure (NII), or Global Information Infrastructure (GII), as a public utility, the way phone service or cable TV service is currently treated. However, the Internet has unique characteristics that contribute to its usefulness, and those, such as two-way access and little central control, need to be maintained.

Viewing the Internet, NII, or GII as a public utility might help to solve some of the problems of public access. It's technologically possible to provide Internet access virtually anywhere. However, there are questions about who will pay for providing the services and how the users will be charged for access. In many countries, the government probably does not have the resources or desire to pay for the installation of equipment and other items for universal access. The Internet appears to be destined to be a private venture with government regulation. So once the decision is made to provide universal access, means of providing the access and paying for the access need to be decided and implemented.

Free-Net

One successful means of providing community access to the Internet and the WWW is a *Free-Net*. A Free-Net allows anyone with a computer and modem to obtain a log-in account and have access to the Internet. Membership in a Free-Net is usually either free to members of the local community or within the means of members of the community. The membership fees cover some expenses, but virtually all the computer systems, modems, phone lines, and other necessary materials are supported by donations or gifts. The expertise and personnel needed for these Free-Nets are provided by volunteers or are supported by donations and membership dues. These are nonprofit organizations that provide access to the Internet only for community and other noncommercial purposes. They usually allow for posting of community calendars, information about health, cultural and governmental events in the community, Internet e-mail, access to some portions of Usenet, and access to other Internet sites and services. Several Free-Nets exist throughout the world. The first, the Cleveland Free-Net, was established in Cleveland, Ohio by T. M. Grundner and others as a means to deliver community health information. Some of these Free-Nets are accessible through Hytelnet and by using a WWW browser. Use the URL **http://nptn.org/CyberStation.Cleveland** to access the one in Cleveland, and use **http://nptn.org/about.fn/By_State.txt.html** to see a list of Free-Nets throughout the United States and the world.

National Public Telecomputing Network

A Free-Net is an example of a community providing its own solutions to some of the problems of Internet access for all its members. In order to address problems on a larger scale and to avoid duplication, some of the people involved in Free-Nets have formed a National Public Telecomputing Network (NPTN). NPTN consists of a confederation of Free-Nets. The purpose of NPTN is to help establish community networks so free, open access is available to link those systems into a common network, and to supplement the services provided by the local systems with network-wide services and resources. This group can obtain resources and services and supply them to the networks that are part of NPTN. For example, the rulings of the United States Supreme Court are made available to the member Free-Nets by NPTN. NPTN is similar to the Corporation for Public Broadcasting and National Public Radio in the United States except that, at the present time, NPTN receives no direct support from the United States government. The URL for the home page for NPTN is **http://nptn.org**.

Internet Security

When you use a computer system connected to the Internet, you're able to reach a rich variety of sites and information. By the same token, any system connected to the Internet can be reached in some manner by any of the other computer systems connected to the Internet. Partaking of the material on the Internet also means that you have to be concerned about the security of your computer system and other systems. The reason for the concern about your system is obvious—you don't want unauthorized persons accessing your information or information belonging to others who share your system. You want to protect your system from malicious or unintentional actions that could destroy stored information or halt your system. You don't want others masquerading as you. You need to be concerned about the security of other systems so you can have some faith in the information you retrieve from those systems, and so you can conduct some business transactions. A lack of security results in damage, theft, and what may be worse in some cases, a lack of confidence or trust.

Maintaining security becomes more important as we use the Internet for commercial transactions or transmitting sensitive data. There is always the chance that new services introduced to the Internet won't be completely tested for security flaws or that security problems will be discovered. While it's exciting to be at the cutting edge, there's some virtue in not adopting the latest service or the latest version of software until it has been around for a while. This gives the Internet community a chance to discover problems. Several agencies are dedicated to finding, publicizing, and dealing with security problems. One site that does this is maintained by the National Institute of Standards and Technology (NIST), United States Department of Commerce. Use your Web to access the NIST Computer Security Resource Clearing House by using the URL **http://first.org/**.

In the section "Privacy and Civil Liberties" we mentioned some of the security or privacy problems associated with e-mail. Since information is passed from system to system on the Internet, not always by the same path or through designated secure systems, it can be monitored. Furthermore, you can't always be sure that the address on e-mail hasn't been forged. It appears that an important way to keep transactions secure is to use encryption techniques. These are similar to the ones discussed in that same section on privacy and civil liberties.

If you access the Internet by logging into a computer system, your primary defense against intrusion is your password. You need to choose a password that will be difficult to guess. This means choosing a password that's at least six characters long. You'll also want to use a password contain upper- and lowercase letters and some nonalphabetic characters. Additionally, the password shouldn't represent a word, and it shouldn't be something that's easy to identify with you such as a phone number, room number, birthdate, or license number. Some bad choices are **Skippy**, **3451234a**, or **gloria4me**. Better choices might be **All452on**, **jmr!pmQ7**, or **sHo$7otg**. Naturally, you have to choose something you'll remember. Never write down your password; doing that makes it easy to find.

Persons who try to gain unauthorized access to a system are called *crackers*. A cracker will, by some means, get a copy of the password file for a system containing the names of all the users along with their passwords. (In some cases the permissions on a password file are set so anyone can read it. This is necessary for certain programs to run. Fortunately, the passwords are encrypted.) Once a cracker gets a copy of a password file, she will run a program that attempts to guess the encrypted passwords. If a password is an encrypted version of a word, a word in reverse order, or a word with one numeral or punctuation mark, it is not too difficult for the program to decipher it. If a cracker has one password on a system, she can gain access to that log-in name and from there possibly go to other portions of the system. So, in addition to creating a good password, you also need to change it regularly.

Because connecting a network to the Internet allows access to that network, system administrators and other persons concerned with network security are very concerned about making that connection. One device or part of a network that can help enhance security is called a *firewall*. A firewall can be a separate computer, a router, or some other network device that allows certain packets into a network. (Remember that all information is passed throughout the Internet as packets.) By using a firewall and configuring it correctly, only certain types of Internet services can be allowed through to the network. Organizations with firewalls often place their WWW, FTP, and other servers on one part of their network and put a firewall system between those servers and the rest of the network. The firewall restricts access to the protected internal network by letting through only packets associated with certain protocols. E-mail can still be delivered and sometimes Telnet to the internal network is allowed. If you are on the protected portion of the network, behind the firewall, then you can access Internet and WWW sites on the Internet, but they may not be able to gain direct access to you. Firewalls also perform logging and auditing functions so that if security is breached, the source of the problem may be determined. To find out more about firewalls, read "Firewalls FAQ" (**http://www.cis.ohio-state.edu/hypertext/faq/usenet/firewalls-faq/faq.html**).

You don't need to be paranoid about security, but you do need to be aware of anything that seems suspicious. Report any suspicious activity or changes to your directory or files to your system administrator. The system administrator can often take actions to track down a possible break in security. Be suspicious if you're asked for your password at unusual times. You should be asked for it only when you log in. Never give your password to anyone. If a program changes its behavior in terms of requiring more information from you than it did before, it could be the original program was replaced with another by an unauthorized user. This is called a *trojan horse*, because of the similarity of the program to the classic Greek tale. What appears to be benign could hide some malicious actions or threats.

One type of program that causes problems for Internet users is called a *virus*. A virus doesn't necessarily copy your data or attempt to use your system. However, it can make it difficult or impossible to use your system. A virus is a piece of code or instructions that attaches itself to existing programs. Just like a biological virus, a computer virus can't run or exist on its own, but must be part of an executing program. When these programs are run, the added instructions are also executed. Sometimes the virus does nothing more than announce its presence; in other cases the virus erases files from your disk. A virus moves from system to system by being part of an executable program. Be careful where you get programs. You can obtain a program that scans your system for viruses and also checks programs you load onto your system for known viruses. Use these virus scanning programs to check new programs you load on your system. Also be sure to have a backup copy of your files so they can be restored if they're inadvertently or maliciously erased.

Getting documents and images from other sites on the Internet won't bring a virus to your system. It comes only from running programs on your system. Viruses can exist in executable programs and also have been found in word processing documents that contain portions of code that's executed called a macro. For more information on viruses, check the hyperlinks at "Other Sources of Virus Information" (**http://www.datafellows.fi/vir-info/virother.htm**).

Internet security is very important to many users, as well it should be. We need to make sure that messages are private and that monetary transactions and data sources are secure. Some of these concerns are enforced by laws and acceptable codes of conduct. A good document to read about security and privacy is "Identity, Privacy, and Anonymity on the Internet" by L. Detweiler. It's available in three parts through the URL **http://www.eff.org/pub/Privacy/Anonymity/privacy_anonymity.faq**.

To see some papers and other resources dealing with electronic commerce, go the Web page ISWorld Net Electronic Commerce Course Page using the URL **http://www.isworld.org/isworld/ecourse/home.html**. Other information about commercial activities on the Internet is available through Commerce Net, **http://www.commerce.net** and FinanceNet, **http://financenet.gov/ec.htm**.

Summary

The Internet has had a tradition of sharing. This includes sharing data, sharing services, exchanging e-mail, having free and generally open discussions, and bringing together ideas and opinions from a diverse population. The rules for behavior, policies for acceptable use, and laws pertaining to activities on the Internet have developed over time. In some cases policies and laws have been adopted from other media, and in other cases the unique qualities of the Internet and electronic communications have been taken into account in establishing laws and policies.

During the transmission of information on the Internet, the information or communication is divided into packets of bytes (characters) that are sent from one system to another. The packets may pass through several different systems, may take different routes to arrive at a destination, and transmissions from one site to another may take different routes at different times. This opens the possibility for intercepting and examining e-mail or other transmissions. Be careful about what you say in e-mail, and think about using encryption techniques so the e-mail can be read only by the recipient. Laws such as the Electronic Communications Privacy Act (ECPA) have been adopted in some countries to ensure the privacy of electronic communications. The ECPA makes it illegal to intercept or read other people's e-mail and requires government officials to obtain a warrant or court order before searching, seizing, or intercepting electronic communications. Laws regulating slander, libel, threats, and harassment deal with electronic communications as well.

The Internet has grown very rapidly, with a sharp increase in the number of users and a change in the makeup of that population. It continues to become more inclusive, representing users from different countries, cultures, and work groups. This causes some strains between some groups of users and others whose actions seem contrary to past acceptable modes of behavior. For example, in the past the Internet was almost free of commercial transactions, and now commercial uses are condoned and encouraged.

In most cases, the information available on the Internet is the intellectual property of someone or some organization and is protected by copyright laws. Check to see if there are any copyright notices on information. Much of it can be shared in an electronic form, provided the author is given credit and it's not modified. Problems arise because it's so easy to make copies of information available in electronic form. There are very few, if any, ways to know whether a copy has been made. This issue needs to be resolved. Some suggest using methods of encryption to protect against unauthorized copying or dissemination.

Access to the Internet or any sort of national or international network involves economic, technical, and political issues. For an individual or organization, the issues are generally economic and technical. One needs to decide the type of Internet service needed (technical issue), and balance that with what is afford-able (economic issue). The political issues generally arise when one thinks about giving community-wide or universal access to the Internet. Is it the government's responsibility to provide this service? Is Internet access as important as other public/private utilities? Some communities have begun Free-Nets, which give Internet and community network access to anyone with a computer and a modem. The National Public Telecomputing Network is a confederation of community networks.

Internet security is an important issue for a variety of reasons, including an individual's desire for privacy, the increased use of the Internet for commercial transactions, and the need to maintain the integrity of data. If you access the Internet by logging into a computer system, you need to take care to choose a password that will be difficult to guess. Furthermore, you should notice and report any unusual circum-stances or modifications.

The Internet is an important place to learn, work, and enjoy yourself. Some of its strengths have come from the diversity in the user population because there is no central control and because there is two-way access. If you can receive information, you can produce information! The Internet has been relatively free of regulation, but it has codes of ethics and acceptable use policies to make it a reasonable and safe place for a variety of activities. As the Internet grows and changes, it needs to maintain its sources of strength and vitality. Whether it will maintain its character will depend on the concerns and actions of its users.

Exercises

These exercises are all small projects. They're meant to give you some focus in thinking about the issues raised in this chapter and to involve you in accessing some Internet sites and resources appropriate to the topics in this chapter.

Acceptable Use Policies

1. a. Does your organization have a statement of policies or procedures for acceptable use of the Internet?
   b. If your answer to part a was yes, get a copy of that policy and read it. Which of the policies would you recommend be changed? Explain your answer.
   c. If your organization doesn't have a policy, then list three or more items you think ought to be in such a policy.

2. Several sites on the Internet have copies of acceptable use policies. You can browse through a list for schools (K-12) by using the URL **gopher://chico.rice.edu:1170/11/More/Acceptable**. Retrieve or browse two of those policies.
   a. How do these policies compare with each other?
   b. What changes would you recommend making to either of the policy statements?

3. Retrieve a copy of "User Guidelines and Net Etiquette" (**http://www.fau.edu/rinaldi/netiquette.html**) by Arlene Rinaldi. Go to the section "The Net: User Guidelines and Netiquette-Index." You'll see it

contains guidelines for working with several types of Internet services. Pick one service you've worked with and compare the guidelines in that document with your behavior and experience.

Organizations

4. Use your Web browser to look at the online resources available from the Electronic Frontier Foundation.
   a. Describe the home page for the EFF, **http://www.eff.org**.
   b. The home page has a hyperlink, **Other Stuff**, which takes you to a list of other resources. Follow the hyperlinks **Other Government Information and Servers—An EFF Index of Global Public-Sector Internet Resources** and **Other Activism, Computing and Nonprofit Organizations**. Write a synopsis of what's available by following those hyperlinks.
   c. Follow the hyperlink **Other Activism, Computing and Nonprofit Organizations** and see what you can find out about two organizations, ones that are affiliated with the EFF. Determine the mission and aims of those organizations.

5. Use the URL for the EFF's FTP archives, **http://www.eff.org/pub/**. You'll see several subdirectories listed. Pick a topic in the area of privacy, civil liberties, or legislation. Using the Internet resources available through that site, write a short paper or create a Web page about any of those topics.

6. Take a look at the home page for the Electronic Privacy Information Center (EPIC), **http://www.epic.org**.
   a. What are some of the items listed under "Hot Topics"? Follow a couple of hyperlinks and describe what you find.
   b. Follow the hyperlink to the **EPIC Online Guide to Privacy Resources**. List the names of five international privacy sites. Follow a hyperlink to one of the sites and describe what's available at that site.

7. The EFF and Computer Professionals for Social Responsibility (CPSR) both have resources available on the World Wide Web. The URL for the CPSR home page is **http://www.cpsr.org/home.html**.
   a. Retrieve or browse statements for each organization that gives its mission and aims. Write a brief summary, at most one page, comparing the two organizations and giving differences between the two.
   b. If you were to join one, which would it be? Explain.

Privacy and Security

8. Retrieve "Identity, Privacy, and Anonymity on the Internet" by L. Detweiler, from the site mentioned in the text. Using the information in that document, provide answers to the following.
   a. What was the Steve Jackson Games case?
   b. List the names and give a short description of three to five Usenet newsgroups dealing with privacy.
   c. What are cypherpunks?

9. One of the more popular anti-virus programs is F-PROT, and there's a free version available from Data Fellows at **http://www.datafellows.com.**
   a. The headquarters for Data Fellows is in Europe. Which country?
   b. Follow the link **Computer Virus Information** from the home page and then the link **Other sources of computer virus information in the net (FAQs, links, etc).** What FAQs are available? Several of the entries represent information in different parts of the world. Which countries are represented? Follow one of the links to a country different from the one you're living in. Write a brief description of what you find at that site.

10. The text mentions some documents available at **research.att.com** dealing with electronic payment and privacy.
    a. What are the names of those documents?
    b. Retrieve one of those documents and write a brief summary.

Free-Nets and NPTN

11. Use Hytelnet or some other method to find ways to access a Free-Net by using Telnet. (One is mentioned in this chapter.) Explore the Free-Net as a visitor. Describe the organization of the Free-Net and some of the services available to members. What is the membership fee? Describe why you would or would not pay a membership fee to join a Free-Net.

12. The site **nptn.org** on the Internet makes information available about the National Public Telecomputing Network. Using your Web browser and the URL **http://nptn.org**, connect to that site and find information that gives the goals and mission of NPTN.
    a. What is the Academy One Program? CyberSolon?
    b. Follow hyperlinks until you get to the "CyberCasting Services Catalog." Pick out five services or items that interest you from the catalog. Explain why you made those choices, stating the mission and goals of NPTN.

13. By following hyperlinks from the home page for NPTN, you can find a a list of Free-Nets in the United States and other parts of the world. (The URL is also mentioned in this chapter.)
    a. Give the names of five Free-Nets in at least three countries.
    b. Using the information in that list, log in to at least one Free-Net on a continent different from your own.

14. The Web page "Rheingold's Brainstorms: Virtual Worlds Linklist" (**http://www.well.com/user/hlr/vircom/**) contains several hyperlinks to virtual communities.
    a. Visit two or three virtual communities. Which did you visit?
    b. Are these virtual communities similar to Free-Net systems? Explain your answer.

Glossary

Acceptable use policy A policy statement from a network or organization giving the acceptable uses of the network for local use and accessing the Internet.

Administrative address The address to use to join a Listserv or interest group and to send requests for services.

Anonymous FTP A means of using FTP (File Transfer Protocol) in which a user starts an ftp session with a remote host through a Web browser, gives the user name "anonymous," and e-mail address as a password.

Archie An information service that helps to locate a file, which can then retrieved by anonymous FTP.

Article A message or file which is part of a Usenet newsgroup.

ASCII American Standard Code for Information Interchange. A code for representing characters in a numeric form. An ASCII file is one which usually contains characters which can be displayed on a screen or printed without formatting or using another program.

BBS Bulletin Board System. A computer and software which provides an electronic forum, message center, and archives of files to its members. Traditionally these have been run by hobbyists through dial-up modem lines. Recently some of these have been connected to the Internet for a variety of organizations.

Binary file A file containing information such as a compressed archive, an image, a program, a spread sheet, or a word processor document. The items in the file usually cannot be displayed on a screen or printed without using some program.

Bit A binary digit—a one or a zero. A bit is the smallest unit of information. Information in computers can be represented as a sequence of bits, and modem and network speeds are often expressed in terms of bits per second.

Bookmark list A list of links to items on the World Wide Web. Usually created by an individual as he uses a Web browser. A good way to keep track of favorite or important sites, these are saved and can be used at any time.

Byte A sequence of 8 bits. Each character in the ASCII code is represented by a byte. The size of files, disks, and memory is often expressed in bytes. For example, a file may have a size of 58,000 bytes, a hard disk may be capable of holding 1 gigabyte (1,000,000,000 bytes) of information, and a computer's memory may be 8 megabytes (8,000,000).

Cache A portion of memory (either in RAM or on a disk) set aside to hold the items retrieved most recently. For Netscape Navigator, this refers to recent Web pages and images. It's used so that items may be retrieved from cache rather than going back to the Internet. Netscape can be set so that, in the case an item hasn't changed, it will be retrieved from the cache.

Client A program or Internet service that sends commands to and receives information from a corresponding program (often) at a remote site called a server. Most Internet services run as client/server programs. Telnet, for example, works this way. A user starts a client program on their computer which contacts a Telnet server.

Compression An algorithm or scheme used to compress or shrink a file. A file in compressed form must first be uncompressed or transformed before it can be read, displayed, or used. Files available through anonymous ftp are often stored in compressed form and must be treated as binary files.

Dial-up access Access to the Internet through a phone line and a modem. Typically gives the user a log-in name and shell account to another computer which has a full IP Internet connection. The user usually has access to only text-based Internet services.

Dial-up IP connection A connection to the Internet through a modem that allows the computer to access the Internet using TCP (Transmission Control Protocol) and IP (Internet Protocol). This allows for the possibility of using any Internet services or resource. Information is sent and received as packets using a modem.

Digest A collection of messages from a Listserv or discussion group sent at regular intervals such as daily or weekly.

Direct IP connection A connection to the Internet made by installing a device (a network adapter or card) into a computer and then connecting the device to a network through a cable. TCP (Transmission Control Protocol) and IP (Internet Protocol) are implemented through software on the computer, information is sent and received as packets, and it is possible to access the full range of Internet services (provided the software for a particular service is installed on the computer).

Discussion group A form of group discussion and sharing information carried on by electronic mail. A discussion group focuses on a single topic.

Domain name The Internet name for a network or computer system. The name consists of a sequence of characters separated by periods such as **www.mwc.edu**.

Download Transfer a file from a remote computer to the computer used by an individual.

E-mail Electronic Mail. A basic Internet service which allows users to exchange messages electronically.

Encryption A procedure to convert a file from its original form to one that can only be read by the intended recipient.

FAQ Frequently Asked Questions. A list, often associated with Usenet newsgroups, of commonly asked questions and answers on a specific topic. This is usually the first place users should look to find answers to questions or to get information on a topic.

Firewall A security device or system, usually a combination of hardware and software meant to protect a local network from intruders from the Internet.

Flame An e-mail message or article in a Usenet newsgroup that's meant to insult someone or provoke controversy. This term is also applied to messages which contain strong criticism of or disagreement with a previous message or article.

Frame Some pages are divided into rectangular regions called frames. Each frame has its own scroll bars, and in fact, each frame represents an individual Web page.

Free-Net A community-based network, allowing access to the Internet for no or a small membership fee.

FTP File Transfer Protocol, which allows computers on the Internet to exchange files. One of the three basic Internet services.

FTP Archive A collection of files available by using anonymous FTP.

Gateway A device or program that transfers information between different types of networks. The networks may have similar functions, but in most cases use different technologies for handling information.

Gopher A menu-oriented system that gives access to documents, files, and other Internet services, regardless of where they are on the Internet. The software for Gopher was created and developed at the University of Minnesota to allow users to browse and retrieve documents in a campus environment.

GUI Graphical User Interface. Uses icons and images in addition to text to represent information, input, and output.

Header A portion of an e-mail message containing information pertinent to the transmission of the message such as the address of the sender, the address of the recipient, and when the message was sent.

Helper application A program used with a Web browser to display, view, or work with files that the browser cannot display. For example, graphic or image files in GIF or JPEG format can be displayed by Netscape Navigator. If an image file of another type were accessed through a hyperlink, then a helper application would be necessary to display it. As another example, Web browsers can work with several protocols but not with Telnet, so to activate a hyperlink that begins a Telnet session. A telnet client, separate from the Web browser, has to be used. The Web browser includes ways of being configured to recognize when to use specific helper applications.

History list A list of Internet sites, services, and resources which have been accessed through a WWW browser to arrive at the current item.

Home page The first screen or page of a site accessible through a WWW browser.

Host A computer on the Internet that allows users to communicate with other computers.

HTML Hypertext Markup Language. The format used for writing documents to be viewed with a WWW browser. Items in the document can be text, images, sounds, and links to other HTML documents, or sites, services, and resources on the Internet.

HTTP Hypertext Transport Protocol. The protocol used by World Wide Web servers and clients to communicate.

Hyperlink Words, phrases, images, or regions of an image that are often highlighted or appear in a different color and can be selected as part of a WWW page. Each hyperlink represents another Web page, a location in the current Web page, and an image, audio, video, or multimedia file or some other resource on the World Wide Web. When selected, the resource represented by the hyperlink is activated.

Hypermedia An extension to hypertext to include graphics and audio.

Hypertext A way of viewing or working with a document in text format which allows cross-references to be followed and then return. This presents a nonlinear means of dealing with text and is accomplished through a computer interface to text.

Hytelnet A guide and a tool for working with resources accessible by Telnet. It presents a hypertext interface to an organized list of Telnet sites. The sites are arranged in categories by the type of service such as a library catalog, database, bulletin board, network information, and includes a glossary.

Inline plug-in A program run on the client computer that extends the capabilities of a Web browser to display certain types of files as part of a Web page within the browser window. Some examples are Adobe Acrobat for viewing and printing of documents in PDF format, Apple Quicktime for displaying video, Macromedia Shockwave for interaction with multimedia, and Progressive Networks RealAudio for audio that's played as it's being retrieved from a remote site.

Interest group Group discussion and sharing of information carried on by electronic mail. An interest group focuses on a single topic. An individual subscribes to or joins an interest group electronically, and all messages sent to the group are distributed by e-mail to the members.

Internet Protocol (IP) The basic protocol used for the Internet. Information is put into a single packet; the packet contains the address of the sender and the recipient and is then sent out. The receiving system removes the information from the packet.

IP address An Internet address in numeric form. Consists of four numerals, each in the range of 0 through 255 separated by periods. An example is **192.65.245.76**.

IP connection A connection to the Internet which provides access to all services, resources, and tools. A computer system with an IP connection has an IP address.

ISP Internet Service Provider. A (usually) commercial service that provides access to the Internet. Fees often depend on the amount and the maximum possible speed, in bits per second, of access to the Internet.

Java An object-oriented and interpreted programming language designed specifically to create interactive applications that can be made part of Web pages.

Java Applet A Java program that can be included as part of a Web page.

JavaScript A programming language based on Java, but not as complex. The statements in the language can be made part of an HTML source file to enable some interactive features such as mouse clicks and input to forms.

List address The address to use to send e-mail to be distributed to each member of a discussion list, interest group, Listserv list, or mailing list.

Listproc   One of the several types of software used to manage and administer a discussion list, interest group, or mailing list.

Listserv   The type of software used to manage a Listserv list, a form of a discussion list, interest group, or mailing list.

Lurking   Reading the e-mail or articles in a discussion group or newsgroup without contributing or posting messages.

Lynx   A text-based World Wide Web browser (software) used for accessing information in a hypertext manner on the Internet.

Mail user agent   The software used to access and manage a user's electronic mail. Some examples are Pine and Eudora.

Mailing list   Group discussion and sharing of information carried on by electronic mail. A mailing list focuses on a single topic. An individual subscribes to or joins a mailing list electronically, and all messages sent to the group are distributed by e-mail to the members.

Majordomo   One of the several types of software used to manage and administer a discussion list, interest group, or mailing list.

Menu bar   The sequence of pull-down menus across the top of the Web browser window. All commands are accessible through the Menu Bar.

Message body   The text portion of an e-mail message.

MIME   Multipurpose Internet Mail Extensions. Extensions to standard e-mail programs making it easy to send, receive, and include non-text files.

Modem   The device used to allow a computer to communicate with another computer over a phone line. It's needed since the computers information is in digital form, and information on many telephone lines is transmitted in analog form. A device to convert from one form to the other is a **mo**dulator and **dem**odulator, hence the term modem.

Moderator   A person who manages or administers a discussion list, interest group, Listserv list, mailing list, or Usenet newsgroup. In most cases the moderator is a volunteer. Messages sent to the group are first read by the moderator who then passes appropriate messages to the group.

Mosaic A World Wide Web browser (software) used for accessing information in a hypertext or hypermedia manner on the Internet. It gives the user a graphical interface (GUI) to Internet services and resources.

National Public Telecommunications Network (NPTN)   A confederation of Free-Net's, community-based networks. Its purpose is to help establish community networks, to link those systems into a common network, and to supplement their services with network-wide services and resources.

Netiquette   A collection of rules for behavior on the Internet and/or Usenet. Short for *net etiquette*.

Netnews   An alternative term for Usenet news; usually used to refer to Usenet news carried on the Internet.

Netscape Navigator   A World Wide Web browser (software) used for accessing information in a hypertext or hypermedia manner on the Internet. It gives the user a graphical interface (GUI) to Internet services and resources. The most popular Web browser.

Newsreader   Software used by an individual to read, reply to, and manage Usenet news.

Packet   The basic unit of information sent across the Internet. Packets contain information (data), the address of the sender, and the address of the recipient.

Personal home page   A Web page used by an individual to give personal and/or professional information.

POP   Post Office Protocol. The way many e-mail programs retrieve messages from a mail server. E-mail is delivered on the Internet to the mail server, and an e-mail program running on a personal computer retrieves that e-mail through POP.

Port number   Some Internet services have a unique number assigned to them which refers to a logical channel in a communications system. Using a port number with a Telnet session, such as **telnet madlab.sprl.umich.edu 3000**, allows for a connection without providing a log-in name.

Posting   An article or message sent to a Usenet newsgroup.

PPP   Point-to-point protocol. A protocol that allows a computer with a modem to communicate using TCP/IP.

Protocols   A set of rules or procedures for exchanging information between networks or computer systems.

Proxy   A special server that runs in the secure portion of a network with a firewall and allows users to access Internet services from that same secure portion of the network. The name and port numbers of a proxy server can be entered in the **Network preferences**, **Proxies** panel of the **Options** menu.

Router   A device (hardware) that transfers information between networks.

Search engine   In the context of the World Wide Web a program that seeks out, visits, and indexes URLs on the WWW. The index is searched for key words or phrases entered by a user. This results in a collection of hyperlinks returned to the user where the hyperlinks are references to sources whose description, title, or content match the words or phrase.

Server   A computer that shares resources with other computers on the Internet. In the context of Internet services, a server is a computer system or program which provides information to other programs called clients. When a user starts a Web browser, she starts a client program, which contacts a Web server program.

Signature   An optional portion of an e-mail message consisting of information about the sender such as her full name, mailing address, phone number, etc. The signature is stored in a file and it's automatically included with each message.

Signoff   A term used in a command to leave, quit, or unsubscribe from a discussion group, interest group, Listserv list, or mailing list.

SLIP   Serial Line Internet Protocol. Software allowing the use of the Internet Protocol (IP) over a serial line or through a serial port. Commonly used with a modem connection to a service providing Internet services.

SMTP   Simple Mail Transfer Protocol. The Internet standard protocol used to transfer electronic mail from one computer system to another.

Subscribe A term used in a command to join or become part of a discussion group, interest group, Listserv list, or mailing list. This term is also used when choosing to make a Usenet newsgroup one of those listed when you use a newsreader.

TCP/IP Transmission Control Protocol/Internet Protocol. A collection of protocols used to provide the basis for Internet and WWW services.

Telnet Allows for remote log-in capabilities on the Internet. One of the three basic Internet services. A user on one computer on the Internet can access and log-in to another computer.

Text file A file containing characters in a plain human-readable format. There are no formatting commands such as underlining or displaying characters in boldface or different fonts. Also called an ASCII file.

Thread A collection of articles all dealing with a single posting or e-mail message.

Toolbar The sequence of icons below the Menu Bar. Clicking on an icon executes a command or causes an action.

Transmission Control Protocol (TCP) A protocol used as the basis of most Internet services. It is used in conjunction with (actually on top of) the Internet Protocol. It allows for reliable communication oriented to process-to-process communication.

Unsubscribe A term used in a command to leave, signoff, or quit from a discussion list, interest group, or mailing list. The term is also used to remove a Usenet newsgroup from the list of those you would regularly read.

Upload To transfer a file from one the computer system being used to a remote system.

URL Uniform Resource Locator. A way of describing the location of an item (document, service, resource) on the Internet and also specifying the means by which to access that item.

Usenet A system for exchanging messages called articles arranged according to specific categories called newsgroups. The articles (messages) are passed from one system to another, not as e-mail between individuals.

Uudecode A program to recreate binary files from the ASCII or text form to which they were converted by uuencode. Used by someone who has received a file or e-mail in uuencode form.

Uuencode A program to convert binary data into ASCII form. Necessary to use to send binary files with some e-mail systems. Used to send binary files on e-mail systems without MIME.

Vt100 A specific type of terminal, most commonly used with Internet services and programs such as Hytelnet, Lynx, and Pine. Many programs work in full-screen mode and need to know the type of terminal they'll be using.

Web browser A program (software) used to access the Internet services and resources available through the World Wide Web.

Web page The information available and displayed by a Web browser as the result of opening a local file or opening a location (URL). The contents and format of the Web page are specified using HTML.

World Wide Web (WWW) The World Wide Web is the collection of different services and resources available on the Internet and accessible through a Web browser.

Netscape Navigator Options and Preferences

Netscape Navigator is relatively easy to use, but it is a complex program. There are a number of options or preferences that can be set to control items related to the browser, e-mail and newsgroups, the way Netscape works with your network, and security. Most of these are set when Netscape is installed and don't have to be changed. Others, like the Internet domain names for the e-mail and Usenet news servers (as we described in Chapters 3 and 5), need to be set before you can start using e-mail and newsgroups with Netscape Navigator. In this appendix we'll describe the preferences or options that can be set with Netscape Navigator and give recommendations for proper settings in some cases.

You get to the options and preferences by clicking on **Options** in the Menu Bar. The **Options** menu contains items that let you set preferences that apply to the Web browser and other elements of Netscape Navigator, and also preferences that apply to the mail and news systems, the way you're using Netscape with your network, and items related to the security used with Netscape. Each of these has a set of panels associated with them—examples of these appear in Chapter 3 and Chapter 5—and the preferences themselves are set in the panels. Once set, click on the button labeled **OK** to save the changes. You get to the panels by selecting an item from the pull-down menu. A number of items following that deal with setting options for the appearance of the Netscape window. These include setting whether or not the Toolbar, Location Pane, Directory Buttons, or Java Console will be displayed as part of the window. You can also set here whether or not images are automatically displayed when they are part of a Web page. If not, you'll need to click on the icon labeled **Images** to see the ones that are embedded in a Web page. You can also choose the encoding, that is, the character set used to display the text on a Web page. Use Latin1 for English. Central European, Chinese, Japanese and Korean are some of the others available. When you've set these options, click on the item labeled **Save Options** to make the changes take effect whenever you use Netscape.

It's easy to change options or preferences, and if you make a mistake it's probably not a catastrophe. Still, you'll want to print or write down the current settings in a panel before you make changes. Then make changes, and if things don't work as you planned, you can always reset them. If you're using Netscape on more than one personal computer, changes made one computer won't carry over to another computer. In other words, the options and preferences are associated with the computer, rather than with an individual.

If you're using Netscape on a Unix computer system, any preferences and options you've set will work whenever you use Netscape on any work station on the same computer system. On Unix systems, the options are associated with an individual.

Netscape has several documents available to help answer questions about setting options. Feel free to use your browser while you're setting options. In fact you may want to have a copy of "Netscape Handbook: Preference Panels" (**http://home.netscape.com/eng/mozilla/3.0/handbook/docs/panels.html**) open in the Web browser window while you're working.

The Preference Panels

We'll go through the preferences to set in each of the panels for the sections:
* General Preferences
* Mail and News Preferences
* Network Preferences
* Security Preferences

To set a preference in any of these categories, click on **Options** in the Menu Bar and then select one of the categories from the pull-down menu. Clicking on any of the preferences brings up a collection of panels in which you set the options. You go from one panel to another by clicking on the tabs.

Figure B.1 shows the panels for General Preferences.

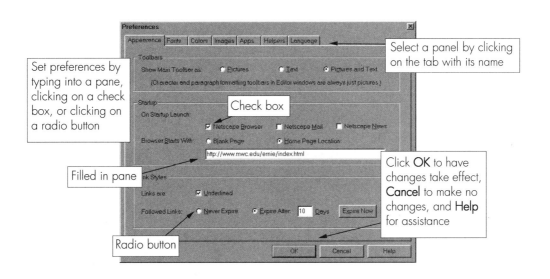

Figure B.1   General Preferences Panels

In the descriptions below, the items in bold font correspond to items—preferences you can set—in the panels.

General Preferences

Appearance. The preferences here affect the way Netscape Navigator looks when you start it and the way hyperlinks appear within a Web page.

> **Toolbars.** You can make the Toolbar appear as **pictures** (icons), **text** only, or both **pictures and text**. Ordinarily, items in the toolbars appear as icons and text. Choosing text only will give more room for a Web page or other items in a Navigator window.

> **Startup.** Netscape Navigator normally starts with the browser. Here you can select a preference so Netscape starts with the **browser**, **e-mail**, or **news** window.

> The next item lets you specify your preferences for whether Netscape will start with a **blank** screen or a **home page**. You can type any URL in the pane for a home page.

> **Link Styles.** Links can be set to appear as **underlined** or not. Once a link is selected, it appears in a color different from those that haven't been selected. This gives a visual clue about hyperlinks followed recently. After some period of time (30 days if the preferences aren't changed), a followed link expires, meaning that its color goes back to the same as links that haven't been followed. Preferences can be set so that followed links **never expire**, expire after the number of days you set, or **expire now**.

Fonts—Fonts and Encodings. Encoding refers to the fonts and characters used to represent text in a Web page. The default is Latin1 (appropriate for English and many European languages) with proportional font Times 12 and fixed font Courier 10. Other encodings include Chinese, Japanese, and Korean. The proportional font is used to display most text and the fixed font is used to display text that's on a Web page but either it isn't in a file that contains HTML or it's surrounded by the HTML tags <**PRE**> and </**PRE**>.

Colors. Here you set colors for **links, followed links, text**, and the window **background** for Netscape. The usual settings are blue for links that haven't been followed, purple for ones that have, black for other text, and gray for the background of Web pages. Any of these can be changed by clicking on the button **Choose Color**. It's also possible to set the background to be an **image file** rather than a solid color. Some documents or Web pages include HTML tags that specify the background, link, and text colors. A preference can be set, **Always Use My Colors**, so the colors selected in this panel override any commands in a Web page.

Images. These items deal with how Netscape displays images. The first preference is **How Colors Are Chosen**. **Automatic** finds the colors most appropriate for the display or monitor that's being used. The other preferences are **Dither** or **Substitute** colors that most closely match the ones available with your monitor.

The two choices for displaying images are **While Loading** or **After Loading**. Displaying the image **While loading** displays the image while it's being loaded, so you may see the image partially or incrementally displayed as it arrives at your computer. Viewing it this way lets you see some of the image (maybe enough of it) before all of it is transmitted. **After Loading** means it's not displayed until it has arrived at your site.

Apps—Supported Applications. Use this panel to give the name of the file that holds the program for each application or program listed. If a pane is blank, that program may not be available from Netscape. **Telnet**, for example, is one of the applications listed. If a Telnet client program is available on your computer then its name/location needs to be filled in here. The applications listed are **Telnet**—a program used for remote log in capabilities (see Chapter 8), **TN3270**—an application similar to Telnet, except that this program emulates an IBM 3270 terminal, and **View Source**—lists the program to use to display the source for a Web page when **Document Source** is chosen from **View** in the Menu Bar. If you plan to edit, change, or save the source for a Web page, you might want to set the **View Source** preference to a program that can work with text files, such as Notepad or a word processor. The last item in this panel, **Temporary Directory**, needs to be set to a folder or directory Netscape can use to store files temporarily. This is needed for some helper applications. When the application is finished the temporary files are usually erased automatically.

Helpers. Following hyperlinks or URLs, a Web browser can retrieve or access various file types. The browser has been constructed to properly display or otherwise make many of them available. For Netscape Navigator this includes text files including files using HTML and image files in GIF, JPEG, or XBM format. When the browser has to work with other types of files, it uses an auxiliary program called a **Helper Application**. These have to be found, retrieved, and installed either by you or someone whose responsibilities include maintaining the computer you use. One place to begin looking for helper applications is the Netscape Web page "Helper Applications" (**http://home1.netscape.com/assist/helper_apps/index.html**) or Netscape Navigator's page on Inline Plug-ins, **http://home.netscape.com/comprod/products/navigator/version_2.0/plugins/index.html**. Many sites that offer files needing a helper application also include a hyperlink to retrieve the necessary program. When you click on a hyperlink that accesses a file type that the browser isn't set to handle, a window pops on the screen telling you about that. This "Unknown File Type" window includes buttons so you can get some help on how to handle the situation, pick an application from the ones on your computer, save the file to your computer, or cancel the operation. One way of working through all this is to add helper applications as you need them. It's a little intimidating at first, but if you follow the instructions, you're likely to succeed and not upset anything. If you don't want to proceed with acquiring and installing a helper application, ask a friend or some other knowledgeable person to help.

Figure B.2 shows an example of the Helpers panel with the application, RealAudio (obtained at **http://www.realaudio.com/products/player/download.html**) installed.

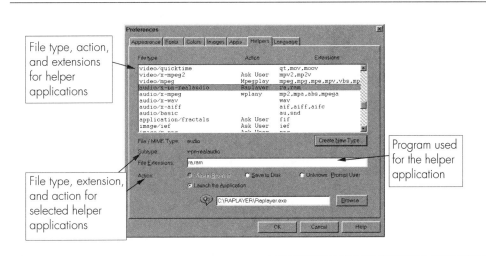

Figure B.2   Helper Application Panel

The list of items in the window shown in Figure B.2 has three headings: **File Type**, **Action**, and **Extensions**. The File Type is a MIME (Multipurpose Internet Mail Extensions) type for the item. The names here, such as **application/zip** or **audio/x-pn-realaudio**, are standard names that help identify the type of information contained in a file. The items under the heading Action either say **Ask User** or give the name of a program such as Raplayer in Figure B.2. If the entry is the name of a program, that program or helper application is started when a file of this type is encountered. Otherwise, the user is asked what to do. Web browsers such as Netscape decide which helper application to start based on the file name extension—the characters after the last dot (.) in the file name. A file name ending with **.gif**, for example, will be treated as a file containing an image in GIF format.

Highlighting an entry in this panel, as shown in Figure 6.2, displays information about it. The **File/MIME** type shown is audio with **sub-type x-pn-realaudio**. The **file extensions** listed are **ra** and **ram**, so a file whose name ends with **.ra** or **.ram** will be associated with this helper application. In the section **Action**, we've specified that the application is **Raplayer**.

To modify or add a helper application for an existing MIME type, first be sure you've obtained a program to use to launch the applications and you know the name and location of the program on your computer. Highlight the entry in the list, click on the radio button labeled **Launch the Application**, and in the pane to the left of the button labeled **Browse**, type the full path name of the file holding the program that works as a helper. Clicking on that button will let you locate the program on your computer rather than typing in its name.

Language. When you send a request to a server for a Web page, either by clicking on a hyperlink or typing a URL, the server gets information from your client. Some of that information includes your language priorities or preferences, which you set in this panel. The languages are represented by codes. The code **en-US**, for example, represents English as it's used in the US, and **fr-CA** represents French as it's used in Canada. If versions of a Web page based on the language code are available, the appropriate one is sent.

To set a language preference, click on one from the **Language/Region** list and click on the arrow pointing right to move it to the box labeled **Accept List**. To remove a language from the accept list, click on it there and then click the left arrow.

Mail And News Preferences

These include the preferences that must be set before being able to use the e-mail and Usenet news features of Netscape.

Appearance—Message Style. Messages can be displayed using **Fixed Width Font** or **Variable Width Font**. A variable width font generally has a better appearance. You can include the text of the original message or article when you reply to, forward, or post a follow-up to an e-mail message or article. Here you can select to have the style of the quoted or included text to be **plain**, **bold**, **italic**, or **bold italic**, and the size of the text **plain**, **bigger** or **smaller**.

Electronic mail can be received by using either **Netscape for Mail and News** or Microsoft **Exchange Client for Mail and News**.

The page layout of folders, list of messages, and the text of messages can be set to split horizontal, split vertical, or stack. With split horizontal the folders, list of messages and text appear as they're shown in Chapters 3 and 5 – the folders and list of messages in the top portion of the screen witht he text below. Split vertical gives an arrangement where the folder and message list are on the left of the screen with the text to the right. Choosing the stack option lists the folders in the top portion of the window, the list of messages underneath, and finally the text of a message or article.

Composition. The preferences here deal with composing messages for Usenet posting or electronic mail.

The two choices for composing messages are **Allow 8-bit,** which deals successfully with the widest range of e-mail servers and **MIME Compliant,** which is fine to use if your using a MIME (Multipurpose Internet Mail Extensions) mail reader.

The panes that follow let you specify e-mail addresses where copies of outgoing **Mail Messages** and **News Messages** will be sent. Leaving the panes blank means that no copy of an outgoing message will be sent. The next two panes are for specifying directories or folders that will hold copies of outgoing messages or articles. Setting these keeps a copy of the messages you've sent out in a file on a local disk.

Selecting the check box along side of **Automatically quote original message when retyping** includes a copy of the original when you reply to or forward e-mail, and when you do the same or post a follow-up to a news article.

Servers. This contains the crucial preferences for e-mail and Usenet newsgroups:

Mail. Netscape needs to connect to an **Outgoing Mail (SMTP) Server** to be able to send e-mail and also connect to an **Incoming Mail (POP) Server** to receive e-mail form the Internet. Either the domain name or IP address of these needs to be given in the first two panes.

The entry in the pane labeled **POP User Name** is the log-in name you use for your e-mail. You'll either get that from a system administrator or your Internet service provider.

The entry in the pane labeled **Mail Directory** is the directory that holds the e-mail on your computer.

If you'd like you can set a **Maximum Message Size** or set it to **None** so there's no limit to the size of a message you can receive. When you check for messages on the POP server, messages can be either **Removed from the server** or **Left on the server.** If you're checking your messages from the computer you use regularly and to conserve space on the server you'll want to remove messages. You can set a preference for how often you'd like Netscape to contact the server to **Check for Mail.**

News. Netscape needs to connect to a **News (NNTP) Server** to receive and post articles in newsgroups. You give the domain name of the server here. You also need to specify the **News RC Directory,** a directory or folder on your disk that holds the files that keep track of which articles have been read. This portion of the panel contains a frame where you specify the number of articles to **Get** from the server when you've opened or selected a newsgroup. The default is **100** and it can be set as high as **3500.**

Identity. Here you specify how you'll be known through your e-mail messages and news articles that you send or post. The entries you give here become part of every outgoing item. **Your Name, Your Email, Reply-to Address,** and **Your Organization** —the name of your agency, company or school. Before you can send any e-mail, you must fill in the pane containing your e-mail address.

The location of your **Signature File** is also specified here.

Organization—General. Specify by clicking on a check box whether Netscape should **Thread Mail Messages** or **Thread News Messages.** Threaded message keep messages on the same topic together.

Sorting. By using the radio buttons, you can specify to **Sort Mail by** and **Sort News by** either **Date, Subject,** or **Sender.**

Network Preferences

The network preferences deal with the way Netscape Navigator works with your network.

Cache. The idea behind cache is to set aside a region or memory and a portion of the disk so that instead recently accessed pages and images can be retrieved more quickly than getting them from the Internet every time they're needed. Both types of cache are used with Netscape, and when it's installed the preferences are set to **600 Kilobytes** of **Memory Cache** and **5000 Kilobytes** of **Disk Cache.** These can be changed, but be aware of any impact increasing these would have on the amount of available memory and disk space in your computer. You specify the **DiskCache Directory,** where the cache is on your disk, here as well.

Using cache gives faster access but you may be using outdated information, in the sense that a Web page or image may have changed since it was placed in the cache. Determining whether an item has changed since it was put into cache is called **Verify Documents** on this panel. You can select documents to be verified **Once per Session, Every Time,** or **Never.** The panel also has buttons you can use to **Clear Memory Cache Now** or **Clear Disk Cache Now.**

Connections. In order to speed up the transfer of information from a remote site to your browser, Netscape Navigator can open up more than one network connection. The more connections there are the more simultaneous transfers can take place, but each is slowed down by the others. The initial value for **Number of Connections** is 4. You can also set the **Network Buffer Size.** This is the maximum number of bytes that can be received in one network data transmission. The initial value is 32 Kilobytes. Setting this higher may give more data in one transmission, but you have to be sure your computer can keep up with that rate of transfer.

Proxies. If your organization or school uses a firewall to improve security on a part of your network, you may have to set some proxy information. A proxy transmits information in and out of the network without allowing unauthorized access. If you're faced with that situation, get the proxy information you need from your system administrator. Many sites with firewalls have them configured so information exchanged through **http,** the protocol for Web pages, can be used without you having to deal with setting up the proper proxy information. The items to set here are **No Proxies, Manual Proxy Configuration,** where you name the sites and ports for proxies, or **Automatic Proxy Configuration**, where you give the URL of the file that has proxies set appropriately for your situation. A resource on the WWW, different than Netscape, for information about this is "Browser configuration for caching" (**http://wwwcache.lut.ac.uk/caching/browsers/**) by Martin Hamilton.

Protocols. Here you specify whether to pop up a box to let you know when you're accepting a cookie or submitting a form by e-mail. A cookie is a piece of information that merchants or others can store on your system in a file named "Cookies.txt". That way the next time you visit the same site the server can determine how long its been since your last visit, which directories or items you visited, etc. This can be used to serve up a Web page that better fits your needs or habits. It's use has been criticized because browsing is no longer anonymous and some feel it's an invasion of privacy. If you choose to be warned, you have the option of not visiting a site that uses this cookie information to track your movements on the Web.

You can select an option to automatically send your e-mail address as the password to an Anonymous FTP site. Many FTP Archives expect to receive an e-mail address as the password for an Anonymous FTP session.

Languages. Click on the check box next to Disable Java to disallow the automatic execution of Java applets. A Java applet is a program that runs or executes on your computer. The programs come from remote sites on the Internet, so there is some concern about security. According to the official documentation about Java, a Java applet poses no security problem on a Microsoft Windows computer system.

Security Preferences

Netscape has the capability, when used with encrypted messages and secure servers, to transmit and receive secure, private transactions. For more information on WWW security, take a look at "Rutgers WWW-Security Issues Page" (**http://www-ns.rutgers.edu/www-security/**), "WWW Security" (**http://union.ncsa.uiuc.edu/HyperNews/get/www/security.html**), and the Netscape Web page "On Security" (**http://home.netscape.com/info/security-doc.html**).

General—Security Alerts. The check boxes in this section determine whether you receive a pop-up alert box when you enter a Secure Document Server, leave a secure document server, view a document with a secure/insecure mix, or submit a form insecurely. It's your choice whether you want to be notified of these events. The other portion of this panel deals with whether SSL (Secure Sockets Layer) Protocol security features of Netscape are in effect. SSL is used to encrypt information passed across the Internet.

Passwords. Here you set a security password on your copy of Netscape. The password is used for giving access to any security certificates you use.

Personal Certificate. A personal certificate identifies you to others on the Internet. Suppose someone receives e-mail that has your e-mail address as the return or reply-to address. How can he be sure it wasn't sent by someone else forging your address? VeriSign issues a digital id—the certificate—that uniquely identifies you to anyone using the Verisign system to authenticate transactions or Internet transmissions.

E-Mail the UNIX Way: Mailx and Pine

Here we'll discuss two e-mail programs that are avaiable to users on many computer systems that use the Unix operating system: Mailx and Pine.

Mailx is common on many Unix computer systems. It's older and a bit more primitive than other e-mail programs available. However, many users have Internet access only through a dial-up or shell account. In these cases, a modem calls a computer system, which uses the Unix operating system to get Internet access. The program that interprets your commands is called the shell, which is where the term shell account comes from. Mailx is completely line-oriented. This means you can deal with information on a single line only. You'll be able to see a list of e-mail messages and you can choose one to read, save, reply to, delete or print, but you can't move to different portions of a screen to enter information. This program is not the easiest to use, but you can do a lot with it.

Pine is a full-screen e-mail system. It's relatively easy to use to compose, read, and manage your e-mail messages. The commands you can use at any stage are always available on the screen, so you don't have to remember them, and on-line help is always available. Pine also has MIME (Multipurpose Internet Mail Extensions), so it's not limited to sending and receiving only text files. A MIME e-mail system can deal with messages that contain nontext items such as programs, images, spreadsheets, and documents to be used with word processing programs. Pine was developed by the Computing and Communications Group at the University of Washington.

Using Mailx

Mailx is a line-oriented e-mail program. Although you see information on several lines, such as a list of messages in your mailbox, the message you're composing, and the contents of a message you're reading, all the commands and actions take place on a single line. You work with e-mail on a message-by-message basis. In this section we'll go over some of the basic ways of using Mailx to work with electronic mail. The topics we'll cover are listed below:

* Using Mailx
* Using Pine

If you're using Mailx, you're most likely working on a Unix computer system. You'll either be at a terminal directly connected to the computer system or you'll access it through a modem or some other sort of communication device. To access your e-mail you first have to log in to the computer. You need to have a log-in name assigned to you and you also have to use a password. When you start you'll see a prompt similar to:

`login:`

You type in your user name or log-in name, press Enter, and then enter your password in the same way. The password won't show up on the screen. When you've typed in the correct information, you'll probably get a message from the computer system giving information about the system or some notices. If you have e-mail waiting for you the system will notify you. It's up to you to act on it. In any case, once you log in successfully and have been notified about e-mail and other things, you'll be able to enter commands. You enter commands to start programs such as Mailx on lines that have a command prompt or shell prompt. (A shell is a program that interprets your commands.) The prompt you see will most likely end with a $ or %. We won't go into the differences here since they don't have much to do with e-mail. Figure C.1 shows a user named mozart logging into a shell account on a Unix system.

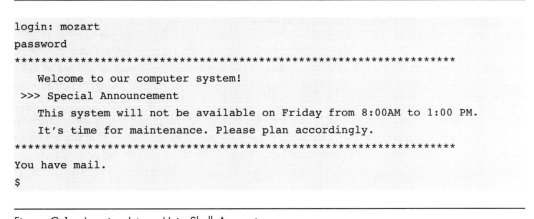

```
login: mozart
password
*****************************************************************
    Welcome to our computer system!
 >>> Special Announcement
    This system will not be available on Friday from 8:00AM to 1:00 PM.
    It's time for maintenance. Please plan accordingly.
*****************************************************************
You have mail.
$
```

Figure C.1   Logging Into a Unix Shell Account

Example C.1   Starting Mailx, Reading a Message, and Ending a Session

You'll want to start Mailx when you have mail to read. Here are the steps to follow:
1. Start a session by typing **mailx**.
2. Read a message.
3. Leave Mailx.

Type **mailx** and press Enter when you have a shell prompt. You'll see a list of messages for you to read or work with. To end or quit Mailx type **q** and press Enter. You can also end a Mailx session by typing x and pressing Enter. That ends the Mailx session without any changes being made to the mailbox, as if you didn't use Mailx at all. Figure C.2 shows some examples.

```
You have mail.
$ mailx
mailx Revision: 70.7    Date: 92/04/16 15:39:44    Type ? for help.
"/usr/mail/mozart": 6 messages 5 new
    1 mozart@s850.mwc.edu  Thu Dec  8 08:06    13/352   a test
>N  2 jacson                Fri Dec  9 08:10    34/934   Art paper
N   3 ernie@s850.mwc.edu    Fri Dec  9 19:13    22/707   Congratulations! Lunch?
N   4 pclark@joj.com        Mon Dec  12 09:14   35/1253  phase 2
N   5 apmills@green.hitech.org Mon Dec  12 09:54 101/5072 Why Invest in Info Tech?
N   6 zebert@abc.edu        Mon Dec  12 11:15   56/2010  Bass (Guitar)
? q
Held 6 messages in /usr/mail/mozart
$
```

Figure C.2   Starting and Ending a Mailx Session

Your messages are listed. You see who sent them, when they were sent, and the subject lines. New messages, the ones marked with **N**, arrived since you last used the command **mailx**. **/usr/mail/mozart** is the full name of the file holding your e-mail; it's sometimes called the system mailbox. When e-mail addressed to mozart is received and processed by the computer system, it's stored in the system mailbox. The question mark **?** is a prompt from Mailx waiting for the next command. After typing **q** and pressing **Enter,** you see the message **Held 6 messages in /usr/mail/mozart**. It says six messages, in this case all of them, were held in the system mailbox for mozart. The next time mozart uses Mailx those six will still be available.

1. Start a session by typing **mailx**.

w⁴w   At the prompt, type **mailx** and press 【Enter】.

You start reading your e-mail by typing **mailx** and pressing Enter. Figure C.3 is an example of a user named mozart doing that.

```
$ mailx
mailx Revision: 70.7    Date: 92/04/16 15:39:44    Type ? for help.
"/usr/mail/mozart": 6 messages 5 new
     1 mozart@s850.mwc.edu     Thu Dec  8 08:06   13/352   a test
U    2 jacson                 Fri Dec  9 08:10   34/934   Art paper
>N   3 ernie@s850.mwc.edu     Fri Dec  9 19:13   20/702   Congratulations! Lunch?
N    4 pclark@joj.com         Mon Dec 12 09:14   35/1253  phase 2
N    5 apmills@green.hitech.org Mon Dec 12 09:54  101/5072  Why Invest in Info Tech?
N    6 zebert@abc.edu         Mon Dec 12 11:15   56/2010  Bass (Guitar)
?
```

Figure C.3   Starting to Read E-Mail with Mailx

A message line starting with **N** indicates new mail, e-mail that arrived since Mailx was last used. A message line starting with **U** indicates unread, but not new, e-mail. Mail previously read and kept in the system mailbox has neither an **N** nor a **U**. The character > before a message line marks the current message. That's the message to act on next. The question mark (**?**) on the last line is the command prompt indicating Mailx is waiting for the next command.

2. Read a message.

*w*ⁿ*w*   To read a message, press Enter. To read any message, type the number of the message and press Enter.

To read the current message press Enter. To read any message, type the number of the message and press Enter. The message you've read stays as the current message until you move on to another. When you choose a message to read, it's displayed one screen at a time. A colon (:) will be at the bottom of the screen. You press Enter to see the next screen or **q** to get back to the **?** prompt from Mailx. The message list doesn't appear at this point. To see the list again type **h** and press Enter. Figure C.4 shows going through those steps. We first press Enter to read the current message, number 4 in this case.

```
From ernie@s850.mwc.edu Thu Dec  8 09:13 EST 1994
Date: Fri, 9 Dec 1994 19:13:25 -0500
From: ernest ackermann <ernie@s850.mwc.edu>
Return-Path: <ernie@s850.mwc.edu>
To: mozart@s850.mwc.edu
Subject: Congratulations! Lunch Next Week?
Status: RO

Congratulations on your award! You're really doing well.
```

```
Are you available for lunch sometime next week? I'd like to see you
again and discuss some plans I have.

Let me know either by phone or e-mail
Ernest C. Ackermann
Department of Computer Science  Mary Washington College
Fredericksburg, VA 22401-5358    540 - 654 - 1320 (Voice)
ernie@mwc.edu                 540 - 899 - 4373 (FAX)
:
(EOF):
??
```

Figure C.4   Reading a Message with Mailx

3. Leave Mailx.

wWw   Type **q** and press **Enter** to quit the Mailx session.

At this point there are a number of things you can do, some of which we'll explain later. To get a list of all the commands to enter when you see the **?** prompt, type **?** and press Enter. If you end the Mailx session by typing **q** and pressing Enter, then any messages you've read will not be returned (unless you take special action) to the system mailbox. Instead they will be put into a file named mbox in your home directory, the directory you start with when you log in. To keep a message in the system mailbox, type the mailx command **preserve** at the current message. You delete the current message so it's not saved anywhere by typing **d** and pressing Enter. It's up to you to decide what to do with messages. When you're done reading them press **q** to quit. The ones you've read and preserved will stay in the system mailbox and be available for reading the next time you enter the command mailx. The ones you've read and haven't preserved will be stored in the file **mbox** in your home directory.

————————————————End of Example C.1————————————————

Reading E-Mail with Mailx

Typing the command **mailx** and pressing Enter reads mail from the system mailbox. However, any file containing e-mail can be read with Mailx. A good example of such a file is **mbox**. You type the command mailx, as at other times when you have a shell prompt, and you follow it with **-f file_name** where **file_name** is the name of the file holding the e-mail you want to read. For example,

```
mailx -f mbox
```

You use the same commands and methods to read e-mail from a file as when reading e-mail from the system mailbox.

Composing and Sending E-Mail with Mailx

Sending e-mail can be done in any of several ways:

* Type **mailx** followed by the address of the recipient, press Enter, and then compose (write) the message. Here is an example of starting to send a message to **mybuddy@great.place.edu**. We go over composing the message below:

```
$ mailx mybuddy@great.place.edu
```

* During a Mailx session, when you have the **?** prompt, type **m** followed by the address of the recipient, press Enter, and then compose (write) the message. Here is another example of starting to send a message to **mybuddy@great.place.edu**:

```
? m mybuddy@great.place.edu
```

* Send a prepared message (in a file) to someone by using the command mailx. Putting -s after mailx causes the next string (the characters in quotes) to be taken as the **Subject:** header for the message. You follow this by the Internet address of the recipient, then the character <, and finally the name of the file to send.

Here is an example where the **Subject:** header is **Report of Market Survey**, the address it's sent to is **mybuddy@great.place.com**, and the message is in the file named report.txt:

```
$ mailx -s "Report of Market Survey" mybuddy@great.place.com < report.txt
```

Composing the message within a Mailx session doesn't give you much flexibility in terms of typing the message. You work with only the current line, and it's cumbersome to make modifications. You can compose the message using an editor on your system and put the message into a file. If you have a Unix shell account you might have to use the editor named vi, but that can be difficult to learn. As an alternative you can compose the message on another system, upload it, and then send it as a file. Sending a file is shown above.

Typing Mailx Followed by the Address of the Recipient

You can send e-mail by typing **mailx**, the address to which the e-mail is to be sent, and then pressing Enter. Once you do that, you'll be prompted to enter a subject for the message. Type an appropriate subject and press Enter. The cursor will move to the next line, and you're ready to start composing or typing the message. This is shown in Figure C.5 where e-mail is going to be sent to the address **mozart@emperor.court.org** with the subject **Great Opera, Wolfgang!**

```
$ mailx mozart@emperor.court.org
Subject: Great Opera, Wolfgang!
```

Figure C.5   Starting to Send E-Mail Using Mailx Followed by an Address

Now you type your message one line at a time, pressing Enter at the end of each line. You can use the Backspace key on a line to make changes on that line, but you can't use the arrow keys to make changes to previous lines. To break off sending the message type Ctrl+C (hold down the Ctrl key, press the C key, and release them). See Figure C.6.

```
Wolfgang,
          I saw the Magic Flute last night. It was wonderful!
How have you been feeling? You looked a little tired last night.
Take care of yourself and stay healthy.
Keep in touch.
```

Figure C.6   Typing in a Message in Mailx

To include a file in the message (such as one holding a signature, as discussed above) type ~r followed by the name of the file, shown in Figure C.7. The numbers **4/172** give the number of lines and characters in the included file.

```
~r /users/ernie/.signature
"/users/ernie/.signature" 4/172
```

Figure C.7   Including a File with E-Mail Using Mailx

To see what the message looks like, type ~p and press Enter. This is useful if you've included files. See Figure C.8.

```
~p
___
Message contains:
To: mozart@emperor.court.org
Subject: Great Opera, Wolfgang!

Wolfgang,
          I saw the Magic Flute last night. It was wonderful!
How have you been feeling? You looked a little tired last night.
Take care of yourself and stay healthy.
Keep in touch.
Ernest C. Ackermann
Department of Computer Science  Mary Washington College
Fredericksburg, VA 22401-5358    540 - 654 - 1320 (Voice)
ernie@mwc.edu            540 - 899 - 4373 (FAX)
```

Figure C.8   Displaying a Composed Message Using Mailx

To end the message and send it on its way, type a period (.) on a line by itself and press Enter as shown below. The shell prompt $ will reappear.

```
.
$
```

During a Mailx Session

If you're using Mailx to read or otherwise manage your e-mail, you can send a message by typing **m** followed by an e-mail address and pressing Enter. You do this when you have the **?** prompt. Figure C.9 is an example where a user named mozart has started reading his e-mail and decides to send a message to someone whose Internet address is **carolc@vienna.opera.com**.

```
$ mailx
mailx Revision: 70.7    Date: 92/04/16 15:39:44    Type ? for help.
"/usr/mail/mozart": 6 messages 2 new
     1 mozart@s850.mwc.edu      Thu Dec  8 08:06   13/352    a test
 U   2 jacson                   Fri Dec  9 08:10   34/934    Art paper
     3 pclark@joj.com           Mon Dec 12 09:14   35/1253   phase 2
     4 apmills@green.hitech.org Mon Dec 12 09:54  101/5072   Why Invest in Info Tech?
>N   5 zebert@abc.edu           Mon Dec 12 11:15   56/2010   Bass (Guitar)
 N   6 ernie@mwc.edu Tue Dec   13 22:19  12/1234  Great Opera, Wolfgang!

? m carolc@vienna.opera.com
Subject:
```

Figure C.9   Sending E-Mail While Using Mailx

The prompt for the **Subject:** header comes up after typing the address and pressing Enter. Composing and sending the message from this point is exactly the same as described in the previous section. The only difference is that after you type the period on a line by itself and press Enter, you'll see **EOT** (for End of Transmission) and get the **?** prompt again, as shown here:

```
.
EOT
?
```

Replying to a Message with Mailx

You reply to the current e-mail message by pressing either

* **R** (uppercase) to reply to the sender, the one listed in the Return-Path: header, or
* **r** (lowercase) to reply to the sender and everyone who received the message

E-mail can be sent to several addresses at once; it can be a group mailing. Including more than one e-mail address on a message sends the mail to a group. For example, the command:

```
mailx Ollie@oregano.mwc.edu mozart@emperor.court.org karl@mmedia.com
```

would send a message to three people. Replying to a group is useful when information needs to be shared. You always have a choice; be aware of the differences. It's easy to press **r** to reply, so remember that that sends a reply to everyone who received the message.

The next example shows how this works. Suppose an e-mail message were sent by **ernie@mwc.com** to three others as shown here:

```
$ mailx Ollie@oregano.mwc.edu mozart@emperor.court.org karl@mmedia.com
Subject:  Reminder: Group meeting Wednesday, 11:00 AM
Just a reminder: we have our group meeting on Wednesday at 11:00 AM.
I'm looking forward to hearing your presentations. Let me know if you're
having any difficulties. I'll treat for lunch after the meeting.

_
lynn
.
$
```

Suppose mozart types **mailx** and presses Enter. He reads a message and decides to reply in two ways: to everyone who received the message, and to the person who sent it. See Figure C.10.

```
$ mailx
mailx Revision: 70.7    Date: 92/04/16 15:39:44    Type ? for help.
"/usr/mail/mozart": 6 messages 2 new
   1 mozart@s850.mwc.edu    Thu Dec  8 08:06   13/352   a test
U  2 jacson                 Fri Dec  9 08:10   34/934   Art paper
   3 pclark@joj.com         Mon Dec  12 09:14  35/1253  phase 2
   4 apmills@green.hitech.org Mon Dec  12 09:54 101/5072  Why Invest in Info
Tech?
>N 5 lynn@abc.edu           Thu Dec  15 14:15  17/121   Reminder: Group
Meeting Wednesday, 11:00 AM
?
Message  5:
From lynn@abc.edu Thu Dec  15 14:15 EST 1994
Return-Path: <lynn@abc.edu>
From: Lynn Aeschbach <lynn@abc.edu>
To: karl@mmedia.com mozart@emperor.court.org ollie@oregano.mwc.edu
Subject: Reminder: Group meeting Wednesday, 11:00 AM

Just a reminder: we have our group meeting on Wednesday at 11:00 AM.
I'm looking forward to hearing your presentations. Let me know if you're
having any difficulties. Ill treat for lunch after the meeting.
```

```
 _
lynn
? r
To: lynn@abc.edu karl@mmedia.com mozart@emperor.court.org
ollie@oregano.mwc.edu
Subject: Re:  Reminder: Group meeting Wednesday, 11:00 AM


Looking forward to seeing all of you.
waM

.
EOT
?
```

Figure C.10 Reply to Everyone Receiving a Message Using Mailx

Everything mozart needs to type is in boldface in Figure C.8. After seeing the list of messages, he presses Enter to read the current message. He types **r** and presses Enter, which generates a response to everyone who received the message.

Replying only to the sender is shown in Figure C.11. When mozart presses **R** a reply is generated to the address given in the **Return-path:** header.

```
? R
To: lynn@abc.edu
Subject: Re:  Reminder: Group meeting Wednesday, 11:00 AM

Thanks for the note, AND your offer to pay for lunch.

waM

.
EOT
?
```

Figure C.11 Reply Only to Sender Using Mailx

Mozart types **R** and presses Enter. This creates a reply to the address of the person who sent the e-mail. The **To:** and **Subject:** headers are created automatically by Mailx. He then composes the message, typing each line and pressing Enter at the end of each line. Typing a period (.) as the first and only character on a line ends the message, EOT appears, and then the **?** prompt.

Saving, Deleting, and Printing Messages with Mailx

Saving, deleting, or printing must be done in a Mailx session. At a **?** prompt type the command **s file_name** to save the current message in the file named **file_name**, type **d** to delete the current message, **u** to undelete the current message (in case you change your mind), and **| lp** or **| lpr** to print the current message (this may be different on your system). Then press Enter.

The current message is the one marked with **>**. To make a message the current message, type its number at the **?** prompt.

When a message is saved to a file that already exists, it is appended to (added to the end of) the file. Otherwise a new file is created to hold the message.

When you give the command to delete a message it's removed from your mailbox when you quit the Mailx session. You can change your mind and type **u** to undelete the current message.

Using Pine

Pine (Program for Internet News and E-mail) is a program that lets users easily work with e-mail. The software was developed and is maintained by the Computing and Communications Group at the University of Washington. It's used in full-screen mode, it contains a relatively easy full-screen editor for composing messages, it has commands to save and organize messages into folders, it has a straightforward way of keeping an address book of Internet addresses, and it allows for sending and receiving both text and nontext messages. The commands you use at each stage are on the screen, on-line help is available, and it's designed to be used without having a manual around to look up commands. Pine can also be used to read Internet News, but here we'll focus on e-mail. The topics covered in this section include:

* Pine Main Menu
* Starting and Leaving Pine
* Reading E-Mail
* Getting Help
* Saving Messages
* Deleting Messages
* Composing and Sending E-Mail
* Replying to a Message
* Forwarding E-Mail
* Working with Folders
* Working with an Address Book
* Adding Aliases
* Working with Nontext Files

Pine Main Menu

When you use Pine you can always go to a screen called the main menu, and from there access any of Pine's major features. See Figure C.12.

```
PINE 3.90   MAIN MENU                       Folder: INBOX  6 Messages


        ?      HELP             -  Get help using Pine


        C      COMPOSE MESSAGE  -  Compose and send a message


        I      FOLDER INDEX     -  View messages in current folder


        L      FOLDER LIST      -  Select a folder to view


        A      ADDRESS BOOK     -  Update address book


        S      SETUP            -  Configure or update Pine


        Q      QUIT             -  Exit the Pine program


    Copyright 1989-1994.  PINE is a trademark of the University of Washington.
? Help                    P PrevCmd                    R RelNotes
O OTHER CMDS L [ListFldrs] N NextCmd
```

Figure C.12 Pine Main Menu

The last two lines on the screen in Figure C.12 list the commands you can use to access Pine's major features. They're all single keystroke commands. If what you need isn't here, press O to see other commands or ? for help. The commands you need for any portion of Pine are always displayed at the bottom of the screen. Pine has lots of on-line help. Press C to go to the portion of Pine where you can compose (write) and send a message. Pine includes a full-screen editor named **pico** (pine composer). The messages you work with when using Pine are either those in your system mailbox or ones you've saved in a file. Pine refers to these files as folders, collections of e-mail messages. When you start Pine, you'll be opening the folder named (by Pine) **INBOX**. This is your system mailbox where all incoming messages are delivered by the computer. You can, however, save e-mail in folders and use Pine to manage and read these folders. Pressing A takes you to the address book. Pine makes it easy to add, delete, and manage e-mail addresses. If you want to make any changes in the way Pine displays messages, prints messages, what file it uses for your signature, or other things, you do that by choosing **Setup**. Press Q to quit.

Starting and Leaving Pine

Example C.2   Starting Pine, Reading a Message, and Ending a Session

How you start Pine depends on the way it's been set up on your computer system. On some systems you type **pine** and press Enter, on others you choose it from a menu, and on others start it by clicking on an icon. Once started, Pine will display a list of the e-mail messages waiting for you. Figure C.13 shows an example of starting Pine. In this case, the program is started by typing pine and pressing Enter.

1. Start Pine

   At the prompt, type **pine** and press ⌷Enter⌷.

```
$ pine


PINE 3.90    FOLDER INDEX                   Folder: INBOX   Message 4 of 6


+    1   Dec   4 mozart             (299) a test
   A 2   Dec   4 Jacson             (847) Art paper
+    3   Dec   6 ernest ackermann   (669) Congratulations! Lunch Next Week?
+  N 4   Dec   7 Pete Clark         (5,087) Phase 2
   N 5   Dec   7 Alisa Mills        (825) Why Invest in Infotech?
   N 6   Dec   9 Zebert             (2,003) Bass (Guitar)



                 [Folder "INBOX" opened with 6 messages]
? Help         M Main Menu  P PrevMsg    - PrevPage    D Delete      R Reply
O OTHER CMDS V [ViewMsg]   N NextMsg   Spc NextPage    U Undelete    F Forward
```

Figure C.13 Starting Pine

Starting Pine lists the contents of the system mailbox, named **INBOX**. The current message, usually the oldest of the new messages, is highlighted, as shown in Figure C.13. The top of the screen has the version number of the program (the higher the number, the newer the software) and the name of the open folder, which is a file containing e-mail. You'll see later how to save messages in folders. The last two lines at the bottom of the screen show commands you can use here. In this case, they're all a single keystroke. To see commands other than the twelve listed here, press **O**. Pressing Enter performs the default action, the command surrounded by square brackets ([**ViewMsg**] here), for this screen. In this case, you'll view or read the current message.

Reading E-Mail

Start Pine and you see a list of messages in your system mailbox, the folder named **INBOX**. Regardless of which folder you've opened, you'll see a list of messages (if there are any). Each message is numbered and the listing also shows the date it was sent, the name of the sender, the number of characters in the message, and the subject. There's also a marking to the left of the message:

* N indicates it's a new message (one that hasn't been read).
* + means it was sent directly to you; the copy you have didn't result from your name being on a Cc: list or on a mailing list.
* A means you've read and sent an answer or reply to the message.

*w*w To read the current message (the one highlighted), press Enter. To read a different message, type the number of the message, and press Enter.

These three possibilities are shown in Figure C.13.

Press Enter to view (read) the current message, the one highlighted. There are several ways to make another message the current message. Press the up/down arrow keys, type in the number of a message, and press Enter. Press the spacebar or minus sign to go to another page of messages (if there is one), or press **N** or **P** to make the next or previous message the current message. Other commands are listed at the bottom of the screen as shown in Figure C.13.

Viewing or reading a message shows it one screen at a time; press the spacebar to go to the next screen. The commands listed at the bottom of the screen tell you what to type to go to the next or previous screen, go to another message, get help, and a few other things we'll discuss later. Figure C.14 is an example of the first screen of a message.

```
PINE 3.90   MESSAGE TEXT              Folder: INBOX   Message 4 of 6 21%


Date: Thu, 8 Dec 1994 09:13:25 -0500
From: Pete Clark <plark@joj.com>
To: mozart@s850.mwc.edu
Subject: Phase 2


    I've been thinking about our work on the first phase of the project and we
ought to take the same approach on the second phase. It seem to me we'll be
spending a lot of time away from our lab, and it will be better if we use an
approach we know will give some results without a lot of setup time.


    Sorry I haven't been able to get in touch with you sooner. It's been
hectic trying to write up our results, plan a wedding, and run a ranch at the
same time. Sometimes I wish I was the one running the lab. It seems so easy
from this distance!
```

```
    Here are some of the preliminary results.


? Help        M Main Menu  P PrevMsg     - PrevPage    D Delete     R Reply
O OTHER CMDS V ViewAttch  N NextMsg   Spc NextPage    U Undelete   F Forward
```

Figure C.14 Reading or Viewing a Message

To get back to the list of messages in the open folder, press I. You can, in fact, give any of the commands you would if you were at the screen with the main menu—? for help, L to list your folders, C to compose a message, and so on.

2. Leave Pine

W[]W   Type Q and press Enter.

W[]W   When asked if you really want to quit, type Y and press Enter.

To leave Pine type Q. You'll see a line letting you know that the open folder (the file holding the e-mail messages listed on the screen) is being closed, and if you deleted or saved any messages, some messages are being deleted. If you only started Pine and read messages, you'd see something like Figure C.15 near the bottom of the screen when you leave or quit Pine.

```
[Closing folder "INBOX". Keeping all 6 messages]
? Help        M Main Menu  P PrevMsg     - PrevPage    D Delete     R Reply
O OTHER CMDS V [ViewMsg]  N NextMsg   Spc NextPage    U Undelete   F Forward

Pine finished
```

Figure C.15 Leaving Pine

────────────────────────End of Example C.2────────────────────────

Getting Help

Pine has on-line help available regardless of which feature you're using. Press ? (question mark) to see the Help screen(s) at any time, except when writing or composing a message and saving a message. In that case press Ctrl+G, represented by ^G, for help. (Ctrl+G means hold down the Ctrl key, press the G key, and release them both.)

There are specific commands to use for on-line help. As with other screens, the commands appear at the bottom of the screen. To save space, only the bottom of the screen is shown in Figure C.16.

```
M Main Menu   E Exit Help        -    PrevPage     Y prYnt     B Report Bug
                               Spc NextPage                    W WhereIs
```

Figure C.16 Commands for Viewing Help

These single keystroke commands are supposed to be self-explanatory, but we'll discuss a few of them. The Main Menu was discussed above. Press the spacebar to go to the next page, and a dash or minus sign (-) to go to the previous page. Yes, you press **Y** to print a page. To look for a word or phrase in whatever you're viewing, press **W** (WhereIs), then type the word or phrase and press Enter.

Saving Messages

You save a message to a folder by typing **S**. The name of the folder is usually taken from the e-mail address in the **From:** header. You'll be prompted for the name of the folder before saving. Pressing Enter saves the message in the folder whose name appears in the brackets, as in Figure C.17. If the folder already exists, the message will be appended (added to) the folder; otherwise a new folder is created to hold the message. It's convenient saving messages in folders. You can save messages based on who they're from, or based on the subject matter of the message. Figure C.17 shows the type of prompt Pine gives if we save message 5.

```
SAVE to folder [apmills] :
^G Help       ^T To Fldrs TAB Complete
^C Cancel   Ret Accept
```

Figure C.17 Saving a Message to a Folder

The ^ represents the Ctrl key. For example, pressing Ctrl+C cancels the action and takes you back to what you were doing with Pine. Press Enter and Pine saves the message in the folder with the name it chose. You can type in a name and press Enter. You may want to press ^T to see the names of folders you already have. You can type part of a name and press Tab to have Pine complete the name to match an existing folder. If you had only one folder, say offers, whose name starts with the letters off, you could type **off** here, press Tab, and the name offers would appear.

Once a message is saved it's marked to be deleted from **INBOX**. If you quit Pine the message will be deleted, but it has been saved. (You can press **U** to "undelete" a message.) It's a good idea to clean out your **INBOX** regularly. If your amount of e-mail is limited because of a quota, cleaning out your INBOX is mandatory!

Deleting Messages

Deleting messages is easy and necessary to keep the amount of e-mail in your **INBOX** and other folders under control. Just press **D** and the current message is marked to be deleted when you leave Pine. You can press **U** to undelete a message. You also get a chance to change your mind when you press **Q** to leave Pine. Here's the type of message you'd see if four files were marked to be deleted:

```
Expunge the 4 deleted messages from "INBOX"?
Y [Yes]
N No
```

If you type **Y** for yes or press Enter, the messages will be removed. You decide.

You can delete messages from **INBOX** or any other folder. You probably face some limit on the amount of space you're allowed for e-mail in **INBOX** or other folders. Think about deleting messages regularly. Take the plunge—expunge!

Composing and Sending E-Mail

Composing e-mail, at a minimum, involves:
* Setting the address of the recipient(s)
* Typing the message and/or including a file as part of the message body
* Giving the command to send the e-mail

Pine also allows several other optional commands or actions:
* Setting the address(es) for others to receive copies of the e-mail
* Sending a file as an attachment to the message (useful for sending nontext files)
* Including other headers as part of the e-mail
* Checking the spelling of the message
* Canceling or postponing the e-mail

You compose and send e-mail once you've started a Pine session by pressing **C** (for compose) any time you can enter a single letter command—reading mail, managing your folders, or working with an address book. If you start Pine by typing in pine and pressing Enter, you start to send e-mail to someone by typing Pine followed by the Internet address of the receiver. For example:

```
pine mozart@emperor.court.org
```

Regardless of which method you use, you'll work with a screen similar to the one shown in Figure C.18.

```
PINE 3.90    COMPOSE MESSAGE                    Folder: INBOX   6 Messages
   To     :
   Cc     :
   Attchmnt:
   Subject :
```

```
__ Message Text __


Ernest C. Ackermann
Department of Computer Science    Mary Washington College
Fredericksburg, VA 22401-5358       VOICE 540 - 654 - 1320
ernie@mwc.edu                FAX    540 - 899 - 4373


^G Get Help   ^X Send      ^R Rich Hdr   ^Y PrvPg/Top ^K Cut Line   ^O Postpone
^C Cancel     ^D Del Char  ^J Attach     ^V NxtPg/End ^U UnDel Line^T To AddrBk
```

Figure C.18 Composing E-Mail—Getting Started

The commands to use with the screen in Figure C.18 are at shown at the bottom. The ^ before each characters represents pressing the Ctrl key. For example, ^G or Ctrl+G means get help; hold down the Ctrl key, press the G key, and release both to see the online help about composing a message. You can use the arrow keys or others to move about the screen. Read the online help to see a complete list of commands.

The initial screen has places for you to fill in the headers **To:** address(es) of primary receivers; **Cc:** address(es) where copies of the e-mail will be sent; **Attchmnt:** name(s) of files to attach to the message; **Subject:** what the message is about (make it brief and descriptive). You move from header to header by typing in the appropriate information and pressing Enter, or you can just press Enter or the down arrow key to skip a field. Separate multiple address with commas if you're sending the same e-mail to several people at the **To:** or **Cc:** headers. Use the **Attchmnt:** header to include files (text or nontext) with the message. You'll want to be sure the receiver can handle working with nontext files sent this way. The receiver's e-mail program has to include MIME (Multipurpose Internet Mail Extensions). Type the name of the file to include; Pine attaches it to the message. To attach several files, use ^J, as shown at the bottom of the screen.

The following line:

```
__ Message Text __
```

marks the beginning of the message body. As you move past that line, you'll see the list of commands changes to:

```
^G Get Help   ^X Send      ^R Read File ^Y Prev Pg   ^K Cut Text   ^O Postpone
^C Cancel     ^J Justify   ^_ Alt Edit  ^V Next Pg   ^U UnCut Text^T To Spell
```

These are the commands to use while writing the body of the message. If you've got a signature file, it will be added automatically here. Check with your local experts or read your local documentation to see the precise name that file ought to have. (On many systems it's named **.signature**.) Type your message; Pine takes care of formatting it. You can use the arrow keys and others to go back to make modifications any time. While you're composing a message, you're using an editor named pico (pine composer) that's included with the program. It's relatively easy to use and gives good results. You can include the contents of a text file by pressing Ctrl+R, typing in the name of the file, and pressing Enter. That's a way to include some previously prepared materials. Figure C.19 shows a complete message.

```
To       : ollie@oregano.mwc.edu, mozart@emperor.court.org, karl@mmedia.com
Cc       : mybuddy@great.place.com
Attchmnt: 1. /users/lynna/futlogo.gif (94 KB) "Our logo"
Subject : Reminder: Group Meeting Wednesday at 11 AM.
__ Message Text __
          Just a reminder, we have a group meeting on Wednesday at 11AM.
I'm looking forward to hearing your presentations. Let me know if you're
having any difficulties getting things prepared. I'll treat for lunch
after the meeting.

Attached is a file containing a sketch for our logo. Let me know your
opinion of it.

Lynn Aeschbach
Director of  Future Studies Cutting Edge Industries
Collonialstown, IA 11111    VOICE 555 - 654 - 1320
lynna@cutting.edge.com      FAX 555  - 899 - 4373


^G Get Help  ^X Send      ^R Read File ^Y Prev Pg   ^K Cut Text   ^O Postpone
^C Cancel    ^J Justify   ^_ Alt Edit  ^V Next Pg   ^U UnCut Text^T To Spell
```

Figure C.19 Composing E-mail—Complete Message

After composing, you can send the message, cancel it, or postpone it. The commands are at the bottom of the screen. When you give the command to send (^X) or cancel (^C) the message, you're prompted to confirm the action. When you give the command to postpone (^O) the message, Pine writes or puts the message to a folder of postponed messages, tells you it's writing it, and then returns to what you were doing when you gave the command to compose a message. The next time you compose a message, you're prompted to see if you'd like to go back to the postponed message(s).

Replying to a Message

You reply to the current message by pressing **R** for reply. You can reply while browsing the list of messages or while you're reading a message. When you press **R** you'll be asked if you'd like to include the original message in the reply as shown in Figure C.20.

```
Include original message in Reply?
          Y Yes
^C Cancel  N [No]
```

Figure C.20 Prompt to Include Original Message

Pressing ^C (Ctrl+C) cancels the reply; you go back to whatever you were doing. In many situations, it's a good idea to include at least a portion of the original message so your reply can be read in context. This is particularly true if you're replying to a message that was sent to a group. Be sure to include only the relevant parts. The default action here, as shown in Figure C.20, is not to include the original message. You must press **Y** to include the original message.

Assuming you don't cancel the reply, you may be asked several questions depending on the headers in the original message. At a minimum, you'll be asked if you want your reply to go to everyone on the list of addresses or only to the person sending the message, if the message was sent to several people. It's your choice; just be sure you don't send something to a group that you'd like to send to an individual. This can be embarrassing, especially if the reply is personal! The other questions you'll have to answer depend on the way Pine is set up, and we won't list all the possibilities here. You can press ^C anytime to cancel the reply.

After you go through the questions, Pine will get the message ready for the reply. You'll see a screen similar to the one in Figure C.18, except the **To:** address(es) will be filled in, the **Subject:** will be set to **Re:** followed by the subject of the original message, and if you said to include the original message, the original message will be on the screen. Now you work with composing a reply the same way you compose any message. You may want to delete lines from the original message and annotate (add your own statements) the original. Figure C.21 shows what a user would see if he started a reply to everyone who received the e-mail in Figure C.19.

```
PINE 3.90    COMPOSE MESSAGE REPLY                Folder: INBOX  7 Messages


To      : Lynn Aeschbach <lynna@cutting.edge.com>
Cc      : ollie@oregano.mwc.edu,
          karl@mmedia.com,
            mozart@emperor.court.org,
          mybuddy@great.place.com
Attchmnt:
Subject : Re: Reminder: Group Meeting Wednesday at 11 AM.
__ Message Text __
On Mon, 11 Dec 1995, Lynn Aeschbach wrote:
```

```
>          Just a reminder, we have a group meeting on Wednesday at 11AM.
> I'm looking forward to hearing your presentations. Let me know if you're
> having any difficulties getting things prepared. I'll treat for lunch
> after the meeting.
>
> Attached is a file containing a sketch for our logo. Let me know your
> opinion of it.
>
^G Get Help   ^X Send       ^R Read File ^Y Prev Pg   ^K Cut Text   ^O Postpone
^C Cancel     ^J Justify     ^_ Alt Edit ^V Next Pg   ^U UnCut Text^T To Spell
```

Figure C.21 Reply to All Recipients—Include Original Message

At this point, you type/compose your reply, deleting lines from the original and including your own as you see fit. When it's complete you can send it off by pressing ^X (Ctrl+X).

Forwarding E-Mail

Forwarding e-mail means passing the e-mail you've received on to another address. You can do this by pressing **F** for forward or **B** for bounce. They're related notions, but different.

When you press **B** for bounce, the current message is sent to another address, not as if it came from you, but as if it came from the person who sent it to you. Pine will ask you for an address to "bounce" or use to send the current message.

When you press **F** to forward e-mail, you're given the chance to add to the original message. You'll be working with a screen similar to the screen for composing a message, except the **Subject:** will be filled in with the subject of the original message followed by (**fwd**), any attachments to the original file will be listed, and the body of the message will include the message being forwarded.

Working with Folders

Pine stores e-mail into files called folders. Listing the messages in a folder shows you what Pine calls an index view of the folder. When you start Pine, you see the list of your e-mail messages in the folder INBOX. That's an index view of **INBOX**. Pine makes it relatively easy to arrange and work with e-mail in folders. When e-mail is saved, press **S** and give the name of a folder. The mail is put into a folder. This way you can save messages from an individual address or you can save messages any way you'd like. Once messages are in a folder you can work with them in exactly the same way you work with messages in your INBOX. You can go through a folder replying to, deleting, printing, forwarding, etc. the messages. Putting e-mail in folders keeps you from having to deal with a hundred or more different messages that aren't organized in any way.

To view your folders, press **L** for **List Folders**. You can do this at the Main Menu, or any time when you can give single keystroke commands (without Ctrl). Figure C.22 is an example of the type of screen you'd see.

```
PINE 3.90     FOLDER LIST                       Folder: INBOX   7 Messages

INBOX                    saved-messages        apmills        bwilliam
cathana                  einstein              ernie          jacson
karen                    listserv              mozart         postponed-msgs
rhoover                  socrates              thodapp




? Help        M Main Menu  P PrevFldr   - PrevPage     D Delete       R Rename
O OTHER CMDS  V [ViewFldr] N NextFldr  Spc NextPage    A Add
```

Figure C.22 List Folders

The current folder is highlighted. The commands to use are at the bottom of the display as shown in Figure C.22. You see that you can delete a folder, add or create a new folder, or rename a folder. To work with the messages in a folder, make it the current folder (press **P** and **N** to move from one folder to another on the screen) and then press **V** or Enter.

Working with an Address Book

Pine includes an e-mail address book that's an integrated part of the e-mail program. You can add addresses by typing them in or having the program take them directly from a message. You give each address an alias or short form so you can use the alias when you're composing or replying to a message, and you can go to the address book to retrieve an address whenever you want to compose, reply to, forward, or bounce e-mail. Furthermore, several addresses can be grouped together so you can send e-mail to all members of a group or organization. It's a good idea to keep frequently used addresses in the address book. That way you don't have to remember people's addresses or save messages and always reply to a previous message.

Adding Addresses

There are essentially two ways to add an address to the address book. One is to take an address from the current message, and the other is to add it by typing it into the address book.

To take an address press **T** while browsing the list of messages or reading a message. Pine lists the address of the author of the e-mail and may list other addresses, such as the one in the **Reply-To:** header. Choose the one(s) you want to add to the address book. While selecting an address press **?** for on-line help. Once an address is selected, press **T** to add the address to the address book. Pine then asks you to enter a nickname, a short name you'll be likely to remember for the address, and then it gives the full name of the person (as it appears in the From: header). You can change the full name if you'd like at this point. Pressing Enter shows the e-mail address that will be put in the address book. Once again you can change it here or press Enter to accept it. Pressing ^C (Ctrl+C) at any of these steps cancels adding the address. If you go on, you'll get a message near the bottom of the screen notifying you the address has been added.

To add an address manually, press **M** to go to the Main Menu and then press **A** to go to the address book. All the addresses saved will be displayed, as shown in Figure C.23. Press **A** to add an address. You'll be asked to enter a full name—last name, first name—for the address, then a single word nickname, and finally the e-mail address. You can press ^C (Ctrl+C) to cancel the addition at any time. Pressing Enter after the last step adds the name to the address book. Addresses are listed in alphabetical order by last name.

```
PINE 3.90    ADDRESS BOOK                  Folder: INBOX  Message 9 of 9

eca          Ackermann, Ernest               ernie@mwc.edu

binky        Ito, Burt                       bito@coco.report.place.us

fba          Leisy, James                    70C17.3671@compuserve.com

cici         Mills, Alisa                    apmills@green.hitech.org

pinebugs     Place to report Pine bugs       pine@cac.washington.edu

angie        Tonsoni, Angela                 atonsoni@great.place.edu

z            Zebert                          rhoover@garlic.mwc.edu

dest         Design Team                     DISTRIBUTION LIST:

                                             karl@mmedia.org

                                             mozart@emperor.court.org

                                             oliver@oregano.mwc.edu

                                             rjmcd@salt.lake.city.ut

? Help           M MainMenu P PrevEntry     - PrevPage        D Delete      S CreateList

O OTHER CMDS E [Edit]    N NextEntry    Spc NextPage A Add   Z AddToList
```

Figure C.23 Address Book

Working with a Distribution List or Group Address. You can also create a distribution list, a list of addresses associated with a single nickname. That lets you send one e-mail message to a group. It's particularly useful if you regularly need to send or share e-mail with several people. To create a distribution list, first go to the address book (press **A** from the main menu) and press **S**. (All the commands you need are at the bottom of the screen.) Now you're prompted for a descriptive long name for the list. Type it and press Enter. Then you're prompted for a short nickname for the list, and then you need to enter the e-mail addresses one at a time, pressing Enter after each one. To stop adding names just press Enter without typing anything. Pine then adds the list to the address book. You can add to a distribution list by first highlighting it and then pressing **Z**. You'll be prompted to add e-mail addresses.

Deleting Addresses. Addresses can be deleted from the address book by first going to the address book (press **A** from the main menu), highlighting an address, and pressing **D** to delete an address. To highlight an address, use the up/down arrow keys or follow the commands at the bottom of the screen. You'll be prompted if you want to delete that address. Press **Y** if want to delete it and **N** if you don't. You can use this to delete individual addresses from a list, delete a complete list, or delete a single address.

Using Addresses. You use the nickname you've assigned to an address when you want to use an address for sending, replying to, forwarding, or bouncing e-mail. Suppose, for example, you have an address in the address book with the nickname "binky," as in Figure C.23. To send e-mail to this address, just type binky in the **To:** or **Cc:** field of a message you're composing. Pine will look up this address and fill in the Internet e-mail address associated with the nickname. You don't have to remember all the nicknames you've saved. While composing a message, press ^T (Ctrl+T) and Pine will take you to the address book. You can then select an address by highlighting it and pressing Enter or **S** to select the address. Pine will put it in the place you left and then lets you continue.

Printing Messages. You press **Y** to print the current message. Why **Y**? Well, the letter P was already used (see Figure C.22). The next question to ask is "Where is it printed?" The designers of Pine realized that you may want to print to different printers at different times. It could be you're working with your e-mail in your room and you'd like to print the messages to a printer attached to your PC, you want to print to a printer connected to the larger system you're using (Pine assumes it's a Unix system), or you'd like to use a customized personal command for printing. This last one is useful to download messages to a personal computer from the system that receives your e-mail.

To set Pine to print to a specific printer, go to the Main Menu (press **M**), press **S** for setup, and press **P** for printer. You'll see a screen listing three possibilities. The first sets the print mechanism so Pine tries to print on a printer attached to your PC. This assumes you're using a program to communicate with the system holding your e-mail. This choice works with most communications programs, but not all. You'll have to try it. Press **1**, then press **Y** to try to print the current message. To print on a printer attached to a Unix computer system, press **2**. Once again press **Y** and check to see if it works. Finally, choose option **3** for your own printer command. When you do, the command for printing is displayed. You can use the command there or enter your own. If you want to download your messages from the system holding your e-mail to another computer, you'll have to know the commands for downloading, which are different in various environments. For example, to download using Kermit from a Unix system, type the command **kermit -is - here.** Then, when you enter **Y** to print, the system holding the e-mail will download the message by Kermit. You need to get your personal computer ready to accept a file transferred by Kermit. Check with your friends or local experts to find out how to do this effectively.

Working with Nontext Files

With Pine you can send and receive nontext files such as images, spreadsheets, files from a word processing program, compressed files, programs, and others. Pine includes these as MIME (Multipurpose Internet Mail Extensions) attachments to messages. They are sent along with a message, but they aren't part of the message body. You need to be sure that your e-mail system can deal with MIME as well as the e-mail system receiving these messages. You may also need to have special software installed to work with the attachments once you receive them; for example, a program to view certain types of graphics files. Pine handles including and extracting a MIME attachment, but it doesn't provide any way to work with the files after they've arrived.

Sending nontext files. You send a nontext file by typing its name in the **Attchmnt:** header or by pressing ^J (Ctrl+J) when you compose a message. In the latter case, it's put alongside the **Attchmnt:** header along with any comments you want to write about it. You have to enter the exact name of the file including any directory information if it's not in your home directory. Some possible entries are **eagle.gif or /users/ ernie/documents/report.doc**. Pine takes care of sending the attached file with your message.

Receiving nontext files. If one or more nontext files have been sent along with a message as attachments, they're listed alongside the **Attchmnt:** header when you're reading a message. An example of a message with nontext attachments is shown in Figure C.24. Exactly what you do to get the attachments depends on which version of Pine you're using.

```
PINE 3.90   MESSAGE TEXT              Folder: INBOX   Message 8 of 9 73%


Date: Sun, 11 Dec 1994 18:36:24 -0500 (EST)
From: ernest ackermann <ernie@mwc.edu>
To: Mozart <mozart@oregano.mwc.edu>
Parts/attachments:
   1 Shown     8 lines  Text
   2          76 KB     File "rept.doc", "word processor output of the report"
   3   OK    129 KB     Image, "image for the report"

Here is my report with text in word processor format and an image for the
cover.


Ernest C. Ackermann
? Help        M Main Menu  P PrevMsg     - PrevPage     D Delete      R Reply
O OTHER CMDS V ViewAttch   N NextMsg   Spc NextPage     U Undelete    F Forward
```

Figure C.24 Message with Nontext Attachments

You either view the attachments on the screen or save them in a file. Press **V**. The attachments are listed, and you can choose to work with them one at a time. You can view an attachment, which is what you might want to do if it's an image, only if the right programs are installed and configured on your computer. Check with your friends, local experts, or the documentation to see if that's possible. In any case, select an attachment from the list and type **V** (again) to view it or **S** to save it. You should always be able to save it to a file and then work with it. You can use it with a program on the system you've saved it on, or you can download it or otherwise transfer it to a system that has the proper software (graphics program, word processor, spreadsheet program, etc.) to deal with it. You can get on-line help by pressing **?** (question mark).

Using Eudora

Eudora is an e-mail program that's become very popular with users of personal computers. It's popular because it is well written, easy to use, and there's lots of on-line help and an extensive user manual available. A version of the program, Eudora Light, is available as freeware (absolutely no charge) and is distributed by many Internet service providers. Eudora is a product of Qualcomm Incorporated, which also sells and provides technical support for a more extensive and robust e-mail program, Eudora Pro. Information about Eudora Light and Eudora Pro is available as part of the World Wide Web through the URL **http://www.qualcomm.com/quest/**. In this appendix we'll be discussing using Eudora Light. Use the URL **http://www.qualcomm.com/ProdTech/quest/light.html** to get the latest version. Installation is straightforward, and instructions are included with the program. Start Windows, create a folder or directory, for example **Eudora,** to hold the program and the Eudora files, move the files **Eudora.exe** and **Eudora.hlp** into the directory, and then run or execute the program **Eudora.exe**.

Eudora is relatively easy to use to compose, read, and manage your e-mail messages. It's a Windows application; you use many of the same commands as with any Windows program. Press **F1**, for example, to access on-line help. The commands are available through pull-down menus on a menu bar, icons on a toolbar, or as keyboard shortcuts. Eudora works well with other Windows applications. Messages can be saved and printed, and text can be copied, cut, and pasted to and from Eudora and other Windows programs. Eudora allows for non-text attachments in MIME (Multipurpose Internet Mail Extensions) format. So you can send and receive all sorts of files, images, video files, audio clips, programs, spread sheets, documents, or anything that you'd expect to receive in electronic form. Messages are kept in what Eudora calls mailboxes. The incoming messages are kept in the mailbox named **In,** deleted messages are kept in the **Trash** mailbox, and copies of outgoing messages are saved, if the user sets that option, in a mailbox named **Out**. The user can create and manage mailboxes as well. Addresses can be saved in an address book Eudora calls **Nicknames**. Eudora also allows the user to set up a list of frequently used addresses it calls the *quick recipient list*. This list can be called up from items in the pull-down menu **Message**.

Eudora is designed to be used on a personal computer that receives its e-mail by using a POP server and sends e-mail to a server using SMTP, in the same way as discussed in Chapter 3. The Internet address or name of theses mail servers needs to be set before Eudora is used the first time. Many Internet Service providers, such as EarthLink, provide a pre-configured version of Eudora that's all set to use. The section "Setting Important Options" below deals with giving Eudora the proper settings.

Eudora Pro and Eudora Light are both full-featured e-mail programs. According to estimates supplied by Qualcomm, there are over 10 million copies of Eudora in use. Eudora Light's features include storing messages on your local computer so they can be read or composed either on-line or off-line (not being connected to the Internet), searching messages by content and sorting based on the headers of messages, including MIME or BINHEX attachments, automatically going to the location given by a URL in a message by clicking on the URL, full compatibility with Unix mail systems, having multiple mailboxes and address books (called *nickname lists*), and others.

We'll cover many of the features but don't have the space to address them all. (Qualcomm makes an excellent user manual for Eudora light (160+ pages), and it's available by anonymous FTP without charge. The URL for the Windows version is **ftp://ftp.qualcomm.com/quest/windows/eudora/documentation/152word.exe**, The topics we'll cover here are:

* Starting Eudora
* Setting Important Options
* Getting Help
* Knowing When New Mail Has Arrived
* Ending a Eudora Session
* The Eudora E-Mail Window
* Reading E-Mail
* Saving, Printing, and Deleting Messages
* Setting Other Eudora Options
* Composing and Sending E-Mail
* Including Attachments
* Replying to a Message
* Forwarding and Redirecting E-Mail
* Working With the Nickname List (Address Book)

Starting Eudora

To start Eudora click on an icon named **Eudora** or **Eudora Light**, or select its name from a menu. The icon looks like a mailbox with the name Eudora underneath as shown here. (The precise appearance of the icon depends on the version of the program.)

Eudora

Eudora

Figure D.1   Sample Eudora Icons

Whether the icon is on the desktop, on the list of programs accessible from the Start menu in Windows 95, part of a program group, or whether you start the program by selecting the name from a menu depends on how it was installed on your computer. Installing the program as part of a disk supplied by your Internet service provider may put the icon in a folder or program group. If you retrieve a version of Eudora Light from Qualcomm, follow the instructions to install it yourself, and if you're using Windows 95, the icon will appear on the program list.

If your Internet connection is active, Eudora will check to see if there's any new mail waiting for you on the e-mail server. Depending on how the program is set, you may have to enter a password for Eudora to connect to the e-mail server. Eudora can be set up so it keeps a copy of your password after you type it once. Be aware that if Eudora remembers your password this way, anyone using your computer can read your e-mail or send e-mail as if it came from you. If the Internet connection isn't active and you connect to the Internet through a modem, Eudora, like Netscape, will initiate the connection by dialing the number of your Internet service provider. Regardless of how you connect to the Internet, after Eudora is started, an Eudora e-mail window opens, Eudora contacts the POP server to see if there's any new mail, notifies you if any new e-mail has arrived, and lists your messages. Figure D.2 shows an active Eudora Window.

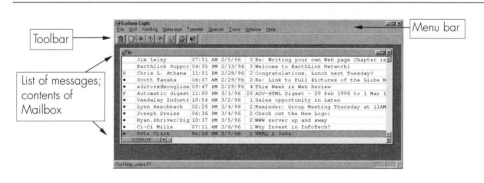

Figure D.2   Eudora Window

Setting Important Options

Before you can receive or send e-mail, some Eudora options must be set—specifically, the Internet names or addresses of the SMTP and POP server(s) and your e-mail address. To set these options click on **Tools** in the Menu Bar and select **Options**. A window similar to the one in Figure D.3 pops up.

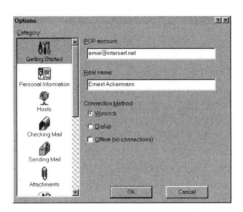

Figure D.3   Options Window for Eudora

We'll go through the options to set in the first five sections. Once options are set click on the button labeled **OK** to have them take effect. If you don't want the changes you've made to go into effect, click on **Cancel**. Some of the items that appear in one category are repeated in others. **Real name:**, for example, appears in **Getting Started** and **Personal Information**.

Getting Started	Fill in the address you've been assigned by your Internet service provider for the POP account. In many cases it has the form your-login-name@domain-name-of-your provider. In Figure D.3 it's **ernie@interserf.net**. Whatever entry you put into the pane labeled **Real name** will be the name that's attached to the **From:** header in outgoing e-mail. It's the name others see when they receive e-mail from you. Put anything you'd like here. Most use their real name, but "Alligator Skids" would work just as well. The last entry to make is the type of connection to the Internet. If you're using a graphical browser such as Netscape, then select Winsock as shown in Figure D.3.
Personal Information	The information entered under Getting Started, **POP account** and **Real name**, also appears here. Two other entries are also set here: **Return address**, the address a mail program uses when someone sends a reply to your message. This can be any valid Internet e-mail address. **Dialup username**, the name used to log in if a dialup connection (not Winsock or TCP/IP) is used to access Eudora. This name is assigned to you and must be correct in order for you to read your e-mail. Note that if you're using a graphical Web browser such as Netscape, you won't have to worry about this setting and can leave it blank.
Hosts	**POP account** appears here again. If it isn't set, fill in the address provided by the Internet service provider (ISP) or system administrator. The name of the SMTP host, again provided by the ISP or system administrator, goes in here. In

many cases, it has the form **mail** followed by the Internet domain name used by your ISP or organization. Some examples are **mail.interserf.net** or **mail.earthlink.net**. There are spaces for some other servers as well, **Ph** and **Finger**. Both of these services, if they're available, can be used to find some e-mail addresses. Check with your ISP or someone locally for information about whether these are available to you.

Checking Mail   Again, you can fill in the name of your POP account here. You can specify how frequently, in minutes, Eudora contacts the POP server to see if any new e-mail has arrived for you. The default setting on this is 15; setting it to 0 means the server isn't checked for new e-mail. Several options dealing with the delivery of e-mail and passwords can be set here as either on or off.

Skip big messages   **On** means only the first few lines of messages over 40K bytes are transferred to your system. **Off** means messages are copied to our system regardless of their size.

Send on check   **On** means messages are copied from the server to your system when you check e-mail.

Save Password   **On** means the password is kept on your PC—only do that if your PC is secure—and **off** means you have to enter the password each time you start Eudora.

Leave mail on server   **On** means that mail copies to your PC is removed from the server—this is what's usually done to avoid build-up of e-mail on the server.

The final setting in this category is the **Authentication Style** used by your server. It can be set to **Passwords** or **APOP**. Check with your ISP or local folks to get this set correctly. In many cases, authentication is handled through passwords.

Sending Mail   The first two entries have appeared previously: **Return address**, the address a mail program uses when someone sends a reply to your message, such as **ernie@earthlink.net**; **SMTP server**, the Internet domain name, such as **mail.earthlink.net**, of the system that your computer sends e-mail to so it can be sent to the Internet. If you leave this field blank, Eudora uses your POP server, and in many cases they are one in the same computer system. The following entries are set as either on or off and affect how messages are sent. Going through them one by one:

Immediate send. On means e-mail is immediately sent to the SMTP server for delivery to the Internet right after you compose it, **Off** means messages are composed off-line (not connected to the Internet) and put in a queue to be sent when you go on-line.

Send on check. On means any messages that have been put in a queue to be sent out are sent immediately whenever Eudora checks the POP server for new mail.

Word wrap. On means Eudora adjusts the line length in outgoing messages so you don't have to be concerned with pressing Enter to fit lines within a message window.

Fix curly quotes. This is esoteric and has to do with how Eudora treats "smart" and "conventional" quotation marks before an attachment. The standard advice is if your recipients have MIME with their e-mail system, there isn't any reason to turn this on.

May use Quoted-Printable. On means Eudora uses an encoding called "quoted-printable" when it has to deal with long lines or special characters; this is useful for dealing with languages or applications that use characters different from those in Western European alphabets.

Keep copies of outgoing mail. On means a copy of each message sent is kept in the **Out** mailbox. **Off** means the messages are put to the **Trash** mailbox.

Use signature. On means your signature file is automatically attached to the end of outgoing messages.

Tabs in body of message. On means Eudora replaces tab characters in outgoing messages with enough blanks to move to the next tab stop, this is useful to maintain the format of a message since the tab settings of the recipient may be different than yours.

Getting Help

On-line help is available by clicking on **Help** on the Menu Bar and by pressing **F1** during a session. Choosing **Help** from the Menu Bar gives the most complete help. As with others Windows applications, you can get a list of Help topics or search through all the information available. Pressing **F1** gives context sensitive help for items on the pull-down menus from the Menu Bar. The Eudora user guide mentioned earlier, **ftp://ftp.qualcomm.com/quest/windows/eudora/documentation/152word.exe**, is an excellent resource for helpful information as well.

Knowing When New Mail Has Arrived

When Eudora starts it checks the POP server for new e-mail since the server was last contacted. if there's any new mail, you'll be notified. While Eudora is running, in the foreground or background, it checks the POP server at regular intervals. The time from one check to another is set in the **Checking Mail** section of the **Options** menu under **Tools** in the Menu Bar; 15 minutes is a good interval so e-mail is checked regularly and you're not interrupted too frequently. When new mail arrives the flag may go up on the Eudora icon, you may here an audio clue, or an letter icon appears in the task bar at the bottom of the screen. The precise form of notification depends on how Eudora is configured. The settings for notification are in the section **Getting Attention** of the **Options** menu under **Tools** in the Menu Bar.

Ending a Eudora Session

Ending a Eudora session is similar to ending other Windows applications. Choose **Exit** from the **File** pull-down menu, press Alt+F4 or click on the **X** in the upper right corner of the window. You can also use the keyboard shortcut Ctrl+Q.

The Eudora E-Mail Window

When Eudora is started, the e-mail window opens, the POP server is contacted, and messages are listed. Figure D.2 shows the Eudora window. It has a menu bar and toolbar consisting of icons just like other Windows applications. We'll go over several of theses items as well as discuss the list of messages.

Menu Bar

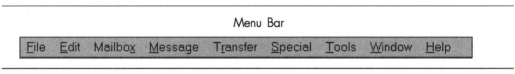

Figure D.4   Eudora Menu Bar

Each of the entries in the Menu Bar represent a pull-down menu. Clicking on the name or using Alt+ the underlined letter shows the items in the menu. Some of the items in a menu are listed as keyboard short-cuts—keys to press to immediately start an action. The first menu, **File**, for example, contains the item **Print ...** Ctrl+P. You can print the currently highlighted e-mail message by pressing Ctrl+P on the key-board at any time, rather than going through the menu. We'll describe each menu item.

File	This menu has entries to close the e-mail window, save the current message in a file, send queued messages (if there are any), check for new e-mail, print messages, and exit Eudora.
Edit	The first part of the **Edit** menu is similar to the one found in other Windows applications; items to **Undo, Cut, Copy, Paste, Clear** (delete), and select all text. Other items used in composing messages present are **paste as a quotation, choose an address from the quick recipient list, search (using Find) a mailbox or message,** and **sort the messages in a mailbox.** Messages can be sorted by any of the fields that appear in the summary: **Status, Priority, Sender, Date, Size,** or **Subject.**
Mailbox	This menu is used to open a mailbox or, if there are several open, to bring a mailbox to the foreground. The item labeled **New** is used to create a mailbox, and the ones created by the user are listed under that item.
Message	Use this menu to deal with sending messages. It contains items to begin composing a new message, to reply to, forward, redirect (bounce) and resend a message if its been rejected by a mail system. Other items deal with attaching file(s) to the current message, changing the queuing and priority options, and deleting the messages. Deleting a message means its moved to the **Trash** mailbox, and if it's deleted from the **Trash** mailbox, it's gone!
Transfer	Has items to transfer (move) messages from one mailbox to another.

Special   This menu could just as well have been called miscellaneous since it contains a collection of different Eudora functions or services. These include entries to create nicknames (entries in an address book), add and remove entries from the quick recipient list, empty trash and compact mailboxes, make sure Eudora forgets your password so it has to be typed in the next time Eudora is started, and to change your password on your POP server. This last item may not be available in many cases since the change is made on the POP server not on the local computer.

Tools   The items here include tools to create, rename, or remove mailboxes, manage the nickname list (address book), set up a signature file, and set the **Options** for using Eudora. Selecting any item brings up a window dedicated to the tool.

Window   One part of the menu deals with ways of arranging (cascade, tile horizontal or vertical, arrange all icons at the bottom of the window, send the current window to the background) the open windows within the Eudora window. The second part lists open windows or mailboxes. Clicking on a name in the list brings the window to the foreground.

Help   The **Help** menu gives access to on-line help by having entries to list the contents or search the contents of the **help** file. A link that lets you subscribe to a mailing list about Eudora is included as well.

Toolbar

Figure D.5   Eudora Toolbar

The toolbar is the sequence of icons, as shown above, just below the Menu Bar. To see a label for the icon, move the mouse pointer to any icon and pause for a couple of seconds. Each icon represents an action that's performed when you click on the icon with a mouse. We'll go over the icons by name from left to right.

Delete   Deletes the current message; copies it to the **Trash** mailbox.

New Message   Opens a window to compose a new message.

Reply   Opens a message window to reply to the current, highlighted message. The reply is sent to the person who sent the message.

Forward   Opens a window to forward the current (highlighted) message to another Internet e-mail address. The outgoing message can be edited or annotated and your e-mail address becomes the reply address.

Redirect   Sends the current message to another Internet e-mail address. The return address isn't changed and there's no signature added. Its almost as if the original message weren't forwarded by you but came from the original sender to the recipient you name.

Nicknames   Opens the list of nicknames. Select a name to use in the **To:**, **Cc:**, or **Bcc:** header; modify a nickname entry, or remove an entry.

Print   Print the current (highlighted) messages.

Reading E-Mail

To read e-mail, you have to have a mailbox opened on the screen. That may happen when starting Eudora. When started, Eudora contacts the POP server to check for new e-mail, and if there is any new mail, it displays the **In** mailbox. Regardless of which mailbox is open, you'll see a list of messages in the **In** mailbox. This list is called a summary list by Eudora. It contains, for each message, the name of the sender, the subject, its size, when it was sent, and whether it's a new message, has been read, or forwarded, replied to, or redirected. Once a summary on the list is highlighted, the message can be read by pressing Enter. To highlight a message, click on it once with the mouse or move to it from another highlighted message by using the up or down arrow keys. You can also open a message by double-clicking on its summary with a mouse. The message being read is displayed in a window within the Eudora window, so the messages window can be closed or minimized to get a less cluttered view of the summary list. Once a message window is open, you can view the previous message by pressing the Alt key and the up arrow key. To view the next message, use Alt and the down arrow key.

Example D.1   Starting Eudora, Reading a Message, and Closing the Window

In this example we'll assume there's a Eudora icon on the desktop and you have to supply a password to contact the POP server.

1. Start Eudora

w⁴⁄w   Double-click on the **Eudora** icon.

Once Eudora is started, it will contact the POP server to check to see if new e-mail has arrived. You'll see a window similar to the one shown in Figure D.6.

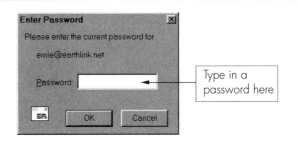

Figure D.6   Enter Password Dialog Box

Type your password into the frame in the **Enter Password** dialog box and click on the **OK** button.

Eudora connects to the mail server, and if you've given the correct password, checks for new e-mail. If there is some new e-mail waiting for you on your mail server, it will be delivered to you; the **In** mailbox will be displayed with the most recent message highlighted. If you don't have any new e-mail, you can open the **In** mailbox, or any other, by selecting it from the pull-down menu **Mailbox**. We'll assume here that some new e-mail has arrived and after typing in the password the **In** mailbox shown in Figure D.7 is displayed.

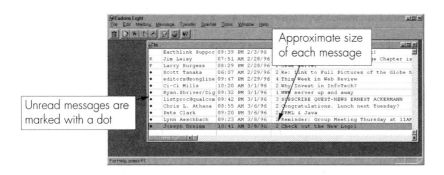

Figure D.7   In Mailbox Message Summary List, Most Recent Entry Highlighted

The **In** mailbox is the one shown in Figure D.7. To open another mailbox click on **Mailbox** in the Menu Bar. You'll see later how to create new mailboxes.

Each listing includes the name of the sender, the subject, and the date it was sent. Messages which haven't been read are marked with a dot in the first column. An **R** marks messages that have been read and replied to, an **F** marks messages that have been forwarded to another Internet address, and a **D** marks messages that have been redirected to another address. In Figure D.7 we have a total of 12 messages, the last nine haven't been read yet. A reply message was sent to the sender of the second message, and the third one was forwarded to another address. The fourth column holds the approximate size of each message. The box in the bottom left gives statistics about the mailbox and shows 12/20K/0K. This means there are 12 messages, their total size is about 20 kilobytes, and no space is wasted in the mailbox. Extra space is used if we delete a message from the mailbox with out compacting it. Compacting a mailbox (select **Compact mailboxes** from the Menu Bar entry **Special**) removes this extra space.

* To read any message, double-click on its entry in the message summary list.
* To read the next message in the list, press Alt and the down arrow key. To read the previous message in the list, press Alt and the up arrow key.

Viewing or reading a message opens a window for the message in the Eudora window. The window for the message holds the Subject at the top and has horizontal and vertical scroll bars. You can use the appropriate keys on the keyboard, for example, Page Up or Page Down, to move through the message.

As you're reading your messages new messages might arrive for you. If they're not delivered immediately, you can check the POP server for them by clicking on **File** in the Menu Bar and then selecting **Check Mail.** Using the keyboard shortcut Ctrl+M also checks for new mail. In this case Eudora contacts the server and checks for new mail. If there is any new e-mail, it's delivered and added at the bottom of the message summary list. Figure D.8 shows what you'd see if you double-clicked on the last message in the list.

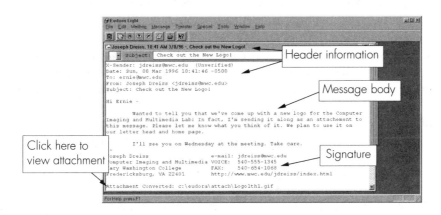

Figure D.8   Opened E-Mail Message With an Attachment

This message contains an attachment. Eudora has removed the attachment, converted it to its proper form, and stored it in the directory **C:\eudora\attach** (on the PC you're using to read the e-mail) in the file **Logo1th1.gif** (its original name). To view the attachment, double-click on its name **c:\eudora\atttach\Logo1th1.gif.**

When you're done reading a message you may want to close its window, and when you're done using Eudora, close or minimize its window.

2. Close the Eudora Window

Press **Ctrl**+Q or click on **File** in the Menu Bar and select **Exit** to close the Eudora window.

————————————End of Example D.1————————————

Saving, Printing, and Deleting Messages

Saving Messages. You can save a message into a file. To save an e-mail message in a file, go to the message summary list and highlight the entry for the message you want to save by clicking on it. Then click on **File** on the Menu Bar and select **Save As..**. A **Save As..** dialog box pops up, the message is saved in a name that matches the **Subject:** header, or you type in the name of the file to hold the message. You can choose to save it with or without the header information. Saving a message to a file is useful if you're going to use the body of the message with some other program. Suppose, for example, your partner sends you a copy of a project she's working on that you'd like to include in a presentation. You might want to save it in a file and then import or copy it into the presentation. Any attachments are automatically put into a file when the message is received.

Saving e-mail in mailboxes you create is a convenient way to organize your e-mail. You may want to have some that deal with a specific topic or project and others that hold the e-mail you've received from one person. You can go through a mailbox replying to, deleting, printing, forwarding, etc. the messages.

To create a mailbox, click on **Mailbox** on the Menu Bar and select the item **New....** A dialog box pops up and you type in the name of the mailbox. You can also create a folder to hold a collection of mailboxes. So mailboxes are useful to manage messages, and folders can be used to manage a collection of mailboxes.

To transfer from one mailbox to another, go to the message summary list and highlight the message you want to save by clicking on it. More than one message can be saved into a folder by highlighting a group of messages. Now click on **Transfer** on the Menu Bar, and then select the name of the mailbox to which to transfer the message(s). The messages are moved from one mailbox to the other.

Printing Messages. To print a message, select it by clicking on its entry in the message summary list and then click on the icon that looks like a printer. You can also use the keyboard shortcut Ctrl+P. If more than one message is highlighted, all of them will be printed. A window pops up, the same you'd see for printing from other Windows applications, and you can select a printer, set options (if necessary), and finally click on the button **OK** or **Cancel**.

Deleting Messages. Deleting messages is easy and necessary to keep the amount of e-mail in the **In** mailbox and other mailboxes under control. Highlight the item(s) in the message summary list and press the icon that looks like a trash can, choose **Delete** from the pull-down menu **Message**, press the Delete key on the keyboard, or use the keyboard shortcut Ctrl+D. Deleting a message sends it to the **Trash** mailbox. You could open the **Trash** mailbox to reclaim a message, in case you delete on by mistake. Deleting a message from the **Trash** mailbox removes it permanently. Messages may still take up space in a mailbox even after they're deleted. To reclaim that space, compact your mailboxes by choosing **Compact Mailboxes** from the pull-down menu **Special**.

Example D.2   Creating a Folder; Saving and Deleting E-Mail

In this example we'll save e-mail into a new mailbox and then delete a message. We'll follow these steps:

1. Start Eudora.
2. Create a new mailbox.
3. Copy two messages to the new mailbox.
4. Delete three messages.
5. Exit Eudora.

1. Start Eudora.

wWw   Click on the **Eudora** icon.

Suppose that after we start Eudora, we see new e-mail has arrived, and the message summary list appears as shown in Figure D.9.

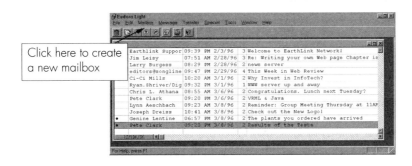

Figure D.9   Message Summary List

We see there are two new messages. In the next step were going to make a mailbox for Pete Clark's messages, and in the meantime, we'll read the new messages first.

2. Create a new mailbox.

We've got two messages from Pete Clark, and we're going to save them into a folder named **pclark**.

wWw   Click on **Mailbox** in the Menu Bar and choose **New ...**

A dialog box pops up where you type the name of the folder, as shown in Figure D.10.

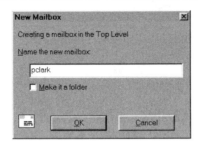

Figure D.10 New Mailbox Dialog Box

Type **pclark** and click on the **OK** button.

A mailbox named **pclark** is created by Eudora. Its name will appear on the list of mailboxes starting with the next time we click on **Mailbox**.

3. Copy two messages to the new mailbox.

Now that the mailbox is created, we can mark two messages from Pete Clark and transfer them into the mailbox named **pclark**.

Click on the entry for the first message from Pete Clark in the message list.

Move the mouse pointer to the second entry from Pete Clark in the message list, press Ctrl, and press the mouse button (left one if your mouse has two buttons).

Figure D.11 shows the messages highlighted.

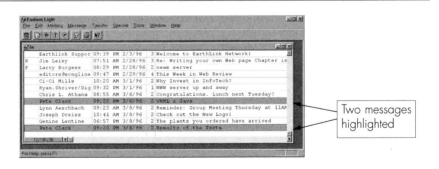

Figure D.11 Messages Highlighted and Ready to Transfer to New Mailbox

Now we're ready to move the messages to the **pclark** mailbox. This will take them out of the **In** mailbox. We can save other messages from Pete, if he ever writes to us again, in the same mailbox.

w⁴ʷ Click on **Transfer** on the Menu Bar.

A menu appears listing the current mailboxes.

w⁴ʷ Click on **pclark**.

The messages will be removed from the mailbox **In** and be transferred to the mailbox **pclark**.

4. Delete three messages.

To demonstrate how to mark a range of messages and delete messages, we'll delete the three oldest messages from the mailbox **In**.

w⁴ʷ Click on the first entry in the message summary list.

w⁴ʷ Move the mouse pointer to the third message but don't click.

w⁴ʷ Press **Shift** on the keyboard and click the (left) mouse button.

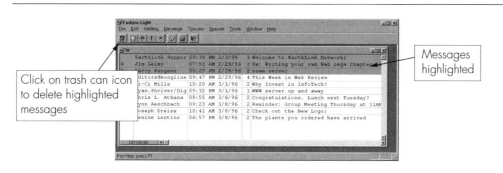

Figure D.12 Range of Messages Highlighted

Figure D.12 shows the messages highlighted. To delete them, we'll click on the icon that looks like a trash can as indicated in Figure D.12.

w⁴ʷ Click on the trash can icon.

This moves them to the mailbox **Trash**. At some point you'll want to delete them from **Trash** as well

5. Exit Eudora.

w⁴ʷ Press **Ctrl**+Q.

———————————————End of Example D.2———————————————

Setting Other Eudora Options

Other Eudora options are set the same way as the options we discussed earlier. Click on the pull-down menu **Tools** and then select **Options...** These options are in the sections **Attachments, Fonts & Display, Getting Attention, Replying, Dialup, Miscellaneous,** and **Advanced Network**. We won't discuss Dialup and Advanced Network here. Dialup isn't used for the type of Internet access discussed in this book and Advanced Network is best left to experts. The Eudora user manual has information on all topics.

Attachments	Here you set the type of encoding, either MIME or BinHex, used for attachments. It's best to choose MIME. Modern e-mail systems use MIME. BinHex is compatible with older Macintosh systems. You also set whether to put text attachments in the body of the message. This is initially set to **off**. In Figure D.8 you saw that attachments were automatically saved in a directory or folder. You set the directory here, and can set an option so attachments are automatically deleted when a message is put into the **Trash** mailbox. You'll probably want to keep attachments when a message is discarded because usually the attachments are more important than the message that carries them.
Fonts & Display	The fonts for screen display and printing are set here along with the default size of rows and columns of the message window. The other options deal with the display including whether to zoom (expand) windows when opening and show all headers, the toolbar, words with the Toolbar, and the status bar, which gives a brief description of menu items and Toolbar icons.
Getting Attention	The settings here deal with what Eudora does when new e-mail arrives. Eudora can open an alert dialog box notifying you that new mail has arrived and giving you the chance to read it, open the mailbox that takes the new mail and display the summary with the newest message last, or play a sound. You can associate any WAV file with the alert sound.
Replying	What should happen when you automatically reply to a message? The options here include replying to everyone the e-mail was addressed to, not only to the sender. If the option is set to **off**, you can generate a reply to everyone who received and sent he message by pressing the Shift key while clicking on the **Reply** icon. Options are also set as to whether to include yourself when a reply is generated—that way you get a copy of each reply—whether to put the addresses in the **To:** field of the original message to the **Cc:** field of the reply, and whether to have the reply keep the priority of the original message.
Miscellaneous	Set an option that determines how to go from one message to another in a summary list if a window displaying a message is open. the default is to use the Alt key with arrow keys, but this can be set to also use only arrow keys. Other options are whether to require a confirmation whenever deleting messages that haven't been read, empty the **Trash** mailbox whenever you leave Eudora (this would help conserve disk space), automatically reply to any alerts after two minutes, and automatically bringing up the next message in the summary list after you've read one.

Composing and Sending E-Mail

You can send a new e-mail message any time you're using Eudora. To send an e-mail message press Ctrl+N, click on **Message** on the Menu Bar and choose **New Message**, or click on the **New Message** icon. In any case a window similar to Figure D.13 will pop up.

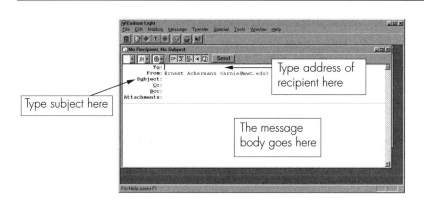

Figure D.13 E-Mail Message Composition Window

The window has places for you to fill in the headers **Send To:** address(es) of primary receivers; **Subject:**, what the message is about (make it brief and descriptive); **Cc:** address(es) where copies of the e-mail will be sent; **Bcc:**, address(es) of where copies will be sent without the recipient being shown those addresses; and **Attachments:**, name(s) of files to attach to the message. You can move from header to header by pressing the Tab key or by clicking on a header with the mouse. Separate multiple address with commas or spaces if you're sending the same e-mail to several people at the **To:**, **Cc:**, or **Bcc:** headers. The boxes across the top are used to set the priority of the message, set whether a signature will be put at the end of the body of the message, set the encoding type (MIME or BinHex) for attachments, use quoted printable for encoding, have the text sent as an attachment, use word wrap, expand tabs in the body, keep a copy of the message, and send the message. To include an file (text or nontext) as an attachment, select **Attach File** from the pull-down menu **Message** or use the keyboard shortcut Ctrl+H. A dialog box pops up that lets you select a file as an attachment. The receiver's e-mail program has to include MIME (Multipurpose Internet Mail Extensions) or BinHex.

There are several options you can use to choose different headers, include files, use an address from the nickname list (address book), and others. They'll be discussed later in this appendix, or you can read about them in the Eudora user guide. To get a message off in a straightforward manner, you need to basically follow these steps:

1. Open the **New Message** Window (Ctrl+N).
2. Fill in the address next to the header **To:**.
3. Fill in the subject next to the header **Subject:**.
4. Compose/type the message body.
5. Send it off by clicking on the icon labeled **Send**.

Figure D.14 shows a message ready to send. It's addressed to several people—the different addresses are separated by commas. The header **Cc:** is used to send a copy of the message to an Internet address. In this case, the message gets sent to four addresses. Three will be listed in the **To:** header and one in the **Cc:** header. There are two attachments. The text in the message body was typed directly into the message using the keyboard. The sections below talk about composing a message and attaching files.

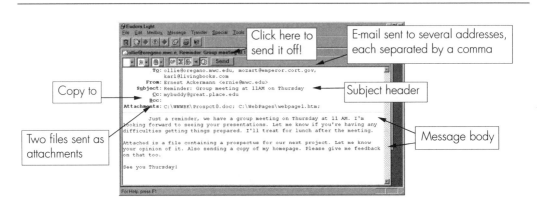

Figure D.14 Composing E-Mail—Complete Message

Composing the Message Body

Type your message into the message body or compose the message using tools or programs with which you're comfortable. You can copy text from another Windows application or Web page. Any text on the clipboard can be pasted into the mail message. To copy/paste between applications, click on **Edit** on the Menu Bar and select the appropriate action. Whether you type your message, include something from another application, or a combination of these, the e-mail program will take care of formatting the text. Type or copy the message and press Enter at the end of a paragraph. You can only send plain text—no underlining, boldface, or italics—in the message body. Anything that's not in plain text format has to be sent as an attachment.

The contents of your signature file are added automatically. To edit or create a signature file click on **Tools** in the Menu Bar and select **Signature**. A window pops up where you type in whatever you'd like to have as your signature; usually your name, postal address, phone number, fax number, and URL of your personal home page.

Including Attachments

Anything that's not in plain text format has to be an attachment if it's sent by e-mail. (Text files can be sent as attachments too.) Select **Attach File** from the pull-down menu **Message** or use the keyboard shortcut Ctrl+H to attach a file to the message. A dialog box pops up from which you select the file to attach or type in its name, and press the button labeled **Open** when you've got the file you want. You can include several files as attachments.

Replying to a Message

You reply to the current message by clicking on the icon for reply (third from the left on version 1.5.4 of Eudora), clicking on **Message** in the Menu Bar and then selecting **Reply** or using the keyboard shortcut Ctrl+R. You reply to the highlighted message or while you're reading a message. Regardless of how you initiate it, a reply a window pops up like the one for a new message, but the **To:**, **From:**, and **Subject:** headers are filled in. The message your replying to is placed in the message with each line preceded by the symbol >. The **Subject:** header will be set to **Re:** followed by the subject of the original message. If the address list in the original one includes several people you can send a reply to everyone on **To:** or **Cc:** list by pressing the Shift key when you initiate the reply. It's your choice; just be sure you don't send something to a group that you'd like to send to an individual. In many situations, it's a good idea to include at least a portion of the original message so your reply can be read in context. This is particularly true if you're replying to a message that was sent to a group. Be sure to include only the relevant parts.

Figure D.15 shows what a user would see if he started a reply to everyone who received the e-mail in Figure D.14.

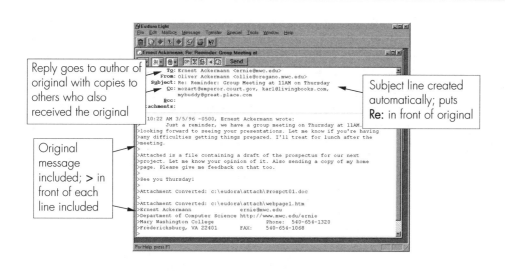

Figure D.15 Reply to All Recipients—Include Original Message

At this point, you type/compose your reply, deleting lines from the original and including your own as you see fit. Use the arrow keys or the mouse to move the cursor to wherever you want to type. Use the mouse to highlight a portion of the text and then the items in the **Edit** menu to copy, cut, or paste portion of the message. When it's complete you can send it off by clicking on the icon labeled **Send.**

Forwarding and Redirecting E-Mail

Forwarding e-mail means passing the e-mail you've received on to another address. You can do this by highlighting one or more entries in the message list and then clicking on the **Forward** icon (the fourth from the left in version 1.5.2 of Eudora) or clicking on **Message** in the Menu Bar and then selecting **Forward**. When you forward a message, the address in the **From:** header is replaced with yours. Redirecting also means passing e-mail along, but the address in the **From:** header isn't changed. The person who receives the message can reply to the original sender. To redirect a message, click on the **Redirect** icon (fifth from the left in version 1.5.2 of Eudora) or click on **Message** in the Menu Bar and select **Redirect**.

When you select messages to be forwarded or redirected, a message composition window pops up like the ones we've seen before. If the e-mail is forwarded, then each line is preceded with the character > just as when you're sending a reply. If the message is to be redirected, then the message appears without any changes. You need to fill in the **To:** header. The message can be edited or attachments added. Click on the button labeled **Send** to send it off.

Working With the Nickname List (Address Book)

Eudora includes an address book called the Nickname List that's an integrated part of the e-mail program. You can add addresses by typing them in or having the program take them directly from a message. You give each address a nickname so you can use it when you're composing or replying to a message. When you're using the New Message window or the similar ones for replying, forwarding, or redirecting a message clicking on the **Nickname** icon (the one that looks like a collection of index cards—the second from the right in version 1.5.2 of Eudora) opens a copy of the Nickname List so you can select an address for the **To:**, **Cc:**, or **Bcc:** header. Furthermore, several addresses can be grouped together so you can send e-mail to all members of a group or organization. It's a good idea to keep frequently used addresses in the Nickname List. That way you don't have to remember people's addresses. Also, you won't have to save messages just because you need an address.

Adding Nicknames. There are essentially two ways to add a nickname and address to the Nickname List. One is to take it from the current message, and the other is to add it by typing it into the Nickname List.

To take an address from the current (highlighted) message click on **Special** on the Menu Bar and then choose **Make nickname..** or use the keyboard shortcut Ctrl+K. A dialog box pops up and you fill in the nickname you want to give to the address. Eudora fills in the e-mail address and name from the appropriate headers in the message. You can add a description or other information to the entry in the address book by clicking on **Tools** from the Menu Bar and then selecting **Nicknames..** or using the keyboard shortcut Ctrl+L. Figure D.16 shows a filled in entry for a nickname.

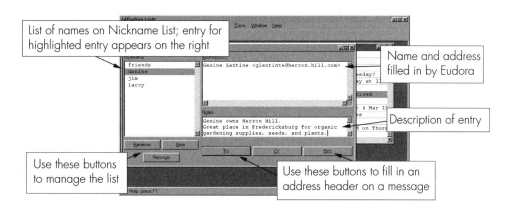

List of names on Nickname List; entry for highlighted entry appears on the right

Name and address filled in by Eudora

Description of entry

Use these buttons to manage the list

Use these buttons to fill in an address header on a message

Figure D.16 Completed Entry in Nickname List

To add an address manually, click on **Tools** on the Menu Bar and select **Nicknames...** or use the keyboard shortcut Ctrl+L. Once the Nickname List is open, click on the button labeled **New** and fill in a nickname. Then click on the pane labeled **Address(es)** and type in the e-mail address(es). Fill in the pane labeled **Notes** to include any other information you'd like about the nickname. These notes aren't sent along with an outgoing message. This is shown in Figure D.16 above.

After you've added the necessary information, close the window. You'll be asked if you want to save changes to the Nickname List. Click on the button labeled **Yes** to save it in the address book. You can change the information for an entry any time by opening the Nickname List, clicking once on the entry in the list, and then changing the information you'd like

Working with a Distribution List or Group Address. You can also create a distribution list, a list of addresses associated with a single nickname. That lets you send one e-mail message to a group. It's particularly useful if you regularly need to send or share e-mail with several people. To create a distribution list, first go to the Nickname List (click on **Tools** on the Menu Bar and select **Nicknames..**), click on the button labeled **New**, type in the nickname, and then fill in addresses in the pane labeled **Address(es)**. Once they're added, a nickname for a group doesn't appear any differently in the list of nicknames than a nickname for an individual. You can add a previously defined nickname to a group nickname.

Deleting Nicknames. Nicknames can be deleted from the Nickname List by first opening the **Nickname List**, then highlighting a nickname(click on it once), and finally clicking on the button labeled **Remove**. To remove an individual address from a group nickname, highlight the group nickname, highlight the address from the list of addresses for that group, and press the Delete key twice. Deleting one that's part of a list removes only that copy of it. Deleting a name from the list of individuals doesn't remove it if it's used in a group nickname. You'll have to take care of that separately.

Using Addresses. You use the nickname you've assigned to an address when you want to use an address for sending, replying to, or forwarding e-mail. Suppose, for example, we want to send e-mail and use the nickname Genine which we've added to the Nickname List as shown in Figure D.16. To send e-mail to this address, just type **Genine** in the **To:** or **Cc:** field of a message you're composing. The address will be looked up in the address book; fill in the Internet e-mail address(es) associated with the nickname. Nicknames are useful with names you'll be using frequently. But you don't have to remember them. Whenever you're composing a message, click on the icon that represents the Nickname List to have it displayed on the screen.

Summary

Eudora is a popular e-mail program. It's fully-featured, easy to use, and a version of it, Eudora Light, is distributed as freeware. It's also relatively easy to install. Once it is installed, you can set the appropriate options so you can begin using it to send, receive, and manage e-mail. Eudora works well with e-mail attachments that are encoded in MIME or BinHex. Messages are received and managed through mailboxes. Incoming e-mail goes into the **In** mailbox. Deleted e-mail goes into the **Trash** mailbox. You can create other mailboxes to manage your e-mail. Commands are entered using pull-down menus from the Menu Bar, clicking on icons in the Toolbar, or using keyboard shortcuts. You read e-mail that you receive by double-clicking on the summary that appears in a list of messages within a mailbox. You can send a new message, reply to an existing message, forward a message, or redirect a message to another Internet e-mail address. Eudora also lets you keep a nickname list or address book for frequently used or important addresses.

Java:
Applets and Scripts

Java—the programming language, Java Applets—programs that come from a Web server and execute as part of a Web page, and JavaScript—programs that are a part of a Web page are significant innovations. Scripts or applets written using Java are used as part of a Web page so that the Web pages become dynamic, including animations, sounds, and interactive programs. Most importantly, the instructions for programs (the applets and scripts) can be passed over the Internet as part of a Web page. This means that programs can be used, executed without having to have the source code or the instructions previously existing on a computer. The programs become part of the World Wide Web. Java allows for truly interactive Web pages and the distribution of information and programs for working with the World Wide Web.

In this appendix we'll discuss just a few of the details of writing programs or scripts using Java. We'll focus on using applets and scripts. Java and Java Script are programming languages that are designed to used in a straightforward manner, but they are not simple. Java is an object-oriented language, considerably less complex than C++. If you're familiar with computer programming and C++, you'll be able to get comfortable with Java in a relatively short amount of time. (There are several excellent tutorials available on the World Wide Web.) If you haven't done much computer programming, you'll need to devote a good deal of effort and time to get comfortable with programming using Java and JavaScripts. This book isn't one that teaches how to write programs, and it would take several chapters to go into the language in appropriate detail. Here we'll include some examples of Java programs, applets and scripts, and go into enough detail to explain them. Whether you're a programmer or not, it's a good idea to take some time to learn a little about Java and why it's important. You'll also want to get an understanding of using Java Applets and JavaScripts in a Web page.

Why Java is Important

Programs written using Java can be distributed on the World Wide Web and executed on several different types of computers. Java is a programming language; it's used to write instructions that can be (eventually) executed by a computer. The statements of the language have a specific format designed so humans can write and read the programs. Computers don't deal with instructions in that form, so before a computer can execute instructions, a translator is necessary. The translator converts the instructions from the Java format to one that a computer can interpret or understand. The translator is called a Java compiler, and produces code in a format called *byte codes*. This means the codes are sequences of bytes, 8 bits—1s or 0s. What's interesting is that these byte codes can be executed on (almost) any computer. That's very important because programs can be developed, and the executable code can be distributed and used by anyone with a program to interpret the code. The term for this is *architecture-neutral*. The programs could be written on one type of computer, a Windows 95 system, compiled on that system, and then anyone with the same or other type of system could execute the instructions. Also, if a Web browser includes the capabilities to interpret code produced by a Java compiler, then the executable programs could become part of Web pages. So Web pages can include small programs or applications, called applets, that do things like provide animations, play sounds, display videos, and perhaps most importantly can interact with the user. Games, spreadsheets, word processors, or almost anything else can be part of Web pages. That's significant because before Java was available, Web pages could be used only to provide information to or collect information (though the use of forms) from users. Now the pages can in fact be used to distribute computing power form a server to a client. The applications are sent by the server to the Web browser, but running the applications and operations on the input from a user can take place on the client system and then collected (if necessary) by the Web server.

Overview of Java, Java Applets, and JavaScript

Java was developed by Sun Microsystems, and the URL for the Java home page is **http://java.sun.com**. Some of the terms used to describe the programming language Java are object-oriented, multi-threaded, architecture-neutral, robust, secure, and high-performance. (Don't worry if those aren't familiar terms.) Since its object oriented, it has classes of objects with certain properties. Tool kits or packages can be constructed to be used in a variety of environments. Its those capabilities combined with the fact that Java was designed to be used in a networked environment, that makes it work so well as part of Netscape and other Web browsers. Using a class called applet and a tool kit called the abstract windows tool kit, takes care of many of the details of making a Java program part of a Web page.

A **Java Applet** is a Java program that's constructed using the class applet and the abstract windows tool kit. An applet is included in a Web page using the HTML tags <**Applet ..specifics about an individual applet**> </**Applet**>. The programs are first written in Java, compiled or translated to byte codes using a Java compiler, and when a Web browser retrieves a page with the Applet tag, the byte codes are sent to the computer viewing the Web page to be executed there. Netscape provides an introduction to Java applets at **http:// www.netscape.com/comprod/products/navigator/version_2.0/java_applets/index.html**.

Netscape Navigator, starting with version 2.0, includes an interpreter (part of the browser software) that will interpret and execute instructions written in a language called **JavaScript**. These instructions are part of the Web page and are translated or interpreted by the browser on the client system. They aren't compiled first, as is the case of Java programs. JavaScript includes several of the features of Java but is meant to be easier to use and develop applications. It includes relatively easy ways, for example, to write instructions that respond to mouse clicks or other mouse movements. A script could collect and verify input from a user before passing it back to a server or an applet. JavaScript has classes and methods developed with Java that are pertinent to developing interactive applications as part of Web pages. Netscape provides a good introduction to and all the details for JavaScript at **http://home.netscape.com/eng/mozilla/3.0/handbook/ javascript/index.html**.

Not every browser or computer can work with Java applets or JavaScript. Netscape Navigator includes the software necessary to interpret the byte codes from the applets and JavaScript on many types of computers.

Before we go on, here's a summary of Java, Java Applets, and JavaScript and how they're used:

Java   Programs are written in Java and then translated to byte codes by a Java compiler. The byte codes are architecture-neutral in the sense that they can be executed on any computer that has a Java interpreter. The interpreter is part of the software making up Navigator. A compiled Java program (byte codes) can be transferred from a server to a client through a Web browser, and the program is then executed on the client's computer. Since Java is an object-oriented language, its features and capabilities make Java a modern, useful, and high-performance language.

Java Applet   An applet is compiled or translated into byte codes and made available to a Web browser through the use of the <**APPLET ..**> tag in HTML. The code is downloaded from its source location by the browser. After the code arrives, it is interpreted by the computer using the browser and the client, and it executes there. In order to include an Java applet on a Web page, you either have the applet in the same directory as the Web page or include a URL to the directory that holds the applet.

JavaScript   A script can appear to be very much like a program, but the script is part of a Web page. It isn't translated first like a Java program. The script is part of the source for the Web page.

Using Applets and Scripts

Using JavaScript or Java Applets (and thus Java) makes it possible to create Web pages that contain interactive elements or items that involve executing a sequence of instructions such as an animation or scrolling marquee.

In this section we'll show how JavaScript and Java Applets are used in Web pages. We'll give a few examples and some resources for collections of applets and scripts to examine. Later, we'll go through some detailed examples of the Java language source code for the Java applets we discuss here.

Using Applets

Sun Microsystems, the developers of Java, maintains the primary Web page for information about the language, **http://java.sun.com**, and a collection of applets, **http://java.sun.com/applets/applets.html**. The largest collection of applets (over 1000 when this was written) is maintained by EarthWeb's Gamelan at **http://www.gamelan.com**. Figure E.1 shows a portion of Gamelan's home page that includes a directory to Java Applets.

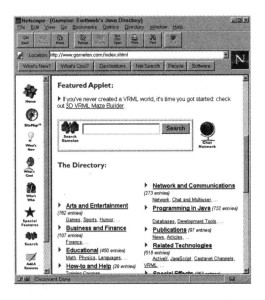

Figure E.1   Directory of Applets at www.gamelan.com

Take some time to explore the sources of applets. There's a pointer to the Java source for each applet and following those links is a good way to learn how to write applets.

We'll show examples of using applets on a Web page by taking a look at "Java Applet and JavaScript Demo" (**http://www.mwc.edu/ernie/java/wwwdemo.html**) shown in Figure E.2. Take a look at the Web page using your browser to see the scrolling marquees.

There are two applets and one JavaScript on the Web page. Here we'll concentrate on the applets. Both applets produce a scrolling marquee. Each has text that continuously scrolls from right to left. That sort of movement is possible only because the applets are executing instructions; they're Java programs. In the first, the scrolling text is built in as part of the program. The second applet allows the person putting the applet on a Web page to specify the text. Take a look at the source for the Web page by clicking on **View** on the Menu Bar and then **Document Source**. Figure E.3 holds a portion of the Web page source for the two applets on the page.

Figure E.2   Java Applet and JavaScript Demo—http://www.mwc.edu/ernie/java/wwwdemo.html

```html
<html>
<head>
<title>Java Applet and JavaScript Demo</title>
</head>

<body bgcolor="#BBBBBB" link="#FFFFFF" vlink="#FFFFFF" >
<center>

<h2>The Java Applet 'Marquee'</h2>
<h4><i>The string is specified in the Java code.</i></h4>
<!-- The APPLET tag is used to insert a Java program into your document.
     'Codebase' specifies the location of the Java program, 'code'
     specifies the name of the Java program, width and height set the
     dimensions of the applet, in pixels.  -->

        <APPLETcodebase = "http://www.mwc.edu/ernie/java/"
                code = Marquee.class
                width = 400 height = 20 >
        </APPLET>
<br>
<a href="http://www.mwc.edu/ernie/java/Marquee.html">The source.</a>
```

> HTML to use the applet **Marquee.class** on any Web page

```
<hr>

<h2>The Java Applet 'Marquee2'</h2>
<h4><i>The string is read in as a parameter in the HTML code.</i></h4>
<!-- In the following APPLET tag, we see a PARAM tag.  This tag is used
     to define parameters to be read in by the Java program using the
     getParameter() method.  This can be seen in the code for
     Marquee2.java -->

<APPLET codebase = "http://www.mwc.edu/ernie/java/"
        code    = Marquee2.class
        width   = 400
        height  = 20 >
        <PARAM Name="text" Value="I was read in using a PARAM tag placed
        within the APPLET tag!" >
</APPLET>
<br>
<a href="http://www.mwc.edu/ernie/java/Marquee2.html">The source.</a>
<hr>
```

> HTML to use the Java applet **Marquee2.class**; note the use of **PARAM**

Figure E.3   HTML used to incorporate the Java applets Marquee.class and Marquee2.class

Each of the applets in Figure E.3 originally came from Java programs, **Marquee.java** and **Marquee2.java**. The programs were translated to byte codes using a Java compiler to produce the files **Marquee.class** and **Marquee2.class**. The files are actually on the computer whose Internet name is **www.mwc.edu** and they are in the directory the servers refers to as **/ernie/Java**. When a Web browser retrieves the page, the byte codes are copied to the client and executed on the computer that's being used to view the page. (By the way, the code is checked to make sure it doesn't do anything unseemly like erase files from the client's disks.)

The HTML tag, **APPLET**, for an applet contains a number of attributes. We'll go over attributes one by one by looking at the code line-by-line.

```
<APPLET       codebase = "http://www.mwc.edu/ernie/java/"
```

This is the beginning of the **APPLET** HTML tag. **codebase** is the attribute used to give the name of the directory that holds the code for the applet. Without **codebase**, the byte codes for the applet are expected to be in the same directory as the Web page.

```
        code = Marquee.class
```

code is the attribute used to specify the name of the file holding the byte codes.

```
        width = 400 height = 20 >
```

width and **height** are attributes that give the size, in pixels, of the portion of the screen that's taken up by the applet. In this case, the applet takes up a space 400 by 20 pixels.

```
</APPLET>
```

This HTML tag ends the specification for the applet.

To summarize: The applet (byte codes) is in the file **Marquee.class** in the directory specified by **http://www.mwc.edu/ernie/java**. The applet takes up a space 400 by 20 pixels on the Web page.

The HTML for the second tag shown in Figure E.3 is similar: **codebase** is the same, the code is in **Marquee2.class**, and the size is the same. This applet was written to take some input from the HTML source for the Web page. That's specified using the tag

```
<PARAM Name="text" Value="I was read in using a PARAM tag placed
within the APPLET tag!" >
```

The name of the variable associated with the input variable **text** and text is given the value following **"Value="**.

You could use either marquee applet on a Web page. (The author hereby gives permission. Be sure you have permission before using someone else's applet without modification.) If you wanted a Web page that had a scrolling marquee with the text **I feel Good!** in a space 450 by 50 pixels you'd use

```
APPLET codebase = "http://www.mwc.edu/ernie/java/"
        code    = Marquee2.class
        width   = 450
        height  = 50 >
        <PARAM Name="text" Value="I feel Good!">
</APPLET>
```

Try it! You'll see the space the marquee applet takes up is a little larger than on **http://www.mwc.edu/ernie/java/wwwdemo.html**, but the scrolling letters aren't any bigger. That's because the size of the letters is specified in the program and not taken as input form the use of the applet.

To know about the possible input to the applet is to read instructions about the applet, read the Java source of the program, or look at the way the applet is already being used on a Web page to see what input variables appear in the HTML tags <**PARAM Name="**..." **Value =**" ...">.

The applets shown here can be used on any Web page since the attribute codebase was set. If **codebase** weren't set, and you had the author's permission to use the applet in one of your Web pages, you could guess at the proper value by knowing the URL for the Web page. Looking at examples of applets at **java.sun.com** you come across the one titled Blinking Text at **http://java.sun.com/applets/applets/Blink/example1.html**. Looking at its HTML source you see

```
<title>Blinking Text</title>
<hr>
<applet code="Blink.class" width=300 height=100>
<param name=lbl value="This is the next best thing to sliced bread! Toast,
toast, toast, butter, jam, toast, marmite, toast.">
<param name=speed value="4">
```

```
</applet>
<hr>
<a href="Blink.java">The source.</a>
```

No value for **codebase**! If you wanted to use the applet (and it was legal to do so), you might guess that this applet would work on any Web page with

```
codebase="http://java.sun.com/applets/applets/Blink/"
```

since the URL for the Web page was **http://java.sun.com/applets/applets/Blink/example1.html** which means **http://java.sun.com/applets/applets/Blink** would take you to the directory holding the applet. Many examples of applets have hyperlinks to the Java source for the program. Retrieve some programs and study the Java source code. After studying some programs, you might be ready to write your own.

Using JavaScript

JavaScript is a language similar to Java. It's designed to be used by people who don't need to use all the rich features of Java, but want to create interactive Web pages that take advantage of some of Java's capabilities. JavaScript has a number of built-in objects and functions that make it relatively easy to work with forms, verify input data, and handle certain events such as the occurrence of a mouse click or other movements of the mouse.

We won't go into many details of the language, but we'll give you enough to get started. If you want to continue to learn JavaScript you'll want to look at some JavaScript tutorials on the World Wide Web, such as "JavaScript-Intro by Voodoo" (**http://www.webconn.com/java/javascript/intro/**) and "JavaScript Authoring Guide" (**http://home.netscape.com/eng/mozilla/3.0/handbook/javascript/index.html**).

We'll look at two examples of Web pages that use elements written in JavaScript. The first is "Java Applet and JavaScript Demo" (**http://www.mwc.edu/ernie/java/wwwdemo.html**) shown in Figure E.2. It's the three buttons on the page labeled **Blue, Red, Green**, which incorporate the use of JavaScript. Here's the pertinent portion of the source for that Web page:

```
We can use JavaScript to allow your http client to change the background
color of this page.
<br>

Click the color of your choice.
<br>

<!-- For JavaScript, we use HTML's FORM tag to 'surround' areas of the
     document that will accept user input.  Here, we define three
     buttons using the TYPE field; the VALUE field is used to specify
     the text that will appear on the button.  'onClick' is a JavaScript
     'event handler' that will perform the action in quotes when the
```

```
button is clicked.  Here, the buttons change the background color
of the page to red, green, or blue.  (The color values are in
hexadecimal, following the pattern 'RRGGBB.')  -->

<FORM>
<INPUT TYPE="button" VALUE="Blue" onClick="document.bgColor='0000FF'">
<INPUT TYPE="button" VALUE="Red" onClick="document.bgColor='FF0000'">
<INPUT TYPE="button" VALUE="Green" onClick="document.bgColor='00FF00'">
</FORM>
```

Figure E.4   HTML Source Using JavaScript from http://www.mwc.edu/ernie/java/ wwwdemo.html

Most of the details are given in the HTML source. JavaScript includes some event handlers, code that senses the motion or click of the mouse. That event handler is used here to change the background color of the Web page. **Document.bgcolor** is an object within JavaScript that specifies the background color of the Web page being viewed by Netscape Navigator. (Take a look at "Navigator Objects" (**http:// home.netscape.com/eng/mozilla/3.0/handbook/javascript/navobj.html**) for more information about these types of objects.) The HTML tag <**FORM**> is used to set up the buttons. When one is clicked on with the mouse, the event handler portion of JavaScript senses or "catches" the action or event, and the background color of the page is changed.

Here's another example of using JavaScript. We'll look at the Web page first. (Why don't you take a look at it on the WWW? The URL is **http://www.mwc.edu/ernie/java/JSquick.html**.)

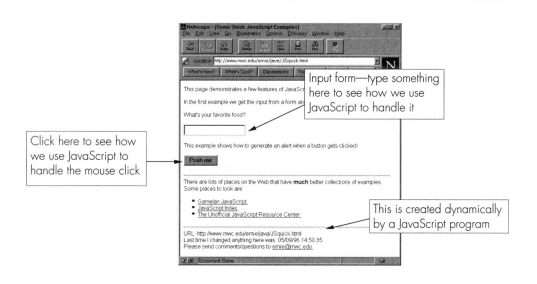

Figure E.5   Web Page "Some Quick JavaScript Examples," http://www.mwc.edu/ernie/java/ JSquick.html

Several features of JavaScript language are used. In the first two we again use JavaScript's event handler capabilities to deal with forms or clicking on a button. While it's not done here, you can imagine that it would be possible to write a JavaScript program to verify the input into a form, before sending it on to a server. Here's the portion of the source from the Web page of Figure E.5 that deals with the first two items.

```
<head>
<title> Some Quick JavaScript Examples </title>

<!--    Define any JavaScript functions in the <Head> section ">
<script language="JavaScript">
function getname(str) {
    alert("There's some ""+ str+" waiting for you in the kitchen.")
  }
function pushbutton() {
alert("Wouldn't a cup of Java be good now?");
  }
</script>

</head>

<body>
This page demonstrates a few features of JavaScript.
<p>
In the first example we get the input from a form and display it.
<p>
<!-- Here's where the functions are used -->
What's your favorite food?
<form>
  <input type="text" name="your Favorite Food?" onBlur="getname(this.value)"
value="">
</form>

This example shows how to generate an alert when a button gets clicked!

<form>
  <input type="button" name="Button1" value="Push me" onclick="pushbutton()">
</form>
```

Two functions—**getname(str)** and **pushbutton()**—are defined in the heading section

getname used here

pushbutton used here

Figure E.6   Excerpt from Source for http://www.mwc.edu/ernie/java/JSquick.html Showing How JavaScript Functions and Its Use

Figure E.6 shows how the input to the forms is handled by some features of JavaScript. The HTML tag <script language="JavaScript"> notifies the browser that what follows, up to the tag </script>, is interpreted as JavaScript.

First, we define some functions that will be accessed in the Web page. The functions are best defined in the heading section so they can be referenced through any statements in the body section of the page. Defining a function is straightforward. You use the keyword function followed by the name of the function and list of parameters that can be passed to the function. For the first one, we have

```
function getname(str) {
```

It takes one parameter, a string of characters. The second function takes no parameters passed to it.

The functions are called or used within the two <FORM> HTML tags. getname is used to treat the input to the first one. It's accessed when the event onBlur occurs. That takes place after an entry is made in the box and the user either clicks the mouse or presses Enter. An alert box is displayed. The second form has a button and the function pushbutton is called when the mouse clicks on the button because of the presence of onclick="pushbutton()".

The information on the last part of the page—the URL for the page and the date last modified—are created automatically by means of the JavaScript program shown in Figure E.7.

```
<!-- This is a short JavaScript program that write the date the page was
last modified. Sure beats having to do it manually each time the
 page is changed. -->

<SCRIPT LANGUAGE="JavaScript">
    var theDate = ""
    theDate = document.lastModified
    thePlace = window.location
    document.write("<hr>");
    document.write("URL: ");
    document.write(thePlace,"<br>");
    document.write("Last time I changed anything here was:");
    document.write(theDate,"<br>");
    document.write("Please send comments/questions to ");
    document.write("<a href=\"mailto:ernie@mwc.edu\">ernie@mwc.edu");
    document.write();
</SCRIPT>
```

Figure E.7   Excerpt from Source for http://www.mwc.edu/ernie/java/JSquick.html Showing How JavaScript Program Accesses Navigator Objects

The program starts with the tag <**SCRIPT LANGUAGE="Java Script"**>, notifying the browser to interpret the following statements as part of a JavaScript program. Two Navigator objects are used. One for the URL of the current page, **window.location**, and the other for the date the page was last modified, **document.lastModified**. From there on, we use the method document to create HTML statements that become part of the Web page.

We use \" in the statement

```
document.write("<a href=\"mailto:ernie@mwc.edu\">ernie@mwc.edu");
```

because a " is used to mark the start or end of a string in **document.write**, but it's also needed so we can get <**a href="mailto:ernie@mwc.edu"**> as part of the Web page. The two occurrences of \" let the " be written to the Web page.

Be sure to follow the hyperlinks on the Web page **http://www.mwc.edu/ernie/java/JSquick.html** to find lots of good examples of the use of JavaScript.

Writing Java Applets

Java Applets are programs intended to be used on Web pages and are written using the Java programming language. In this section we'll briefly describe the language Java, describe how to obtain a Java compiler and accompanying software that's needed to develop Java applets, and discuss the applets used in the Web page shown in Figure E.2 and it's source in Figure E.3.

Brief Description of Java

The Java language was developed by Sun Microsystems. It's object-oriented, interpreted, architecture-neutral, multi-threaded, and secure. Object-oriented means that the a programmer can focus on the design of a program rather than the tools to construct it. The elements of a Java program are objects or classes which contain properties and methods (functions) for manipulating the objects. One class is the applet class which specifies several methods that can be used to present and manipulate applet objects. The language is interpreted. A programmer writes a program in the Java language and uses a Java compiler to translate the instructions into byte codes. These byte codes may be passed from one computer to another on the Internet. If the receiving computer has a Java interpreter, the byte codes are interpreted into instructions that can be executed one at a time. The two computers don't have to have the same types of processors because the byte codes don't depend on the processor or architecture (architecture neutral). Programs can be written and compiled on a computer that uses a particular version of a Unix operating system, for example, and the byte codes can be interpreted on a computer that uses the Windows 95 operating system. This allows for easy distribution of executable, interpreted programs. Multi-threaded means that several activities, such as animations can take place at the same time as someone is scrolling through a window, entering data, or selecting items on a Web page. The language is secure in the sense that it is designed to not allow Java code to be modified and carry viruses. Also, Java applets cannot contain code that modifies files on a computer.

There are several complete descriptions of the language available on the World Wide Web. Some of these are "The Java(TM) Language Environment: A White Paper" (**http://www.javasoft.com:80/doc/**

language_environment/) "The Java(TM) Language—An Overview" (**http://www.javasoft.com/doc/Overviews/java/index.html**), and "The Java Tutorial" (**http://java.sun.com/tutorial/**).

The Java language system is distributed as the Java Developer's Kit (JDK). It has everything you need to write and compile applets. It also contains several demonstration applets. The JDK, along with installation instructions, is available from Sun through the URL **http://www.javasoft.com/products/JDK/1.0.2/index.html**. A detailed set of instructions for installing the JDK on a Windows 95 computer system, written by Phil Filner, is available through the URL **http://www.bcpl.lib.md.us/~pfilner/jdkhowto.html**.

In brief, you need to follow these steps:
1. Set certain system or environment variables including PATH to be sure you can invoke the Java compiler from any directory.
2. Create a folder to hold your Java programs, for example, **html**.
3. Use Netscape to Download the JDK archive from Sun. (The URL for the Windows 95 version is **ftp://ftp.javasoft.com/pub/JDK-1_0_2-win32-x86.exe**.)
4. Move the archive to the root directory and unpack it. This creates a directory/folder named **java** which includes folders named **bin**, **demo**, **include**, and **lib**. A file named **src.zip** may be present, and you can unpack that if you'd like. The directory lib contains a file named **classes.zip**. Do not unzip or unpack this. It contains the classes you use to write applets and should not be modified.

Once you have the Java Developers Kit you're ready to develop, write, and test Java programs and applets. The process proceeds in these steps.
1. Work in the folder or directory that will hold your applets.
2. Using any editor or word processor that can save files in text or ASCII format write a program and save it in a file whose name ends with **.java**, for example, **num1.java**.
3. Working in an MS_DOS window compiler the program using the command **javac num1.java**
4. You'll be notified on the screen if there are syntax or other errors. When there are no errors the compiler creates a file named **num1.class**. That's the file that contains the byte codes.
5. Create a Web page that holds the applet, for, example **num1.html**.
6. View the applet using a Web browser or the command **appletviewer num1.html**.

Remember that the applet needs to be in the same directory as the Web page, or you need to specify the codebase attribute.

Example Applet Programs

We'll take a look at the example applet programs in the Web page **http://www.mwc.edu/ernie/java/wwwdemo.html** shown in Figures 7.2 and 7.3. The Java source code for each is available from the Web page. The first program, **Marquee.java**, is shown in Figure E.8 below. The programs contain lots of documentation, comments written between /* and */, to explain the programs. We'll give a brief overview of the program and include some annotations in the listing in Figure E.8.

The program begins by importing two classes that are necessary for this type of Java applet. The class **java.applet.*** is needed for all applets, and **java.awt.*** is the abstract windows tool kit that allows for such things as scrolling and managing windows. A class **Marquee** is declared to be an extension of the applet class. That means we can define specific methods and objects for **Marquee** and it inherits (has available to it) all the methods and objects for the **Applet** class. We need to include **implements Runnable** since we'll be using a thread to actually display and scroll the text in the marquee on the Web page. The function or method **init** is then defined. When it's called, it will set the size of the applet's window, the background color (white), the position and width of the message, and it calls the function **run** to begin scrolling the text. The method **paint** is used to update the screen. The final method, **run**, in the class continuously scrolls the text in the window.

```
/* import the java.applet class (necessary for all applets) */
import java.applet.*;
/* import the java.awt (Abstract Windows Tool kit) classes */
import java.awt.*;


/* declare a class Marquee that can use all variables and functions
   from the Applet class.  The Runnable interface is needed to
   provide functions that will allow for the execution of the
   applet; the Runnable function used here is run(). */
```

The class **Marquee**, declared here, includes all methods and objects from the **Applet** class

```
public class Marquee extends Applet implements Runnable {

/* define a Thread, t.  Think of a Thread as a process; it can be
   started and stopped as necessary within the code. */
   Thread t;
```

The message in the scrolling marquee can't be modified because it's hard-wired as part of the program

```
/* define a String, msg, to hold the text we wish to scroll */
   String msg = "Welcome to the Wonderful World of JAVA!";

/* define an integer, msgWidth, to hold the length of the string in pixels. */
   int msgWidth;

/* define an integer, pos, to hold the current X position of the text. */
   int pos;

/* define an integer, yLoc, to hold the Y position of the text. */
   int yLoc = 15;

/* init is the first function called in a Java applet. */
```

init is automatically called when the applet starts; here is where the size of the window, background color, and other properties are set—**init** finishes by calling **start**, which in turn calls **run**

```
public void init()
  {
/* resize the applet window to 400x20 */
   resize(400, 20);


/* set the Background color of the applet to white in the form
   (Red, Green, Blue) with integer values ranging from 0-255. */
   setBackground(new Color(255, 255, 255));


/* use the getFontMetrics function to get the width of the string, in pixels. */
   msgWidth = getFontMetrics(getFont()).stringWidth(msg);


/* set the initial position of the text to the right side of the applet window. */
   pos = size().width;


/* set t to be a new Thread within 'this,' the Marquee class. */
   t = new Thread(this);


/* start the thread.  This calls the run() function. */
   t.start();
  }


/* the paint function is called whenever the window needs to be updated; the
repaint() statement also calls this function.  Here, we use it to draw the msg
string at the coordinates specified by the pos and yLoc variables. */
public void paint(Graphics g)
  {
   g.drawString(msg, pos, yLoc);
  }


/* t.start() calls the run() function.  Here, the while loop
   will iterate continuously; each iteration will repaint the
   applet (drawing the string five pixels to the left of its
   previous location), and pause for 100 milliseconds.  If the
   complete string has scrolled off to the left side of the applet
   window (pos <= -msgWidth), reposition the string to the
   right side of the applet window. */
```

```
public void run()
  {
    while(true)
    {
      repaint();
      pos -= 5;
      try
      {
        t.sleep(100);
      }
      catch(Exception e)
      {
      }
      if (pos <= -msgWidth)
      {
        pos = size().width;
      }
    }
  }
}
```

> This loop continues until the window is closed or we go on to another Web page, always scrolling the text set above

Figure E.8   Java Source Program Marquee.java

The second program, **Marquee2.java**, is similar to the first except that the text for the scrolling marquee is specified on the Web page rather than in the Java program. The statement that sets this up in **Marquee2.java** is

```
msg = getParameter("text");
```

appearing in the method **init**. The corresponding statement in **Marquee.java** is noted in Figure E.8.

The programs need to be compiled using the commands

```
javac Marquee.java
javac Marquee2.java
```

These commands produce the files Marquee.class and Marquee2.class. They can then be included as applets in a Web page as shown in Figure E.3 above.

Information, Tutorials, and Examples on the WWW

As you'd expect, there are several sources of information about Java, Java Applets, and JavaScript on the World Wide Web. Several have been mentioned previously. Several are listed here for easy reference.

Java Language and Java Applets

Java Home Page
http://java.sun.com

The Java Language Tutorial
http://java.sun.com/tutorial/index.html

Setting Up and Using the Java Developer's Kit
http://www.bcpl.lib.md.us/~pfilner/jdkhowto.html

The Perpetually Unfinished Guides to Java
http://phanouri.bevc.blacksburg.va.us/AWT/JavaTutorial.html

The Java Corner
http://sunsite.berkeley.edu/java-corner/

Gamelan: EarthWeb's Java Directory
http://www.gamelan.com

The World Wide Web Virtual Library:
The Java Programming Language
http://www.acm.org/~ops/java.html

JavaScript

JavaScript—Intro by Voodoo
http://www.webconn.com/java/javascript/intro/

JavaScript Authoring Guide
http://home.netscape.com/eng/mozilla/3.0/handbook/javascript/index.html

The JavaScript Index
http://www.c2.org/~andreww/javascript/

Summary

The Java programming language, Java Applets, and JavaScript are all important developments. They can be used to provide dynamic and interactive elements to Web pages.

Programs written using Java can be distributed on the World Wide Web and executed on several different types of computers. The programs are translated, using a Java compiler, into a format called *byte codes*. The byte codes can be executed on any computer with a Java interpreter, and the same byte codes are produced regardless of the type of computer used to develop the program.

Java was developed by Sun Microsystems. Some of the terms used to describe the programming language are object-oriented, multi-threaded, architecture-neutral, robust, secure, and high-performance. Since its object oriented, it has classes of objects with certain properties. Tool kits or packages can be constructed to be used in a variety of environments. It's those capabilities combined with the fact that Java was designed to be used in a networked environment, that makes it work so well as part of Netscape and other Web browsers. Using a class called applet and a tool kit called the abstract windows tool kit, takes care of many of the details of making a Java program part of a Web page.

A Java applet is included in a Web page using the HTML tags <**Applet ..specifics about an individual applet**> </**Applet**>. The programs are first written in Java, compiled or translated to byte codes using a Java compiler, and when a Web browser retrieves a page with the **Applet** tag, the byte codes are sent to the computer viewing the Web page to be executed there.

Netscape Navigator, starting with version 2.0, includes an interpreter (part of the browser software) that will interpret and execute instructions written in a language called JavaScript. These instructions are part of the Web page and are translated or interpreted by the client. They aren't compiled first, as in the case of Java programs. JavaScript has several of the features of Java but is meant to be easier to use and develop applications. A script could collect and verify input from a user before passing it back to a server or an applet. JavaScript has classes and methods developed with Java that are essential to developing interactive applications as part of Web pages.

There are several excellent collections of examples of applets and JavaScript, tutorials, and other helpful material available on the World Wide Web. Java is important and it's use is becoming widespread. It's worth spending some time learning something about the language and examining some of its uses.

Index

A

Administrative address, 117
Adobe Acrobat, 35
Advanced Research Projects
    Agency (ARPA), 27–28, 303
Andreesen, Marc, 3
Anonymous FTP, 270–283
Archie, 283–287
    priority, 287
    servers, 283, 286–287
Archie client, 283
Archived files, 281
ARPANET, 27–28, 303–304
ASCII files, 211, 275

B

Berne Union, 310
Berners-Lee, Tim, 3
Bina, Eric, 3
BinHex, 281
BITNET, 27
Bookmark list, 10, 34
Bulletin board system (bbs), 133
byte, 275

C

C++, 383
Carnegie Mellon University, 289
CERN, 3
City.Net, 13–18
Civil liberties, 305–311

Berne Union, 310
    copyright, 310–311
    intellectual property, 310–311
    libel, 308–310
    offensive material, 308–310
    Universal Copyright Convention, 310
    unwarranted search and seizure, 307–308
Cleveland Free-Net, 29, 313
Client, 10
Client/server, 23
Commercial activity on the WWW, 316
Common file extensions, 281
Compressed files, 276
CompuServe, 29, 304
Computer Resource Clearing House, 314
Copyrights, 28
Corporation for Public Broadcasting, 313
Crackers, 314

D

Department of Commerce, 314
Department of Defense, 303
Detweiler, L., 316
Deutsch, Peter, 283
Dial-up IP, 26
Direct IP connection, 26
Discussion group, 20, 116
    flame, 116
    lurking, 116
    moderated, 116
    posting, 117
    subscribe, 116

unsubscribe, 117
Discussion lists, 129
Domain names, 24–25, 304
Dot (.), 276

E

E-mail, 10, 20, 21
    etiquette, 88–89
    finding an address, 86–87
    headers, 84–85
    message body, 83
    nontext files, 89–90
    sending, 87–88
    signature, 85
E-mail addresses, 83–84
E-mail privacy, 305–306
EarthWeb's Gamelan, 384
Electronic commerce—payment, publishing,
privacy, 316
Electronic Communications Privacy Act
    (ECPA), 306
Electronic mail, 10
Emtage, Alan, 283
Encryption, 306
EPIC Online Guide to Privacy Resources, 307
Etiquette, 26–27, 128–129
Eudora
    address book, 380–382
    attachments, 376, 378
    checking mail, 365
    closing the window, 371
    composing e-mail, 377–378
    curly quotes, 366
    deleting, 368, 372–376
    e-mail window, 367
    edit, 367
    ending a session, 367
    file, 367
    font and display, 376
    forwarding e-mail, 368, 380
    getting attention, 376
    Help, 366, 368
    hosts, 364
    leave mail on server, 365
    mailbox, 367
    message body, 378
    message, 367
    miscellaneous, 376
    new mail, 366
    new message, 368
    nickname list, 380–382

    nicknames, 368
    options, 363–365, 375
    outgoing mail, 366
    password, 365
    personal information, 364
    printing, 366, 372–376
    quoted-printable, 366
    reading e-mail, 369–371
    redirecting e-mail, 368, 380
    replying, 368, 376, 379
    saving, 372–376
    send on, 365
    sending e-mail, 365–366, 377–378
    signature, 366
    skip big messages, 365
    special, 368
    starting, 362–363
    tabs, 366
    Toolbar, 368
    tools, 368
    transfer, 367
    using, 361–382
    window, 368
    word wrap, 366
European Laboratory for Particle Physics, 3
Excite, 172–177

F

FAQ—International E-mail accessibility, 25
FAQs *see* Frequently Asked Questions
File extension, 276
File Transfer Protocol (FTP), 21, 259, 269–275
    anonymous, 270–275
    URL format, 270
File types, 275
    .arc, 275, 281
    .au, 275, 281
    .avi, 275
    .bmp, 275
    .com, 25
    .edu, 25
    .fli, 275
    .gif, 65, 275, 281
    .gov, 25
    .jpeg, 275
    .jpg, 63, 275, 281
    .lzh, 275, 281
    .mil, 25
    .mov, 275, 281
    .mpg, 275
    .net, 25

.org, 25
.tar, 282
.taz, 282
.text, 275, 282
.tgz, 282
.tif, 275
.tiff, 275
.txt, 212, 275, 281–282
.uue, 282
.wav, 275, 281
.Z, 273, 281
.zip, 275, 282
.zoo, 275
Archie, 283–285
Archie servers, 286–287
compression, 276–277
finding with anonymous FTP, 282–283
Gopher, 287–291
retrieving, 277–281
searches, 285–286
Finer, Phil, 395
Fire wall, 315
Free-Net, 313
Frequently Asked
    Questions (FAQs), 25, 159–160
FTP *see* File Transfer Protocol

G

Galaxy, 186–191
Gateway, 26
GIF, 65
Global Information Infrastructure (GII), 311
Global Network Navigator, 177–180
Gopher, 259
    about, 287
    Carnegie Mellon University, 289
    directories, 289
    finding resources, 289
    Michigan, University of, 289
    Minnesota, University of, 289
    subject trees, 289
    URL format, 289
    using, 287
    Veronica, 291
Graphical User Interface (GUI), 10
Grundner, T.M., 313

H

Heelan, Bill, 283
History list, 34
Home page, 5, 35

HTML, 207
    introduction, 216
    links, 230–234
    tags, 215, 217
Hyperlinks, 9–10, 34–35
Hypermedia, 9–11
Hypertext, 9–11
Hypertext Markup Languages (HTML), 10
Hypertext Transfer Protocol (HTTP), 10
Hytelnet, 264–269
    finding resources, 264–269

I

Identity, privacy, and anonymity
    on the Internet, 316
Illinois, University of, 282
Infoseek Guide, 191–193
Interest group, 19
Internet, 19–29
Internet domain name, 24–25
Internet Protocol (IP), 22
    dynamic, 26
    static, 26
Internet security, 313, 316
InterNIC, 29
IP *see* Internet Protocol

J

Java, 33, 383, 385
    architecture-neutral, 384
    brief description, 394–395
    byte codes, 384
    compiler, 384
    example applet programs, 395–398
    examples on the WWW, 398–400
    importance, 383–384
    information on the WWW, 398–400
    JavaScript, 390–394
    overview, 384–385
    tutorials on the WWW, 398–400
    using applets, 385–390
    using scripts, 385–390
    writing applets, 394–395
Java Applets, 385
Java Developer's Kit (JDK), 395
JavaScript, 33, 384–385, 390–396
    init, 396
    paint, 396
    run, 396
JPEG, 63
Jughead server, 291

L

Lharc, 281
Lists
 archived files, 126
 communicating, 121–123
 digest mode, 125
 etiquette, 128–129
 file retrieval, 126
 finding names and addresses, 127–128
 hiding your name, 124
 joining, 119–121
 leaving, 123
 message suspension, 125
 service requests, 124
 subscriber lists, 124
List address, 117
Listproc, 117
Listserv, 20, 116
Lycos, 194–200

M

Macromedia Director, 35
Mailx
 composing, 341
 deleting, 346
 printing, 346
 reading mail, 340
 replying, 343–345
 saving, 346
 sending, 341
 starting a session, 337–340
 using, 336–346
McGill University, 283
MCImail, 304
Michigan, University of, 289
Milo's public key, 306
Minnesota, University of, 289
Mosaic, 3, 304
Mouse, 36

N–O

Naplayer, 281
National Center for Supercomputer
Applications (NCSA), 3
National Information Infrastructure (NII), 312
National Institute of Standards and
Technology (NIST), 314
National Public Telecommunications
Network (NPTN), 29, 311, 313
Nelson, Ted, 11

Net Directory, 6
Netscape Communications Corporation, 3
Netscape Mail
 address book, 111–113
 composing e-mail 107–109
 deleting messages, 102–105
 forwarding e-mail, 110
 Help, 95
 mail and news preferences, 93–95
 Menu Bar, 96–97
 opening and closing, 95–96
 printing messages, 102
 reading e-mail, 99–101
 replying to messages, 109–110
 saving messages, 101–102
 sending e-mail, 107–109
 setting options, 92–95, 105–107
 Toolbar, 97–98
Netscape Navigator, 4–9
 after loading, 330
 appearance, 330
 bookmark list, 48
 bookmarks, 65–70
 cache, 334
 colors, 330
 content area, 42
 directory bar, 41
 disk cache, 334
 disk cache directory, 334
 document source, 331
 document view, 42
 e-mail, 79–114
 finding text, 43
 fonts, 330
 general Java, 335
 handbook, 36
 Help, 57–59
 helpers, 326
 history list, 47
 images, 328
 link styles, 330
 local files, 65
 location bar, 43
 mail, 333–334
 mail directory, 333
 mail icon, 44
 mailing, 60, 64, 90–114
 maximum memory size, 333
 memory cache, 334
 Menu Bar, 39–41
 network buffer size, 334

network preferences, 334–335
news, 333
News RC directory, 333
number of connections, 334
POP server, 333
preference panels, 329–335
preferences and options, 70–73
printing, 60, 64
Reply-to address, 334
save options, 328
saving, 60, 63
scroll bars, 44, 45
searching a page, 45
security alerts, 335
security preferences, 335
site certificates, 335
status bar, 44
stop icon, 46
temporary directory, 331
thread mail messages, 334
thread news messages, 334
Toolbar, 41–42
using, 50–57
verify documents, 334
while loading, 330
your e-mail, 334
your name, 334
your organization, 334
Netscape News, 139
Nevada (Reno), Univeristy of, 292
News server, 133
Newsgroups, 161
Newsreader, 133, 137
NSFNET, 31, 303–304
Open text, 200–204

P–R

Packet-switched network, 22–23
Packets, 22–23, 305
Peter's PGP Page, 306
Pine
    adding addresses, 357
    address book, 357–359
    composing, 352–354
    deleting addresses, 352, 358
    distribution group, 358
    folders, 356–357
    forwarding, 356
    Help, 350–351
    main menu, 347
    nontext files, 359–360
    reading e-mail, 349–350
    replying, 354–356
    saving, 351
    sending, 352–354
    starting a session, 348
    using, 346–360
PKUNZIP, 276
PKZIP, 276
Point to Point Protocol (PPP), 24
Pretty Good Privacy (PGP), 306, 307
Protocols, 10, 259
Real Audio Player, 35
Router, 24

S

Search engines, 165
Searches
    exact match, 285
    regular expression, 285
    subcase match, 285
    substring match, 285
Server, 10
Signatures, 159
Sound file, 35
Sun Microsystems, 383, 384
Swedish University Network, 276

T

Telnet, 20, 259–264
    configuring your browser, 261–264
    protocols, 259
    URL form, 261
    when to use, 260
Text files, 211
Threads, 136
Top-level domains, 25
Transmission Control Protocol (TCP), 22
Trojan horse, 315

U–V

Uniform Resource Locator (URL), 10–14
Universal Copyright Convention, 310
Unix
    operating system, 311
    shell account, 311
URL, 211
Usenet, 20, 134–161
    ending a session, 143–146
    etiquette, 158–159
    FAQs, 159–160
    finding newsgroups, 160–161

how it works, 135
local level, 135
mailing an article, 151–152
Netscape News, 139
news window, 146–150
newsgroup categories, 136
newsgroups, 161
passed and stored, 135
posting, 153–157
printing an article, 152
reading articles, 150–151
saving articles, 151
setting news preferences, 140–141
signatures, 159
starting a session, 141–143
threads, 136
working with it, 138–141
writing, 153
User's Network (Usenet), 29
uudecode, 282
Veronica, 292
Nevada (Reno), University of, 292
searching, 292–295
Virtual connection, 22–23
Virus, 315

W–Y

Web browser, 1, 3, 34–44, 304
Mosaic, 3
Netscape Navigator, 3, 4–9
obtaining one, 74
starting, 37
stopping, 37
window, 38
Web pages, 1, 34, 207
author's comments, 218
bold, 221
bookmarks, 65–70
creating a Web page, 240–248
description, 212–215
emphasized, 221
head and body, 217
headings, 219
HTML tags, 215, 217
images, 234–237

introduction to HTML, 216–247
italic, 221
line breaks, 219–221
links, 230–234
lists, 224
local files, 65
mailing a page, 64
nested lists, 228
paragraphs, 219–221
preformatted text, 221
publishing on the WWW, 252–253
quoted text, 221
resources, 253–254
saving items from a page, 63–64
shadow lines, 219–221
special characters, 223
structure, 217–223
style guides, 249–252
table of tags, 237–238
title, 218
tools, 248–249
URL formats, 238
viewing source version, 215
WebCrawler, 204–206
WinZip, 281
World Wide Web (WWW), 1, 2, 304
directories, 165–166
Excite, 172–177
Galaxy, 186–191
Global Network Navigator, 177–179
Infoseek Guide, 191–193
Lycos, 194–200
Open Text, 200–204
search engines, 165
search tools, 183–186
searching, 181–183
subject-oriented directories, 167–171
Web pages, 166–167
WebCrawler, 204–206
Yahoo, 168–171
World Wide Web publishing, 252–253
World Wide Web Virtual Library
(WWWVL), 49–58
X-Windows, 2
Yahoo, 6, 168–171